INSIDE THE FDA

The Business and Politics Behind the Drugs We Take and the Food We Eat

Fran Hawthorne

John Wiley & Sons, Inc.

Published by John Wiley & Sons, Inc., Hoboken, New Jersey
Published simultaneously in Canada

For general information on our other products and services, or technical support,
please contact our Customer Care Department within the United States at
800-762-2974, outside the United States at 317-572-3993 or fax 317-572-4002.

Wiley also publishes its books in a variety of electronic formats. Some content that
appears in print may not be available in electronic books. For more information
about Wiley products, visit our Web site at www.wiley.com.

Library of Congress Cataloging-in-Publication Data

Hawthorne, Fran.
    Inside the FDA : the business and politics behind the drugs we take and the
food we eat / Fran Hawthorne.
        p. cm.
    Includes bibliographical references.
    ISBN 0-471-61091-7 (cloth)
    1. United States. Food and Drug Administration.   2. Pharmaceutical policy—
United States.   3. Food adulteration and inspection—United States.   I. Title.
    RA401.A3H39 2005
    353.9′98′0973—dc22

                                                            2004022067

Printed in the United States of America

10 9 8 7 6 5 4 3 2 1

To the generations:
my parents,
Lillian and Edward Hawthorne,
and my children,
Mallory and Joey

Contents

Introduction

The Holiday Inn in Bethesda, Maryland, is an unassuming stucco building tucked sideways off a slow commercial street, across from a Pizza Hut, a gas station, and a mini-mart. You enter from the side driveway and climb up a wide, curving staircase to reach the Versailles II ballroom on the second floor.

On a sunny February morning in 2004, as week-old snow lingered in piles at the edge of the sidewalk, it was standing room only in that ballroom. Some three hundred people had come—parents, grandparents, siblings, and friends, bearing posters and white satin ribbons—to talk to the United States Food and Drug Administration about the medicine that had killed someone they loved.

The long room was decorated in shades of beige and blue, with textured beige wallpaper, beige-and-brown carpeting in a *fleur-de-lis* motif, and a turquoise ceiling studded with 16 crystal chandeliers. At one end, three tables had been arranged in a large "U" for the two panels of 36 outside experts who had been summoned to advise the FDA, along with a few agency staffers. Facing them were rows of burgundy-and-purple brocade chairs, a battery of TV cameras, and a microphone for the audience.

They came from Rhode Island and California, from Texas and Colorado, Arizona and Pennsylvania. Most of them were middle-aged, the men in business suits, the women in nice slacks. One mother quoted the Book of Revelations; another wore a button supporting Democratic Senator John Edwards for president. A 10-year-old girl read an Archie comic book, while a boy of about six played with his GameBoy. In the hall outside the ballroom, one blonde woman asked another, "Was your daughter suicidal?"

They came with tales of the anguish and horror that they and their families had lived through after a teenage son, daughter, grandchild, or friend had started taking an antidepressant medication legally prescribed by their doctor and approved by the FDA. While on the medication, the teenagers had killed themselves, or someone else, or tried to. The families blamed the drugs, and they wanted the FDA to do something to prevent more horror stories.

Tom and Kathy Woodward. Their 17-year-old daughter Julie had hung herself in the garage six months earlier, after seven days on Zoloft.

Terri Williams. Her 14-year-old son Jacob had hung himself in the attic with a belt while taking Prozac. A friend held up a picture of Jacob in his football uniform.

Corey Baadsgaard with his father, Jay. Corey had used first Paxil, then Effexor. Then he woke up in a juvenile detention center one morning. Apparently, he had carried a hunting rifle to school and held his class hostage, but he didn't remember any of that. "These drugs are hell. Look what they've done to my son!" Jay Baadsgaard shouted, his voice hoarse. He strode out of the ballroom, slamming the door behind him.

Glenn McIntosh. His daughter Caitlin hung herself in the girls' bathroom in her middle school when she was 12; she had been using Paxil and Zoloft. She had been a straight-A student and had hoped to be a veterinarian.

Eileen and Todd Shivak. Their 11-year-old son Michael had taken Paxil. He was still alive. But he had tried to slash his wrists in class, had run in front of a moving car, and was now afraid of doctors, teachers, and police. "His peers think of him as a freak," the Shivaks said.

One after another, more than 60 people spoke.

The medications had all been approved by the FDA years ago, starting in 1988, for adults. Millions of people said the pills had saved them from unbearable depression, anxiety, compulsive behavior, panic attacks, and stomach pains. Yet the medicines had been controversial almost from the start, because of their ability to alter people's moods and personality so powerfully. Almost 13 years earlier the FDA had convened a similar meeting of outside experts to discuss whether these pills led to suicidal tendencies in adults; some of the same people now in the audience at the Holiday Inn had been there, too. Back then, emotions had been so intense that the chairman of the advisory panel had worn a bulletproof vest. The Church of Scientology had condemned Prozac. A small study by two Harvard researchers had seemed to show that people on Prozac were prone to suicidal thoughts, and patients and their families had sued Eli Lilly and Company, the manufacturer of the drug. In 1989 a Kentucky printing press operator named Joseph Wesbecker had killed eight co-workers plus himself with an assault rifle and wounded a dozen others a few weeks after he started taking Prozac. The FDA panel back then recommended further research. Still, the FDA had decided that the drugs were beneficial and safe for most people, based on the weight of scientific studies, and should stay on the market.

For patients under 18, there was the added concern about how these powerful chemicals might affect brains that were still developing. Children's brain chemistry is different from that of adults. So even if the drugs were completely safe for adults and helped ease their depression, that did not mean they were necessarily safe or helpful for children. Only Prozac had ever been officially authorized as an antidepressant for this age group. Studies on the other drugs (most of them belonging to a class known as selective serotonin reuptake inhibitors, or SSRIs) had not clearly shown that they worked significantly better than a placebo, or fake drug.

Nevertheless, doctors could legally prescribe any of the medications for any age, and they did: The usage rate for children under 18 jumped more than threefold from the early 1990s to 2001, according to a study by Washington State University; the FDA reported that almost 11 million prescriptions for that age group were written in 2002.

If there was no sure proof that the SSRIs were effective for youths, neither had any clinical trials on patients clearly and definitively demonstrated that the medications increased the risk of suicide—or at least, that was what the medical community believed. The companies that produced the drugs, anxious not to lose this rich market, insisted that the families' stories were only anecdotal—though heartbreaking—aberrations. What made things even more difficult to sort out was that the patients taking the pills were unhappy to begin with, by definition, and might have tended toward suicide with or without the medications. It was also hard to define what to consider a "suicide attempt." Slapping yourself on the head? Stabbing yourself with a pencil during an exam? For that matter, even as the use of the antidepressants had been rising, the overall rate of teenage suicide in the United States had dropped in the late 1990s. So maybe the pills were actually helping to reduce the number of suicides.

The FDA had issued a warning specifically about Paxil in June 2003 after the drug's manufacturer, GlaxoSmithKline, submitted studies that showed a higher level of what might be suicidal thoughts and incidents among adolescents and younger children taking that drug, compared with patients taking a placebo. (Most of the data about Paxil was not made public, and the New York state attorney general, Eliot Spitzer, sued GlaxoSmithKline a year later for withholding the trial results.) In October came a stronger FDA warning about the whole group of antidepressants. The warnings did not forbid doctors from using these medicines, however. There still seemed to be no definitive proof, either that the drugs led to an increased risk of suicide, or that any drug but Prozac worked in youngsters. The FDA commissioned Columbia University to conduct yet another study. Meanwhile, in December, the British equivalent of the FDA took a stronger step, warning doctors in the United Kingdom to shun all antidepressants but Prozac for children.

Most of the speakers at the Holiday Inn called for stricter labels on the drugs, and some urged that only trained specialists, not generalists or pediatricians, should be allowed to prescribe them. Some demanded an outright ban. They wanted the FDA to protect their children. Yet many of them were skeptical that the regulators would.

Dawn Rider exuded an air of competence and confidence; she was a tall woman with a bright red jacket and long, thick, dark hair. Her 14-year-old son had died after taking Prozac. Then her husband was given Paxil to help him cope with the death, and his attempt to withdraw from that drug destroyed their marriage, she told the crowd in the ballroom. During the lunch break, I asked her what she hoped the FDA would do.

"I don't have a lot of faith in the FDA," she replied. "There's too much sway from the pharmaceutical industry." She pointed particularly to the fact that Mitchell E. Daniels Jr., a former Lilly executive, had been the White House budget director and was running for the Republican nomination for governor of Indiana. (He would later be elected.) And somehow it was only Lilly's drug Prozac that had been approved for children. "I was sitting there, watching them [on the FDA panel] today. I almost noticed bored expressions."

"It's clear that the FDA is a political entity," Tom Woodward told the three dozen panelists. "Under the Bush administration, the FDA is putting the drug industry over the interests of the public."

The FDA?

The Food and Drug Administration, the agency that was created in 1906 to make sure that Americans were never again poisoned en masse the way Upton Sinclair described in his novel *The Jungle*? That poll after poll has always shown is one of the most trusted arms of the entire government?

For almost a century, the FDA has been the *Good Housekeeping* seal of approval, the Nobel Prize, and Ivory soap (99 and $^{44}/_{100}$ percent pure) combined. No medicine or medical device can be sold in the United States unless the FDA pronounces that it is safe and that it works. No packaged food can make health claims unless its label is approved by the FDA. Americans count on this agency to make sure that we have a steady stream of wonderful new pills that are potent and perfectly safe at the same time, as well as a supermarket full of goodies that we can gobble up without worrying about food poisoning. We also count on this government agency to be on our side against powerful drug and food companies and to resist political pressure. We trust the FDA so that we do not have to stop and read the label of every can of soup and bottle of aspirin we buy. In fact, we pretty much assume that it will protect us from everything short of nuclear war.

Undoubtedly, most Americans do not completely understand how this influential government office works. We probably overstate its clout in some categories, like restaurants, and don't realize how far its power extends into other areas, like microwave ovens and pet food. Some people think it tests every drug that is sold, and or that it inspects all food products. (Neither of these is true.) Still, we know the basics: If the FDA lets us down, we are not just personally disappointed, betrayed, and angry. We could be dead.

To say you have lost faith in the FDA is like saying motherhood and apple pie have gone rotten—literally, in fact, since the FDA is supposed to ensure that apple pie is safe to eat if you buy it prepackaged from the supermarket. (Not if you eat it in a restaurant, however.)

So how could this mighty agency that we have relied on for a century mess up so badly? Why didn't it catch the suicide problem before it ever approved the first SSRI? How can it be legal for doctors to give teenagers drugs that the FDA never approved for kids? Why didn't the FDA know about the GlaxoSmithKline studies? The parents who came to the Holiday Inn had once trusted the FDA to keep their children safe. And it had failed them.

Before I started covering health care as a reporter and editor at *Institutional Investor* magazine in the early 1990s, I probably had more or less the same vague knowledge of the FDA that most Americans do. Luckily, I never had much reason to be concerned with the products it oversees. I come from a healthy, long-lived family, and my husband, my kids, and I have rarely needed a prescription except for the occasional antibiotic. Nor have I had to be a caretaker for my parents or other aging relatives who do take a lot of medication. As for the "F" in FDA, well, I've always worried more about the calories in my food than any contaminants.

Once I began writing about the pharmaceutical industry and health insurance, I got to meet the FDA that the drug companies know. To these companies, it is the all-powerful, arbitrary, nitpicky naysayer that keeps their desperately needed medicines off the market until they run a zillion unnecessary tests to prove things they already proved. The agency is unreliable, one week saying it wants to help manufacturers get their products out to patients quickly, then the next week panicking after too many reports of dangerous side effects. It is mysterious; there is no way of knowing just what a company must do to move its product past the regulatory box-checkers. At best, the FDA is a bunch of bureaucrats who mean well but are scared to be the first to approve something new. Most of all, the agency must be obeyed. It is almost impossible to get through a 10-minute interview with a pharmaceutical executive without hearing at least one complaint or fear about the FDA.

Of course that is a one-sided view, and the other side can overwhelm you as soon as you walk into an advisory committee hearing, such as the one at the Holiday Inn. There were so many stories at that hearing that I stopped taking notes. It was too much suffering, too many horrible new examples, one after another, without enough time to absorb the horror of the first ones. And it was painful to be there, to picture my own kids' faces—to be too lucky. The drug companies were wrong; the problem was not that the FDA was keeping good medicines off the market in order to enforce overly stringent rules. The problem was clearly that the FDA had given in too easily to the drug companies' pressure, had skimped on its due diligence, and had let dangerous products into the marketplace.

I wondered how it felt to be one of the FDA staffers listening to those stories at the Holiday Inn, knowing that maybe something you had done had caused a family so much pain. A few weeks after the hearing, I asked Dr. Robert J. Temple that question. Heavyset and a bit shorter than average, with longish salt-and-pepper hair that flips over his collar, a thick mustache, round eyeglasses, and thick dark eyebrows, Temple is the FDA's associate director of medical policy and its resident expert on clinical drug trials. He started working at the agency in 1972, just as it was in the midst of laying out the scientific processes that would define modern drug testing, and he has been in the midst of it ever since. In his job capacity, Temple was one of the three dozen people at the U-shaped table, though he was not a member of the advisory panels and could not vote on any recommendations. He gave a short laugh at my question. "They're very moving stories," he replied calmly. "The fundamental problem," and he leaned forward as though to share a secret, "is you don't know whether in fact their attribution is correct. Long before there were antidepressants, people committed homicides and suicides. It's well known that depression is a cause of suicide."

In other words, yes, the families' tales were sad, but heartbreak is not scientific proof. Just because someone takes Pill A and then commits Act B, that does not prove that A caused B. What else was happening in the person's life that could have led to Act B? What had other people done when they were taking Pill A? The FDA could not base its decisions on emotion. First and foremost, before worrying about drug companies' profits, before even worrying about consumers' anxieties or medical needs, the FDA had to look at the science.

Maybe. But as a reporter at newspapers in California and New Jersey over the years and as the former political reporter for *Institutional Investor*, I have spent enough time covering politics at the local, state, and federal levels to know that the FDA's decisions could not always be purely scientific. The FDA is a government agency. Its commissioner is appointed by the president. Its budget and commissioner have to be approved by Congress. Its officials can be hauled before a congressional committee for interrogation at any time. Its major decisions are usually vetted by the Department of Health and Human Services, if not the White House. On top of all that, the FDA regulates the industry—pharmaceuticals—with the most powerful lobbying force in Washington, D.C. Of course all those players try to influence FDA decisions on issues they care about, and of course, the FDA gives in when the pressure is too great. If there are three hundred parents whose children become violent after taking drugs like Paxil and those three hundred parents shout loud enough, Congress, the White House, the pharmaceutical industry, and the FDA will hear. Marion Goff of Rhode Island, one of the parents at the Holiday Inn, knew exactly what she was doing when she brought a friend to the hearing—Stephanie Chafee, wife of Republican senator Lincoln Chafee.

Chafee stood nearby, silently, while Goff told the FDA experts how one of her twin daughters, then age nine, had taken Zoloft and Paxil. Goff had once found the girl on the window ledge, with one leg already out the window. The girl had also tried to stab herself repeatedly.

And there is a lot more to the FDA jigsaw puzzle. Now that I was covering health care, I naturally began noticing constant references to the FDA in the news, even in the most unlikely articles. The agency warned pregnant women against using sophisticated ultrasound equipment to take "souvenir" pictures of embryos. Blood banks complained that the FDA was making them ask too many questions of potential donors, about AIDS, West Nile disease, and SARS. A factory in China, certified by the FDA to manufacture ingredients for various medicines, was dumping untreated chemical waste. Cell phone users wanted the FDA to find out if their phones might cause brain cancer. Was there anything the agency didn't regulate? Indeed, it seemed to have its finger in many of the most controversial and important pies at the American supper table: genetic engineering of plants and animals, abortion, mad cow disease, obesity, drug prices, cloning, Baby Boomer vanity drugs, illegal steroid use by athletes, drug ads on TV.

How could I fit something this huge into a single book?

As it turned out, perhaps the grieving parents at the Holiday Inn should not have been so cynical. At the conclusion of the hearing that afternoon, the two scientific advisory committees recommended that the FDA immediately issue stronger warnings to doctors about the risks to children, without waiting for Columbia University to complete its analysis. In its official decision a month and a half later, the agency went even further. First, it asked the manufacturers themselves to place warnings right on package labels, which were more likely to be seen by doctors and patients on an ongoing basis. It also put out a health advisory to physicians and other caregivers to "closely monitor all patients being placed on therapy with these drugs for worsening depression and suicidal thinking," especially at the beginning of treatment—*all* patients, not just children.

This was pretty impressive. The FDA really listens to ordinary people, acts fast, and bucks the big drug companies. The *New York Times* claimed the new warnings were a break with the FDA's normal, more cautious procedures, because there was no clear-cut evidence of danger from "well-controlled" human trials.

But then several newspapers reported that, in fact, even before the hearing at the Holiday Inn, the FDA did have such evidence—and kept it hidden. In studying data from more than 4,000 participants in clinical trials, an FDA drug safety analyst, Dr. Andrew D. Mosholder, said he found that children on antidepressants were almost twice as likely to become suicidal as those on placebos. The agency refused to let him testify about his findings at the hearing and never showed the panelists his report, however. With the incident hitting newspaper headlines across the country, the chairman of the Senate Finance Committee, Charles Grassley of Iowa, launched an investigation that came up with further charges of FDA manipulation. "You don't just ask someone to clam up," the senator told the *Wall Street Journal.* "If there's any doubt, they ought to put out the caution to the public at large." All that was on top of the Paxil trial results that GlaxoSmithKline and the FDA had kept from the public.

So had the FDA actually tilted in favor of the pharmaceutical companies by squelching reports critical of their drugs, even while it seemed to be listening to the patients?

Well, that was not necessarily the case, either. Bob Temple, the expert on clinical trials, told reporters that Mosholder's report was "premature" because too much of the underlying data was unreliable—for instance, some of the supposed examples of suicide attempts were vague and might not have been real attempts. He said the FDA did not want to spread unsubstantiated fears, thereby discouraging severely depressed people from getting treatment that might help them. And FDA officials claimed the law did not allow them to reveal GlaxoSmithKline's proprietary trial results. Even before I had a chance to ask, Dr. Steven Galson, the acting head of the FDA's Center for Drug Evaluation and Research, insisted in an interview with me that "stories that we're somehow suppressing people, that's the farthest from the truth."

Later that summer, the Columbia University report did back up Mosholder's findings, but only after digging into the data more deeply. Finally, another meeting of outside experts in September called for yet stricter warning labels, and the FDA officialdom agreed to implement those changes. In fact, the agency said it would even go back and reanalyze its data on adult suicidal behavior. Temple admitted that all the clinical trials, taken together, seemed to show "an increase in suicidal thinking and action."

At a hearing soon afterwards, members of Congress from both parties pounded on the FDA for hiding Mosholder's report and other information. "The FDA's lack of cooperation," declared Congressman Joe L. Barton of Texas, "leaves me wondering whether this is sheer ineptitude or something far worse." "No agency charged with the public health should have behaved with such indifference to the public safety as is evidenced in this case," intoned Congressman Peter Deutch of Florida. The House and Senate both launched investigations.

Two more possibilities, then. Maybe the brouhaha over the Mosholder report proved that the FDA truly operates the way Temple described it, as an ivory tower of pure science. It is so careful and so insistently scientific that, even under tremendous pressure from consumers, the press, and politicians, it will not issue half-baked announcements until it has all the facts. And if new data cast doubt on its previous findings, it is so scientifically pure that, rather than stonewall, it will pore through all of its research yet again.

Or maybe, like any institution, it just tried to cover up its own mistakes.

Protector of the consumer? Pawn of industry? Pure scientists? Political plaything?

Now I really needed to write this book. I had to put all the jigsaw pieces together and decide what the FDA is—this sprawling, scientific, political, nitpicky, pioneering, admired, feared, detested, trusted agency.

CHAPTER 1

Case Study: Chasing Cancer

Garo Armen, Russ Herndon, Pramod Srivastava, and Renu Gupta started practicing at nine in the morning on the day after Labor Day, 2003. They gathered in a small, green-carpeted conference room just off the seven-floor atrium of the DoubleTree hotel in Rockville, Maryland, half an hour outside Washington, D.C. Across from their room, bathed in the atrium's soft yellow light, three small waterfalls trickled down an indoor stone wall.

Okay, what would the reviewers from the Food and Drug Administration be likely to ask when they met that afternoon?

The four of them worked for a New York City company called Antigenics Inc., one of countless new, small firms trying to use a niche of biotechnology to tackle cancer. Srivastava and Gupta, both born in India and deeply interested in philosophy, were the scientists. Herndon was the businessman, outgoing and boyish-looking. Armen was pretty much everything: CEO, co-founder, fundraiser, public spokesman, elder statesman, and driving force.

Antigenics' particular approach was based on work that Srivastava had begun as a graduate student 25 years earlier at the Centre for Cellular and Molecular Biology in Hyderabad, India. That work focused on a kind of protein known as heat-shock proteins, or stress proteins, which are found in all cells of all living organisms, including cancer cells. Under normal circumstances, these proteins play a major role in transporting another kind of protein called antigens within a cell (and thus they have an even more colorful nickname, chaperones). Antigens, for their part, stimulate the body's immune system to respond to infection or disease. In theory, you could extract and purify the heat-shock proteins that had chaperoned an antigen that stimulated a response to a certain cancer. Then the extracted heat-shock proteins could be made into a vaccine that would contain some trace of that specific antigen and its cancer—the "antigenic fingerprint" of that cancer. If a patient got that vaccine, unique to his or her cancer, the immune system might be reprogrammed to home in on cancer cells bearing the antigenic fingerprint. It would not prevent anyone from getting cancer, but it could stop the cancer from spreading.

That was the theory, anyway. A number of universities and research institutes in the United States and Europe were also studying the heat-shock protein process, and so far the buzz about Antigenics among scientists and on Wall Street was cautiously positive. The vaccine, which was called Oncophage, had already proved itself in animal experiments, in tests for safety, and even in the first stage of clinical trials on cancer patients. A trial of colorectal cancer patients had just reported some good news about survival rates. Now 650 people with kidney cancer and 350 with skin cancer were participating in further tests at more than 130 sites around the world.

As soon as doctors removed a patient's tumor, the specimen was frozen in dry ice and rushed to Antigenics' labs in Woburn and Lexington, Massachusetts, both near Boston. There, scientists had 24 hours in which to extract the heat-shock proteins—they needed a minimum of seven grams of tumor—and process them into a vaccine. For the next three weeks the vaccines were tested for purity, sterility, and composition. Finally, at least four vials were flown back to each patient and injected—one a week for four weeks, then biweekly. The stuff looked like a small glass of Sprite.

Of course, these were only tests. Oncophage was still far from being a safe, workable drug, let alone a cure for cancer. The Antigenics scientists figured they would need at least two more years of clinical testing, checking to see if the cancer had spread, before they would be ready to seek official FDA approval. So there really wasn't much reason to be hanging out at the FDA's headquarters in Rockville.

But Antigenics had requested this special meeting because a problem had cropped up. The FDA had recently reorganized. Some 200 reviewers who specialized in protein-based drugs, including staffers who had been working with Antigenics for almost a decade, were about to be shifted to a different branch of the agency. That meant that a whole new crew of scientists would be taking over the review of Oncophage—scientists who did not know Antigenics' people, its drug, or its history.

What made the situation even dicier was that Antigenics wasn't exactly following standard operating procedure. Over the past several years, the company had been negotiating off and on with the FDA in hopes of convincing the regulators that its drug was unique and should be able to bypass some of the normal requirements for quality control. Antigenics was hardly alone; biotech firms right and left were flooding the FDA with revolutionary science, demanding exemptions and challenging traditional testing standards.

For instance, in order to make sure that volunteers in experimental drug trials—and, ultimately, patients in the general population—are not swallowing something dangerous, the FDA obviously needs data from the manufacturer about the potency and safety of the drug being tested. But the agency also goes a step further, asking manufacturers to explain how they will test their drugs to obtain the potency and safety data. The idea is to reassure doctors that the drug they are prescribing is consistent bottle after bottle and that the method of measuring is accurate. So the manufacturers have to provide details about the tests they use to check a drug—known as *assays*—even before a human subject can swallow the first pill or be injected with the first dose.

With a traditional chemical drug, measuring is fairly routine. However, vaccines are much more variable because they are made from living material, which is inherently inconsistent. And vaccines made to order from the patient's own tumor are even more variable, a totally new creature for the FDA. "It's not straightforward, because it's a personalized cancer vaccine," Dr. Elma S. Hawkins, a veteran of the industry, explained to me a couple of months after the meeting in Rockville, when she was Antigenics' vice chairman. Garo Armen had been talking with Dr. Philip Noguchi, acting director of the FDA's Office of Cellular, Tissue, and Gene Therapies, to get advice on developing the assays.

Another problem, Hawkins said, is that everything just happened too quickly. Since there are only about 35,000 people in the United States with kidney cancer, Antigenics had been told it would take ten years to recruit its goal of 650 patients. Instead, it filled its ranks in less than three years. "We accrued patients fast into a trial that everybody said was impossible to do. The clinical trial went at lightning speed." But the paperwork of collecting forms from each trial site did not go as speedily. "Not everything was documented at the FDA the way they would like it to be," Hawkins said.

So Antigenics had neither collected all the data that it was supposed to, nor given the FDA the explanation of its assays. Now the new FDA reviewers had sent Antigenics a letter asking for some of that missing information.

A little before two o'clock, the Antigenics crew headed past the Twin-brook Metro station, some three blocks to the FDA headquarters. The 18-story, dark brown-and-grey monolith stands out in its spare, suburban Maryland neighborhood mainly because of its ugliness and bulk. Row after row of windows and steel look down onto a gently sloping hill marked with scattered stands of skinny trees. In front, the building crams almost right up against the street, with room for just two wooden benches, seven large concrete planters—the kind that are built for security, not beauty—and a single bike rack. Across the street sits a strip mall with a video store, a surplus furniture outlet, and a mailing service.

As soon as the group from Antigenics got to the meeting, Armen could tell there was a bigger problem than they had practiced for. "When I saw the body language, I knew something was going on," he recalled later. "I tried to soften them. That backfired. I tried to tell them about the fact that we were doing this because it was supported by an enormous amount of science and that we were doing it because there was a terrific unmet need. They didn't even look at me."

Antigenics couldn't document how it would test the safety of the drug that it was putting into its subjects?

Then the FDA, in good conscience, could not allow any more people to be placed at risk.

As of that moment, the kidney trial was placed on partial clinical hold. No new patients would be permitted to try the vaccine.

Dr. Garo H. Armen is short and trim, with thinning hair, a light brown goatee generously flecked with grey, and what seems a perpetual small smile of confidence. "Never ever in the last ten years"—the lifetime of Antigenics—"did I ever think about giving up," he insisted, eight weeks after the clinical hold was issued.

He was born in 1953 to an Armenian family in Istanbul, Turkey, which meant that his forebears had somehow survived the massacres and mass deportations of Armenians in the Ottoman Empire during the late nineteenth and early twentieth centuries. His father, an auto parts dealer, sent him to the United States in 1970 because the 17-year-old was getting a little too outspoken about Armenian independence. Armen headed for New York City, to the semi-suburban borough of Queens, where he had some distant relatives. Besides, the local public university, Queens College, charged only $200 tuition and offered an English course for students who did not speak the language. Armen blended easily into the borough's ethnic stew of Italians, Irish, Jews, Greeks, blacks, Poles, and Puerto Ricans.

Because he was interested in science, Armen studied chemistry at Queens College and earned a PhD in physical chemistry at City University of New York in 1979. At Brookhaven National Laboratories in nearby Long Island, he did research on photosynthesis and energy production. But by then Armen had discovered the thrill of the stock market.

In 1981 he took his science background to Wall Street and became a stock analyst specializing in chemicals at E. F. Hutton & Company. Five years later he moved to Dean Witter Reynolds as a senior vice president of research with a specialty in chemical and pharmaceutical companies. (Biotech firms like Antigenics may have a reputation for self-destructing after short-lived bursts of glory, but so far it is Armen's two Wall Street alma maters that have disappeared. Hutton was acquired by Shearson Lehman Brothers in 1988, and the Dean Witter name was erased in 2001, four years after the company merged with Morgan Stanley Group Inc.)

Next leap: In 1990 Armen opened his own money management firm, Armen Partners. Instead of just analyzing stocks for others to buy, he did the buying and selling himself, taking a cut of 20 percent of any profits he made. At its peak, Armen Partners was handling $75 million of Armen's own money plus that of select wealthy individuals. His specialty was biotechnology companies.

Naturally, he got a lot of hot tips about the newest cures for cancer or obesity. "Most of them didn't turn out to be anything," Armen recalled. A few did, however. He made his name launching a cancer business for Immunex Lederle. There was also an Irish company named Elan Corporation that was working on an intriguing approach to Alzheimer's disease. Then, on June 15, 1993—Armen is very precise about this—a scientist named Dr. Pramod K. Srivastava showed up with an idea about how heat-shock proteins could be purified and made into a vaccine for cancer. Another hot tip. But this one seemed more promising than most.

Like Armen, Srivastava was an immigrant with a passion for science. His background was about as elite as it gets in India: He came from the northern city of Allahabad, one of the most important places in both Hindu mythology and modern Indian history, and from a relatively high-ranking caste of professionals in the Hindu hierarchy. His father was a civil servant and retired Army officer. There is, moreover, hardly a scientific discipline or foreign language that Srivastava hasn't studied. He has a bachelor's degree in biology and chemistry, a master's in botany, a PhD in biochemistry, and at age 47 he enrolled in medical school at the University of Connecticut (where he also ran the Center for Immunotherapy of Cancer and Infections Diseases). Having earned his degrees on three continents, Srivastava has at least a working knowledge of Bengali, English, French, German, Hindi, Japanese, and Urdu.

At graduate school in Hyderabad in the early 1980s, Srivastava more or less stumbled into cancer research after a friend showed him a cancer cell in a lab. "I couldn't get over how weird and strange the cancer cells looked, how different from the normal cells," he later told an interviewer. Scientists had already managed to vaccinate mice against cancer by injecting them with weakened tumor cells, so Srivastava broke that process down to the next level. Using a centrifuge, he separated the tumor cells into various components, then tried vaccinating mice with different sample parts. The one that worked, he found, was the heat-shock protein. However, as he kept experimenting, he realized that the heat-shock proteins had to be bound to short pieces of other proteins called peptides. Then Srivastava put aside his research for a few years to come to the United States for a postdoctoral fellowship in genetics at Yale University.

After their first meeting in New York, Armen and Srivastava continued to talk periodically for ten months. "Every time we peeled a layer," Armen said, "it looked better and better." Armen also had a personal reason for his interest, because his mother had had breast cancer. Although it seemed to go into remission, she died of a stroke when he was 19.

Finally, in 1994, Armen decided to junk Wall Street, essentially close up his money management firm, and leap to a new career once again. He and Srivastava formed Antigenics to commercialize the heat-shock protein idea. Armen contributed $250,000 of his own money and raised $150,000 from private investors such as a former Dean Witter analyst and the founder of the hedge fund Oracle Investment Management in Greenwich, Connecticut. (He did not tap the investors in Armen Partners because "I thought that would be unethical. This was a very, very early stage development," far riskier than the kinds of investments his firm typically made for its clients. Ten years later, Armen claimed, those same investors pounced on him for keeping them out of such a good deal. "You can't win," he sighed.) The new firm rented a small office on the ninth floor of one of the most famous landmarks in New York, the art deco Rockefeller Center complex on Fifth Avenue. Srivastava and about eight other scientists continued to work in his lab at Fordham University several miles north in the Bronx.

Armen and Srivastava decided to start with pancreatic cancer, kidney cancer, and a kind of skin cancer known as melanoma. There were a couple of reasons for this approach: People with those particular diseases have few alternative treatments. Also, Antigenics would need a tumor big enough to provide seven grams for processing, and not all varieties of tumors are that large. But Garo Armen had no intention of limiting himself to kidneys, pancreases, and skin. The company's methodology—its platform, in scientific jargon—could work for all cancers, he believed. In fact, he told me, because it is based on the immune system, the Antigenics approach could have applications for neurological diseases, cardiovascular disease, infectious diseases, and conditions associated with aging. "If we execute well, we have the technology to become the Microsoft of this industry—that level of dominance. We believe that we are the masters of the immune system."

No, he didn't just mean the Microsoft of cancer. He meant the Microsoft of all biotechnology.

Russell H. Herndon had just finished a speech at a meeting of the Biotechnology Industry Organization, the main trade group for biotech firms, when Garo Armen and Pramod Srivastava came up to him one day in 1994. As the vice president of regulatory affairs at Genzyme Corporation—a relatively big and established company, for a biotech—Herndon handled paperwork and conversations with the Food and Drug Administration. Among other things, he had dealt with the regulators on a type of cell therapy based on the principal of using the patient's own body to heal itself. An easy conversationalist, with light hair and round, brown eyes, Herndon had earned a bachelor's degree in biology, taken courses at Harvard Business School, and worked for an eclectic collection of other small firms before Genzyme.

For their part, the pair from Antigenics knew the science behind their heat-shock proteins, and they knew the business world. They had plans

for moving ahead on their research, raising more money, possibly part-
nering with a big pharmaceutical company, and marketing their vaccine.
But they had no idea how to approach the government, how to get the
approvals they would need to test their drug in humans, or even what
approvals were required.

"We've just formed this company, and we would love to get your advice
as to who we should talk to at the FDA, and what sorts of questions they
might ask," they said to Herndon. "What would the product be classified
as? What are some of the problems we might encounter?" It was the
beginning of Garo Armen's crash course in the FDA.

There are four basic steps that any company must take in moving a
potential drug from lab to market in the United States: tests on animals
(known as preclinical trials), trials on a small group of healthy volunteers
to ensure that the drug is safe (known as Phase I clinical trials), then two
progressively larger trials on people with the disease to test both safety
and effectiveness (known as Phase II and III clinical trials). Animal trials
are not regulated by the FDA, but in order to test anything on humans, a
drug company must submit what is called an investigational new drug
application, or IND—a huge document that summarizes the animal test
results, explains the manufacturing process, and outlines the human testing plans in detail. Then, after Phase III, the company files an application
to actually start selling the drug. For vaccines like Oncophage, the filing
is called a biologics license application, or BLA; for chemical-based drugs,
it is a new drug application, or NDA. (There is more on this process in
Chapter 5.)

By 1995 Armen figured he was ready to seek the FDA's go-ahead to
start Phase I testing on humans, and he came up with what he thought
was the brilliant idea of having the IND prepared by the medical staff at
Memorial Sloan-Kettering Cancer Center in New York, where Srivastava
had worked following his stint at Yale. The hospital had experience handling the FDA's red tape, after all. But that plan did not last long. As
Armen put it, in his typical blend of European formality and ironic self-
awareness, "After a few months I came to the realization that the movement at Sloan-Kettering was at such a snail's pace that my temperament
didn't allow me to put up with it." Antigenics would have to file its own
application with the FDA.

So Armen contacted Mark Boulding, a partner with the Washington,
D.C. firm of Fox, Bennett, and Turner who, he had been told, specialized
in regulatory law. Boulding met him at Srivastava's Fordham labs.

Armen quickly learned that the FDA's safety requirements are levels above what he had been accustomed to. For instance, he could not simply hand in his animal toxicity test results. "Our experience with animals suggested no toxicity. That didn't matter. We had to run [separate] toxicology testing" on human subjects in Phase I. Moreover, the manufacturing process that Antigenics had been using to churn out samples for research purposes at Fordham would have to be upgraded. "We had to have a certain quality of air; certain parts of the manufacturing had to be segmented to guard against cross-contamination."

"All of a sudden, lightning went over my head," Armen recalled. "The FDA was not a trivial thing. I said, 'Holy Moses, we have to go and bring in some talent that really understands this stuff.'" But he said he was not upset at the work that lay ahead. "I was happy, because I now knew what needs to be done."

Throughout this time Armen had kept in contact with Russ Herndon, calling him every six months or so with more questions. As far as Herndon was concerned, Antigenics had a fascinating scientific theory that probably was not as good in reality as it sounded. Meanwhile, one of his colleagues at Genzyme, Elma Hawkins, was analyzing Antigenics for another reason. It was her job to scout out possible acquisitions for Genzyme. And she wanted Antigenics.

Hawkins is a native of South Africa who retains a slight accent and a calendar from that country on her office wall. In a peripatetic career, she spent her adolescence in London, including two years studying at the Royal Ballet, then headed back to Pretoria for college. A professor on sabbatical from the University of Alabama recruited her for her PhD in medicinal chemistry, with a specialization in cancer. From there Hawkins went to Warner-Lambert Company in Michigan, where she shepherded three widely varying drugs through the FDA, and to Boston, where she did research at Tufts University and grew skin at a biotech. After orchestrating Genzyme's purchase of that biotech, Hawkins created the new company's molecular oncology unit. She is short and sturdy, with rimless oval glasses and wavy, red-brown hair that brushes her shoulders.

"I was so impressed by the thoroughness of the science. It was a really different way of approaching the treatment of cancer," she said of her first view of Antigenics. But unless the company could get the FDA to approve its plans for Phases I, II, and III, it was not worth buying. So Hawkins offered to help teach Armen the ropes of working with the regulators. The next thing she knew, she was commuting from her home in Boston

to Antigenics' New York headquarters every weekend—without pay—
from February through July of 1996. "I didn't think he'd take me up on
that offer to that degree," she admitted a little ruefully.

That spring, Armen also spoke for an hour on the phone with Phil
Noguchi, the FDA official. "I said we want to file an IND, but we want to
have a pre-IND meeting—I didn't know what the hell those terms are."

A pre-IND meeting occurs when people from a drug company meet
with the FDA staff to discuss the specifics of their plans for human trials.
The idea is that if the company can find out what the FDA wants in the
IND beforehand, then it should be easier to write an application that will
be approved. This can be particularly important for a fledgling biotech
like Antigenics. It's probably the scientists' first application, so they need
to understand the process. And their cutting-edge technology may be
new to the FDA. As Armen described things, "I thought it was critical
for us to sit down with the agency and explain to them the nuances of our
technology. The world's first personalized protein therapeutic—there's
no regulation that governs a personalized protein therapeutic. Unless we
acquainted the agency with the kind of details that were critical, we would
be at a disadvantage." He cited one potential stumbling block: Drugs in
Phase I are supposed to tested only on healthy volunteers. By definition,
however, the Oncophage vaccine could not possibly be tried on healthy
people, because it had to be made from the trial subjects' own tumors,
and therefore, Antigenics needed people with cancerous tumors. The FDA
agreed to waive the Phase I rule.

Noguchi, Armen's main contact at the regulatory agency, is hardly a
scary figure. Slightly built, his straight black hair speckled with grey, he
speaks calmly and quietly, as careful as Armen is charismatic. He wears the
sparkling "summer blue" uniform of a captain in the U.S. Public Health
Service Commissioned Corps. (Many people at the FDA are members of
this little-known branch of the national uniformed services, which was
founded in 1798 to care for sick and injured merchant marines.)

He, too, has an immigrant's story, but this one goes back through two
generations of racism. Noguchi tells it without any apparent bitterness.
His grandparents came from Japan, took up farming near Sacramento,
California, and then were interned with other Japanese-Americans during
World War II. After the war, his father had to sweep floors for a while
despite a degree in architecture and engineering from the University of
California at Berkeley; his mother, a nurse, rode in the back of the bus
with "coloreds" in Washington, D.C.

By Phil Noguchi's generation, at least, things had gotten better. He was born in Sacramento in 1949 and moved to Washington, D.C. for medical school at George Washington University. There he joined a Public Health Service summer internship program, working in the National Institutes of Health's Division of Biological Standards; when the division was transferred to the FDA in 1972, he followed with it. Then Naguchi heard about a deal where the program would pay his tuition ($2,600 a year at the time) if he promised to spend two years doing research for the government. He signed because of the money. But he stayed, he said, because of the scientific camaraderie and respect. "Everyone's opinion makes a difference. You're a junior staff scientist, but if your research has been in a certain area of monoclonal antibodies, and you review a protocol, that factors into how the FDA reviews a particular program."

FDA rules prohibit Noguchi from talking specifically about Antigenics or its products, but he is certainly mindful that science is changing rapidly all around the six-floor outpost where the Oncophage reviewers work, some two miles from the main FDA offices. "When there are areas involving new techniques," he explained, a couple of months after Antigenics was placed on the clinical hold, "what we strive to do is to be open about what we have requested and why. Each product is looked at individually. Together, we can brainstorm and come up with tests that are going to be meaningful. Almost anything that's being done out there can be accommodated." However, he also warned that when it comes to vaccines made from a patient's cancer cells, which a number of companies besides Antigenics are working on, "the mechanism of action isn't known. We have had a plethora of trials in which the results are highly inconsistent." To Armen, the FDA as personified by Noguchi seemed flexible and reasonable. "Phil Noguchi said, 'We will work with you. We're not going to stop this product from being developed. We're not going to ask you to do something that is scientifically impossible.'"

In order to prepare for the pre-IND meeting, Armen, Hawkins, Srivastava, and a few other scientists from Antigenics created a slideshow of over 40 slides, outlining the rationale and the science behind their vaccine, and also detailing the animal toxicity data. It was not difficult, according to Armen: Each person worked on the preparations for two to three days a week over several weeks, "pulling data, analyzing, tabulating so it was compatible with the agency's standards." The meeting itself lasted two hours and was relatively low-key. Armen was pleasantly surprised by the sophisticated level of queries from the ten or so FDA staffers. "What impressed me was their questions about taking it to the next level, and the next." The bottom line: "They said go ahead, prepare the IND."

The only problem was, Genzyme had decided not to acquire Antigenics after all. At around $75 million, Elma Hawkins said, the price tag was just too high, considering that "all there was, was Garo and Pramod and a bunch of patents." But that did not signal the end of Hawkins' relationship with the company. "Garo in his very persuasive way told me, 'On Monday you'll come and work for me.'"

Armen had set a goal of getting the IND approved by the end of 1996. Since the FDA has 30 days in which to make its decision—if the agency does not reject the submission within that time, it is automatically approved—that essentially meant filing the massive application by around Thanksgiving. The filing would run 1,600 pages in three volumes, with six copies of each.

"Elma put in 24/7 for a month and a half," Armen said. As the self-imposed deadline neared, about five other staffers joined her for all-nighters. "At three in the morning we're all standing there, punching holes, assembling volumes and volumes of work," Hawkins recalled. "I read and reread everything." Spouses were lassoed to come in and proofread. The firm's five printers spit out copy after copy. The group ordered in pizza and Chinese food and took turns grabbing naps on the floor and the couch in Armen's office; amazingly, in all the frenzy, no tomato or soy sauce spilled on the pages. "There were nights I never slept. All I was seeing was the deadline," said Hawkins. Luckily, her old ballet training had taught her how to focus with little sleep. By the last night, Armen said, "eleven of us were working until two-thirty in the morning." Driving home on the Long Island Expressway, "it was the first time ever that I fell asleep at the wheel"—just for a few seconds.

But they made it. They filed around Thanksgiving and got the go-ahead by late December. A year afterwards, Hawkins went back to reread that IND. "I found maybe one spelling mistake."

The first Phase I trial began in November 1997 with pancreatic cancer patients at Memorial Sloan-Kettering—patients who were given perhaps a year more to live. In other words, they might be spending the last year of their lives helping science. And they didn't have much to lose.

Ten people ultimately joined the trial, but it was hard to find appropriate subjects. "I'd hear about the patient in the morning and grab my little box of Styrofoam and dry ice," Hawkins recalled. She would wait in the operating room while doctors removed the tumor, hovering, trying to make sure they saved seven grams for her after doing their biopsy. (If the cancer had spread to the liver, the doctor simply sewed the patient back up; the patient would not live long enough to participate effectively in a trial.) Then Hawkins would grab her precious grams of tumor, pack them in the dry ice, and dash for the Delta Air Lines Shuttle—she was building up frequent flyer miles—to Antigenics' Massachusetts lab for processing. She repeated this dash every week or two for several months. Then she stopped playing courier, and the samples were more officially delivered by Federal Express.

Because the FDA, in approving the IND, had essentially approved Antigenics' blueprint for all three phases of trials, Hawkins and her colleagues did not expect much contact with the regulators for the next few years. Every year they were required to submit a report detailing both the number of patients enrolled in their ongoing tests and the number who had experienced what is known as an adverse event—which means not just side effects from the drug, but any sort of medical complication. In addition, Antigenics would need to file a formal request for a new protocol before beginning any subsequent trial, describing what it intended to study, the names and background of the scientists (known as investigators) who would be conducting the study, the criteria that would be used to determine toxicity, and samples of the informed consent form that patients had signed. The new protocol request is typically about one-inch thick and takes about a month to compile, Hawkins said, but she implied that it is no big deal; it is organizational work that the company would want to do anyway, even if the FDA did not exist. After all, a company would certainly need to line up its investigators and make sure they were qualified, and patients by law have to give their informed consent. So, even while the test on pancreatic tumors at Memorial Sloan-Kettering was under way, Antigenics launched two more—a study of 36 people with melanoma and another involving 42 kidney cancer patients, both at the University of Texas M.D. Anderson Cancer Center in Houston.

The bigger problem was that more trials demanded more money. In November 1999 Garo Armen went back to his Wall Street and pharmaceutical contacts for an infusion of $39 million. That still was not enough, and so in February 2000, with exquisite timing, Antigenics sold its first shares of stock to the public. This move raised $67.3 million. A month later, the stock market slide began.

Antigenics plowed ahead. After six years of sporadic conversations, Armen lured Russ Herndon to join him full-time as chief operating officer, over lunch in 2001. (Later, the company would reorganize and Herndon would become president of commercial operations.) As the work expanded, Antigenics began constructing an 80,000-square-foot, two-story, corrugated-metal second home in an office park in Lexington, Massachusetts, a suburb of Boston best known for the battle that launched the American Revolution. By winter 2004, the facility would replace the Woburn labs and house most of Antigenics' 220 employees, including all of its manufacturing work, with options to double the space and a lease that could be extended to 30 years. The company also moved its New York operations to larger quarters on the 21st and 22nd floors of another building at Rockefeller Center. Connected by an internal spiral staircase, the new digs combine elegant, dark, wood furniture and paneling with industrial blue-grey carpet and basic white walls and cubicles. Armen's small executive suite, overlooking the Rockefeller Center skating rink, has a foldout bed for his next all-nighter.

And the trials grew; in addition to the kidney, melanoma, pancreatic, and colorectal studies, the Oncophage vaccine was being tested on lung cancer and lymphoma, and Antigenics also was investigating a genital herpes vaccine and a vaccine for leukemia. Because the target populations for its kidney and melanoma uses are so small, Oncophage was granted so-called "orphan drug" status from the FDA, which provides tax credits and an extra stretch of marketing exclusivity to companies that make medicines for rare diseases. And because Oncophage is aimed at life-threatening conditions that have few other treatments, the FDA also put the drug on its "fast track" designation, which meant the agency would consider the application under somewhat more lenient criteria than normal. "You take advantage of everything you can," Herndon told me.

In the midst of all this work, Elan—the Irish company with the Alzheimer's drug that Garo Armen had invested in back in his Wall Street days—blew up. It was by that point a global, $2 billion company, and Armen was on the board of directors. However, it suddenly halted the Alzheimer's trials because patients were developing a potentially deadly brain inflammation. Moreover, investors and Wall Street analysts started raising questions about the company's accounting methodology, a convoluted system that involved 55 separate joint ventures and partnerships and evoked all-too-recent memories of the collapse of Enron Corporation. In July 2002, after the stock had plunged 96 percent and the two top executives resigned, Armen was named chairman. Investors did not blame Armen or the other board members for the mess; indeed, Wall Street was impressed with the fact that Armen personally answered questions at his first press conference as chairman, rather than handing the burden off to Elan's remaining managers. But the pressure to fix the company was intense. So now, on top of running Antigenics, Armen had to reassure Wall Street about Elan while finding ways to shed its assets, lay off workers, and do something about those joint ventures and partnerships. It took six months before a new chief executive was hired.

Then the FDA reorganized the way it reviewed protein-based drugs. And the Antigenics crew set off for their meeting in Rockville.

Armen said he asked just two questions after the FDA reviewers read aloud their prepared statement putting Oncophage on clinical hold. "What does this mean?" and "How am I going to explain this?"

As he recalled, one of the FDA people told him, "I don't care what you tell investors." Armen replied: "I don't mean investors. What am I going to tell doctors and patients who have no treatment options—'I am going to take a potential hope away from you'?"

In fact, the clinical hold did not mean that Antigenics would have to pull its treatment away from anyone. Patients already in the Phase III trial could continue. New patients could even be admitted to other trials. The only change was that no new patients could begin the Phase III kidney and melanoma trials.

But it was also a fact that Armen did have to worry about investors. A ruling like this is what Wall Street calls a "material event"—something that could have a significant effect on a company's finances. After all, if Antigenics never managed to supply enough information to get the hold lifted, the FDA would be unlikely to ever approve the drug. No drug, no revenue. The four Antigenics executives knew that they would have to make a public announcement by the next day, which would not be fun.

Because everything must be precise when it comes to science, government regulations, and financial statements, Armen and his colleagues wanted a copy of the statement that the FDA staff had read aloud to them. That way, they could use the exact wording in their own public announcement. There would be no misunderstandings or misinterpretations. Sorry, the FDA reviewers told them, but the statement could not be given out until it had gone through the agency's formal review process—certainly not today.

In the end, the FDA staffers read the letter aloud again, slowly, several times, while the four from Antigenics scribbled it down like stenographers. Then Armen and his colleagues headed back to the DoubleTree hotel.

"Holy crap," Herndon remembered thinking. "We've got to figure out what it is they want and get it to them as fast as possible." Armen later described his own reaction as "disappointed," though not angry. Srivastava saw things differently. "My friend," he said to Armen, "obviously the outcome of this meeting is not very heartening. But we will be better off a couple months down the road." After all, Srivastava was sure Antigenics had the patient data the FDA wanted, just scattered at dozens of trial sites and not in the right format. And the company had been working on the assay details, planning to submit an explanation in a couple of months anyway. So all that was needed was to gather the data and speed things up a bit. Once that was done, Srivastava predicted, "we would no longer be one of a thousand companies out there. Our standing amongst the FDA would rise by the way we addressed the issue."

Noguchi, the FDA official, would not, of course, talk about how serious Antigenics' particular situation was, but he pointed out in one of our interviews that a clinical hold can be issued for any range of reasons, from minor to major, from missing paperwork to fatalities. It could be that "you didn't tell us in any detail who you are going to test, you didn't tell us enough about how you are going to make the product." It could be that the FDA does not think the investigators have sufficient credentials for this kind of work. A month after Antigenics was put on hold, the same thing happened to a New Jersey company called DOV Pharmaceutical, Inc., because the FDA wanted more safety information about its anti-anxiety drug. When 18-year-old Jesse Gelsinger died during a clinical trial of an experimental gene therapy technique at the University of Pennsylvania in 1999, followed by two patients developing leukemia during a trial in France, the FDA threw a temporary hold on some trials using a similar type of gene therapy (which involves trying to insert a therapeutic gene into a patient's cells, typically by having a benign virus deliver the gene).

"It's simply an administrative mechanism that we have. We have to have some reassurance about the quality of things. We're dealing with human subjects, human safety, and the rights of human subjects. We tend to be conservative, and rightly so," Noguchi explained. Besides—and this is where things can get tough for companies like Antigenics, that make their products out of biological material rather than synthesized chemicals—"you have to demonstrate that this is a product that you can make consistently, that you have some idea of the quality and potency. This is all to help the physician. We are not looking to have something that works sometimes but not all the time."

When a clinical hold is announced, Noguchi added, "Wall Street may go completely bananas, or they may not do anything at all. It's given a mystique by the investment community."

Back at the DoubleTree, the group from Antigenics rented a small conference room on the fifth floor for an hour to strategize. Their first priority was to draft a press release for investors plus a statement for the staff, both of which would have to be ready early the next day. They would also have to start working on a plan to collect the data that the FDA wanted. Armen, Gupta, and Srivastava then took the train back to New York while Herndon flew to Lexington. From the train, Armen called his vice president of corporate communications, Sunny Uberoi, to warn him to prepare for a marathon. In fact, Armen, Uberoi, and then chief financial officer Jeff D. Clark stayed at the Rockefeller Center headquarters until two in the morning, went home to grab a couple of hours sleep, then returned at 5:30 to get the press release out by 7 AM.

Like any PR, the public statements tried to emphasize the good news—that the FDA had no concerns about the drug's safety, that the other trials were not impacted. The three-paragraph press release took until the third sentence to mention the clinical hold. In standard, soothing corporatese, it quoted Armen promising that "we expect to provide the FDA with the required information within the next six to eight weeks." In fact, Srivastava had thought the job could be done in four weeks, but the rest of the gang decided to give themselves some breathing room.

The company held a conference call with investors at 9 AM, and two hours later the staff assembled—the New Yorkers in the corporate boardroom, the far larger Massachusetts crowd via teleconference. The stock dropped by a dollar, to around $13 per share, which was a pretty considerable chunk, though not as bad as other companies on hold have suffered. (Dyax Corporation, another small firm working on a cancer treatment, plunged from $14.41 to $10.26 a couple of years later, for instance.) Armen fielded queries from his worried staff for an hour. And after that, for the next seven weeks, it was almost like the days when the company had been putting together the IND, with people working 24/7 in the labs in Massachusetts. Patient forms had to be collected from the trial sites, some of them going back years. The assays they had been using had to be analyzed and described. "We had to find a way of characterizing the product more precisely, in a way that the FDA is satisfied with," Elma Hawkins explained. The company gathered the data that it thought would satisfy the government. Then it waited.

Of course, during this time other work had to go on. There were some promising results from trials that were not on hold, perhaps buttressing Garo Armen's vision that his product could be applicable for a wide range of cancers. The ten patients in a Phase I trial for pancreatic cancer at Memorial Sloan-Kettering reported a median survival rate of two and a half years, almost twice as long as patients in standard therapy. And the *Journal of Immunology* published an analysis showing that Oncophage produced a significant reaction in patients with skin cancer and colorectal cancer—an increase in the production of T-cells that could attack the cells specific to those types of cancer. Staff began moving into the new Lexington, Massachusetts, facility. But the clinical hold overwhelmed everything, and the stock price, after a short pickup in late September, slid lower and lower, even below $10.

Armen came to the realization that nearly ten years of lessons on living with the FDA had not been enough. Antigenics needed more people, full-time, who knew how the agency thinks. "The clinical hold was a reality check," is the way Uberoi, the communications vice president, described it. So Dr. Renu Gupta, who had been only a consultant to Antigenics when the hold was first issued, was hired full-time as senior vice president of development. Following time-honored industry tradition, the firm also brought in an FDA alumna, Taylor Burtis, as senior director of regulatory affairs.

Gupta, petite and precise, could not have found a more perfect job. Her father, an Air Force officer named Amar Mapb Verma, had died of kidney cancer in 1997 at age 70. Since then, "I have been on a quest to make a greater effort toward the research of agents for the treatment of kidney cancer," the daughter said.

On November 20, Taylor Burtis asked Russ Herndon to step into her small, white-walled office, just a few doors down the hall in the Lexington building. He had to stay calm, Burtis advised, so that nobody passing by and looking through the window would notice any emotion. The FDA had just called to say they were off clinical hold.

Afterwards, Antigenics officials would claim that they had not been particularly worried about being able to provide the right information or getting the hold lifted. They did admit to being pleasantly surprised that the FDA moved so fast, and with no further questions (although it would take until the following July for the last red tape to be sealed). The stock spiked briefly. "It was—I don't want to say vindication, that's too adversarial. It was a great relief. We did it, we were on the right path; if you work with the FDA you get there," Elma Hawkins summed up.

"Look," said Armen, "they have a whole bunch of boxes that need to be checked. It is our obligation to make sure the boxes are checked."

Even with that vote of confidence, Oncophage was hardly ready to go on pharmacy shelves, and Antigenics was hardly in a position to pick a fight with the FDA. That May, the company's regulatory crew hoped to troop back down to Rockville for another meeting, this time to ask the FDA to approve Oncophage after just one successful Phase III trial, rather than the traditional two. That rule-bending has become increasingly common for urgent cases like cancer. Also, the company would go over the next trials' "housekeeping details," as Armen put it. "How we are getting data, how we are bringing outside reviews of data. We will ask the FDA if they have any suggestions to tweak any part of it. Maybe they want five independent radiologists instead of one or two [assessing the test results]. So that our application won't be rejected. If the data are good but because of some stupid reason they get thrown back, that doesn't help anyone."

In preparation, Renu Gupta was on the phone with FDA staffers about once a month. Antigenics was also amassing an information package that the FDA had to receive at least two weeks before any meeting could be held. The package would run about 300 pages, with the data so far from the Phase I, Phase II, and animal trials, Antigenics' analysis of the data, and detailed plans and timetables for the next tests. It also had to include, according to FDA regulations, "a list of the specific objectives/outcomes expected from the meeting," "a proposed agenda, including estimated amounts of times needed for each agenda item and designated speaker(s)," and "a list of specific questions grouped by discipline." Interviewed early into the process, Gupta figured it would take eight to ten people working less than full-time three months to prepare the package.

During that rush of preparations, Antigenics dropped its idea of asking the FDA to let it get by with just one trial—at least for now. Instead, it would start a second trial while it continued to gather results from the first one. According to a formula understood only by statisticians and the FDA, 214 of the 650 patients in the first trial would have to show signs of a recurrence of their cancer, including patients getting Oncophage as well as those getting a conventional treatment like chemotherapy. A sample that size would allow a meaningful comparison of the rate of recurrence among Oncophage versus non-Oncophage patients. If the ones with Oncophage had a significantly lower rate, then that would be the time to go back to the FDA, show off the results, and ask if this was strong enough proof of the vaccine's effectiveness to cut short the second trial and file for approval. Antigenics expected to have the data by winter. "Before the results are out, it would be very unproductive to have this kind of discussion. That's a hard sale. We don't want to force them to fix into a position they couldn't reverse later on," Armen explained. Besides, he sensed a change in attitude at the FDA—more of an insistence on going by the book—tied in with the staff transfer. However, the second trial, if it ran its full course, would cost the company $15 to $20 million and delay things an extra year and a half, to mid-2006 or even later.

As it turned out, once Gupta submitted the briefing material, the FDA wanted some additional information, and the meeting had to be put off two months until late July. (Armen was right on the money in one of his predictions: the FDA did, indeed, ask for a third radiologist to assess trial results, as a tie-breaker.) In addition, the agency requested yet more background on the assays that Antigenics would be using to test the drug's potency; that was another 300-page submission. On top of all that, virtually the entire FDA review staff changed yet again. Even Phil Noguchi transferred to a different part of the agency. So now about ten people from Antigenics' regulatory and clinical staff were spending an hour or two per week on the phone and e-mail trying to bring the newcomers up to date, plus sending copies of material they had already submitted. Armen guessed it would take the new FDA people a few months to catch up.

It was a heck of a maiden voyage for a company trying to cure cancer. To be fair, it was also far from the norm. FDA staff "have been gracious enough to admit," Armen told me with a wry smile, "that this has not been an optimal way to deal with our situation." At least the 90-minute July meeting went well, according to Armen—in fact, the agency even asked Antigenics whether its method of electronic data collection could be used as an oncology standard. Then it was on to the next step.

About 25 staffers from all parts of the company were already beginning to write the 400 to 900 volumes—that's 400 to 900 *volumes*, not pages; each volume has several hundred pages itself—that Antigenics would be submitting to the FDA when it finally sought approval for Oncophage. The huge section on clinical trials would have to wait, of course, but they could get a head start on the rest by gathering the data and drafting the portions about animal tests, safety, and manufacturing. Also, Antigenics was preparing to file its second IND application, this one for its herpes vaccine, which Armen figured to be a lot easier than Oncophage's. In November, Gupta checked the protocol for the second kidney trial with the FDA's medical reviewer. Even though this protocol was "quite similar" to the one for the first trial, Gupta said she would not start the trial or mail the protocol to the investigators until "all the i's are dotted and all the t's are crossed. I want to know from the FDA if we're ready to go."

To pay for these plans, Antigenics had amassed a nest egg of $135 million from its various stock sales and private offerings, which Armen claimed would see the company at least up to the conclusion of the first trial. (Like most biotechs, it had yet to actually make a profit.) At that point, "if the data is positive, our ability to raise money will not be an issue," Armen said dismissively. And if not? "We'll have to scramble like any biotech with bad results." In addition, executives were talking with a dozen or so bigger drug companies about some sort of partnership in which the larger company's sales force would also pitch Oncophage. Meanwhile, the chief financial officer went back home to Texas, and Antigenics hired a new one from Ireland. "For investors," wrote *Bloomberg Markets Magazine* earlier that year, "the next 12 months will provide the best indication of whether betting on Antigenics was worth the wait."

In the main lab on the first floor of the Lexington building, on a wintry Wednesday in 2004, a 26-year-old research associate named Ben Roscoe was working on the future of Oncophage by watching liquid drip.

The lab stretches over 2,000 square feet, the size of a small restaurant, one alcove after another. Each alcove, or bay, covers about 670 square feet, consisting of a row of beige, glass-doored cabinets above a black countertop, then a narrow aisle, then a black countertop with computer monitors sitting on it, then a second black countertop with computer monitors, then another narrow aisle, then another black counter underneath beige, glass-doored cabinets.

What Roscoe was aiming to do that Wednesday afternoon was to purify a synthesized protein that would be used, in turn, to purify one particular patient's Oncophage vaccine. The protein had been engineered by Antigenics scientists to contain an amino acid sequence that binds to nickel. That would allow Roscoe to use a purification technique called immobilized metal affinity chromatography, which takes two hours and involves several steps. First, a gel-like solid containing nickel ions was put in a tall, clear plastic column, and a solution containing the special protein was poured in. Next, a clear liquid buffer was added to wash the nickel-protein combination, in order to control acidity and alkalinity and to remove contaminants. After that Roscoe had used a dropper to contribute yet another clear liquid, a chemical called imizadole, which would bind the nickel to the protein. The column was then attached with a large metal clamp to the top of a beaker sitting on the countertop. So now Roscoe, sitting on a tall stool at one of the center counters in his bay, in white lab coat and plastic goggles, was watching as the leftover buffer slowly dripped from the bottom of the column into the beaker. Eventually, that excess would be spilled out. What remained was the target protein.

After the protein did its job purifying the Oncophage sample, the patient would get his or her vaccine. Antigenics scientists would track the disease's progress in that patient, and in dozens of others—and in more trials. Some patients, hopefully, would stave off a recurrence of their cancer for a few more months, or even years. Once it had enough evidence, Antigenics would be back to the FDA with hundreds more pages of data. Then it would launch further trials. It would take more data to the FDA: more all-nighters with the printer spitting out copies, and more meetings where the FDA might send it back to redo something or might give a thumbs-up. And this process would go on and on.

Meticulous, yes. Nitpicky, exciting, risky, potentially life-saving, potentially life-threatening, and no doubt wasteful of paper. Also probably difficult to streamline much.

And that was only if Antigenics was lucky enough to have a drug that worked.

CHAPTER 2

Beyond Science

Leaving the FDA's drab Rockville headquarters, where the Antigenics executives learned of their clinical hold, it's about a five-minute drive to the modern, white, six-floor office building that Phil Noguchi's staff in the FDA's Center for Biologics Evaluation and Research (known as CBER) share with an accounting firm, an insurance company, and several other private businesses. Right next door, overlooking a development of brick townhouses, another medium-size leased office building houses some employees from a different arm of the FDA, the Center for Drug Evaluation and Research (CDER).

Drive about 20 miles southeast to College Park, Maryland, and you're at the sprawling, brand-new offices of a third FDA branch, the Center for Food Safety and Applied Nutrition (CFSAN). Including its parking lot, the four-story building spreads across an entire block, centered around a sunny, book-lined atrium.

Or, from Rockville, take the Metro train three stops toward Washington, D.C., to the Bethesda, Maryland, campus of the National Institutes of Health (NIH). The main offices of CBER are in a five-story, red-brick building there, tucked just under a small hill.

Elsewhere in Rockville, the FDA's Center for Veterinary Medicine (CVM) is almost hidden in a nondescript corporate park, without even a sign on the outside of its low-slung brick facility. The Center for Devices and Radiological Health (CDRH) sits in yet another standard-issue corporate park in

Rockville. Still more CDER and CBER staffers, including Robert Temple, the expert on clinical trials, work out of a brown-brick office building around the corner from a shopping mall, so new and obscure that some of their offices are not even listed on the lobby directory.

From these buildings—plus several dozen others in the Washington, D.C. area—plus a one-million-square-foot facility near the Pine Bluff Arsenal in southeastern Arkansas, plus over 100 other offices and labs around the country, and a new headquarters complex in Maryland that is scheduled to take in most of the Washington-area staff by the time it is fully built in 2010—the FDA puts its imprint on roughly one-quarter of the U.S. economy. It decides whether fresh peaches are moldy and whether the labels on canned peaches are misleading. It determines whether drugs like Oncophage are safe and effective enough to be sold, whether the advertisements about them are accurate, and whether doctors need further warnings once they are on the market. It checks the dyes in face cream, the record-keeping at blood centers, even the radiation in airport X-ray scanners. Pet food to pacemakers, lip gloss to lettuce, cell phones to sperm banks, the 10,800 doctors, scientists, reviewers, inspectors, and other employees of the FDA are supposed to make sure, as best as they can, that when consumers swallow, insert, apply and buy food, drugs, medical devices, cosmetics, radiation-emitting gizmos, and biological products, they know what they're getting, they won't be poisoned or injured, and (in the case of drugs and devices) the purchases will work as intended.

Think of almost any headline relating to food or medical safety, and it probably was handled by one of the five main branches of the FDA in those scattered offices—the alphabet soup of CBER (pronounced Seeber), CDER (or Seeder), CFSAN (often called Sifsan), CVM (sorry, no nickname), and CDRH (occasionally called Sidrah). Agency inspectors tested milk, fish, and water for radiation after the partial meltdown at the Three Mile Island nuclear plant in 1979 and investigated millions of bottles of Tylenol after seven people died from poisoned capsules in 1982. Following the September 11 terrorist attacks and the anthrax scare of 2001, when several letters containing deadly anthrax spores were mailed, the agency scrambled to assess the quality of the nation's available smallpox vaccines and then set out to persuade private industry to make new ones. In November and December of 2003 alone, the FDA held hearings or issued statements on the following: how "mad cow" disease might be spread in animal food, an athlete's death from the diet supplement ephedra, crossing the border to Canada to fill prescriptions, the safety of meat and milk from cloned animals, dangerous levels of methylmercury in fish, differences in studying new drugs in men versus women, the risk of eating imported green onions, and the use of genetic tests in new types of personalized drugs.

There's more. The FDA is pushing—and being pushed—to expand its turf still further, into issues of pricing, medical ethics, people's lifestyles, the secrecy of clinical trials, the way companies develop drugs, even the choice of which drugs to develop. In 2004—for the second time—it came close to getting authority to regulate tobacco, which would have been one of the biggest prizes of all. These changes could well boost the agency's reach over the U.S. economy closer to 30 percent.

We Americans, by and large, have liked what we have gotten. We take for granted that our food, medicine, and devices are safe because of the FDA. We don't worry every time we open a can of peas or a bottle of pills. "The public perception is, 'I feel the government protects my food and drugs and cosmetics,'" summed up Dr. Mark Novitch, who spent 14 years at the agency, including a year as acting commissioner in the mid-1980s.

Not just the American public, in fact. Manufacturers of drugs and devices all over the world also submit themselves to the FDA's Phase I, II, and III application process and pull together volumes and volumes of data for review, just like Antigenics. Of course, this is mainly because the United States is the biggest market on the planet, and foreign companies need the FDA's imprimatur in order to sell their products to tens of millions of American customers.

But even that is not the whole story of the FDA's clout. Consider the Swiss firm Bioring, which was founded in 2000 in a small town near Geneva specifically to fill a niche created by the FDA: The FDA had refused to approve the devices manufactured at that time for babies and children with defective heart valves because the devices were not biodegradable. Any children using the devices would have to return to the United States periodically for follow-up surgery, and the agency feared that those from poorer nations would never be able to. So Bioring decided to invent a biodegradable device. Chairman and Chief Executive Raymond Andrieu foresees a market of 30,000 infants per year—a market that exists almost solely because of FDA policy.

The FDA is probably not much stricter than the only other regulator that matters, the European Medicines Evaluation Agency. According to a report by Tufts University's Center for the Study of Drug Development, released in March 2004, the two regulatory bodies took almost exactly the same amount of time, on average, to approve new drugs—17 months for the European agency and 16.7 months for the FDA. Some products come out first in one place, some in another, although rejections are a bit more likely in the United States than in Europe. Nevertheless, there is just a feeling in other countries that approval from the American regulator adds a unique luster. "If you want something regulated from a health point of view, anywhere in the world, you look to the FDA," said Dr. Lester M. Crawford, who has been at the agency off and on since 1978, including two stints as acting commissioner. In a separate interview, Franz B. Humer, chairman and CEO of the pharmaceutical giant Roche Holding Ltd.—which is based in Switzerland—echoed the sentiment: "If a clinical trial is FDA-approved, it has a seal of quality."

Or is that seal overrated?

Almost every week there are warnings or recalls regarding various drugs, medical devices, or food products for safety reasons. In some cases, dozens of people have become very sick or even died. Why didn't the FDA stop the sale of those products?

At the same time, the FDA still hasn't approved some drugs that seem to work so well in Europe, or herbal remedies that the Chinese have been using for thousands of years. What takes the FDA so long? If desperately ill people are willing to take a chance on a new medicine, why won't the agency let them?

One of the two main industries that the FDA regulates, the pharmaceutical industry, is famous for its political clout. It is always among the biggest donors to election campaigns. It has buddies in the White House and on Capitol Hill. It blocks legislation that it does not like and helps write bills it favors. Food companies are no slouches politically either. If these businesses have so much influence on Congress and the president, can the FDA be immune?

For that matter, science itself has become less academic and more politicized, as scientists reach deeper and deeper into areas that many people see as the jurisdiction of God, not humans—research involving genetic engineering, embryonic stem cells, and human cloning, for example. Can the FDA ignore those public pressures?

The FDA likes to see itself as being as pure as the food and drugs it approves—scientifically, politically, and ethically. As Bob Temple asserted with the antidepressants, the agency likes to claim that all of its decisions are made purely on the scientific data. In fact, the FDA is staffed by a corps of dedicated, careful scientists. But it is, and always has been, buffeted by the conflicting demands of scientific accuracy and public pressure, of industry and consumers, and by the contradictions between two types of public need. That is why the agency is so often in the headlines; the scientific issues it confronts are also issues of important public policy. It has at times given in to some of the less-than-pure forces—not often, but more than officials would care to admit. For instance, at various periods the review staff has moved faster in approving drugs, then slower, then faster, partly because of practical factors like its budget, partly because of the quality and quantity of the applications it receives, and partly because of the political pressure for speed. It is not necessarily a bad thing for a government agency to be responsive to the views of society or the pain of consumers, like the parents at the Holiday Inn, of course. But for good or ill, all these pressures have grown more powerful in recent years.

Economists talk about Type I and Type II mistakes, which essentially boil down to risk of commission versus risk of omission. A Type I mistake occurs when the FDA approves a drug, people start taking it by the tens of thousands or more, and then a lot of those people develop a horrible physical malfunction that is traced to the drug. A Type II mistake occurs when the FDA takes a long time to approve a drug, and during that waiting period patients suffer and die from the disease that the drug would have treated. The classic Type I case is thalidomide—which the FDA never approved—the notorious sedative taken in the 1950s and 1960s by pregnant women throughout Europe who then gave birth to thousands of babies with missing limbs and other birth defects. The anguished parents who came to the Holiday Inn for the hearing on antidepressants might argue that the FDA made a Type I mistake in approving Prozac, Paxil, and the like, especially without attaching any warnings for teenagers. The classic Type II mistake involves AIDS in the mid-1980s, when activists accused the FDA—fairly or not—of holding up badly needed experimental drugs because it insisted on following a stringent review process to the letter. Another Type II example might be Erbitux, the cancer drug that famously snared lifestyle doyenne Martha Stewart in a stock-dumping scandal in 2001. The FDA refused to consider the drug's application because of serious problems with its clinical trials. So manufacturer ImClone System Inc. ran some new trials, which produced virtually identical results. Two years later, the FDA approved the same drug it had originally shunned. Meanwhile, cancer patients were deprived of a potential treatment for two years, investors lost millions of dollars as ImClone stock sank, and Martha Stewart and the CEO of ImClone eventually went to prison on charges related to selling stock holdings before the FDA refusal was public. (Chapter 11 explains the ImClone story more thoroughly.)

It's a truism that the FDA—with the long approval process that bogged down Antigenics, with its demand for mountains of data, with its never-ending questions—fears Type I mistakes more than Type II. Therefore, supposedly, it insists on meticulous review before it will let a drug onto the market. It is also a truism that one reason the FDA fears Type I mistakes so much is that those are the kind of mistakes for which Congress and the public are most likely to criticize the FDA. Assume that a certain drug might cause ten deaths from side effects—but save a thousand people's lives, posited Frank R. Lichtenberg, a professor of economics and finance at Columbia University's Graduate School of Business. "Those ten deaths are highly visible; those people's relatives are going to be able to sue. The thousand people, their story is not going to get told. Therefore, you might imagine that the FDA might be excessively conservative." Famously, a former commissioner, Dr. Alexander M. Schmidt, said in a speech to the National Press Club in 1974:

> In all of the FDA's history, I am unable to find a single instance where a Congressional committee investigated the failure of FDA to approve a new drug. But, the times when hearings have been held to criticize our approval of new drugs have been so frequent that we aren't able to count them. The message to FDA staff could not be clearer. Whenever a controversy over a new drug is resolved by its approval, the Agency and the individuals involved likely will be investigated. Whenever such a drug is disapproved, no inquiry will be made.

That is actually not an unreasonable bias for a regulatory agency. To continue with Professor Lichtenberg's example, it is usually pretty clear when a drug causes ten deaths, but who can be sure the drug would have saved the thousand others? In general, it is better to err on the side of safety. Only after it is certain that a proposed drug is safe should the FDA let people experiment with treatments that may not actually be better than the proven safe ones already on the market. Even with those precautions, in most years the FDA has to issue a few dozen safety alerts for drugs, medical devices, and dietary supplements. (This is separate from the more frequent, temporary recalls of specific batches of drugs because of a problem at a single manufacturing plant.) Drugs with the FDA's imprimatur kill over 100,000 Americans each year and put 1.5 million others into the hospital, according to the *Journal of the American Medical Association*.

Why do any bad drugs slip through? Every drug has side effects, some serious, some less so. It would be impossible for the FDA to root out every potential problem before giving a new medicine the go-ahead. Typically, a drug is tested on, at most, a few thousand people in clinical trials before it is submitted for the FDA's appraisal. If it causes a certain serious side effect in just 1 out of 1,000 patients, or even 15 in 1,000, those few instances are unlikely to be apparent in the trials. Similarly, if a new drug induces problems only when patients are also taking a second medication for a completely different ailment, the clinical trials are not going to catch it; no company can test every new drug in combination with all the thousands of existing prescription drugs, let alone over-the-counter pills and herbal remedies. These so-called adverse reactions emerge only after the general public has been using the new medicines for a while. In a population of 250 million, with over $200 billion worth of prescription drug sales per year and tens of thousands of drugs, devices, and diet supplements—well, that's not a lot of Type I mistakes.

For that matter, the number of Type II mistakes does not seem all that high either. FDA officials say they approve 75 percent of the drugs that are submitted after Phase III, and they have cut the amount of time they take to make their decisions by more than half since the early 1990s. So how many patients are really being denied good drugs?

To FDA staff it seems as if they're damned if they do, damned if they don't. "If a drug has a problem and is removed or even has the labeling changed, it is on the news and people are faulting the agency for approving it. If a new drug is hyped in the news, people are faulting the agency for not approving the drug faster. It is all part of the ebb and flow. When you are being criticized by both sides, you are probably doing things right." These words were spoken recently by Jere Goyan, a low-key California pharmacist who served as FDA commissioner under President Jimmy

Carter in the late 1970s. But they could almost be a slogan, the way FDA officials repeat them so often.

Those staffers—who face the flak from both sides; who catch, or don't catch, the side effects; who demanded more paperwork from Antigenics; who listened to the parents at the Holiday Inn and analyzed the studies on antidepressants and turned down Erbitux—are largely MDs and PhDs who prefer doing their science with test tubes and computers rather than directly with patients. Often, like Noguchi, they are straight out of graduate school or the Public Health Service. Some taught first at universities or worked in different branches of government, mainly the NIH. They could easily double their salary, in far more luxurious quarters and under a lot less public pressure, if they went to pharmaceutical companies. And many do: The agency's turnover rate is typically eight percent a year, according to Lester Crawford; the Government Accountability Office (formerly the General Accounting Office) in 2002 said that was higher than in the federal government as a whole.

Yet the staff has an amazing esprit de corps. Over and over, employees and ex-employees use terms like "mission" and "protecting the public health" without apparent irony. They carry around copies of the basic food and drug statute. Quite a few of them stay 20 years or more, leaving only because the government retirement incentives at that point are too good to pass up.

Gerald F. Meyer is one of those. He spent 22 years at the FDA, from 1972 to 1994, and 14 years before that in other government jobs. At the FDA, he started in the congressional lobbying office, went on to run management and operations, and then became deputy director of CDER and, briefly, the acting director. After he retired, he took on part-time consulting work for lawyers and drug companies. He walks slowly nowadays; he is white-haired and heavy, with dark grey eyebrows and a deep, hoarse voice. He does not seem to be the sentimental type. He matter-of-factly noted that he switched majors in college from chemistry to business because "I liked science but didn't have a lot of aptitude for it." Certainly, he can be curt when he is not impressed by something, like calling Health and Human Services Secretary Tommy G. Thompson "a joke" or Dr. David Kessler, the activist but controversial chief who headed the FDA through most of the 1990s, "the worst commissioner in my entire tenure."

How did he feel about working at the FDA? "I do love the place. You know you're on the right side of the issue. What they do is help make the world a better place to live."

Dr. Jay P. Siegel is another long-timer. He left as the director of CBER's Office of Therapeutics Research and Review—that is, the office that oversaw Antigenics' Oncophage vaccine—in 2002 after 20 years at the FDA, partly because of the reorganization that also shook up Antigenics, partly because of the government's retirement incentives. (More on the reorganization in Chapters 11 and 12.) Now he heads research and development at Centocor, Inc., a subsidiary of Johnson & Johnson that is based on the outskirts of Philadelphia and makes drugs for arthritis, an intestinal inflammation called Crohn's disease, and other conditions. "My salary with bonus is five times higher than it was [at the FDA]," he pointed out. "I could have left the agency any time. I was there for a reason: It was to protect the public health."

Most people, including officials at the FDA itself, date the agency to the federal Food and Drug Act of 1906. Peter Barton Hutt, the FDA's chief counsel from 1971 to 1975 and its unofficial historian, prefers to start in 1862, when the newly created U.S. Department of Agriculture set up a laboratory to analyze food samples. It could also be argued that the modern FDA did not really take shape until the laws were revised in 1938 and 1962. Now the twenty-first century is forcing more changes, more rapidly than ever before.

The FDA is revamping the way it reviews drugs and the kinds of tests and proof it requires, in order to adapt to the new science that companies like Antigenics are pursuing. But it is an almost impossible race to keep up with. Biotech firms complain that the FDA's rules just don't work for their specialized genomics-based products, which are custom-made and should have fewer side effects. Making matters worse, the agency may have shot itself in the foot with the recent reorganization of Jay Siegel's office, which could weaken a historic tradition of doing original scientific research.

The FDA has begun to redefine the meaning of its mandate—safety and efficacy—in ways that could explode its jurisdiction. Does efficacy mean simply making sure that a diabetes drug works as promised to help patients process insulin? Or should the FDA also be urging these patients to eat right and exercise so that perhaps they can manage their diabetes without needing any medication at all? And how effective is a drug if people do not use it because they cannot afford it? The FDA has taken steps to look at both those questions, and while it subsequently shied away from the affordability issue, public anger may push it back. But if dieting tips and price controls are now added to the FDA's job description, it is going to have to buck the angry opposition of both the food and the drug industries.

The FDA must deal with two types of growing and often contradictory consumer activism—consumers who file suit every time a drug has a bad side effect, and those who demand a miracle cure for arthritis or Alzheimer's disease immediately. The pressure from both will only get stronger as the Baby Boomers who learned to protest in the 1960s now hit their prime prescription-buying years.

The FDA has also been handed a whole new role as a soldier in the war on terrorism. This involves more than just the added workload of keeping track of 25,000 shipments of imported human and animal food every day and trying to get drug companies to develop new vaccines against bioweapons. Without any public discussion, the antiterrorism assignment has turned the FDA from an agency that largely reacts to what it is given, into an agency that attempts to root out problems before they happen.

The FDA may need to consider, for the first time, the ethics of the drugs it evaluates, not just their safety and effectiveness. Thanks to ever-advancing science, we already have drugs that bulk up our muscles and whisk away our wrinkles; soon we may be able to pop a pill to help us ace our SATs, or forget bad memories, or change our personalities dramatically. Someday, too, we will undoubtedly be able to clone human embryos, harvest their near-miraculous stem cells, and use those cells to develop medical treatments; scientists in South Korea have already gotten as far as the harvesting. But should we? Although the FDA may argue that its role is merely to decide whether the drugs work safely, politicians and religious leaders will turn any "yes" or "no" into a socio-political statement.

The FDA is facing pressure to do more than file away the data it gets when drugs are tested. Angry physicians, patients, and politicians want it to make more of the results public. The agency itself would like to see further trials done after drugs are on the market, because the pre-approval trials cannot catch those 1-in-1,000 adverse reactions. However, the regulators have to figure out a way to scientifically collect and analyze this kind of data, without revealing drug companies' trade secrets.

As society and science evolve, the FDA's portfolio will keep growing. Issues that it thought had been settled, for good or ill—the safety of genetically modified food and animals, herbal remedies and dietary supplements, cigarettes, mad cow disease, prescribing of drugs for unapproved uses, television commercials—are demanding a second look as unexpected side effects crop up, people use products in changing ways, manufacturers develop different versions, and public opinion changes. Moreover, scientists constantly bring new questions out of their labs, like producing food from cloned animals. Any of these—anything that sparks consumers' hopes or fears—can become a political football.

The FDA's role, in short, is growing more and more beyond science and into public policy. To do this expanding job right, therefore, the FDA will have to draw on not just its 100-year history of scientific and regulatory experience and its public-spirited staff. It will also have to draw on its mixed history of alternately holding off and bending to pressure from industry, consumers, and politicians alike. It will have to do a better job of juggling. But first, it will have to stop pretending that it is above the fray— it has to jump in.

CHAPTER 3

The First 100 Years

. . . as for the other men, who worked in tank rooms full of steam, and in some of which there were open vats near the level of the floor, their peculiar trouble was that they fell into the vats; and when they were fished out, there was never enough of them left to be worth exhibiting— sometimes they would be overlooked for days, till all but the bones of them had gone out to the world as Durham's Pure Leaf Lard!

With those few words from the novel *The Jungle* in 1906, the Food and Drug Administration was essentially born.

From then on, it would ride back and forth on waves of public health crises, political theories of government, budget cuts, scientific discoveries, bureaucratic reshuffling, and consumer outrage.

The production of food and drugs, like so much else in American history, began as a domestic chore and was gradually transformed into a commercial commodity. During the Colonial era, women made medicines for their families by collecting herbs according to instructions handed down by their mothers and shared around the community. Only if an ailment was beyond their repertoire did Colonial moms head to apothecaries. These all-purpose experts—who were also known as doctors—set bones, pulled teeth, and sold candles and tobacco, in addition to concocting salves, potions, and lozenges from a basic list of several hundred herbs and animal parts. By the early 1800s, however, the doctors were buying their medicines from a new breed called pharmacists, who mixed fine chemicals that they ordered from specialty chemical companies. A few decades later, even the pharmacists would be overtaken by companies that premixed the chemicals into medicine—the forerunners of today's giant pharmaceutical manufacturers.

As medicine gradually expanded beyond the known ingredients, it was harder for consumers to be sure of what they were using. There were a few attempts to establish standards. Some Colonial doctors published manuals for self-treatment of disease, and these could include advice on drugs as well as diet and bloodletting, according to the Pulitzer Prize–winning book *The Social Transformation of American Medicine* by Paul Starr. In 1820 a group of 11 physicians created the U.S. Pharmacopeia, which listed recommended remedies for various ailments and the guidelines for making them. (The organization still exists today, analyzing the makeup of drugs and providing advice on purity testing, run out of offices down the street from the FDA's main building.) But no federal laws regulated what could or could not be put in the store-bought concoctions or—in some ways just as important—what could be claimed on the label.

Enterprising hucksters soon realized the potential gold mine in this state of affairs. All they had to do was pour a "secret formula" into a fancy bottle, slap on a label asserting wondrous properties, and then advertise in the newspapers that were just starting to flourish. By 1849 there were some 600 of these so-called patent medicines; by the late 1800s, you could buy Kick-a-poo Indian Sagwa and Wheeler's Nerve Vitalizer and Mrs. Winslow's Soothing Syrup and Lydia Pinkham's Vegetable Compound to cure—well, to cure almost anything, according to the labels. (Diabetes and cancer were as big then as they are now.) The medications might actually contain some of the same minerals and herbs that the Colonial mothers and physicians had used. But they might have heavy doses of opium, morphine, heroin, cocaine, or alcohol as well. Who could tell? Or, for that matter, the "medicines" might not be much more than colored water. In *Tom Sawyer*, written from 1874 to 1875, Tom's Aunt Polly is a big fan of something called Pain-Killer, which, judging from its effect on the family cat, must have contained a good helping of some stimulant. In this free-for-all era, with no rules on contents, testing, or labeling, patients and doctors could not be sure that even legitimate drugs had the right ingredients.

Food was hardly any safer. As with medicine, Americans were less and less likely to eat what they grew themselves, so food, too, became a commodity mass-produced by profit-making corporations. Moreover, as people migrated from the farm to the city, food had to be transported over long distances without spoiling. Thanks to ever-growing science, manufacturers had a whole new array of chemicals and preservatives at their disposal to put into this commodity. Sometimes the chemicals and preservatives were used to try to keep the shipments fresh during the long trek to the cities. But the new ingredients were also added to disguise the smell and look of bad food, or to unfairly puff up foods sold by weight like flour and bread. Philip J. Hilts, in his history of the FDA, *Protecting America's Health: The FDA, Business and One Hundred Years of Regulation*, describes a slew of fraudulent practices, including some creative uses of cheap laboratory-made glucose. Add brown coloring and a dead bee, and it could be sold at a markup as honey. Add some hayseeds and pulped apple skin, and *voilà!*—strawberry jam.

Why was there no public uproar when patients swallowed the phony "medical" potions and didn't get better? Partly, of course, it was because even legitimate medicine was not very good, so people were not necessarily surprised if a remedy did not work. Besides, in the mid-1800s there was no sense of consumer rights, no innate assumption that people had a right to know what they were ingesting and to be protected from unscrupulous business practices. When the patent medicine era began, after all, half the United States did not think all human beings had a right not to be bought and sold as slaves. There were few labor unions and no government consumer protection agencies. Industrialization was just coming into place. America had not yet figured out how to deal with commerce that stretched beyond the local community.

Still, laws regulating food and drug purity were not unheard of. As the FDA itself points out on its official Web site, more than 600 years earlier, in 1202, King John of England had issued the Assize of Bread law prohibiting the adulteration of bread with ground peas, beans, and other fillers. A number of states and even municipalities had laws that set weight and measurement standards for food, or that authorized inspections of certain foods like bread.

The first real national clamor to do something in the United States arose out of patriotism. During the Mexican War of 1846 to 1848—the war that would ultimately add California and areas of Arizona, Colorado, Nevada, Utah, and Wyoming to the U.S. map—American troops in Mexico were given adulterated, diluted, and otherwise impure medicines. Famously, 87 percent of the fatalities in that war came not from bullets but from cholera, dysentery, yellow fever, and other diseases. That did not necessarily mean, of course, that the tampered medicines caused all the deaths. Nevertheless, it was a jolt to the nation, and doctors and pharmacists urged the government to do something to protect its citizens. So Congress passed the Drug Importation Act of 1848, which required that imported drugs be inspected for quality and purity at the port of entry. But the measure proved virtually toothless. It set no uniform standards for the quality and purity that it mandated. The customs inspectors who were supposed to inspect the imported drugs were political hacks with no training. And the law did nothing to regulate drugs made domestically.

Over the next 58 years, as the patent medicine advertising blitz swamped the nation's newspapers, there would be 100 more attempts to pass some sort of national food and drug protection bill. None of them succeeded. Meanwhile, Great Britain enacted a food law in 1860 and a law covering the sale of food and drugs in 1875, which, among other things, banned putting poisonous chemicals and other dangerous ingredients in food and allowed medical officers to inspect the products. Without waiting for Congress, 23 states approved legislation on food adulteration between 1874 and 1895.

At the same time, huge social changes were sweeping across America, fueled by a burgeoning belief in the rights of ordinary citizens. To curb the power of the railroads and the big oil trusts, the first of the great reform laws—the Interstate Commerce Act and the Sherman Antitrust Act—were passed in 1887 and 1890, respectively. Workers began finding their political muscles, organizing the National Grange for farmers in the 1870s and the American Federation of Labor in 1886. (Their muscle proved limited, however. Over the next eight years dozens of protesters and strikers would be killed in the Haymarket riot of 1886, the Homestead strike of 1892, and the Pullman strike of 1894.) The Populist and Progressive movements burst onto the scene, with their calls for a shorter work week, a graduated income tax, and an end to child labor. William Jennings Bryan ran for president in 1896, 1900, and 1908 promising to represent the common man, declaiming in his first run, in opposition to the gold standard, that "you shall not crucify mankind upon a cross of gold." Elizabeth Cady Stanton launched the National Woman

Suffrage Association in 1869 and, with allies like Susan B. Anthony, campaigned for women's right to vote. In this spirit of public reform, muckraking journalists, most notably at *Collier's Weekly* and *Ladies' Home Journal*, published exposés about the patent medicines.

Even without an overarching law governing the safety of food and drugs, the federal government had been able to take some action by presidential order. In 1862 Abraham Lincoln created the Department of Agriculture (USDA) and appointed a chemist named Charles M. Wetherill to work there. Wetherill promptly set out to determine if adding sugar to grape juice in the process of winemaking, in order to increase the alcohol content, constituted "adulteration." (He decided that it didn't.) That work grew into a full-fledged Bureau of Chemistry, and in 1883 Dr. Harvey W. Wiley, a chemistry professor from Purdue University, was appointed to head it. He would later become the patron saint of today's FDA.

As Philip Hilts describes him, Wiley was a tall, skinny farm boy from Indiana who learned medicine through a combination of old-fashioned apprenticeship and modern university study. After fighting for the North in the Civil War, he got his M.D. from Indiana Medical College, followed by a bachelor of science degree from Harvard. He then studied some more under the world's great German chemists. Back in his home state, Wiley became head of the science department at the brand-new Purdue University and was also named state chemist.

When he came to Washington, Wiley started by investigating some of the patent medicines and suspicious foodstuffs that were flooding the country. To test the safety of common preservatives, he set up a "poison squad" of healthy young men who were monitored as they ate foods with gradually increasing amounts of additives. The results—severe indigestion, stomach pain, bowel trouble, headaches, and more—shocked Wiley, Hilts says in his book. Over the next two decades, Wiley threw himself into the cause of food and drug safety: He went on the lecture circuit, issued reports to Congress, organized meetings, investigated more products, and campaigned for food and drug laws. Still, little happened. The only products that got any regulatory attention were vaccines and other biological drugs—that is, medical products made from living organisms—which were the most common forms of legitimate medication at that time. After 14 children died from contaminated antitoxins and smallpox vaccines, Congress in 1902 passed the Biologics Control Act, requiring that manufacturers be licensed to ensure safety and purity, which would ultimately prove to be a model for the FDA. But when it came to regulating food and most drugs, the industry opposition—from wholesalers to meatpackers to whiskey distillers to patent medicine concocters to retail grocers—was too powerful. Until 1906, that is, when Upton Sinclair published *The Jungle*.

Historians have often pointed out that Sinclair was not in fact campaigning for stronger food and drug laws. He had a much bigger agenda—he was trying to promote socialism. But his novel, essentially a soap opera about a Lithuanian immigrant named Jurgis Rudkus and his extended family, focused readers' attention on food because it takes place mainly in the slaughterhouses of Chicago, with harrowing descriptions of how cows and hogs were butchered and processed, workers were injured, and the few government inspectors were misled. (The scene describing the men who fell into the vats of Durham's Pure Leaf Lard is probably the most infamous.) Amid the public outrage that followed, and with strong support from women's clubs and President Theodore Roosevelt, Congress finally passed the Food and Drug Act of 1906—the first wide-ranging, national legislation on food and medical safety—as well as a tougher law on meat inspections under a different arm of the Department of Agriculture.

While the 1906 law marked the official beginning of the FDA and established the principle that the federal government could regulate food and drugs on a broad scale, it did not really authorize much regulation. In fact, if that law were all the United States had today, the FDA could probably fit into a couple of rooms in Rockville, and we would still not be sure what we were swallowing.

The Food and Drug Act made great sweeping declarations—it was illegal to manufacture and ship across state lines any "adulterated" and "misbranded" food and drugs—but failed to pin down the details. Most important, the law applied primarily to what was said on the label, not what was actually in the bottle. Government regulators were given no authority to look inside the container, let alone test the ingredients, to ensure that the contents would not harm the public.

If a manufacturer made any statement on the label about what the contents were, then the statement had to be true, but of course the manufacturer could just as well say nothing. There was no requirement to list the ingredients of patent medicines. Other medications had to reveal just certain specific ingredients, including marijuana, alcohol, opium, cocaine, morphine, and a few poisons. So a bottle could contain a poison not on that list, and if the label were blank, there was no way the government could stop the public from swallowing it. Even the weight and measurement of the contents did not have to be disclosed. Nor did the law apply to advertisements or any other promotional material. Food, meanwhile, got a few more rules: It could not be missing a key ingredient or be "filthy, decomposed or putrid." Also, food processors could not try to disguise violations.

Another big problem was that the only enforcement tool the government had was a bludgeon—the courts. If the regulators thought someone was violating the law, they could not simply investigate and issue an order to stop. They had to take the culprit to court, where the burden of proof was on the government and the process could drag on. Thus, a dangerous product could be sold for years before it was finally halted.

And that was not all: The Supreme Court ruled in 1912, in a case involving something called Dr. Johnson's Mild Combination Treatment for Cancer, that the new law did not prevent manufacturers from falsely claiming any power or cures for their products. In other words, someone could put water in a bottle, accurately label the bottle as containing water, and then—legally—claim that this bottle of water would cure cancer. Congress quickly passed the Sherley Amendment in an effort to overcome that problem, but in some ways it made things even tougher by requiring the government to prove that manufacturers intended to defraud buyers with their false labels. It is almost impossible in a court of law to prove intent.

The job of enforcing this loophole-ridden legislation, such as it was, went to Wiley's Bureau of Chemistry. Eventually, the bureau would be reorganized and renamed the Food and Drug Administration. But by the time Wiley died in 1930, his life's work seemed to have withered to skin and bones.

It took a political upheaval, a scientific upheaval, and a health crisis to add some muscle to that skeleton. By 1933 the United States was awash in all sorts of products, from cosmetics to pesticides, that had not been envisioned in 1906 and thus had clearly not been regulated. Meanwhile, mysterious miracle cures and phony food products were still being peddled. When Franklin D. Roosevelt won the presidential election of 1932 promising a new burst of government activism, Walter G. Campbell, Wiley's successor as head of the FDA, decided this was the time to propose a regulatory overhaul. The second Roosevelt quickly signed on to rewrite the law that the first Roosevelt had championed. But industry was just as vehemently opposed as it had been during the earlier go-around. Congress chipped away at the proposal, and the bill flopped weakly around the Capitol for four years like a fish on the deck of a sailboat.

Then, in 1937, Massengill Company of Bristol, Tennessee, decided it needed a way to package its antibiotic sulfanilamide in a more tasty liquid form. It mixed the drug with the solvent diethylene glycol, added raspberry extract for flavor, and started selling the new drug, called "Elixir of Sulfanilamide," that September. Within weeks, patients began dying; eventually, 107 would be killed, mostly children. It turned out that the diethylene glycol solvent was toxic.

But it was apparently legal. There was, after all, no requirement in the law to test drugs on humans or animals before selling them. And there was apparently no complaint about the elixir's label.

The dramatic headlines gave politicians the impetus they needed to finally pass the Food, Drug, and Cosmetic Act of 1938, a much stronger law that established the framework for what the FDA does today. Probably its most important provision was that drug manufacturers have to show scientific proof that their products are safe before they can sell them—in other words, to stop any future elixirs of sulfanilamide from getting to market. The measure also eliminated the Sherley Amendment's requirement that the government prove intent to defraud, authorized factory inspections, and brought cosmetics and therapeutic devices under the FDA's aegis.

With some fiddling, that 1938 statute carried the United States another decade and a half. (The biggest milestone occurred in 1940, when the FDA was transferred out of its birthplace in the Agriculture Department to what would become the Department of Health and Human Services, or HHS.) By the mid-1950s, however, the law was again becoming outdated. World War II had introduced penicillin to the public on a wide scale, and now pharmaceutical research was exploding with the development of "miracle" drugs like sulfas, antibiotics, and steroids. In addition, the flowering of suburbia meant that food was being trucked over greater distances. Still, another political gale and another health crisis would have to arrive in order for major change to occur. This time, the catalysts were a stubborn, populist senator named Estes Kefauver and a drug named thalidomide.

During the late 1950s, Kefauver—a Democrat from Tennessee who liked to play up his country roots by sporting a coonskin cap—was looking for a new crusade. He had already held well-publicized hearings on organized crime, the auto industry, and the steel industry. He had been among the first to call for censuring Joseph McCarthy and was one of the rare Southerners to support civil rights. He had been the vice presidential nominee in 1956 but had lost. Now, Dr. Irene Till, a staffer working on his subcommittee on antitrust and monopoly, had an idea: A few years earlier, when her husband had gone to fill a prescription for an antibiotic, he had been taken aback by the high price. Not only that, but all the alternative antibiotics his doctor suggested sold for exactly the same price. How about investigating prescription drug costs?

In subcommittee hearings that ran off and on from December 1959 until October 1960, Kefauver grilled the top executives of major pharmaceutical companies in front of the public and the press. Why did they sell drugs for 17.9 cents per pill when it cost less than 1.6 cents to make them? For the drug companies, the PR battle was lost as soon as headlines hit the newsstands proclaiming markups of 1,118 and even 7,079 percent.

The hearings delved into other issues as well, such as drug advertising, and Kefauver had a slew of ideas for reforming the FDA. Among them: Before a medicine was allowed on the market, the FDA should evaluate whether it actually worked, not just whether it was safe. Naturally, the industry opposed the measure, and despite its weakened public image it still had clout in Congress. Nor did the feeble FDA under then Commissioner George P. Larrick or the White House under President John F. Kennedy give Kefauver much support. (There was little rapport between Kefauver and Kennedy, who had been rivals for the vice presidential nomination in 1956 and the presidential spot in 1960.)

Meanwhile, a German company called Chemie Grünenthal was marketing a new sedative throughout Europe that supposedly helped ease nausea in pregnant women. A U.S. company, Richardson-Merrell, Inc., bought the rights to sell the drug, known as thalidomide, in America, and in September 1960 it applied to the FDA for approval. But the FDA, even back then, was more strict than Germany about authorizing new drugs. The American reviewer, Dr. Frances Oldham Kelsey, was bothered by the sketchiness of the supporting data that were supposed to prove safety. In particular, she asked about birth defects. Over the next year, Richardson-Merrell would repeatedly pressure her to give the drug her okay while dodging her questions. Then reports started trickling in from Europe about a high number of babies born without arms or legs, with their hands, feet, toes, or fingers growing out directly from their trunk. The reports increased; in all, approximately 10,000 babies would be born with birth defects resulting from thalidomide use during the 1950s and 1960s. Several thousand more died before birth, the vast majority of them in Europe. (In addition, the drug was given out to about 20,000 American patients on a trial basis, and the FDA has estimated that 17 thalidomide babies were born in the United States.) Americans were horrified by the possibility that a mass disaster could have happened to them—if not for the dogged caution of the FDA. Frances Kelsey was a hero. Chemie Grünenthal pulled the drug from the European market in November 1961. And Senator Kefauver finally had the momentum to pass a strong—indeed, revolutionary—FDA bill.

The irony is that what had started with a hearing on drug prices and later got political cover from a scandal about an unsafe drug ended up as a measure that had little to do with either issue. The Kefauver-Harris Amendments to the 1938 Food, Drug and Cosmetic Act were passed unanimously by both houses of Congress in 1962, mandating that drugs must be shown to be effective as well as safe through "adequate and well controlled" scientific studies before they can be sold in the United States. It was not enough to put some supposedly innocuous ingredients into a bottle. Consumers had to have some assurance, based on scientific evidence, that what they were taking had worked for people with similar medical problems. It was the first time the federal government had applied that principle since the 1902 law on vaccines and biological drugs.

In addition, the new law included two important provisions meant to make sure that people were aware of the possible dangers of taking a particular medication. Drug companies had to report any adverse reactions (or serious side effects) to the FDA, and advertisements had to include a complete discussion of the product's risks. Also, in the one area that directly related to the thalidomide disaster, the measure laid out strict rules for conducting human trials and making sure that participants give their informed consent for undergoing the procedure. Not only did the FDA have to grant approval before a drug could be sold, but manufacturers could not even test a drug on humans without the regulators' authorization.

Forty years later, there are still critics who claim that requiring manufacturers to prove efficacy is a Type II mistake that needlessly delays patients' access to good products. They scoff that Frances Kelsey, after all, managed to keep thalidomide off the U.S. market perfectly well without any help from Senator Kefauver. But that view is far out of the mainstream. What the 1962 amendments essentially did was to codify Kelsey's courage and careful attention into law, while also adding other protections. If the 1938 Food and Drug Act laid the foundation of the agency, the Kefauver-Harris Amendments put in the kitchen, living room, and bedrooms that make it a real house.

Over the next 30 years, a series of more laws and amendments, more public health crises, advances in science, a revived consumer movement, weak or short-lived commissioners, and political pressure would continue to redefine the FDA.

The growth of consumer activism and new government agencies during the presidencies of Lyndon Johnson and Richard Nixon took nips out of the FDA in some spots while adding tucks in others. For two decades starting in the 1940s, the agency had prosecuted illegal drug use and even sent undercover inspectors to catch drug dealers; but in 1968 it lost its authority over narcotics and illegal drugs to a narcotics bureau that was established in the Justice Department. When the Environmental Protection Agency (EPA) was created in 1970, it took away a lot of the FDA's responsibility for pesticides. In addition, jurisdiction over nonmedical consumer goods like toys and household chemical products shifted to the new Consumer Product Safety Commission (CPSC) in 1973.

On the incoming side, the agency gained an assortment of duties in 1969, including sanitation programs for milk, shellfish, food service, and interstate travel facilities, such as bar cars on trains. Regulation of biological drugs like Antigenics' vaccines—the ones covered by the separate 1902 law—came over to the FDA from the National Institutes of Health, in 1972 (along with Phil Noguchi). In 1971 radiation was dumped in the FDA's lap as the Bureau of Radiological Health was transferred from the Public Health Service. The National Center for Toxicological Research, the branch of the FDA that conducts scientific research and testing, was established—not in Washington or Rockville, however. It was situated near the Pine Bluff Arsenal in Arkansas because the Pentagon happened to have space in an empty biological warfare facility and "there was a strong congressional delegation in Arkansas" pushing for it, in the words of Dr. Daniel A. Casciano, the center's director. The commissioner for most of the Nixon years, a surgeon-turned-management consultant named Dr. Charles C. Edwards, is usually credited with establishing professional management standards, hiring top-notch administrators, and standing up to industry pressure to some degree.

Because clear scientific evidence was now required before drugs could be approved, the FDA had to develop standards for conducting "adequate and well-controlled" trials. In doing so, it essentially created the modern science of clinical trials that governs the way the pharmaceutical industry works today.

Most companies back in 1962 practiced what is called empirical science—essentially, trial and error. "The way everybody did trials was to start at the low dose and titrate up to higher doses until everybody got sick," explained Bob Temple, the agency's associate director of medical policy and expert on clinical trials, only partly exaggerating. This may seem a logical way to do things, but it is actually unscientific (apart from being risky). If a patient reacts to a drug at a particular dosage level, investigators cannot be sure whether the reaction is due to that specific dosage, or to the compounded effect of taking a lot of doses over an extended period, or to the progression of the disease over time.

The FDA came out with its first set of regulations in 1970 and a revised version in 1985. Among other things, it recommended a more organized method of testing, by comparing sets of patients on different, predetermined dosage levels against control groups on a placebo. The method is known by a variety of terms—double-blind, randomized, placebo-controlled, and dose-response. The FDA had the clout to do this, of course, because it could declare that this type of trial was necessary to prove a drug's efficacy.

The new approach also meant the FDA had to beef up its own staff by hiring experts such as statisticians. As Richard Cooper, the agency's chief counsel from 1977 to 1979, put it: "Under the 1962 law, the FDA demanded a new level of scientific rigor in studies submitted to show the effectiveness of new drugs. The FDA pushed the envelope."

(The main exceptions to the rigorous trial demands are generic drugs, which are low-cost copies of name brands. In this case, the idea is that the generics should be able to get approval based on the original drugs' clinical trials, because they are virtually identical to those drugs; to require their own trials would be like asking the first drugs to redo their whole submission. And if generic manufacturers did not have to spend tens of millions of dollars repeating the patient trials, they could charge far lower prices. In 1984, that principal was enshrined in the Drug Price Competition and Patent Term Restoration Act—usually known as the Hatch-Waxman Act in honor of its prime sponsors, Republican Senator Orrin Hatch of Utah and Democratic Congressman Henry Waxman of California.)

As usual, tragedies extended the FDA's power. An estimated 200,000 women suffered miscarriages, pelvic inflammatory disease, and unplanned pregnancies from the Dalkon Shield, an intrauterine birth control device marketed by the A.H. Robins Company in the early 1970s, and at least 17 died. The FDA had never approved the Dalkon Shield—nor forbidden or recalled it, for that matter, because it never had the authority to regulate medical products other than drugs and biologics. That spurred the passage of the Medical Device Amendments in 1976, which gave the FDA the right to review devices ranging from tongue depressors to pacemakers for safety and effectiveness more or less the way it oversees drugs.

One of the high points of the era, however, came during a different crisis, the Extra Strength Tylenol scare of 1982. "It was a Thursday morning, and someone walked in and said, 'Seven people are dead in Chicago and it looks like it's been traced back to lots of Tylenol,'" recalled Mark Novitch, who was then the deputy commissioner. "The first thought I had was, 'Is this the beginning of something even more horrible? Are we going to hear about more deaths?'"

Novitch gathered the regulatory affairs staff in a thirteenth-floor conference room at the Rockville headquarters and immediately called Johnson & Johnson, the manufacturer of Extra Strength Tylenol. By that time Johnson & Johnson had already identified four lots that the suspect capsules came from. The FDA issued a public warning against the product, and it asked Johnson & Johnson to pull the affected lots off the shelf. J&J went even further: It recalled all 31 million containers of the product—all its lots—a step that would be heralded in business classrooms for years to come as an example of the best in corporate behavior.

Once the capsules were safely out of shoppers' reach, the FDA's main concern was to reassure consumers. "We were fairly certain that this was a local issue," Novitch explained, two decades later. "But we had to convince the public of that. When it hit the news there was panic that nothing was safe." So the agency sent inspectors throughout the country to test millions of samples of Tylenol—plus aspirin, cold medicine, and other over-the-counter medication, for good measure. The agency also rushed out new regulations requiring tamper-resistant packaging, and Congress quickly passed a law making it a crime to tamper with the tamper-resistant packages. Eventually, police would determine that someone had most likely bought the capsules at a store, crudely injected them with cyanide, and then replaced them on the shelf, but no culprit was ever arrested.

Along with the rise of both consumer activism and the FDA's visibility came heavier political pressure. The FDA abruptly discovered the limits of its power in 1977 in a confrontation over something almost sacred to

Americans—their right to drink diet sodas. Scientific studies had shown that the low-calorie, artificial sweetener saccharin causes cancer in animals. Under the Delaney clause of the Food Additives Amendment of 1958, any food additive that causes cancer in humans or animals, no matter how minute the quantity, must be prohibited. So the FDA's commissioner, Dr. Donald Kennedy, announced plans for a partial ban. But industry, politicians, and medical groups protested that the agency was overreacting. The soda-drinking public, having already lost one artificial sweetener, cyclamates, to the Delaney clause, was not about to be denied its Diet Coke and Diet Pepsi again, and Kennedy was simply outgunned. He was new, he was unused to Washington, and, he had not spent years dealing with the pharmaceutical or food industries. Congress overruled him, passing the first law preventing the FDA from banning a specific food additive.

The pressures only grew. In 1980, Republican Ronald Reagan was elected president bearing a radical new agenda of deregulation and smaller government. The FDA commissioner at the time was Jere Goyan, the pharmacist from California, appointed by the Democrat whom Reagan defeated, Jimmy Carter. Goyan was visiting San Francisco for the New Year's holiday when he got a call a two o'clock in the morning from what he describes as "a fairly low-level member of the Reagan transition team." The staffer told him he was fired. "I have become known as the first commissioner fired with a change in administration," Goyan told me. He would not be the last.

In terms of scandals and politics, the 1980s would prove the FDA's worst decade since the passage of the 1938 law.

Political pressure. Reye's syndrome usually begins when children get a viral infection like chicken pox. Starting with nausea and vomiting, then possibly seizures, it leads to death in about one-fifth of cases. Another high percentage of patients suffer mental retardation. By 1981 the federal Centers for Disease Control (CDC) had found a strong link between the disease and aspirin and sent the data to the FDA. But the aspirin industry protested vigorously to the Reagan White House. The FDA, first under Dr. Arthur Hull Hayes Jr., a clinical pharmacologist, and then under Dr. Frank Young, a former dean of the medical school of the University of Rochester and a born-again Christian, was simply a yo-yo. The secretary of Health and Human Services—the FDA commissioner's boss—ordered the FDA to prepare warning labels for aspirin bottles, then withdrew the order under pressure from industry and the White House. A new HHS secretary ordered a weaker set of warnings; then that order, too, was withdrawn. The FDA never fought back for stronger action, at least not openly. It was not until a public interest group sued the FDA and Congress passed a law that the FDA finally required warning labels in 1986.

Approving dangerous products. Now that the FDA had authority over medical devices, it had granted approval in 1979 to the Bjork-Shiley artificial heart valve. Ultimately, 85,000 units were sold worldwide. But time after time, the crucial struts that controlled the flow of blood kept breaking. The FDA claims that the manufacturer, Shiley Inc. of Irvine, California, never told it of problems the company knew about even before gaining approval and then repeatedly delayed filing reports on the recurring breakdowns. Still, the FDA must have known that Shiley had recalled the device three times for repairs from 1980 to 1983. The FDA's acting commissioner admitted to Congress, a few years later, that his agency "should have made swifter decisions." In the end, some 500 people died, and Pfizer Inc., which owned the valve maker, pulled the device for good in 1986.

Not approving beneficial products. When tissue plasminogen activator, or TPA, was developed by the new biotech company Genentech, Inc. in 1987, it seemed the ultimate treatment for dissolving blood clots that can precipitate heart attacks. It was faster and more powerful than the only existing clot-dissolver, the generic streptokinase. Still, TPA had its disadvantages: It was far more expensive than streptokinase, and at the dosages being tested it could cause potentially fatal bleeding into the brain. In addition, streptokinase had data to prove that it actually saved lives, which most scientists assumed would be a result of dissolving clots but which Genentech had not specifically proved with TPA. A panel of outside experts, in the longest and one of the most controversial meetings in FDA history, took the super-cautious route: The panel voted to recommend that the FDA reject TPA. Later that year TPA was approved at a lower dose that caused fewer side effects, and journalist Stephen S. Hall, author of the 2003 book *Merchants of Immortality* (about scientific attempts to extend human life), calls the drug "a staple now in virtually every emergency room in the developed world." So you could say that the FDA saved lives by sending Genentech back to reformulate a better dosage level, but most people see it the other way—that the FDA delayed an effective drug for no good reason.

Underenforcing. Of course food is not regulated as closely as drugs—manufacturers do not have to prove safety and efficacy before being able to sell their macaroni-and-cheese mix. If a food claims to have medicinal benefits, however, it is to some degree treated like a drug and must prove its claims scientifically. Manufacturers started getting more and more creative with their claims in the 1980s until finally, in 1984, Kellogg Company flung a challenge in the FDA's face by outright advertising its All-Bran cereal as helpful in preventing cancer. It had no scientific backup for that assertion beyond a statement from the National Cancer Institute declaring that in general, a "high-fiber, low-fat diet may reduce the risk of some kinds of cancer." The industry waited to see what the FDA would do. The FDA did nothing. After that, in a tidal wave reminiscent of the patent medicine days of a century earlier, food products poured onto grocery shelves advertising their wondrous effects upon human health.

Overreacting. In March of 1989, after an anonymous tip to the U.S. embassy in Santiago, Chile, an FDA inspector pounced on three suspicious-looking grapes from that country in a shipment of tons of fruit unloaded on the docks of Philadelphia. The find was rushed to the nearest FDA lab, where testers announced evidence that two of the grapes had been injected with cyanide. Fulfilling its duty to protect the American consumer, the FDA slapped an embargo on all fruit shipments from Chile. The trouble was that a follow-up FDA test found no cyanide, and even the first results were not consistent with the science of how cyanide usually reacts in fruit. Pretty soon people were questioning whether the FDA had poisoned the grapes itself, Chile was suing the United States, and the FDA had become a laughingstock.

Bribery. Once the Hatch-Waxman Act opened the door wide to generic drugs, something odd began to happen. Certain generic makers always seemed to get their products approved much faster than everyone else. Three of the non-favored companies testified at a congressional hearing in 1989 that their competitors had been making payoffs to FDA reviewers and that broad hints had been dropped that they, too, ought to pay up. Not only that, but some of the favored drugs that were waved through were never properly examined at all. Five FDA officials and more than 40 generic company employees were eventually convicted of felonies. (Frank Young, the commissioner, was never personally implicated.)

Budget cuts. Just as the FDA was trying to cope with its new responsibilities for regulating scientific trials, its increased authority over devices and biologics, and the demands of a more muscular consumer movement, the Reagan administration was stripping away the money and staff it would need to do the jobs. For instance, in his first budget, in 1981, President Reagan wiped out nearly one-tenth of the agency's staff of 7,500. Reagan had made it clear back in the campaign that he thought taxes were too high and government was too big and that both were impeding free enterprise. Regulatory agencies were a particular target. From now on the Office of Management and Budget would have to approve new regulations, based on a cost-benefit analysis. Several FDA initiatives to give consumers more information about the side effects of drugs and the ingredients in packaged food were stopped cold, and even enforcement actions were halted in mid-investigation, according to Hilts.

The FDA's biggest black eye during the 1980s involved AIDS, or acquired immune deficiency syndrome. What makes the complex disease so tough to fight is that it pits a person's own defenses—his or her immune system—against itself. The human immunodeficiency virus (HIV) that triggers AIDS transfers its deadly genetic information into the DNA of so-called helper T-cells in the immune system, which weakens the body's ability to fight back. Moreover, the virus can lie dormant for years before erupting fiercely and unexpectedly. Then, with the immune system less able to stop it, the virus can move almost at will to any organ, or multiple organs.

The epidemic began slowly, with some unusual cases of pneumonia in 1981. Then came reports of a rare type of cancer. With increasing speed, the disaster spread, 180 dead in 1981, then 500, 1,600, 41,000 by 1988, hitting the gay community and intravenous drug users in particular. All the while, the federal government seemed frozen. President Reagan did not even utter the word "AIDS" for five years. Nor were many Americans all that worried about a disease that seemed to target what they considered marginal—if not disreputable—segments of society. Desperate AIDS patients sought any kind of treatment, even heading to Mexico and Brazil for the newest miracle cures, in violation of the federal law against importing unapproved drugs. But there was no cure, nothing that seemed to stop the fatal progression of the complicated disease. Furiously, the playwright and AIDS activist Larry Kramer called one FDA official a murderer.

Drug companies initially were reluctant to shell out tens of millions of dollar in research and development for a condition that was so difficult to treat, that could be so dangerous to handle, and—so it seemed—that had such a limited and unpopular clientele. When Burroughs Wellcome finally agreed to open up its vast inventory of chemicals for testing, scientists at the NIH and Duke University did the actual work, at government expense. One of the compounds seemed promising, so in 1985 Burroughs filed to begin clinical trials for azidothymidine, or AZT. The FDA set in motion the normal application process, with a couple dozen healthy people to be tested for safety in Phase I, then several hundred AIDS patients in Phase II along with a control group on a placebo. As the Phase II trial results came in amazingly strong, the FDA agreed to let the drug skip Phase III and go straight on the market, slashing years off the normal process. AIDS finally had its first treatment.

So why were AIDS activists angry at the FDA? For one thing, by then it was already 1987, and people had been dying for six years. They had felt ignored by the government and stigmatized by society. As well, the AIDS community blamed the FDA for what was really the fault of the drug companies.

Still, there is plenty of criticism to lay on the FDA itself. The agency could have used its bully pulpit to urge the pharmaceutical industry to delve into research. It was slow to screen the blood supply, which allowed AIDS to spread more quickly into the wider community and infect celebrities like tennis star Arthur Ashe. Mark Novitch, who was either the deputy or acting commissioner in the early years, exemplified the FDA's hands-off approach when he recalled the first time he heard of this odd disease. Some people from the Centers for Disease Control had come to tell him about an unusual number of cases of pneumonia clustered in Los Angeles. His response was not: What can the FDA do? It was: "There was little we could do until the NIH and CDC and researchers could present something that would be ready for FDA action. It was a research issue."

Moreover, before and after AZT, the FDA was slow in approving other AIDS drugs. In his 1994 book *The FDA Follies*, Herbert Burkholz describes one example—ganciclovir, a drug for an inflammation of the retina known as Cytomegalovirus retinitis (CMV), which is caused by a herpes virus and can lead to blindness. The drug's potential seemed so hopeful that the FDA let the manufacturers of two versions, Syntex of California and Burroughs Wellcome, give it away for free under what is known as a "compassionate use" basis, or special access for people with fatal conditions, even before human trials were completed. However, the agency proceeded to reject Syntex's formal application to market ganciclovir, saying that the trials had not been conducted with the proper control group on a placebo, as required by law, and the data were inadequate. To the AIDS community, this was outrageous nitpicking over a badly needed drug that the "compassionate use" experience had already shown could save thousands of people from blindness. To the FDA, however, it was careful, proper science. Perhaps that is a debatable issue. But as Burkholz points out, when the FDA finally approved the drug a year and a half later, the decision was based on "nothing more than the original data recooked and served up with a touch of finesse...no placebo-controlled trials had been performed, and much of the information was still anecdotal." So tens of thousands of AIDS victims had to risk blindness for a year and a half, waiting for a perfectly good drug.

Dr. Janet Woodcock, who was then an official at the Center for Biologics—she later became director of the Center for Drugs, and now is the agency's acting deputy commissioner for operations—sighed as she remembered the atmosphere in those days: "People said, 'Any drug with any possibility should get on the market. The FDA is killing people.'"

At any rate, years of pent-up anger homed in on the FDA. On October 11, 1988, AIDS activists, patients, relatives, and friends brought their protest to Rockville—1,000 of them, from all across the United States. Among the group was Matt Sharp, then a 32-year-old ballet dancer from Oklahoma City, newly diagnosed with the disease. He had organized a contingent from his hometown and wore a sign on his back noting where he was from so that the local media could find him for an easy interview. (They did: He got on the TV news that night.)

Back then, the FDA "was viewed as apathetic in their approach to listening to people who were dying of HIV. They shut the door to us," said Sharp, who is now the director of treatment education for an AIDS information and support group in Chicago. "There was a lot of discrimination. That was the general mindset. It was the same thing that was going on all across the country."

Sharp was "new and a little bit frightened" when he first walked the three blocks from the Metro station just before seven o'clock on the morning of the demonstration. As he arrived at the hulking agency headquarters, "it was unbelievably angry and charged and energetic. People were fired up, linking arms trying to stop people from going into the building, police on horseback, always some scuffle taking place." Demonstrators, who had promised nonviolence, raised a black flag on the building's flagpole and hanged Reagan and Frank Young in effigy. Sharp can remember protestors crawling along the tops of police buses to stop them from moving, and others crawling into the building to drop banners in the hallways. Some people carried placards with slogans like "FDA red tape killed me." Others poured what looked like blood onto the street. "We made the government stand still that day," Sharp said.

Many staffers working at the FDA claim it actually was not hard to bypass the demonstration and continue business as usual. Dr. Carl C. Peck, who headed CDER at that point, typically got to work at five o'clock in the morning anyway, so he slipped in before the demonstrators arrived and simply stayed until they had gone, at around five in the evening. Gerry Meyer, the loyal 20-year veteran and Peck's onetime deputy, brown-bagged his lunch to avoid facing the crowd by going out to eat, although he did look out his window a few times to watch them. "You couldn't hear anything, because they were outside," recalled Jack W. Martin, who was then associate commissioner for public affairs.

Clearly, though, the protests and the plight got to the FDA. Breaking with its hard-won requirement that drugs must prove safety and efficacy, which had taken the disasters of sulfanilamide and thalidomide to carve into law, the agency established two new programs, known as a "treatment IND" and "parallel track." They allowed AIDS patients (and others) access to promising experimental drugs early in the development process, long before their safety and efficacy had been proved. The main requirements were that the patients had to have a life-threatening disease, there had to be little other effective treatment available, and the manufacturer had to continue with its properly controlled trials. FDA officials at first insisted that they were not really setting a precedent, pointing out that beta-blockers, calcium channel blockers, and cancer drugs had been made available for years under similar "open protocols" or the "compassionate use" arrangement undertaken with ganciclovir. But the two new programs were at the least a more formal version of the earlier ones, and even the FDA Web site bluntly says that parallel track was developed "in response to AIDS." A decade later, the FDA would continue finding ways to allow access to experimental drugs for patients with serious or life-threatening diseases. Some scientists, meanwhile, worried whether important information about side effects or potency was being missed because of all these shortcuts.

By then, Frank Young, the commissioner, was worn down. So was his staff. The FDA was desperate for a knight in shining armor.

People either love or hate David Kessler.

Consider two interviews, less than three months and some three hundred miles apart:

"Kessler was the worst commissioner in history. Everything David did was calculated to advance his own career," declared Peter Barton Hutt, the tall, silver-haired, impeccably patrician lawyer and historian who was the agency's chief counsel in the early 1970s; he now represents major drug companies and trade associations at Covington & Burling, a Washington, D.C. law firm.

"David Kessler was a wonderful person to work for—extremely bright, hard-working, disciplined, and on top of that he's just the nicest person you could ever work for. He captures what public service is all about," said Jerold R. Mande, a short, speed-talking, slightly boyish-looking Yale University official who was Kessler's executive assistant for most of the commissioner's six years and four months on the job.

What most people can agree on is that David Kessler is brilliant and driven: An M.D. as well as a lawyer, he was the director of medicine at Albert Einstein College of Medicine in New York City by age 32 and was appointed to succeed Frank Young in November 1990 when he was just 39. At that point, he had no political record other than some stints working for Orrin Hatch, the conservative Republican senator from Utah (and cosponsor of the Hatch-Waxman law on generic drugs).

Kessler dove into the agency like a hundred new brooms and a hundred hurricanes. Less than six months after his arrival, he decided to make the point, loud and clear, that the FDA would now be enforcing the laws on food labels. He focused on an orange juice brand made by Procter & Gamble called Citrus Hill Fresh Choice. Only the fine print pointed out that, well, it was not exactly fresh. It was made from concentrate, which meant that after the oranges were picked, the liquid was evaporated, the concentrate was stored, and then water, pulp and other ingredients were added in to turn the product into juice again. The FDA tried to negotiate a new label with Procter & Gamble. When that failed, the agency sent federal marshals to cordon off a warehouse where 24,000 cartons of Citrus Hill were stored. P&G soon changed its label.

To Kessler, as he proclaimed in a speech to food industry lawyers just as the marshals were making their move, the action would "send a clear message that the FDA will not tolerate such violations of the law." To critics, it was a publicity stunt. Gerry Meyer called it "one of the silliest, most embarrassing things." (Kessler, in a book he wrote about his years at the FDA, entitled *A Question of Intent*, is only somewhat more polite in his disparagement of Meyer as "the professional who has seen everything and was implacable in his views.")

Citrus Hill's days would probably have been numbered anyway, because Congress in 1990 had mandated new labels for food packages that were supposed to make the contents and their nutritional value much clearer to consumers. In particular, the labels were to show what proportion of the average person's daily diet would be provided by the nutrients in the particular food. However, the details—most notably, how many calories should constitute an appropriate average daily diet—remained to be decided. The Agriculture Department called for a standard of 2,350 calories, largely because it did not want to discourage people from eating beef, which it regulates and which is high in calories. Kessler said that standard might lead people to overeat, so he recommended 2,000 calories. The two agencies were so uncompromising that they ended up taking the dispute all the way to the Oval Office in 1992 for President George H.W. Bush to resolve, which was virtually unheard of. Since when does the president have to be brought in to decide the numerical value of a chocolate chip cookie? Armed with a paper tray-liner from a McDonald's outlet listing 2,000 calories as an average daily diet, Kessler won. (The FDA chief later said he would have resigned if he had lost that battle.)

But in one sense the labels backfired: They roused the makers of diet supplements and herbal remedies, who feared that the next step would be for their companies, too, to come under regulation for the first time. Those industries launched a powerful PR campaign that scared voters into thinking their vitamins were going to be taken away. The consumers and lobbyists persuaded Congress to pass a law in 1994 specifically exempting the supplements and herbs from FDA labeling regulations or safety tests.

This was a serious setback for the FDA. The new law essentially meant that supplements and herbs would be treated the way drugs and food had been before 1938—that manufacturers would not need to prove that their products worked or were even safe before putting them on the market. Nor would they have to report side effects. In the public mind, these products were "natural," which meant they must be safe. After all, hadn't people been gathering medicinal herbs for hundreds of years? Moreover, the law assumed that they were being used only as a sort of addition to the consumer's diet, an extra nutritional boost.

In fact, herbal remedies and supplements are not always harmless. Supplements have been linked to strokes, cancer, kidney and liver damage, and rashes—and besides, they sometimes do not even produce the health benefits that they claim. But in order to prevent a dangerous herbal remedy or supplement from being sold, the FDA has to wait until it causes serious injuries or deaths, and then prove that the product was at fault. The supplement ephedra might never have been banned in 2003 if it had not been a well-known baseball player, Baltimore Orioles pitcher Steve Bechler, who died after taking it.

Meanwhile, as supplements regulation faltered, Kessler was taking on Dow Corning Corporation and other manufacturers of silicone-filled breast implants, as well as plastic surgeons and their patients. The implants had been on the market since before the FDA had authority to regulate them under the Medical Devices Amendments of 1976. Now the FDA was trying to work backwards, to make sure after the fact that there was scientific proof of the implants' safety. Certainly millions of women had been wearing them quite happily for 30 years. Yet for many other women they had turned into miserable, painful intrusions that hardened, broke, leaked, and left hideous scars. After a series of contentious public hearings, Kessler ended up cobbling together a disputed compromise that was more diplomatic than logical: The implants would be allowed in breast reconstruction after cancer surgery—that is, for a real medical need—but manufacturers were asked to withhold them if the reason was only cosmetic. (That hardly settled the issue. Dow Corning filed for bankruptcy in 1995, and nine years later, when another company applied to sell a new version of the implants, the FDA staff and a panel of outside experts disagreed about whether to let the product on the general market.)

In an era of seemingly endless federal budget deficits, it was a pipe dream to think the FDA would ever get more resources out of the U.S. Treasury. So Kessler tried another approach to fatten his agency's wallet. A proposal had been bouncing around since the Reagan era that would have drug manufacturers essentially finance their own FDA reviews by paying user fees. Theoretically, the fees would go for hiring more staff, thus enabling the agency to approve (or reject) applications faster. The idea was controversial among consumer groups, who worried that it would give the pharmaceutical companies too much influence over reviews. In addition, there was fear that the White House and Congress would subtract the fees from the FDA's existing budget, meaning no net gain at all. Nor were manufacturers all that happy at the prospect of paying more money to the government. But Kessler championed the proposal as a source of needed new money, and his imprimatur gave it credibility among most consumer groups. The first Prescription Drug User Fee Act, or PDUFA, was passed in 1992, charging drug makers an annual fee of $50,000, plus $6,000 a year for each product already on the market and $100,000 for each new application. Just as significantly, it set deadlines for how long reviewers could take to come to their decisions. The measure was due to expire five years later but was renewed twice with increasingly tough deadlines, and similar laws for devices and animal drugs eventually followed. The number of reviewers and the funding available to the FDA did, in fact, go up, while review times went down.

Of all his whirlwind of activity, Kessler may be best known—and most controversial—for his attempt to regulate tobacco as a drug. From a public health perspective, cigarettes are an uncomfortable anomaly. As the leading cause of preventable death in the United States, they are clearly bad for public health. Yet they may be bought far more easily than most medicines, without a prescription or even a brochure spelling out all the risks in detail. There is only a brief warning on the package that virtually everyone ignores and an age requirement that teenagers have been evading for decades. The FDA has never regulated cigarettes because—it was assumed—they are not food, drugs, cosmetics, or medical devices.

For an activist like Kessler, that anomaly was probably unbearable. In *A Question of Intent*, he claims that going after tobacco was not his idea. Rather, he says, the suggestion first came from Jeff Nesbit, the agency's head of public affairs at that time, whose father was dying of cancer. In addition, a number of consumer groups, led by the Coalition on Smoking or Health, had filed petitions seeking some sort of FDA action. Even then, cigarettes took a back seat for a while to more pressing matters, like orange juice.

But once he started, Kessler bore into the tobacco industry. From the fall of 1992 until he left office in February 1997 to become dean of the Yale University School of Medicine, Kessler and his staff pored over patent applications and old legal depositions, and tracked down whistle-blowers and customs documents throughout the southern United States and into Brazil. They visited gleaming tobacco company headquarters and one-plow farms, testified in Congress, lobbied President Bill Clinton, read 710,000 letters from the public, and prepared for trial. Kessler hired or reassigned about a dozen staffers specifically for the effort, and his book acknowledges an FDA "tobacco team" of 89 people. He was so wrapped up in the quest that he personally conducted several interviews, fed questions to his staff during other interviews, and went to the Library of Congress to do his own research—surprising the librarian.

Some FDA veterans complain that the rest of the agency suffered from Kessler's single-minded focus on tobacco. With the investigation sucking all the oxygen out of the air, other things just got ignored. Even Carl Peck—who headed the Center for Drugs during part of that time and who calls Kessler "a personal hero of mine" for his campaign on cigarettes—admitted that "Kessler didn't have a clue what I was doing. He was off working on tobacco." In fact, Peck posited that tobacco distracted Kessler so much that he did not fight hard enough against the diet supplement industry. "A more attentive commissioner might have kept [jurisdiction over] supplements. Frank Young wouldn't have let that happen."

The Kessler team developed a novel theory that a cigarette is actually a device for delivering a drug, nicotine. They even unearthed documents that quoted tobacco company officials saying things like, "In a sense, the tobacco industry may be thought of as being a specialized, highly ritualized and stylized segment of the pharmaceutical industry." Kessler never tried to go so far as to ban cigarettes, which would have been politically if not legally impossible. Instead, he concentrated on the marketing side as a way to keep teenagers from taking up smoking. President Clinton was persuaded, and in 1996 he issued a regulation that would allow the FDA, among other things, to forbid vending machine purchases, cartoon characters in publications aimed at children, promotional giveaways, mail-order sales, and free samples. Then the U.S. Supreme Court killed that effort cold, ruling in March 2000 that the FDA did not have the legal authority to regulate tobacco.

Still, most observers say the seven-and-a-half-year effort was not a waste. The evidence the FDA dug up, showing that the tobacco companies knew they were selling a dangerous product, buttressed a growing public anger. It is undoubtedly because of Kessler's work that the industry in 1998 reached a settlement with 46 states requiring the companies to pay $246 billion over 25 years and putting some restrictions on marketing. Kessler's efforts probably also paved the way for a bill granting the FDA limited jurisdiction over tobacco, which passed the Senate in 2004, although opposition from the Republican leaders of the House of Representatives later killed the proposal. "The debate has moved a long way in the ten years since David Kessler took action. There's a much broader base of support for the concept," said Matthew L. Myers, who was originally with the Coalition on Smoking or Health and then became president of the National Center for Tobacco-Free Kids, another anti-smoking advocacy group in Washington, D.C.

In the midst of all this, a political upheaval rocked the federal government: Republicans took over both houses of Congress in 1994, for the first time in four decades. Many of these new officeholders were even more anti-government than Ronald Reagan had been, while others were furious at Kessler's regulatory activism. Along with critics who had been complaining for years that the FDA took too long to approve drugs, they came together to propose a set of "reform" bills that would drastically curtail the FDA's authority in the name of getting medication out to people faster. Drugs could be marketed without FDA review, as long as they were reviewed by certified private agencies—which did not exist. Drugs for serious and life-threatening conditions could get on the market without any standardized human tests at all. Kessler fought back, with support from public interest groups and many members of Congress. Ultimately, the most extreme measures were watered down, and an FDA Modernization Act was passed in 1997 in conjunction with a reauthorization of the user fee law, speeding up the deadlines for completing reviews.

If the FDA wanted a respite from the Kessler whirlwind, fate had other plans. With a Democratic president, Bill Clinton, and a partisan Republican Congress that fiercely disagreed with him—plus a move to impeach the president over his affair with a White House intern—it took nearly two years after Kessler left in February 1997 to find a replacement whom the Senate would approve. In the meantime, Dr. Michael Friedman, an oncologist and former professor who had been the deputy commissioner of operations, stepped in. He had barely filled his coffee cup before disturbing reports started to surface about deaths and serious side effects from the diet drugs Redux and Pondimin. Then the blood pressure medication Posicor. The painkiller Duract. The antibiotic Raxar. The diabetes drug Rezulin. Altogether, a dozen drugs that the FDA had originally approved were pulled off the market in just four years (during Friedman's tenure and that of his successor). The agency had never had such a disastrous safety record.

Meanwhile, the usually quiet animal part of the FDA was also about to erupt. Europe had been struggling for more than a decade with so-called mad cow disease—formally, bovine spongiform encephalopathy, or BSE—among its herds. The disease is spread when animals eat food containing the remains of infected animals, and it destroys the brain by causing brain tissue to become spongy and full of holes. Bad as it was to have herds of cattle infected, matters worsened in 1996 when England reported the first cases of a related disease in human beings, apparently a result of eating tainted beef. While at that point there were no recorded cases in animals or humans in the United States, McDonald's had announced that it had stopped buying beef from Britain. So the FDA was under tremendous pressure to do something to protect the American food supply. Consumer groups wanted a law as strict as Great Britain's ban on feeding any mammal remains to "food animals." The cattle industry, however, wanted as little restriction as possible, claiming it would cost companies hundreds of millions of dollars if they had to throw out dead animal parts instead of using that as feed. After more than a year's delay, in August 1997, the FDA issued a compromise regulation declaring that cattle feed could no longer contain the remnants of dead cattle, goats, sheep, deer, and certain other mammals. However, cows would still be able to eat dead horses, pigs, poultry, and cattle blood products, while poultry, and pets could eat anything. For the moment, the dam held.

It was a heavy load for a commissioner who was only supposed to be keeping the chair warm for a permanent successor while an angry Congress hovered and "reform" remained under debate. When I asked him to describe his tenure, however, Friedman diplomatically called it "a very lucky and happy time." He went on, "What can be more satisfying than to have important public health issues where you're surrounded with very talented, knowledgeable, effective people, where the whole group feels you're having an impact?"

In December 1998 the Senate finally confirmed as FDA commissioner Dr. Jane E. Henney, a press-shy oncologist from Indiana and a long-time medical administrator at the University of Kansas, the University of New Mexico, and the National Cancer Institute. Into her lap got thrown an even hotter potato: RU-486, known as the abortion pill, a synthetic steroid that can help induce abortions early in pregnancy by interfering with a fertilized egg's ability to adhere to the lining of the uterus. Advocates—including most of the medical world—saw it as a safe, humane alternative to surgery, and it had been safely used in Europe for a decade. To opponents of abortion, however, it was simply murder in pill form. The decision whether or not to approve RU-486 was so controversial that a public hearing in 1996 was held in a special windowless room protected by armed guards and metal detectors. It was undoubtedly the most controversial decision the regulators had made affecting women's health or reproduction since they were confronted with the first birth control pill in 1960. Henney gave the FDA's approval in September 2000.

From then on, Henney was in the bull's-eye of the Christian right. And when George W. Bush took over the White House after the disputed election of 2000, she was fired within days.

Again, it took almost two years to name an FDA commissioner. One potential nominee was opposed by the pharmaceutical industry as being too pro-consumer, while another was blackballed by Senate Democrats as too favorable to industry. As the search dragged on, staffers "found it disturbing and demoralizing," said Dr. Michael Greene, a professor of obstetrics, gynecology, and reproductive biology at Harvard University who consults regularly for the agency. The FDA's far-flung constituencies were tired of a vacuum at the top. Companies like Antigenics with innovative scientific techniques needed a chief who had the clout to authorize changes in the approval process. Legislation passed after the terrorist attacks of September 11, 2001, had given the FDA responsibility for helping companies develop vaccines against bioterrorism; who would set the standards for this new mandate? Drug industry executives, consumer advocates, and members of Congress all pressed the Bush White House to find someone fast.

When Dr. Mark B. McClellan became commissioner in November 2002 at age 39, the agency finally seemed to be back on course. He was a Kessler with better political connections and without the controversy, another youthful overachiever bearing two professional degrees—in McClellan's case, an MD and a PhD in economics. Everybody—Democrats and Republicans, consumer groups and pharmaceutical makers—seemed to like him.

Short and boyish-looking, with a receding hairline, a round face, and the faintest Texas twang, he comes across as charmingly self-effacing yet bursting with energy. Even one of the candidates he beat out, Dr. Alastair J. J. Wood, assistant vice chancellor at the Vanderbilt University School of Medicine—he is the candidate who was opposed by the drug industry—said he had been "very impressed" with McClellan when the latter, as a White House economics staffer, had previously reviewed Wood's own nomination. "He's certainly a thoughtful person, a person you'd like to have on your faculty," commented Wood, who still speaks in the rich accent of his native Scotland, with "certainly" coming out "saretanly." (Coincidentally, Wood joined the board of Antigenics in 2004.) In addition to all the other qualifications, McClellan had two more: His younger brother, Scott, was the White House press secretary, and his mother, Carole Keeton Strayhorn, was a Texas politician with ties to the Bush family.

McClellan soon had more balls in the air than even an economist could count. There was something for everyone: faster approvals of new drugs, faster approvals of cheaper generic drugs, new food labels, new restrictions on animal feed to prevent mad cow disease, new guidelines to deal with scientific advances like that of Antigenics, a special committee to study obesity, a crackdown on the use of performance-enhancing steroids by athletes, a crackdown on importing cheap drugs from Canada, a crackdown on drug-mixing by pharmacists, a renewed crackdown on dangerous diet supplements despite the1994 law, bar codes on medicine in hospitals, more testing of drugs on women. . . .

And then, 16 months later, McClellan, too, was gone. He was named to head another agency in the Department of Health and Human Services, overseeing the federal health insurance programs Medicare and Medicaid and implementing a controversial new law on prescription drugs. Since the presidential election was less than eight months off, there was no attempt to name a lame-duck replacement at the FDA. So it would be at least a year before the FDA had another leader.

Once again, with public pressure bearing down, with revolutions in science, ethics, politics, and consumer attitudes demanding regulatory rethinking—Rockville waited.

CHAPTER 4

"You Don't Know Which Agency Is in Charge"

Federal health officials in the mid-1980s started noticing a troubling increase in the occurrence of *Salmonella enteritidis*, or SE, a type of food poisoning that comes mainly from eating fresh eggs infected with the salmonella bacteria. At its mildest, SE causes diarrhea, abdominal cramps, and fever; at worst, it can lead to kidney disease, meningitis, rheumatoid arthritis, heart disease, and death. Indeed, it has been known to kill hundreds of people each year, and tens of thousands of cases of illness are reported annually.

While the Salmonella bacteria can be destroyed by thorough cooking, people eat eggs in lots of ways that do not involve high enough heat—as sunny-side-up eggs, Caesar salad dressing, egg nog, and Hollandaise sauce, to name a few. So, other safety measures are necessary before the eggs ever reach the restaurant table or the grocery store shelf. There are various possibilities: Regulators could inspect henhouses more rigorously, insist that eggs be refrigerated at colder temperatures, or mandate warning labels on egg cartons. Pennsylvania started a pilot program in 1992 that included requiring chicks to come from flocks that had been monitored for SE, testing of manure samples, and pasteurizing of infected eggs.

In 1997 the Center for Science in the Public Interest (CSPI), a consumer advocacy group founded by three lawyers who had worked with Ralph Nader, petitioned the federal government to adopt Pennsylvania's program nationwide. There was just one problem: "You don't know which agency is in charge of infected eggs," recalled Caroline Smith DeWaal, director of the CSPI's program on food safety.

The U.S. Agriculture Department's Agricultural Marketing Service inspects egg facilities regularly for cleanliness and grades the eggs based on yolk size. Another arm of the Agriculture Department, the Food Safety and Inspection Service, tracks diseased animals and also inspects facilities that make egg products, like powdered eggs. The FDA is supposed to keep infected food out of retail stores and recall eggs that have caused outbreaks of food poisoning. The Centers for Disease Control (CDC) issues advisories to state health departments, nursing homes, and hospitals. "If the chicken is sick, USDA is in charge," DeWaal summarized. "If the chicken is not sick but lays infected eggs, the FDA is in charge."

According to the CSPI, the Agriculture Department and the FDA started out in 1988 with a voluntary joint program under which the industry would rein in potentially dangerous processes that could lead to a salmonella outbreak. But a year later, the cooperation had fallen apart, and each agency was working on its own mandatory program. The Agriculture folk announced theirs first, so the FDA dropped its tougher version. Then Congress stepped in, passing a law in 1991 authorizing the Agriculture Department to require that eggs be kept at 45 degrees Fahrenheit (or colder) after they are packed and while they are transported. The same law also ordered the FDA to ensure that restaurants maintain that temperature. However, the FDA does not inspect restaurants; state and local health departments do. The FDA in 2000 put out a notice advising consumers and retailers to refrigerate and thoroughly cook eggs, but that was still voluntary. Finally, in September 2004, the agency proposed rules that would require strict tests, pest and rodent control, cleaning and disinfecting procedures, and other processes for egg farmers.

The confusion over eggs is not a fluke. Because the FDA has such a sprawling jurisdiction, running from cell phones to salad to saccharin and beyond, it inevitably bumps up against other government agencies with authority over closely related products. The Agriculture Department (USDA) is by far its biggest neighbor, but the FDA also frequently overlaps with the Federal Trade Commission, the Environmental Protection Agency, state regulators, and a whole alphabet soup of government entities. When it does, the FDA is at a bureaucratic disadvantage. It is not a Cabinet department like Agriculture. It is not an independent agency like the EPA. It is not headed by someone with a direct mandate from the voters, like a city. So when it collides with another agency and loses, the public health issue at stake might be decided by the other agency's regulations—whether tougher or weaker. Or there might just be a tangle.

On the face of it, the organizational chart seems very simple. The FDA's Center for Biologics regulates biological products and procedures, such as blood banks, tissue, and vaccines; the Center for Drugs handles all other medications; the Center for Veterinary Medicine does animal food, drugs, and devices; the Center for Food Safety oversees food products and additives for people; and the Center for Devices has a hodgepodge of responsibilities, from medical devices like pacemakers and breast implants, to radiation-emitting machines like microwave ovens. In addition, the National Center for Toxicological Research in Arkansas does behind-the-scenes research and testing, such as developing methodologies that both FDA inspectors and industry scientists might use to understand molecular processes, or analyzing drugs after a lot of serious side effects have been reported.

So, the Center for Food Safety and Applied Nutrition at the FDA regulates the safety of all food other than poultry and meat, which are the province of the Agriculture Department.

Except for so-called game meats like venison and ostrich, which actually fall to the FDA. Also bottled water, for which the EPA develops the standards while the FDA takes on the labeling and safety. And eggs, in which case, as the CSPI found, the jurisdiction is shared. (But the chicken, whether or not it came first, is handled by Agriculture.) Meanwhile, alcoholic beverages come under the aegis of the Bureau of Alcohol, Tobacco, Firearms, and Explosives in the Department of Justice and the Alcohol, Tobacco, Tax, and Trade Bureau in the Treasury Department

Fish are a different kettle of—well, anyway. The EPA regulates fish that are caught recreationally, but if they are sold commercially, they fall to the FDA. That created a problem when scientists realized that certain species of fish—particularly tuna, the most popular fish eaten in America—tend to absorb high levels of methylmercury, a form of mercury that can damage the growing brains of fetuses and young children. The EPA recommended a strict weekly limit on the amount of fish that pregnant women and children should consume. The FDA wanted a higher limit, arguing that since fish are a good, low-fat source of protein and Omega-3 fatty acids, it did not want to discourage people from eating that food. Consumer groups protested that the FDA's first proposal in 2001 was too generous, especially for tuna, and was hard to understand besides. The FDA revised it, moving closer to the EPA's version. In December 2003, the FDA held a special public hearing at which it produced a new alternative that it had coordinated with the EPA. Finally, the following March, the two agencies issued a joint policy that recommended eating a variety of fish, with special warnings about tuna and a list of other species to be avoided completely.

As for meat, the Agriculture Department is in charge of meat for human consumption, but the FDA takes care of meat fed to animals. This meant, when the first case of mad cow disease appeared in the United States in December 2003, that the Agriculture officials were frantically trying to find all the steaks and hamburgers that might have been processed from that one sick cow, while the FDA was analyzing what the cow might have eaten.

Furthermore, the FDA regulates the drugs that are given to the animals that the USDA regulates (except for biologic drugs, which the USDA keeps charge of). In early 2004, Agriculture inspectors discovered that veal calves in two slaughterhouses in Wisconsin had been implanted with synthetic testosterone to stimulate growth, a practice the FDA had banned. So the USDA kept the calves out of the food supply temporarily, until the testosterone had left their systems and the FDA decided that they could be sold for meat.

While food is still growing in the field, the EPA joins Agriculture and the FDA in sharing responsibility for the pesticides that are used: The EPA sets the level at which a residue may remain on crops, and the other two agencies make sure those levels are not exceeded once the crops are harvested and sent to market. The USDA also has the mandate to block the spread of plant pests.

Things get more complicated if food is genetically modified—that is, if a gene from one organism is transferred into the genetic make-up of another. The Agriculture Department regulates the field-testing of genetically modified plants. The EPA regulates bioengineered plants that are altered in order to make their own pesticides. The FDA regulates whether these plants and animals are safe to eat. This is not much regulation: When the issue first arose in the early 1990s, the FDA more or less punted. It decided that genetically modified food was essentially the same as natural food and therefore there was no requirement for safety testing.

Then Europe, worried about the potential long-term risks to human health and the environment, put a moratorium on the importation of virtually all genetically modified food. So then it became a trade issue, which fell into the domain of the U.S. trade representative.

That's not the only place where the FDA tackles trade. Under its post–September 11 mandate, the FDA is supposed to ensure that imported foods are not somehow contaminated by terrorists. To do that, it has to work with yet a new set of partners, the Customs and Border Protection agency.

Then there are restaurants. State and local governments are responsible for inspecting them—remember the confusion about enforcing egg temperatures—but the FDA has drawn up a voluntary Model Food Code that the locals can adopt. The current version includes eight chapters and seven annexes, covering issues from clean fingernails to sewage disposal to contaminated utensils. "These are things we highly recommend," said Dr. Robert E. Brackett, who heads the FDA's Center for Food Safety. "We would like it if every state would adopt it."

Brackett, who has silver hair combed back from his face and thick, dark eyebrows, was barely into his job and obviously still being cautious about how he phrased his comments when he discussed the FDA in the winter of 2004. A microbiologist, he had been a professor at the University of Georgia, then the FDA's food safety director for three years. Now he had the tough task of following a popular and unpretentious predecessor, Joseph A. Levitt, who had just retired.

In fact, most states do follow the FDA's code, partly because of the agency's strong reputation, partly because the industry prefers to have one set of consistent requirements, and no doubt partly because it is a lot easier to latch onto existing rules than to write new ones from scratch. The FDA, industry representatives, and local health authorities also talk formally at least every other year in a meeting known as the Conference for Food Protection.

The senior vice president for quality and logistics at Jack in the Box Inc., Dr. David M. Theno, gave me an example of how the Model Code works: Back in the mid-1990s, restaurants sought to change the requirement that hamburgers and other meat had to be cooked at 155 degrees Fahrenheit for 15 seconds to kill *E. coli* 0157:H7 bacteria. Rather than a single, fixed limit, the industry wanted a range that would balance temperature with cooking time. "We went in and made the case to them [the FDA], why we were requesting a variance. They called us back a couple of times for clarifications," Theno said. After the FDA staffers wrote an opinion supporting the change, Theno and his industry allies had to lobby the states to actually implement it. Ultimately, they succeeded, and the code now has a chart that lists 17 different time and temperature combinations.

Still, the states and locals often pick and choose among sections of the Model Code, or add their own rules. In the early 2000s, the FDA was pondering whether restaurants should be required to list the calories, carbohydrates, and other nutritional content of the food on their menus, as packaged goods do. Without waiting for Washington, six states and the District of Columbia went ahead and introduced bills to do exactly that.

In fact, labels on the packaged food sold in supermarkets are another issue entirely. Under the 1990 law, it is the FDA's job to approve these nutritional listings, which show how the food's various nutrients fit into an average daily diet. But the FDA does not set the requirements for the average daily diet—that was the issue President George Bush had to settle. The FDA relies on guidelines from the National Academy of Sciences, the USDA, and the Department of Health and Human Services. And the Federal Trade Commission (FTC) oversees food advertising. So as soon as a health claim migrates from the back of a box of cookies to the TV screen, it leaves the FDA and goes to the FTC. When KFC (owner of the Kentucky Fried Chicken chain) in October 2003 launched an ad campaign oddly proclaiming that fried chicken is good for your health, it was the FTC that investigated.

Altogether, Eric Schlosser, the author of *Fast Food Nation*, has calculated that a dozen federal agencies and 28 congressional committees oversee food in some way. The classic example of absurdity that everyone points to is pizza: The FDA regulates frozen cheese pizza, but once a slice of pepperoni is put on it, Agriculture takes over.

So much for food. Now, drugs are indisputably the bailiwick of the FDA—that is, medical drugs. Illegal drugs like heroin and marijuana go to the Drug Enforcement Administration (DEA). Drugs that can be used both ways, such as prescription painkillers, are shared between the agencies. Both the FDA and the DEA have to decide whether the drug falls under Schedule II (those like methadone or morphine, which can be dispensed only in a clinic or office with bulletproof glass and under other strict conditions—the highest level of control for a drug with a medical use) or the less restrictive Schedules III and IV (drugs like valium, which can be bought at a pharmacy with a prescription and taken at home). There is also the White House Office of National Drug Control Policy, which is mainly a cheerleader but sometimes urges policies on the other two agencies.

In this dance of drugs, the DEA usually wants to control a product's availability more tightly than the FDA does. For instance, the DEA in 2003 asked an FDA panel to narrowly limit the uses for which certain painkillers could be prescribed; the agency refused. Dr. Charles P. O'Brien, vice chair of psychiatry at the University of Pennsylvania School of Medicine and founder of a drug treatment clinic there, said he was told by FDA advisors that the FDA and DEA quarreled for two years over how to classify buprenorphine, an alternative to methadone that reduces an addict's desire for heroin.

Sometimes pharmacists, rather than purchasing pills from drug manufacturers, mix their own concoctions from chemicals they buy in bulk, a practice called compounding—reminiscent of drug-making 200 years ago. Typically, they do this on a case-by-case basis in order to personalize a prescription, leaving out a dye for an allergic patient, for example. FDA officials are worried about the danger if pharmacists create end products that the regulators never approved. However, it is legally none of the FDA's business; a 2002 Supreme Court decision wiped out a provision of the 1997 Food and Drug Administration Modernization Act that had given the FDA authority. Compounding therefore falls mainly under the jurisdiction of state boards of pharmacy and also under the DEA, which is investigating pharmacists who compound narcotic painkillers.

Another important distinction is that individual states, not the federal government, license doctors. Thus, there is virtually nothing the FDA can do if a physician chooses to prescribe a drug for a condition the FDA has not authorized, as long as the FDA has approved that drug for *something*. (This practice, called off-label prescribing, is discussed in more detail in Chapter 6.)

Of course, when a crisis erupts—an outbreak of food poisoning, say, or tampering with medicine bottles—the Centers for Disease Control gets involved along with the FDA. The CDC tries to trace back the route that the infection or outbreak has taken, from the victim to the poisoned food to the store where the food was bought to the manufacturer. The FDA's role is to pinpoint exactly what element in the food or drug caused the problem.

All that—food and drugs—is the simple part. Moving over to the Center for Devices and Radiological Health, "the regulation of devices is particularly complex. There are many overlapping programs," explained Dr. David W. Feigal Jr., who headed that center from 1999 to 2004.

Feigal is an easygoing internist from California with thinning blond-grey hair who talks a mile a minute without seeming to rush. He taught both epidemiology and biostatistics at the University of California at San Francisco School of Medicine, then moved south to teach medicine at the UC campus in San Diego. In a 12-year FDA career beginning in 1992, he worked in all three of the agency's major medical centers—Drugs, Biologics, and Devices.

Some of the complexities of devices regulation that Feigal outlined are:

The Nuclear Regulatory Commission licenses nuclear radiation therapy—for instance, injecting nuclear seeds via a catheter into the body to look for signs of cancer—but the FDA regulates it.

The Department of Energy and the FDA share jurisdiction over ultrasound equipment.

The FDA oversees lab tests sold publicly, but the Centers for Medicare and Medicaid Services, or CMS, has responsibility when laboratories make their own tests.

And Feigal did not even touch on the potential cross-connections with the Consumer Product Safety Commission. Some distinctions are obvious: Contact lenses, FDA. Baby cribs, CPSC. Household appliances, CPSC— except those that emit radiation, like cell phones and microwave ovens, in which case the FDA takes over. How about exercise machines? They are intended to have an effect on the human body, which would seem to make them medical devices. But of course they also can be bought without any medical supervision. "The FDA has worked out with CPSC that they're consumer products, not devices, unless they're used for therapy," said Richard Cooper, who was the FDA counsel in the late 1970s and is now a partner and corporate attorney with the über-firm of Williams & Connolly. Tall, grey-haired and gaunt, Cooper is an intimidating presence despite his soft voice, clearly loyal to his experience at the FDA, and clearly brilliant. David Kessler in his book called Cooper "a man of enormous intellect." Less than 20 years after leaving the FDA, Cooper would face off against Kessler in court during the fight to regulate tobacco, representing the cigarette giant R. J. Reynolds Tobacco Company.

Finally, all these turf distinctions can be—and have been—disrupted any time Congress creates new agencies, eliminates old ones, or shifts jurisdiction.

Looking at this mass of interwoven lines, many people would throw up their hands and scream. There is no point trying to draw an organizational chart. A number of consumer groups, including the CSPI and the

Consumers Union, have suggested moving food regulation out of both Agriculture and the FDA into a new, consolidated agency.

By necessity, the various bureaucracies over the years have worked out ways of getting along. Take the issue of lab tests, said Feigal: "CMS [the Medicare and Medicaid center] looks at the lab's proficiency, the quality of the lab and the technicians, whether tests are reproducible. It studies quality control in hospitals." By contrast, "the FDA is looking at marketing. There really isn't the kind of conflict you're thinking about. We don't need CMS." In the case of food ads, attorney Cooper said, "the FTC accepts the FDA's medical expertise." Brackett, the FDA's food center director, pointed to the fact that the FDA and the Environmental Protection Agency finally did reach agreement on methylmercury in fish. And anyway, isn't it a good idea to get another department's perspective?

Still, even loyal FDA-ers concede that all this jurisdiction-sharing can be cumbersome. Conferring with sister agencies when there is a disagreement can add months to the decision-making timetable. Look at how long it took the EPA and FDA to reach agreement on methylmercury, or the DEA and FDA to classify buprenorphine. A particular annoyance for the Center for Foods is the voluntary aspect of the Model Food Code. When a state does not follow the code, "it can be frustrating," said Dr. Joseph Madden, who retired in 1997 as the center's strategic manager for microbiology.

I asked Jere Goyan, the FDA chief under President Carter, if coping with the overlap was difficult. "There are so many that you can't even think about that," he replied calmly. "It's a fact of life." Back in the 1970s, he met with his counterparts at the EPA and the CPSC every month or so, but they did not really coordinate regulatory matters. It was more to talk politics and worry about the rising clout of the Republican Party.

For outsiders like DeWaal of the CSPI, trying to determine who inspects infected eggs, it is worse than cumbersome or frustrating. It can be impossible to find their way through the web of interlocking lines, and therefore impossible to get their point across to the right person. Even when the lines are distinctly marked, they do not always connect. "Agencies are not speaking well enough to one another. They are not working together," said Karen Taylor Mitchell, executive director of a fairly new food safety group called Safe Tables Our Priority (abbreviated STOP), which was formed in 1993 after an outbreak of food poisoning from Jack in the Box hamburgers. To cite one example: Mitchell said that after two people were infected with *Salmonella* poisoning from eating packaged tomatoes at the 2002 Transplant Games at Disney World—a sort of Olympics for people who have received organ or bone marrow transplants—STOP badgered the FDA to recall the tomatoes. In a time-honored bureaucratic shuffle, "the FDA said they hadn't gotten all the information from the CDC. We called the CDC; they said the FDA had all the information."

Michael Friedman, the acting commissioner who replaced David Kessler in the late 1990s, said that he held discussions with other agencies, including Agriculture and the White House, about ways of reorganizing the lines of authority. "We certainly thought about a more consolidated food and food safety program, just looking for efficiencies."

When the FDA butts heads with other parts of the government, who wins? Undeniably, the FDA gets a lot of respect. One reason is its vast reach. The only federal agencies that might even come close in scope are the Federal Trade Commission and the Federal Communications Commission, with their jurisdiction over the way Americans interact, suggested Frank Lichtenberg, the Columbia economics professor who has been an advisor to the FTC. As one of the oldest federal consumer agencies, the FDA has also had more time to establish its reputation. And there is a definite cachet attached when your mandate involves life-and-death decisions.

But all other clout evaporates before the 500-pound gorilla of political influence, the Department of Agriculture.

From its nineteenth-century beginning as the Bureau of Chemistry within the USDA, the FDA has seldom been able to wield as much power as its former parent. For starters, Agriculture is far bigger: Its budget in 2004 was $21.5 billion, compared with a mere $1.7 billion for the FDA. While the FDA may oversee 25 percent of the nation's economy, Agriculture handles that icon of American lore, the family farm. And the United States has a lot more farms than drug companies. Two-thirds of all the land in the lower 48 states is used in some agricultural capacity. "The USDA has vastly more reach in the Congress," Michael Friedman summed up. "There are many, many states that have important agricultural activities, so the Department of Agriculture has historically been very important to some extremely potent congressional seats. That's just a historic reality."

Within the hierarchy of government, moreover, never underestimate the importance of being a Cabinet department, like Agriculture, versus a mere "administration" within a Cabinet department, which is what the

FDA is. When the Center for Veterinary Medicine has a disagreement with the USDA, "it could go all the way up to the [Agriculture] secretary," noted Dr. Stephen F. Sundlof, the CVM's lanky, leathery-faced director. In which case, he conceded, Agriculture has a built-in advantage: Its secretary, one of just 15 Cabinet officials, outranks the FDA commissioner. Sure, the FDA chief could call on his or her boss, the secretary of the Department of Health and Human Services, for equal clout, but that means trying to catch the attention of someone who has other priorities besides food and drugs.

Worse, the FDA's budget is still under the control of the congressional agriculture committees, even though the FDA was formally transferred out of the Agriculture Department in 1940. This is because members of Congress do not easily give up jurisdiction over anything that may enable them to allocate money to their district or collect campaign contributions from people affected by that jurisdiction. So the FDA is fighting for dollars from politicians whose main concerns are all those beloved family farmers and the big campaign contributors from the agriculture and meatpacking industries.

"These are very smart, very good individuals who I liked very much," Friedman said, choosing his words diplomatically as he talked about the congressional committee members and their staff. "But they didn't have the science background of some of their counterparts who were reviewing the CDC, NIH, and so forth. What it meant was, you always need to spend time to make sure these smart people get the background they need." Even after the background briefings, he went on, "it's pretty clear their first constituency would be an agricultural one."

His fellow ex-commissioner, Jere Goyan, agreed, with a caveat: "The Agriculture Committee controlling the budget does put the USDA in a better position than the FDA. But no matter who controls the budget, there will always be issues and never enough money."

Probably most important, the two federal bureaucracies simply view the world in diametrically opposed ways. Agriculture officials often come from the meatpacking industry or trade groups. By contrast, FDA commissioners—Jane Henney, Kessler, Goyan, Frank Young—are generally hired from academia, hospitals, or the NIH (although they and lower-level staff frequently go to work for drug companies after they leave the FDA). The Agriculture Department's mission is to promote the beef industry as well as regulate it; the FDA has only the regulatory side. When the two agencies clash, Agriculture is typically pushing for less stringent requirements than the FDA. The dispute over food labels in 1992, when Agriculture wanted to set a higher-calorie standard in deference to beef producers, is a classic example. In short, Agriculture has a reputation for being cozier than the FDA with the industry it oversees.

And the FDA looks down on Agriculture for that. "I know that most people at the FDA feel that a person cannot be a regulator and at the same time an advocate for the industry. I think that some of the people in the Department of Agriculture are more concerned about the health of the industry than the health of the American people," Goyan said to me. Added Mitchell of STOP, during her interview, "There's no love lost between the two agencies, and that hinders food safety."

Until the 1960s, the post of FDA commissioner had effectively been just a promotion through the ranks of the agency. President Lyndon Johnson gave it new gravitas by bringing in a respected outsider, Dr. James Goddard of the CDC, and since then nearly all commissioners have been MDs from outside (with the exceptions of President Carter's two appointees, Donald Kennedy and Goyan, who were outsiders but not MDs). Still, it remained just a managerial job two ranks down from Cabinet level, hired by the president the way any executive might hire a subordinate.

Burned by the disasters of the 1980s, some members of Congress, most notably then Senator Al Gore of Tennessee, decided the agency needed a chief with more institutional clout. They wanted a chief with an independent power base who could not be easily fired and might be less subject to politics. One way to do that, they concluded, would be to give the commissioner a fixed six-year term, more or less like the director of the Federal Bureau of Investigation or the chairman of the Federal Reserve. The White House balked, so Gore came back with another option: require the Senate to confirm the appointment. By definition, that would declare that the job was on an order of magnitude with the assistant secretary of a Cabinet department, who also has to be confirmed. Along with that change, the commissioner would now report directly to the secretary of HHS. Both those provisions elevated the job one level in the bureaucracy—no small matter when standing toe to toe with another agency. Finally, by putting a debate and vote on the public record, Senate confirmation would make it hard for a president to appoint an unqualified political or industry hack. "You must go through the deliberative process, an important additional layer of public review and accountability," pointed out Jerry Mande, who was Gore's health care aide at the time. The proposal was, Gore later said to the Senate Labor Committee during a follow-up hearing in March 1991, "a clear statement of Congressional intent that the independence and integrity of FDA be enhanced." The measure was enacted as the Food and Drug Administration Act of 1988, and David Kessler was the first commissioner to be officially confirmed by the Senate.

(After Gore was elected vice president in 1992, his initiative would come back to haunt him: In 1997 and 1998, with the Republicans in control of the Senate, it took nearly two years to find a replacement for Kessler acceptable to both President Clinton and the Senate. Mande said he and his boss nevertheless did not regret their bill. "I still think from the standpoint of how government should operate, it's the right thing to do," he said. Mande spent the 1990s alternately working for Gore, then Kessler at the FDA, then Gore at the White House. In 2001, he joined Kessler once again, this time at Yale University, where he became associate director for policy at the cancer center of the School of Medicine; but in 2003, Kessler left Yale for San Francisco.)

Making the FDA position subject to Senate confirmation undoubtedly gave it more cachet as well as publicity. Carl Peck, the respected former head of CDER and now director of the Center for Drug Development Science at Georgetown University, believes that the political clout that came with a Senate imprimatur is what enabled Kessler to go after tobacco. "You can take on something you have no authority to do—you can do things because it's a politically appointed leadership."

But apparently the FDA still does not have as much cachet as Medicare and Medicaid. When Commissioner Mark McClellan moved to the Medicare/Medicaid job in March 2004, no one seemed to doubt that it was a step up, especially with a controversial new law on prescription drugs to implement.

CHAPTER 5

Truckloads of Paper

om Garvey still remembers the first time he reviewed a new drug application at the FDA.

It was for a gastrointestinal drug called Reglan, made by A. H. Robins Company, back in the mid-1970s. "It had been put in my office by the supervisory consumer safety officer. She took me by the ear and said, 'Here's an NDA.'" Garvey looked at it—all 300 volumes. "It was choking my office, this great thing. I said, 'Get me out of here.'"

The supervisor sat him down, Garvey recalled, "and showed me, one by one." There were only 10 to 12 key volumes that Garvey, as the officer in charge of reviewing the drug's medical properties, had to read himself. Most of the others would get farmed out to the toxicologist, statistician, and other specialists working on the review.

Short, red-faced, and a little plump, Dr. Thomas Q. Garvey III now has hair, a goatee, and a mustache all the same brilliant shade of snow-white. He talks almost nonstop, interspersed with plenty of jokes and Yiddish expressions picked up from his mother. He originally joined the Public Health Service and subsequently the National Institutes of Health to avoid the draft during the Vietnam War. After the war he went to Massachusetts General Hospital for a fellowship, then returned to the NIH, where he met up with an old Harvard classmate, Bob Temple (the FDA associate director of medical policy who was at the Holiday Inn hearing on antidepressants). Temple urged him to transfer to the FDA, and Garvey spent five years at the agency, rising through three promotions to become supervising medical officer in the cardio-renal division, where he oversaw other doctors doing reviews on heart and kidney drugs. During his tenure, Garvey said, he personally ran the main review on what would become the blockbuster Tagamet for heartburn and supervised the review for another big heartburn drug, Zantac. He also continued working part-time at the NIH while keeping up a small private practice. He left the FDA in 1981 for family reasons, and decided that he liked working from home so much that he never went back. Today, like many former FDA reviewers, Garvey is a consultant to the industry he once regulated. As president of his own firm in Potomac, Maryland, he helps write drug applications for biotech and pharmaceutical companies, including such big players as Merck & Co., GlaxoSmithKline, Lilly, and Genentech.

"It can be done," Garvey said of reviewing an NDA. "You start reading. You try to get over the panic, over the immensity of it all. You read around. You sit there late at night and go line by line." (In the case of Garvey's first effort, Reglan was ultimately approved.)

Imagine what someone goes through to prepare for a presidential debate, to study for the bar exam, to defend a PhD thesis in an oral grilling, to proofread Proust's *In Search of Lost Time*, to work without sleep for four days in a row—and then put that all together. That is a little bit what it is like to work on an application to sell a new drug in the United States. On both sides—for the company that is submitting the application, and the FDA division reviewing it—the work is careful, intense, efficient, repetitive, scientific, arbitrary, and painstaking all at once. There must be data documenting every change in the condition of every patient tested, and those data must be cross-referenced several places in the NDA. Every decimal point must be accurate. A lot of money is riding on the reviewer's decision. So are a lot of lives.

More than anything else, this approval process is what defines the FDA. It lies at the heart of the Type I versus Type II question and creates the most headlines. "The FDA has to be super careful before approving any new drugs because our health is in its hands." "No, the FDA goes overboard, asking ridiculous questions and holding up medicines we desperately need." "Industry has too much influence and pushes the FDA to go too fast." "No, the FDA unfairly treats industry as an enemy." That is the basic debate, and no matter how many efforts the FDA undertakes to streamline the process, the debate never seems to change. Industry will apparently never be satisfied if it has to wait more than a week to start making money. Consumer groups will apparently never be satisfied if a single patient ever dies.

In fact, the process probably could be tightened up a bit—almost anything in life can be made more efficient, especially with constantly improving technology, whether it is typing reports or comparing molecular reactions. As the FDA's role inevitably changes in light of all the new issues it faces, from scientific advances to bioethics to consumer pressure, some of the changes may help approvals move faster, and some may drag things down. But ultimately, the approval process has to be slow and careful. The FDA has to focus on Type I mistakes, because the risks of allowing a dangerous drug on the market are simply so much higher than the risks of not allowing a good one. The first type of risk is that the status quo will be disrupted and people will die much sooner than they otherwise would. The second type is simply that people will not gain an improvement—that the status quo will remain.

Under tremendous pressure from industry and Congress, the FDA in recent years has made huge strides in speeding up its reviews. Critics worry that patients are being put at Type I risk and that the powerful pharmaceutical companies are exerting too much influence. Actually, the real danger lies less in the speed of reviews than in the mindset behind it. The FDA has definitely moved closer to Type II.

The chanciest, most creative, and most exciting part of developing a new drug actually has nothing to do with the FDA. It involves the very first steps—choosing a disease to target and finding a molecule that seems to work on the disease.

Drug companies select their targets for reasons of public need, glory, profit, convenience, and luck. They look for diseases with a big and ongoing market, which means chronic, serious conditions that affect middle-class Baby Boomers who have health insurance, like high cholesterol, arthritis, and diabetes. They also want to be in the areas where cutting-edge science is taking place, like cancer and Alzheimer's disease. And they may focus on a disease because they had noticed that a drug they already make for another condition seems, coincidentally, to have an impact on this one.

Traditionally, researchers at a drug company, a university, a private research lab, or the National Institutes of Health would test hundreds of thousands of molecules that they had been storing in laboratory "libraries" against their disease target. The advent of computerized tools and the mapping of the human genome made the process more efficient, enabling researchers to home in faster and more precisely on the structure of the target, but the basic principle has remained the same: Try to find a match-up of molecule to disease process. For instance, if a certain disease is caused by signals sent to a cell, there might be a molecule that attaches itself to a receptor on that cell and blocks it from receiving the signals.

The most promising of the molecules are tested for safety in animals, to see how well the molecule is absorbed into the blood, how it affects the animals' body chemistry, and other issues relating to the way it works. At least two different animal species are generally used, one of them almost always a rodent. At the end of this time, of 5,000 molecules that scientists begin with, typically 4,995 will have been dumped.

Only then does the FDA come into the picture.

When the drug company has a molecule that seems to work against the target and to be safe in animals, then it prepares its investigational new drug application (IND), which is its formal request for permission to test the drug on humans. This is the application that kept the staff at Antigenics working all day and night just before Thanksgiving of 1996. The IND contains the major results from the animal tests along with details on the composition of the drug and the way it is manufactured. But the heart of the application is the trial protocol, which spells out in excruciating detail exactly how the company plans to conduct its human tests: how many people will be tested at what dosages for how long and at which locations; how these volunteers will be chosen; and what endpoints, or yardsticks, the company will use to evaluate whether the drug works.

Even before filing the IND, most companies send their lead scientists plus representatives from the manufacturing side down to the behemoth at Rockville for a pre-IND meeting with key FDA staffers, as Antigenics did with its slide show. This is probably the company's first contact with the FDA, and it is basically an effort to sound out the agency in advance—to try to make sure the IND is written in a way most likely to be approved and to find out what information the FDA wants. Do the safety findings from the animal tests look solid enough to justify proceeding to humans? What qualifications will the FDA require for the investigators who will be conducting the trials? What kinds of manufacturing controls need to be in place to ensure purity? Is the starting dose big enough? For a company like Antigenics with an innovative approach, the meeting is also a crucial chance to explain its science to reviewers who may never have seen anything like it.

In 2004 the FDA decided to give drug companies even more help, by drawing up standardized guidelines, drug by drug, for considerations like how long the human trials should last and what the endpoints should be. "These are going to spell out for companies exactly what our expectations are. For conditions that are particularly complex and challenging, it's difficult for the company to know what's expected," explained Steve Galson, the acting director of the FDA's Center for Drug Evaluation and Research. He said the agency would begin with obesity and diabetes because they were complex conditions, pharmaceutical makers were crowding into those fields, and there seemed to be confusion as to what the FDA requires as proof. "In the future, I would hope we would have these kinds of guidelines for every condition."

Because all that is really involved is planning, the pre-IND meeting and the IND submission are usually pretty stress-free. In fact, it is essentially a default call: Unless the FDA says "no" within 30 days of the submission, the company may proceed.

But sometimes problems can arise. Among the touchiest topics is the question of where the drug fits in the FDA bureaucracy. Does a drug for skin cancer go to CDER's skin division or its cancer division? Some products are so innovative that it is not even clear whether they are drugs or devices. Manufacturers would prefer to slide in as a device (which would technically be an Investigational Device Exemption, or IDE) because the approval process is a lot faster and less expensive. Where a drug might need to be tested on several thousand patients over at least six years, a device could be done in just a few hundred patients over three years. That's because of the nature of the products—devices do not usually invade the body the way a drug does.

Linda Alexander runs Minnesota-based Alquest, Inc., a contract research organization, which is a type of consulting firm that helps clients maneuver through the regulatory process. Around 2001, she was advising a small, privately owned company in Washington state that was developing a device to dissolve blood clots after a stroke. When a person suffers a stroke, the clot must be dissolved quickly to avoid serious brain damage.

Drugs like TPA and streptokinase can do this, and some researchers have been experimenting with catheters that snake up to the clot to either deliver a shot of a dissolver drug or even pluck out the blockage. Alexander's client had the idea of adding a power source to the catheter—Alexander will not give any details about that power source except to say "think light or sound"—that would activate the drug when it hit the target. The drug that the company planned to use had been approved for dissolving clots in other parts of the body but not the brain.

The client had finished more than two years of animal tests and was ready to file with the FDA—as a device, it hoped. Alexander's staff spent around three months, off and on, preparing a report of a couple hundred pages that detailed all the animal and lab tests and explained the design. Then Alexander headed to Rockville to meet with the reviewers to discuss classification. She knew the reviewers would be skeptical: "Catheter delivery to the brain is something the FDA is not thrilled about. The vessels in the brain are very fragile, and they tend to twist and turn. Trying to get the catheter through is tough." After an hour and a half, she had her answer: It's a drug. Alexander appealed the decision to the division chief, then the FDA ombudsman, but lost again. Since the human trials would now be so much more complicated and expensive, the client tried to hook up with a big pharmaceutical company, but it could not find anyone willing to partner. In 2002, it went out of business.

Alexander said she understands the FDA's reasoning—to a point. "When they make a classification, they base it on the primary mode of action of the product. But it prevents new technology from coming to the forefront. You have to prove the drug all over again."

A Type II mistake or necessary caution? It seems like necessary caution. Clearly the part of the product that would have the key impact on the patient was the drug, not the catheter or the power source. Furthermore, the drug had never been approved for brain clots. So this was more like an application for a brand-new drug that happened to be attached to a catheter with an odd power source, rather than an application for a new device. It is a shame that the company went out of business. But as even Alexander admitted, you don't want to monkey around with the brain.

The next half-dozen years are the meat, potatoes, and entire main course of the drug approval process—the clinical trials, the time when companies test their hoped-for drugs on ever-growing numbers of people, according to the protocol approved in the investigational drug application. The results depend on a combination of luck, skill, patience, careful attention, the basic nature of the disease and the molecules being tested, and how much scientists understand about the functioning of the human body. If things do not work out well in these trials—and about nine-tenths of the time, they don't—there will be no drug.

The Kefauver-Harris Amendments require only that tests on humans must be "adequate and well-controlled." Defining those terms is where the FDA comes in.

The trials are held in groups of 20 or 50 or so all over the world, with hospitals, medical schools, and other sites competing intensely for the privilege. In Phase I, the drug is tested just for safety on a few dozen healthy volunteers over a period of a year or so. Assuming the drug proves safe, the company moves to Phase II, where the drug is given to several hundred people who suffer from the condition it is supposed to treat. This phase, which typically lasts about two years, starts to look at whether the drug actually works, as well as continuing to monitor safety. Finally comes Phase III, which is essentially a bigger version of Phase II, with several thousand patients being monitored for safety and effectiveness over three years or more.

Probably the biggest debate has to do with what to compare the new drug against—in other words, the "control" part of Kefauver-Harris. It is normal scientific practice for only half the subjects in a trial to actually be given the drug being studied; otherwise, there would be no way to compare the effectiveness. It is also an ironclad rule that neither the patients nor the investigators conducting the trial can know exactly who is getting the real drug. The question is, what should the rest of the group get? Should the new drug be tested against a placebo, which is a sugar pill that has no effect on the body, or against another drug for the same condition, if one exists?

Virtually everyone agrees on two circumstances in which placebos cannot be used. When people have life-threatening conditions, it would be unethical to deny treatment. Also, antibiotics have to be compared against each other, because a new antibiotic that is less powerful than what is already on the market is actually dangerous—it could enable bacteria to develop resistance.

Otherwise, the tradition has been to test against placebos. Bob Temple of the FDA argues that a placebo is needed to establish a baseline. With a placebo, researchers can see what happens when a patient is untreated, whether the condition would have cleared up naturally without any drug. Antidepressants are probably the classic example of the benefits of using a placebo. Trials of antidepressant drugs are notoriously unreliable because the initial condition and the "proof" are so subjective. In a standard antidepressant trial, the drug beats the placebo only half the time. That just leaves too high a proportion of uncertainty to allow an existing antidepressant to be the yardstick for measuring a new drug.

But by the early 2000s, there was a growing international criticism of the placebo tradition, for two basic reasons of ethics and economics. When a placebo is used, half the test subjects by definition are not getting treated for their condition. How can scientists ethically allow suffering when they know that a treatment is available? And second, only a direct comparison between drugs can show if a newer, usually more expensive medicine is really any better than the old cheap version. This is especially important because drug companies have a tendency to churn out a lot of "me-too" drugs that are very similar to popular medicines already on the market, and then pump tens of millions of dollars into advertising them. (There is more on these points in Chapters 13 and 14.) "Doctors don't want to know if this new drug is better than a sugar pill. They want to know if it's better than the drug they're already using," Dr. Marcia Angell, a respected former editor-in-chief of *The New England Journal of Medicine* and author of a book castigating the pharmaceutical industry, *The Truth About the Drug Companies*, has said. Still, the FDA and Temple held firmly for placebos, for the most part.

Another hotly debated aspect of defining "adequate and well-controlled" involves how many different dosages of the drug should be tested. Temple said the FDA tries to prod companies to experiment with a variety, to improve the chance of finding the optimum balance between potency and side effects. However, if a study expands into "multiple thousands" of subjects, Temple conceded, "that gets pretty daunting," and the FDA may not press the point. In which case, probably just the higher doses, not lower ones, will be tested, because those are more likely to show strong results. Dr. Jay S. Cohen, a physician and author of the 2001 book *Over Dose*, is probably the most prominent critic of the whole issue of dosage. He charges that after testing at the higher levels, the pharmaceutical industry rarely ratchets down to try less potent amounts. The danger of a too-high dose, as the blood-clot medicine TPA showed, is that it might cause serious side effects. In a study of nearly 500 drugs approved between 1980 and 1999, according to Carl Peck, CDER found that 20 percent had their original dosage altered after going on the market, and "80 percent of the time it had been reduced to lower dosage because of safety problems."

While placebos and dosages remain controversial, other changes in clinical trials procedures have been greeted more with the reaction, "What took you so long?" For instance, the FDA waited about 30 years to acknowledge that women, children, and ethnic minorities get sick. Drug companies traditionally sought out only healthy, fairly young men for their trials, on the theory that this group would have relatively few medical problems that could complicate the results. Until 1993, in fact, it was official FDA policy to exclude from trials women aged 14 to 50—that is, women of childbearing age. "They were protecting women from themselves," said William W. Vodra, who was the agency's associate chief counsel from 1974 to 1979. The reviewers feared that women's menstrual cycles might affect the trials and also that the experiments might affect the women's ability to have children

The catch is that most of the population that will be taking the drugs are not healthy young men. By eliminating people whose medical conditions might "complicate" the findings, the FDA and the companies were also eliminating any chance of learning how the drug would work in the real world or interact with other conditions or medications. Women and men with the same diseases, for instance, can be affected differently and respond differently to the same medication—as Pfizer discovered in early 2004, when it gave up efforts to test its impotence drug Viagra on women. Even race can make a difference. One notable example is that blacks do not do as well as whites on standard heart failure and hypertension drugs. And almost no testing was ever done on children, whose bodies, too, are quite different from that of a 40-year-old—just ask the angry parents at the hearing on antidepressants and teenage suicide. But doctors historically just gave children adult medicines in reduced dosages.

So the FDA started trying to encourage testing on neglected demographic groups. In 1989 it published guidelines for studying drugs in the elderly, and in 1993 came similar guidelines for males and females. Tabulations of trial participants by gender, race, and age became mandatory in 1998. Going a step further, the agency in 2000 approved plans for clinical trials of a heart failure combination drug called Bidil, from the startup company NitroMed, to be tested *only* in African-Americans. If it worked, this could be the first drug approved solely for one specific ethnic group—an approach that raised fresh controversies over whether race should be a scientific category for clinical trials.

The attempts to bring in children were even more difficult. In its 1997 FDA Modernization Act extending the user fees, Congress added a provision giving pharmaceutical makers six more months of patent protection against cheaper generic rivals if they tested their product on children—whether or not the tests showed that the drugs actually helped children, and whether or not the drugs even treated diseases that affect children. According to FDA statistics, over the next six years drug companies offered to test 336 medications under that provision, and ultimately 63 were granted new pediatric labels. (In another, if inadvertent, result, it was GlaxoSmithKline's attempt to get the six-month extension for Paxil that led to the studies that showed the possible links to teenage suicide.) Critics, however, charged that drug makers simply took advantage of the law to rake in huge profits for an extra six months by testing drugs that were big sellers but would rarely be given to children, such as products for arthritis and ulcers. Meanwhile, companies were not testing the drugs that the law was aimed at—less profitable medicines, particularly biologics, that actually were being used for kids.

Since the six-month carrot did not seem to be producing enough genuine pediatric testing, the FDA tried to add a stick. In 1998 it announced that if companies would not voluntarily test certain commonly prescribed drugs and biologics on children, it would order them to do so. The U.S. District Court for the District of Columbia struck that rule down in October 2002, saying the agency had exceeded its authority. Congress had to pass a special law 14 months later specifically giving the FDA the go-ahead.

Conducting a trial is meaningless, however, unless the investigators know just what it is the trial is supposed to measure—that is, the endpoint. With traditional diseases, it was relatively easy to define the marker. Did an anticholesterol statin reduce the level of "bad" (LDL, or low-density lipoproteins) cholesterol? How much did an antihypertensive lower blood pressure? For cancer, the endpoint historically was how many people were free of symptoms five years after beginning treatment. But as companies started pursuing more difficult targets with innovative approaches, they asserted that new sorts of measurements were needed, and the FDA increasingly was willing to accept more flexible yardsticks, so-called surrogate endpoints. (More on that can be found in Chapter 12.) So a cancer drug could be approved even if patients still had symptoms, as long as they demonstrated other signs of measurable improvement. One of the most common yardsticks was showing that a tumor had shrunk, which presumably indicated that the drug had managed to slow the spread of the disease. Or the yardstick might be that it took longer before a malignant polyp returned.

During this lengthy interim of testing, the drug company does not usually have much contact with the FDA. The two sides communicate mainly via updates at required intervals. Every year an annual product report is submitted listing the number of people being tested, any adverse reactions they have had, and the trial plans for the following year. Also, companies must report any changes to their protocol. If patients experience reactions to the drug that are serious, unexpected, and life-threatening—say, a heart attack or stroke—the company cannot wait for the annual report. It has to let the FDA know within seven days. The adverse-event reports typically run eight to ten pages per patient, including the patient's medical history and some information to put it in context—"This is the third heart attack in this study," "This is actually lower than the ordinary rate for this population without the drug."

In 1995 the FDA proposed even more reporting of adverse events, which naturally raised protests from the industry, as all rule-tightening anywhere does. The agency claimed that the original system simply had too many loopholes, because it allowed companies to decide that bad reactions in patients were not serious enough to report or were unconnected to the drug, before the situation was fully investigated. In particular, the revised rule might have prevented the disaster that occurred in a 1993 trial of the hepatitis B drug fialuridine, or FIAU: Five of the 15 patients died, and two more were saved only by liver transplants, because the side effects were at first thought to be due just to the illness itself, not the drug.

Critics retorted that the change would create mounds of paperwork for too little benefit. Dr. Henry I. Miller, a former FDA official and one of the most outspoken advocates of shrinking the agency's power, claimed in his book *To America's Health* that the proposal would increase per-patient costs and paperwork more than sixtyfold. He also argued that it is extraordinarily difficult to determine whether a drug was the cause of a side effect if a patient has several medical conditions. (When I tried to interview him about the FDA, he talked briefly but then told me to go buy his book. Which I did.) Less dramatically, drug safety specialist Peter J. Tichy estimated that the change would mean five times as much reporting work at his company, Alteon Inc., a biotech in New Jersey that focuses on cardiovascular disease, aging, and diabetes. One thing no one could accuse the FDA of, at any rate, was rashness: It took until the end of 2004 to make its new guidelines final.

Type I nitpicking? Type II exaggeration? Most likely the complaining companies are overreacting. Miller's point about proving culpability actually buttresses the case for more reporting—let the FDA analyze the data before anyone jumps to any conclusions. But the FDA has to be careful itself not to overreact to every report of bad side effects.

When other problems crop up that do not involve serious side effects, it can be a judgment call whether to notify the FDA. One day in mid-February 2004, Taylor Burtis of Antigenics learned that there had been a lapse at an Oncophage test site in Italy a few weeks earlier. Every time a patient's tumor sample is collected in the operating room, it is given a number, which is then supposed to be recorded both in a log book and on the container the sample is placed in. Apparently, the same number had been assigned to samples from two different patients in Italy. Since Oncophage is made from a patient's own tumor, this double-counting would seem to render both the samples useless. Antigenics could not risk giving one patient a vaccine made from another patient's cancer.

However, Antigenics had a system of backups. Each sample actually gets four identifying markers: the number it is given in the operating room, plus the patient's initials, date of birth, and insurance policy number. In this case, the other three identifiers on both samples were all accurate and distinct. Furthermore, the two samples were taken from surgeries three weeks apart. After an emergency meeting of her materials review committee—11 staffers from quality assurance, quality control, manufacturing, regulatory affairs, and clinical—Burtis decided to go ahead and process the two patients' batches of vaccine. "There's no chance they could mix it up," she said. No need to discard the samples, and no need to check with the FDA.

Even when they have good news, companies do not rush to call Rockville. It is a balancing act, a rough determination of how significant the news is and the credibility of the source. Some promising data that's about to be published in a scientific journal? Probably. An interim report from the company's advisory board of outside experts? Probably not.

While Antigenics was moving toward filing its new drug application for Oncophage and finishing its Phase III trials, Renu Gupta said she talked to the FDA "on a formal basis" at least once per quarter and, informally, once a month. A larger company like Eli Lilly, with several dozen drugs in clinical trials or post-marketing studies at any given time, "would fly a planeload of people to Washington two times a week" to meet with FDA staff, recalled Dr. W. Leigh Thompson, who spent 12 years at the giant Indiana pharmaceutical maker, from 1982 to 1994, as chief scientific officer, executive vice president, and other positions. (In 2003, the FDA gave him a special citation for "multiple innovative contributions to public health and well being.")

Something else the FDA has power over is the product's name. The company can suggest anything it likes, but the FDA wants to make sure it could not be confused with another drug on the shelves. And as the years go by, with new medications joining old ones, that task has gotten harder. (What also makes it tough is that drug companies have a propensity for using the same few letters, like X, Z, and V.)

Already, there are Vytorin (cholesterol) and Viagra (impotence); Xenical (obesity) and Xanax (anxiety); Prozac (depression) and Procrit (anemia); and a whole lot more. Novartis had to change the name of its innovative cancer drug at the last minute because the FDA thought the European version, Glivec, might be confused with the diabetes drugs Glynase and Glyset. The American compromise: Gleevec.

At some point during the clinical trials, a company with a drug that treats a life-threatening condition or a condition with no other therapy available usually applies for the various designations that allow it to speed up the review process, as Antigenics did. Under fast-track authority, a drug can be approved using a surrogate endpoint, and companies can submit a portion of the application even before the whole thing is completed. Accelerated approval also allows the use of surrogate endpoints. Priority review means the FDA promises to review the product within six months. With Subpart E designation, a drug does not need all the safety data that are generally required.

These designations are supposed to be limited to extremely serious illnesses. Most famously, they have been used for AIDS and cancer drugs, but others can apply, too. More than 50 medications for various conditions—especially diabetes and obesity—got fast-track status in 2003, according to the Tufts University Center for the Study of Drug Development in Boston. Diabetes and obesity qualified because they have been labeled epidemics and they can lead to more serious health problems. Then there is Lipitor.

In clinical trials in the early 1990s, the future drug was showing impressively strong results in lowering levels of the so-called bad cholesterol. Desperate for a blockbuster right away, the Parke-Davis Research division of Warner-Lambert Company sent about ten people down to Rockville to try to persuade the FDA to give it priority status. However, four similar drugs, called statins, were already on the market. There was no urgent need for Lipitor. Dr. Irwin Martin, who was then vice president of regulatory affairs at Parke-Davis and is now an industry consultant, remembers facing ten or so staffers from the FDA for an hour or two. As Martin recalled, the FDA told the Parke-Davis contingent, "Better doesn't get you faster. It has to be significantly different." Lipitor might well be approved eventually, but it would need to wait in line.

While Martin and his colleagues in regulatory affairs were not surprised or upset at the response, those from R&D and marketing, who were not so used to the FDA's ways, were "maybe a little chagrined," Martin said. The company went back to rethink its approach. On an offhand suggestion from the president of R&D, scientists turned to a group of children with a rare genetic defect that interfered with their ability to clear cholesterol from their bodies. These children had such excessive levels of LDL cholesterol that they were at risk of heart attacks before they were 20 years old, yet no drug they had tried so far had worked. It was a niche group—no more than 100 of them in the United States. But it was a genuine medical need. In a test of ten of these patients in South Africa, Lipitor lowered LDL levels by an impressive 30 to 40 percent. So Parke-Davis brought its revised application to the FDA, with a new protocol for conducting Phase III trials on the niche group of children. This time, it was promised the priority review.

Martin admitted to me that "that was a bit of a stretch. They [the FDA] knew full well what we were doing in the market"—that is, that Parke-Davis was not going to all this trouble just for a drug to treat 100 kids. He told me the FDA understood that once it got the priority approval, Parke-Davis would be joining the four existing statin makers to pitch Lipitor to the broader market of over 24 million Americans at risk for cholesterol problems. In fact, that is exactly what Lipitor did after it was approved in December 1996. And with a lower price and a more powerful initial dose than its rivals, it quickly grabbed the lead in sales. (Warner-Lambert was later swallowed up by giant Pfizer, which today markets Lipitor.)

Could the FDA have practiced a bit more Type I caution here and denied the priority review? Regrettably, no. If Parke-Davis could prove that there was a population in dire need of treatment and that its drug would treat that population safely and effectively, the FDA could not ethically deny that group of kids their Lipitor as fast as possible—even if it knew that it was actually handing Parke-Davis an early birthday present. Of course, the FDA had even less authority to deny approval just because there were already so many similar drugs. Remember, it does not usually do drug-to-drug comparisons. So Parke-Davis was free to market its drug to the max.

Toward the end of Phase II comes the next major get-together, known as the pre-Phase III or end-of-Phase-II meeting, to prepare for the final round of clinical trials. As in the pre-IND meeting, the company tries to determine whether its plans for Phase III—statistical, eligibility, treatment, and endpoint—are going to be satisfactory. The company asks FDA staff very specific questions: Will 500 patients be enough? How long should the next stage last? What statistical method should be used? Are the right questions being asked in the trial, and does the FDA think that a trial organized in this way will answer the questions? Naturally, the company would like to limit the number and size of trials it has to conduct, without skimping so much that the application gets knocked down, because each additional patient can cost another $10,000 to $30,000.

The guidance goes both ways: If the company is getting pointers on how to shape its application, the FDA is getting to know the drug, so that it is not hit cold when the NDA is finally filed. "A meeting of the minds is had there," Dr. Richard Pazdur, director of the Division of Oncology Drug Products at CDER, explained to a congressional subcommittee in 2002. "It locks the FDA and the sponsor into an agreement, and that has to be so that the FDA does not have the complaint that we are arbitrary and capricious in our decisions." As with most meetings, the FDA is supposed to write up minutes summarizing the important points and send all parties a copy within 30 days, just to make sure everything is clear.

But now the stakes are a lot bigger than with the pre-IND meeting. The company has probably put in over nine years, from the very first screening of molecules, and tens of millions of dollars, if not several hundred million. Hopes are high. "Wall Street has been following every element of this with microscopic attention. They're already going, 'How long will it take to get the data? How long will it take to get the product approved?' You're spending money hand over fist with no revenue coming through the door to speak of. Everybody wants to see a product," summed up Don Drakeman, CEO of Medarex, Inc., a New Jersey biotech that makes genetically engineered mice for creating human antibodies.

A company can devote a full day getting ready for the meeting. Dr. F. Xavier Pi-Sunyer, chief of endocrinology, diabetes, and nutrition at St. Luke's-Roosevelt Hospital Center in New York City—among other titles— said that companies have asked him to come in and pretend to be an FDA staffer at a mock run-through. He raises the kinds of issues he thinks the FDA might, especially about side effects.

It was at the pre-Phase III stage of discussions, many experts say, that ImClone went wrong with its famous cancer drug Erbitux in December 2001—the drug that would ultimately bring down Martha Stewart for lying to investigators about her sale of ImClone stock. The FDA says it warned ImClone, starting in the summer of 2000, that its Phase III trials needed the standard comparisons involving patients on chemotherapy, patients who take Erbitux plus chemotherapy, and patients who take Erbitux alone. When ImClone nevertheless submitted an application containing Phase III results without all those comparisons, the FDA refused to consider it. (The story is, of course, much more complicated. The FDA says there were other problems with the application, such as missing data and trials that tested too few patients. ImClone officials have argued that they were never adequately warned and were, in fact, encouraged by being granted fast-track status.)

If Phase III goes well, the company girds for the biggest pile of paperwork yet, preparing the NDA, the formal application to start selling the drug.

All the horror stories that are cited about the FDA—the trucks pulling up to Rockville filled with bound volumes the size of phone books, the trial results recorded in excruciating detail, tens of thousands of pages, weeks of preparation and then months of waiting for an answer—all these are essentially true. And they are mainly about the NDA.

The NDA is the FDA's last big chance to make sure a drug is safe and effective before it is unloaded onto a trusting public. So the FDA is extraordinarily careful. It needs to see a great deal of detail, to make sure it is not missing any warning sign.

An NDA includes a listing of virtually every piece of data collected on every single patient tested in every single trial of the particular drug. (Depending on the disease, data might be collected every day, once a week, or once a month.) These are only lists of numbers, of course. For any patients who die during the study or drop out because of side effects, the actual case reports from which those numbers are taken—the ones researchers might write up at the bedside, also known as source documents—must also be included.

Altogether, an application typically encompasses some 100,000 to 200,000 pages, bound into maybe 400 volumes, plus backup copies. Thanks to electronic filing, the whole thing can now be put on a few CD-ROMs with hyperlinks to patient data or data tapes. But in the olden days, yes, companies usually rented trucks to deliver their NDAs to Rockville. (It was cheaper than registered mail.)

To give me an idea of what this encompasses, Dr. Pi-Sunyer walked me to a room down the hall from his small office at St. Luke's-Roosevelt on the Upper West Side of Manhattan. Born in Barcelona, Spain, Pi-Sunyer fled the Franco dictatorship with his family when he was an infant, heading first to Mexico, then to New Jersey. He has bright white hair, dark eyebrows, aviator-style rimless eyeglasses, and a craggy face with a lightly bent nose, and after decades in the United States, he speaks English today without any trace of a foreign accent. As a specialist in diet and diabetes, he has done clinical trials for three decades for all the big pharmaceutical companies, including work on a diabetes drug for Lilly and an insulin inhaler for Pfizer. Calmly, matter-of-factly, he unlocked the second room. Along one entire wall, maybe 12 feet long, three glass-doored wooden bookshelves were filled with blue, white, and green loose-leaf binders. Each binder, one to three inches thick, was a patient; each color was a trial.

Then we walked across the hall to a small computer lab. In bookshelves scattered around the room were sets of four-inch-thick binders containing the protocols and rules for various trials. There were plenty more from older trials, stored in a warehouse, because the FDA requires scientists to keep their records for five years after a study ends, and inspectors may visit the trial sites for an audit at any time.

It is easy to make fun of the FDA's rules for submitting paperwork. Its instructions can go into details as picayune as how to number the various tables, how wide to make the margins, and what type font to use. "A *fully paginated* document with a table of contents, appropriate indices, appendices, cross references, and tabs differentiating sections is recommended [italics in original]," the agency advises in its "Guidance for Industry," in discussing the backup documentation to submit when requesting a meeting. "I was amazed at how anal the process was," Garo Armen of Antigenics said. He added that he understands the reasoning: "You want the review process to be relatively cookie-cutter. If they have to shift gears"—to get used to a strange type font or numbering system—"it will be less efficient."

"If it's clear, it's concise, it's organized, it's grammatical, it's to the point—it's beautiful," said Tom Garvey.

This is one area where the FDA undoubtedly could ease up. Is it really necessary to remind pharmaceutical officials who have been through at least 18 years of schooling to use page numbers and appendices?

B y the time a company gets to the point of filing an NDA, the obvious failures—which is to say, over 90 percent of what the researchers started with—have been dropped. This leaves the companies in a strange position of both confidence and anxiety. Most drug makers do not go to the trouble of compiling the tens of thousands of pages for an application unless their molecule has shown promising results in its clinical trials. Moreover, the FDA already has a good idea of what it will find in the NDA and it has not told the manufacturer to stop. So the odds should be pretty high, right? "It would be unthinkable for a public company to submit an NDA or BLA that they did not think was approvable. Most observers—and certainly plaintiffs' lawyers—would regard that as fraud," declared C. Boyd Clarke, a veteran of the pharmaceutical industry for more than a quarter-century as a marketing official at Merck and now the chief executive of Neose Technologies Inc., a biotech just outside Philadelphia that specializes in proteins.

Yet FDA approval is hardly a given. According to Janet Woodcock, the former head of CDER, the agency approves about 75 percent of all NDAs. This is a sizable rejection rate, though not nearly as bad as you might think from all the industry complaints. Irwin Martin, for one, did not take Lipitor's green light for granted. "So many years away from the market, you tend not to get overbubbly," he said.

Four things can happen to the NDA once it is submitted. Very rarely, the FDA will not even consider the application and will issue a "refusal to file" letter, which is what happened to ImClone. That essentially says the filing has so many holes that it is not worth even trying. Assuming the agency does review the application, it can approve it, or it can reject it in one of two ways. For years the two rejections were known as "approvable" letters (for minor problems) and "not approvable" letters (major problems), but in mid-2004 the agency announced that it would eliminate the two categories of rejection and simply issue something called a "complete response letter." After that, depending on a company's response, the rejection would be classified either Class 1 (minor) or Class 2 (major). Any drug that is rejected can try again if new tests produce better data, as ImClone ultimately did with Erbitux.

The most likely explanations for a drug's being turned down are that the trial was not conducted according to the protocol that had been mapped out with the FDA, the trial results are not clear, or the trials show only a small improvement among patients. Unfortunately for the drug industry, as the target diseases get more complex, clear or significant trial results become less common. Cancer is the obvious example. It would be easy to measure if every cancer drug kept patients alive for five years without symptoms, but these drugs rarely do. They might shrink a tumor in 10 percent of the people tested. They might delay the tumor from spreading for an extra month. Is that good enough?

Once it arrives in Rockville, the NDA is usually parceled out among a chemist, a pharmacologist, a statistician, a toxicologist, perhaps a microbiologist, and the lead reviewer, or medical officer, who is the MD specializing in that type of drug and who coordinates the others. Back when everything was submitted on paper, "the volumes were put into a little cart like a library cart that got taken around," recalled Dr. Robert R. Fenichel, who spent 12 years reviewing drugs at the FDA, ending as deputy director of the cardio-renal division in 2000. Whenever a chart went from one specialist to the next, a sticker would be slapped on it.

(Keep in mind, of course, that at any one time each reviewer is probably working on not just this application, but also five to nine other NDAs, some INDs, the annual reports from ongoing INDs, and supplementary reports for drugs that were previously approved.)

The reviewers' job is essentially to search the volumes of data for two patterns: the side effects, deaths, and dropouts, in order to determine safety, and the progress of improvement in the endpoints that the FDA and the company agreed on, to gauge effectiveness. "You don't take anything for granted," summed up Tom Garvey. Chapter 7 gives more details of what the reviewers want to know and what questions they ask, but here is the kind of thing they would look for: Let's say two patients had dropped out of a trial because of liver problems. It is crucial to try to determine if those problems were caused by the drug. For starters, the reviewer would want to see if there was anything in the two dropouts' medical histories that might show a predisposition to liver-related difficulties. He or she would also look at how the drug worked and where it might intersect with the functioning of the liver. And the reviewer would investigate other cases where people quit the trial for reasons that seemed unrelated to liver problems, because there might be a correlation after all.

Meanwhile, the chemists are interested in the nitty-gritty of how and where the drug is made, focusing on consistency, purity, and potency. Dr. Steven R. Koepke spent nine years at the FDA as a reviewer and then deputy director of one of CDER's divisions of new drug chemistry. Now he works in the heart of Washington, D.C. at a contract research organization called PharmaNet, Inc., one of those new consulting firms, like Alquest, that help pharmaceutical makers navigate the application process. Burly and silver-haired—he looks like he would be more comfortable out on a farm than in his firm's half-empty luxury offices—Koepke explained what he used to analyze:

In terms of chemical composition, he would need the paperwork from three different lots of the drug. He would have to make sure that the correct amount of each ingredient went into the drug, and also that it was kept at the right temperature during each stage of preparation. (There is an allowable range for each of those measurements.) He also examined the manufacturing plant: "What chemical suite [room] was it made in, and what was being made in the suite next door? You want to make sure the room is enclosed so you don't get cross-contamination." For a typical NDA, it would take him three or four days just to read through his set of 3 to 12 volumes and take notes on what looked good, what looked like a problem, and what the key issues were.

The ultimate goal of the whole review is determining what the drug's label may claim regarding the allowed uses, dosages, and side effects. (The technical term "label" is a little misleading: This is not like the label on the outside of a can of soup. Also known as the package insert, it is really the brochure that goes inside the package.) These claims are crucial because the wording on the label is the drug's introduction to the world. It influences how doctors view the medication, whether insurance companies will reimburse the cost, and what may appear in TV advertisements.

Companies, naturally, want the fewest and weakest restrictions and the widest possible usages. Should pregnant women "use caution" or "avoid" the drug? "It's essentially the company's wish list," said Tom Garvey, and "each wish has to be supported by data."

When the reviewers finally finish, according to Fenichel, the cardio-renal deputy, they typically write one page of review per volume of NDA—in other words, a total report of several hundred pages. But that is only the first stage of a drug review.

Next, the team leader, or secondary reviewer, boils the report down to maybe 50 pages. This reviewer is the one who actually recommends whether the drug should be approved and what the label should say. From there it goes to the division director and then, in the case of drugs that are significantly different from what is already on the market, to another level of management, the office director. (That is the equivalent of Phil Noguchi or Jay Siegel.) At each level, the reports get progressively shorter. If a manager at any point disagrees with a predecessor's opinion, an explanation must be written; but insiders agree that hierarchy counts—the highest-ranking person's opinion will usually win out.

Between the second and third reviews, the most controversial and innovative drugs, devices, and biologic products get special scrutiny from advisory committees of outside experts—which have become controversial themselves.

The practice started in the 1970s, to answer critics who claimed the FDA was isolated from "the real world." In fact, there is nothing like this in Europe, and many pharmaceutical executives both there and in the United States find it amazing that these meetings—technical discussions of proprietary drugs—are held in public at all.

The committees consist of roughly a dozen physicians, professors, and other scientists, as well as one representative each from industry and consumer groups, many of them highly respected experts in their fields. This is where the controversy starts.

Drug companies sniff that the consumer representatives too often do not know what they're talking about. Consumers charge that some scientist-members are biased because they do extracurricular consulting work for the industry. In one case in 1997, according to newspaper reports, the chairman of the Cardiovascular and Renal Drugs Advisory Committee presided over the debate on Roche's blood-pressure drug Posicor even though he was still conducting a trial of the drug. At least he abstained on the final vote. Three years later, newspapers reported that a committee member who was a paid consultant to then-Glaxo Wellcome Inc. (it became GlaxoSmithKline after a merger) actually voted to approve Lotronex, a drug for a kind of gastrointestinal condition called irritable bowel syndrome, which was made by Glaxo.

In fact, the experience and qualifications of the members vary widely. The two committees meeting on antidepressants included scientists from prestigious places like Brigham and Women's Hospital in Boston, the Mayo Clinic, Baylor College of Medicine, Cornell University, UCLA, and the CDC. But there were also members from less-heralded institutions such as the Veterans Administration, the University of Pittsburgh, the University of Texas at San Antonio, and a private practice in Virginia. A California nurse was a consumer representative, and a doctor from Johnson & Johnson was an industry rep. Altogether, there are 16 of these committees for CDER—30 for the FDA as a whole, plus 24 subcommittees—each specializing in a certain discipline like anti-infectives, pulmonary-allergy drugs, or cardiovascular and renal disease.

The biggest controversy has to do with just how much authority these committees actually have. But we'll get to that a little later.

The preparation for an advisory committee meeting is intense on both sides. At a small firm, "you close down the company and focus on the meeting," said Kenneth I. Moch, chief executive of Alteon, the New Jersey biotech.

Short, blue-eyed, and talkative, with closely cropped hair that is turning from brown to gray, Moch never stays still. He jumps up to check something on his computer screen or squeezes a cardiovascular pumping ball while he sits. His conversation ranges from Neil Simon's play *Biloxi Blues*, to the unpublished poem of James Whitcomb Riley that he found in his late grandfather's papers, to the scientific underpinning of Alteon's research. Another family heirloom, an original manuscript that the novelist John Galsworthy gave Moch's grandfather, is displayed on a wall of his corner office in a corporate park in the low hills of suburban Ramsey, New Jersey, along with the requisite photos of his wife and kids.

It is Alteon's theory that glucose-protein links develop in the tissues as people age, making the tissues stiffer, which in turn contributes to problems like heart failure, high blood pressure, and kidney disease. Alteon also theorizes that diabetes accelerates the stiffening. The company has yet to reach Phase III—indeed, just a couple of months before my visit, it had suffered a bad setback when results from one of its Phase II trials showed that its lead drug did not reduce high blood pressure significantly more than a placebo did. However, Moch knows the whole Phase I-through-III process from 25 years at other companies, including a firm he founded that used stem cells from umbilical cord blood in transplants. With a BA in biochemistry from Princeton and an MBA from Stanford, he has also been a management consultant and a venture capitalist.

Moch and Barbara A. Regan, Alteon's medical writer, calculated that 20 staffers might spend 20 percent of their time for six weeks getting ready for an advisory committee hearing, and full time or overtime in the last week or two. They will do practice runs, with the lead scientists giving their planned presentation and colleagues trying to anticipate what the advisory committee might ask. (Regan figured that they correctly predict about half the questions.) In addition, the company has to prepare briefing books and Power Point slides with data from trial results that can go back years.

Meanwhile, the committee members have received from the FDA staff a list of specific issues regarding the drug that the agency wants more information about. At the hearing on antidepressants, there were seven key issues, including "Should the FDA provide additional advice to practicing physicians regarding the use of these drugs?" and "Any thoughts you might have on alternative approaches to demonstrating benefits in this population." The day before an advisory panel meeting on a controversial type of emergency birth control known as Plan B, in December 2003, Alastair Wood showed me a stack of background papers and folders five-and-a-half-inches tall. That is actually about half the size of a normal set of briefing papers, he said. He had been reading the papers in his spare time for nearly a week.

The committees usually meet for a full day or even two at one of a handful of indistinguishable hotels near Rockville. It might be the pink-and-green ballroom with three huge crystal chandeliers in the lower level of the Hotel Washington, two blocks from the White House. Or the beige-and-blue Versailles II ballroom of the Bethesda Holiday Inn, where the panel on antidepressants met. Or, most likely, the newly renovated, pale yellow ballroom of the Hilton in Gaithersberg, Maryland.

The bulk of the meetings can be as dry as the NDA data. After all, these are largely scientists asking other scientists for precise details on questions that may turn on the smallest measurement of white blood cells. In a discussion of powdered infant formula: Was there any information on the *Enterobacter sakazakii* bacteria's resistance to sterilization? In a discussion of fertility treatments: Does ooplasm transfer increase the chances of the egg's being fertilized?

Still, the committees are often dealing with some of the most heatedly debated issues in American society—abortion, teenage sexuality, cloning, and genetic engineering. The meetings can definitely get emotional. While no one lobbies the members at their home or office, advocacy groups, patients, scientists, and sometimes even politicians will show up at the hearings in force, along with TV cameras, as they did for the antidepressants, Plan B, and methylmercury in fish. People who have been injured by a drug will walk up to the microphone and try to gulp out their story before they cry. So will people suffering from a disease who want that drug.

Dr. Douglas L. Archer, deputy director of the foods center from 1989 to 1994 and now a professor of food science and human nutrition at the University of Florida, was on the advisory committee looking into methylmercury. He said he is not fazed by all the public attention—not after 20 years in the fishbowl of the FDA.

Archer is a no-nonsense kind of person, short and rotund, with thinning silver hair, rimless glasses, and a thick silver mustache. He originally came to the FDA in 1974 by accident and, he thought, for a short-term gig. As an officer in the U.S. Army Reserve and a newly minted PhD, he was due to be sent to the Signal Corps but requested a transfer to the Public Health Service (through the same uniformed Commissioned Corps program that Phil Noguchi joined). That made Archer eligible for a health-related job in several government agencies. It just so happened that the FDA was the first to call. "My thinking was, I would stay two or three years, then go to academia." He stayed for 20, disliking the heavy workload and increasing politicization but enjoying the sense that "every day you feel you're doing something important." Two things finally pulled Archer away: He was eligible for a nice retirement package and he had a "no-brainer" job offer from the University of Florida. Now, as an outside expert, he sits on his old Center's Food Advisory Committee.

Even if the committee members can stick to their science and try to ignore the tears and TV cameras, the decisions are rarely as straightforward as a scientific experiment. After all, the committees are convened for the tough questions, not the easy calls. With methylmercury, for instance, Archer said, "There are big question marks about the numbers being thrown around, about what levels of mercury are appropriate." Alastair Wood said bluntly, "I don't think I've ever left an advisory committee feeling good about it. You're voting on something when there are two sides to the story. If it was clear-cut, there wouldn't be a need for an advisory committee."

Over time, much of the public has come to assume that these committees actually make the decisions, whether to approve, recall, or relabel a drug. What else is all this brainpower for? In fact, the committees can only issue recommendations. Traditionally the FDA has usually done what the panels recommend. In recent years, however—especially with the kinds of controversial products that Archer and Wood have been handling— more and more daylight has been creeping between the FDA staff in Rockville and the outside advisors.

In the fall of 2003, a divided advisory panel voted nine to six to allow silicone-filled breast implants back on the market for general use, under certain conditions to protect women in case the implants leaked or ruptured. Soon afterwards, the committee's chairman (who had not been allowed to vote, by committee rules) wrote to Commissioner McClellan urging him to ignore the panel's advice and reject the implants. Two months after that, the FDA officially declared that it was delaying a final decision because it wanted more information about why the implants ruptured, and what a rupture could do to a woman's health.

David Feigal, who was then the head of the devices center, which has jurisdiction over the implants, insisted to me that there was no real disagreement between the committee and his office. "We did not take them [the implants] off the market and put them on again; that would be back and forth. We have continuing safety concerns. They identified the issues." In fact, going back to the days of David Kessler, the FDA has been unable to come up with a straightforward "yes" or "no" on the troubled implants.

Within just a few months of the waffling on implants, FDA staff and advisory committees also disagreed about the safety of milk and meat from cloned animals. And the agency brass flat-out rejected the recommendation of Alastair Wood's committee to allow the emergency contraceptive pill Plan B to be sold without a prescription. (More on that in Chapter 11.) "We don't necessarily slavishly follow the advice," Janet Woodcock said curtly, when I asked her about the disagreement over Plan B. "They're *advisory* committees, not *decision* committees."

Even once a drug or device is on the market, no one says good-bye to the FDA. For one thing, medications that are approved using alternative endpoints must do post-market studies "to verify and describe the drug's clinical benefit," according to the FDA Modernization Act. If a lot of people seem to be having serious reactions or even dying, the FDA may demand stricter warnings on the label. (Even the FDA admits it does not do enough monitoring, and this is discussed more fully in Chapters 8 and 15.) Sites where clinical trials were held are subject to audit for several years, especially if there were problems, which is why Dr. Pi-Sunyer keeps so many files. Drug and device manufacturing plants anywhere in the world whose products are sold in the United States can get a visit from FDA inspectors at any time, with little or no notice, to make sure they are adhering to what is called GMP, or good manufacturing practices. Some conditions are sure to trigger an inspection: the launch of a new product, a significant number of adverse reactions among patients, or a previous manufacturing violation. Altogether, agency officials annually make over 20,000 inspections of food and drug facilities.

"It's like having a policeman show up at your door," explained one quality operations manager at a manufacturing plant of a major U.S. pharmaceutical company, whose job includes making sure that products meet all the specifications and serving as the liaison to the FDA. "Your assumption is you haven't done anything for them to inspect, but..." The manager's voice trailed off. (The manager wanted to remain anonymous because the pharmaceutical company, like most of its peers, is very touchy about having employees quoted.)

About four FDA inspectors will probably show up for the inspection, staying anywhere from one day to three weeks. They will tour the plant and also pore through the records, asking technical questions: What chemicals are used in the quality tests? How are the solutions prepared? Why is the procedure done this way? They may question the line workers and even ask them to demonstrate how a required procedure is followed.

Schiller is a family-owned company based in the small town of Baar in northern Switzerland that makes cardiac defibrillators and other devices that are sold in the United States. With no more than a day's warning, three or four FDA inspectors show up every couple of years at its four-floor headquarters-and-factory building, perched quietly on a street of two-story, pastel stucco homes, said Alessandro L. Züsi, the international sales manager. Züsi seemed very casual about this. The inspectors stay no more than four days, they inspect samples and records, and work goes on. "The people are quite nice. They're strict, but they quite clearly know the business of what they're doing," Züsi said. In its 30-year history, he went on, Schiller has never had a serious problem with an inspection.

Perhaps Schiller does not need all those check-ups, but not every company has such a great record. It was just such a regular inspection that caught mysterious black particles in vials of Celestone, a corticosteroid used for premature babies with undeveloped lungs, at a Schering-Plough Corporation plant in Puerto Rico. Inspections at Schering-Plough and elsewhere have also uncovered asthma inhalers produced without enough of the key ingredient (which consumer advocates claim may have caused the deaths of 17 people), inadequately trained workers, and a couple hundred more violations in a typical year.

The question of inspections hit the headlines with flu vaccine in the fall of 2004. The British counterpart of the FDA abruptly shut down the Liverpool, England factory that made half of the vaccine for the United States, because batches were contaminated with bacteria. FDA inspectors had in fact found similar problems during a routine visit the prior year. But the agency said the violations were not that serious, and over the next 14 months the manufacturer, Chiron Corporation, assured the regulators that it was fixing the problem. Critics charged that the FDA should have gone to England and made more inspections itself, rather than relying on the manufacturer; the FDA claimed it didn't have enough staff. Congress launched an investigation.

So in the end, the approval process comes down to the basic debate over how long versus how careful. Is the FDA spending too much time checking and double-checking details on new drugs because it is overly afraid of taking a risk? Or does the FDA need to be extremely careful in order to keep the next thalidomide off the market? And the corollary: Is the FDA too hostile to the drug companies, or too cozy?

As the NDA review time started stretching to two years or more in the early 1990s, the debate shifted in favor of the side demanding speed. By 1993, according to the FDA, even high-priority drugs—those that promised a breakthrough for a life-threatening condition or a condition with no other treatment—were spending 20.5 months in the burrows of Rockville. Almost no one defended the FDA's record, not even the FDA. Bob Temple conceded that "it's hard to say you're accomplishing anything with 26 months." The libertarian Cato Institute in 1985 estimated that each one-year delay in bringing a new drug to market meant an extra 32,000 to 76,000 deaths per decade of patients the drug could have saved.

The main problem, the FDA asserted, was lack of money, which translated into lack of sufficient staff and technology. "Any reviewer who worked on an application would have to prepare a report, then you would have to wait for it to be typed and move on to the next level. A lot of time was wasted waiting for a report to be typed," Mark Novitch, the acting commissioner in the mid-1980s, recalled. The long delays spurred the rush of drastic Republican proposals in Congress in the mid-1990s that would have wiped out much of the FDA's authority.

Although those measures failed, Congress did pass PDUFA (pronounced "puhdoofa," the law establishing user fees) and its two renewals. Not only did the new laws provide an influx of money, to be used for hiring more reviewers, but they also set deadlines for completing reviews, including the six-month limit for priority drugs. And things in fact began to move faster. The median time it took the Center for Drugs to finish a new drug application dropped to a low of 12 months for standard drugs in 1998, although the numbers started creeping higher again after that. For priority drugs, the FDA pretty much adhered to PDUFA's six-month requirement from 1997 through 2001. (It slipped drastically in 2002 to 19.1 months, a problem the agency attributed to "a few applications with unusually long regulatory histories." The next year CDER was nearly back on track, at 7.7 months.) The agency then set a goal of speeding up even more by 2007, aiming to lop a month off of priority drug reviews and two months off the rest.

CBER was generally slower than CDER, but it, too, picked up its pace. Its median review time for new BLAs (the biologic equivalent of new drug applications) went from 13.8 months in 2001 to 12.8 months in 2002. The efficiency efforts also got an assist from electronic filing and other technological advances. AIDS activists played a role, pushing the agency to think of creative new ways to speed things along, like treatment INDs and parallel track access.

By the fall of 2003, James C. Greenwood, who at that time was a Republican congressman from Pennsylvania and who had been one of the leaders of the mid-1990s congressional charge, was singing the praises of Mark McClellan and telling me, "They have a requirement to get products to people that need them as expeditiously as possible. I think that they have changed their approach [from the 1990s]." The steam pretty much fizzled out of Washington's bash-the-FDA blaze.

But among the constituencies that deal directly with the FDA, equilibrium never lasts for long. Consumer groups pointed to an unusual spate of recalls in the late 1990s and worried that the FDA was sacrificing quality for speed. Drug and devices company officials, for their part, continue to complain about FDA slowness and bureaucracy (especially when they are not quoted publicly). Dr. Daniel Vasella, chief executive of the drug giant Novartis, dropped a hint of a laugh as he said, "That will never change. Of course if you have a great drug and if you think it works, everybody in a company wants to take it to market."

Since it was hard to criticize NDA approval times any more under PDUFA, the industry and its allies switched to another complaint. The real issue, they said, was not what the FDA did once it had the application in hand, but rather that it takes too much time and money for companies to get to the point of even filing the NDA, because the FDA demands so many trials to prove safety and efficacy. Famously, drug companies tend to bat around figures like 12 or even 15 years to get the average drug to market, and $802 million to $1.7 billion as the average cost. Even if those estimates are accurate, however, they include all the years of early development trying to find a molecule that seems to work against the disease target, which is something companies would have to do even if the FDA did not exist. (More on this in Chapter 7.)

For further ammunition, critics cited the fact that the number of new drug applications submitted to the FDA had been slipping for years. In 1997 CBER had received 33 original biologics license applications; by 2003 that had plunged to just 14. CDER's 72 approvals in 2003 were just a little more than half as many as it had processed in 1996.

Certainly, the demand was huge. There were not enough drugs for cancer of all sorts, for Alzheimer's disease, for depression, and for anxiety. New vaccines and antibiotics are always needed, although drug companies rarely clamor to make these because they are not very profitable. As well, aging Baby Boomers were queueing up for not exactly life-saving treatments that would wipe away wrinkles, improve their sex lives, ease their heartburn, and grow hair on their heads (men) but not on their faces (women).

The FDA, naturally, insisted that it was not being unreasonable in its requirements or its reviews. It said the complexity of science was the reason that applications were slower to trickle in. The medical conditions that the drug companies were tackling were more complicated and difficult than the earlier generation of infectious and cardiovascular diseases, so of course drug development would take longer. And the fancy new sciences of genomics and proteomics were not producing miracle tools as quickly as expected.

Still, the agency clearly heard the industry's complaints, and it said it wanted to help. With great fanfare, it released a report in the spring of

2004, dubbed its "critical path" report, that cited the slowdown in drug applications and promised an unprecedented "aggressive, collaborative effort to create a new generation of performance standards and predictive tools." The FDA would not merely analyze a drug's safety and efficacy after it had been developed. Together, even before the drug ever existed, the FDA, the pharmaceutical companies, and other "stakeholders" with an interest in the issue would try to figure out ways to harness innovative scientific approaches and get drugs out to consumers faster. The regulator would act like—well, almost like a partner in a business venture with the companies it was regulating.

This new attitude on the part of the FDA raises several troubling concerns. For one thing, the agency made essentially no attempt to defend the principal of Type I caution. It apparently bought the argument that speed of approvals is the most important criterion.

Furthermore, the critical path plan, as many commentators pointed out, risked blurring the line between regulator and regulated. Certainly it is important for the FDA and the drug companies to have steady communication, as they do in the various meetings during the clinical trial process. The FDA has to make its standards clear and—just as important—be open to the industry's arguments for changing those standards. It is also a terrific boon for society when the FDA *independently* conducts research that may produce better scientific tools, which it then makes available to all of industry, the way the National Center for Toxicological Research does in Arkansas. As the scientific and ethical questions behind medicine become more complex and the demands of society grow, the FDA has to become more assertive beyond its traditional role of safety and efficacy. No argument there.

But the "critical path" sounds a little too "uncritical." Was there a risk that FDA officialdom would feel a personal stake in the drugs it had helped bring to fruition or the drug companies it had worked with? Could the reviewers still be objective? In the constant debate over balance and bias, was the balance tipping too far in the direction of speed and industry coziness?

There are ways the FDA can be efficient, fast, sensitive to industry, on top of cutting-edge science, and still safe. Just take another look at thalidomide. The only catch is that the new story of thalidomide raises a whole different problem than the one from Estes Kefauver's day.

CHAPTER 6

Case Study:
The Return
of Thalidomide

The name has come to symbolize the worst that can happen when people are not protected from dangerous drugs. A drug that was used too cavalierly, causing horrible side effects. A drug that was loose on the market in Europe, Asia, and Canada without proper studies because the regulatory systems were so weak. A drug that Americans were saved from only because of the vigilance of their government. The drug that spurred the passage of the Kefauver-Harris Amendments and made the FDA what it is today. Many Americans can still remember seeing the pictures in *Life* magazine of the babies born to women in Germany and England, babies with hands and feet like flippers growing out of their shoulders and trunk.

Thalidomide. And now it is sold legally in the United States, with the approval of the FDA. In fact, it is Exhibit A for those who want to show that the FDA is indeed willing to take risks in order to get innovative medicines out to the public. Michael Friedman, who was the acting commissioner when the FDA approved thalidomide in 1998, has called that decision one of his most significant accomplishments.

The story of thalidomide's resurrection began in Israel in the 1960s. Even as the drug was being withdrawn from the market in Europe and blocked in the United States, a doctor at Hebrew University in Jerusalem was prescribing it as a sedative for patients with leprosy. After all, it was effective at helping people sleep, and its most infamous side effect—birth defects—would not be an issue for these patients. To his surprise, he noticed that the drug also alleviated a kind of lesion and nerve deterioration common in leprosy, known as erythema nodosum leprosum, or ENL.

At Rockefeller University in New York City, meanwhile, Dr. Gilla Kaplan—an immunologist who, coincidentally, was born in Israel and went to Hebrew University for her undergraduate work—was studying immune responses in leprosy patients. Picking up on the thalidomide research, she discovered that the drug appeared to inhibit a protein called tumor necrosis factor alpha (TNF-alpha), which is produced by immune cells and causes inflammations. Her discovery was significant because TNF has been implicated in other, more common conditions such as rheumatoid arthritis, tuberculosis, Crohn's disease, and cancer-related weight loss. In turn, anything that worked for those ailments might also relieve some of the secondary complications of AIDS patients, who often suffer from tuberculosis and severe weight loss. Kaplan and her colleagues asked themselves, "Can we dampen the TNF response in other diseases?" Could the scourge of pregnancy actually help in treating tuberculosis, arthritis, or AIDS?

The answer, Kaplan found as she studied TB patients, seemed to be an amazingly strong "yes." Not only did her patients stop losing weight, they even were gaining. Then Kaplan gave thalidomide experimentally to AIDS patients and got the same result. The news started to percolate through the AIDS community. But the drug was still illegal in the United States.

While all this was going on, a small biotech named Celgene Corporation in suburban New Jersey, 40 miles from Kaplan's lab, was undergoing a transformation. Created in 1980 as a unit of the chemical giant Celanese, it had originally focused on environmental biotechnology, such as using enzymes to clean up pollutants. After it was spun off in 1986, in connection with Celanese's merger with Hoechst, the new company began doing work on biotech pharmaceuticals as well. Its specialty was single-isomer drugs, which are mirror-image forms of existing medications, but with fewer side effects. After the firm got an assignment to make a single-isomer drug for tuberculosis in 1991, top officials headed out to see one of the experts on the disease—Gilla Kaplan.

As the story has been told at Celgene, the meeting was petering out when Kaplan mentioned, "By the way, I've discovered that thalidomide seems to be very interesting."

Although scientists and pharmaceutical executives were intrigued by what seemed a second shot at thalidomide, everyone tiptoed around it at first. Kaplan had trouble attracting drug companies, and Celgene had a tough sell with investors. "I would go to cocktail parties, and I would have eyebrows raised," recalled John W. Jackson, a veteran pharmaceutical executive who became Celgene's chairman and chief executive five years after the fateful conversation with Kaplan. Still, Celgene took on the drug. Personally, Jackson said he was fascinated, not queasy, when he heard about his new company's controversial product.

Jackson is tall and wiry, with craggy features and dark hair just starting to grey at the temples. He grimaces when asked about his slight English accent; the truth is that his mother is British and he was raised in England from age six until he went to college, but he tried to get rid of the telltale pronunciation while he was at Yale University and then in the Marines. After heading back to Europe for his MBA at the prestigious business school INSEAD, Jackson spent 25 years at Merck, American Cyanamid Company (now part of Wyeth), and a small medical consulting firm before Celgene recruited him, looking to beef up its pharmaceutical credentials.

The most important group to convince of thalidomide's merits was neither pharma executives nor investors, but the FDA. Early on, Kaplan happened to meet David Kessler, then the commissioner, at a dinner at Rockefeller University. As she remembered it, she asked him, "How would the FDA handle a request to test thalidomide?" His surprising answer: "The FDA would consider a protocol based on potential toxicity, based on news, not based on history."

In fact, the FDA soon had a strong reason to seek out a legitimate thalidomide manufacturer that it could regulate. The drug was spreading fast through the underground network without any controls whatsoever. It was openly used in Brazil, where leprosy is a major problem, and as word spread about its effectiveness in halting weight loss, AIDS patients in the United States started forming buyers' clubs to import the drug illegally from Brazil. Matt Sharp, the AIDS activist from Oklahoma who demonstrated at FDA headquarters in 1988, ran one such club in San Francisco, with thousands of members. Although the club required a doctor's prescription and gave out advice pamphlets, using this new thalidomide was hardly the same as buying a drug that had gone through the FDA approval process and been produced at an FDA-inspected plant. "Coming in with no warnings, it was a disaster waiting to happen. It's a miracle that no babies were born with birth defects," Jackson said.

Around 1994, according to Jackson, the FDA actually asked Celgene—plus two other small companies, some Canadian thalidomide victims, and their lawyers—to come to Rockville to discuss bringing back thalidomide strictly for AIDS patients. As Jackson tells it, the FDA was so eager to get the drug approved that it even allowed Celgene to do a retrospective study, which is almost unheard of. In a normal drug application, scientists plan a clinical trial in advance in hopes of achieving certain declared endpoints. But in a retrospective study, the scientists work backwards, looking at historical data of patient use in order to discern patterns. Celgene combed through 20 years' worth of data from the Hansen's Disease Center in Louisiana, which had been using thalidomide for leprosy, to see if patients' symptoms worsened when they stopped taking the drug or improved when they started.

Meanwhile, at Children's Hospital Boston, another doctor was noticing that thalidomide seemed to inhibit the growth of blood vessels, which can be a factor in cancer. The wife of a cancer patient in New York City, who had been searching the United States for possible treatments, asked the hospital to try it on her husband. If it worked, that could open up yet another world of possible uses for this apparent miracle drug—a miracle drug with horrible side effects.

In 1996, Celgene did what would have been unthinkable 34 years earlier, when the Kefauver-Harris Amendments were passed: It filed a new drug application for thalidomide. However, it did not file for cancer, which it was just starting to study, or even for the purpose that the FDA had sought, AIDS weight-loss. It filed for the limited ENL condition in leprosy, which affects only a couple thousand people in the United States. That is where Celgene had the strongest data.

By all accounts, this was not an easy call for the FDA, even though the agency had essentially asked Celgene to apply. Jackson said people at the FDA's top levels were supportive, but lower-ranking reviewers were skeptical. Some wondered why Celgene had applied for the leprosy indication when everyone knew it was actually going to be used for AIDS. Others worried that there were not enough safeguards to prevent a patient on thalidomide from becoming pregnant.

For its part, Celgene tried to lay the groundwork. Nervously, the vice president of sales and marketing, Bruce Williams, called Randy Warren, the president of a Canadian thalidomide victims' association, and arranged a get-together in the spring of 1997. It was awkward for both sides, but they followed up with a continuing series of phone calls. Warren, who was born with malformed legs and no hips, kept emphasizing his fears of a new rash of birth defects. Yet he also sympathized with the idea that the drug could help other patients, and he was somewhat reassured when the Celgene officials said they were experimenting with a safer, second-generation product that could eventually replace thalidomide. The victims persuaded Celgene to sharpen the drug's warning labels against pregnancy.

The FDA advisory committee meeting at the Gaithersberg Hilton in the summer of 1997 lasted two days. Celgene officials practiced for nearly a week beforehand and brought in leprosy experts to speak on the drug's behalf. The FDA, meanwhile, had appointed a thalidomide victim to the committee as a nonvoting member. In Jackson's opinion, the turning point came when the thalidomide victim took his turn at the microphone.

"He was sitting in his wheelchair, and he gave this very impassioned speech—'Who am I to deny people the chance?' There were actually tears in the eyes of several people on the advisory committee. I actually felt the same way," Jackson said, and he dabbed at one eye, six years later.

"The easy thing would be for the agency to say, 'No, we took it off the market once,' and never let it back on," Michael Friedman told me. "Knowledge changes. You need a public health agency that responds to new knowledge, whether taking a product off the market or putting it on—all the relevant information, all the risks and benefits."

The advisory committee voted to recommend approval, and a year later the FDA made it official. There was a big condition to the approval, however: To try to prevent any more grotesque birth defects, Celgene would have to put in place one of the strictest regimens that had ever been seen for controlling access to a drug. This kind of control, known as risk management, is a significant change from the way the FDA usually operates. Typically, the agency just sends a drug out onto the market with the side effects and warnings on the label. After that it is up to the doctor to decide which patients should get the drug and to alert them to any complications—in other words, it's the MD, not the FDA, who practices medicine. Now, with thalidomide, the FDA was getting more directly involved in selecting and warning patients. It is an approach that has been used sparingly since then, most notably with the acne drug Accutane, which can also cause horrible birth defects.

Celgene and the FDA spent a year working out what would become known as the STEPS program, or System for Thalidomide Education and Prescription Safety. Any woman of child-bearing age who wants to fill a thalidomide prescription must have a negative pregnancy test before starting and biweekly tests afterwards, and must promise to use two methods of birth control. All patients sign an informed-consent document saying they are aware of the risks, agree to use condoms, and see a video about thalidomide's side effects. As another precaution, patients can get only a four-week supply at a time. Before renewing, they answer a checklist of questions. Even Jackson's 80-year-old aunt was asked about her sex life.

Michael S. Katz, a senior vice president at the giant consulting firm Booz Allen & Hamilton Inc. and a user of thalidomide, dialed into Celgene's automated phone line to demonstrate the monthly drill for me: What's your Social Security number? Have you shared your thalidomide with anyone? Have you donated blood? Have you had sex without a condom? All told, the phone questionnaire took less than two minutes.

The FDA's other main concern, before it would approve thalidomide, had to do with the brand name. Celgene had originally planned to call the drug Synovir. "Generally, the agency won't let you use a trade name that's too close to the generic name," Jackson explained. But this time the agency insisted on a name similar to thalidomide, seeing that as yet another way to remind users about the dangers. Celgene came up with Thalomid.

Have these safeguards been enough? After five years on the market, Jackson said, no birth defects had been reported from thalidomide. Every now and then the FDA makes minor changes in the STEPS program, and Graham H. Burton, Celgene's senior vice president for regulatory affairs, said he talks with FDA officials about once a week. They might discuss new information Celgene wants to hand out via the STEPS program, or some demographics on the drug's customers.

But the stories of Mike Katz and Jackson's aunt highlight what has become a new controversy regarding thalidomide and other drugs. Neither of these two patients was taking thalidomide for leprosy. Both were using it for a cancer of the blood called multiple myeloma, for which thalidomide had not been approved.

Myeloma essentially involves a breakdown of the functioning of plasma cells. Normally, plasma cells produce a variety of antibodies that fight infection. Multiple myeloma cells, however, produce only one form of the antibodies. Those cells grow out of control, crowding off other plasma cells that could make more useful antibodies. The myeloma cells can also attach themselves to body tissues, such as bone, to produce tumors.

For Mike Katz, the first hint of trouble came in 1989, when he noticed a slight twinge in his right hip after exercising. "I didn't think much of it," he said, "until a trip to Hong Kong. I got off the plane and found myself limping quite badly." He was given MRIs and x-rays for nine months, but doctors could not figure out what was wrong. Then the myeloma tumor broke through the back of his pelvis and was discovered on an x-ray.

The median survival time for multiple myeloma is less than three years, but Katz—at least, as of spring 2004—was going strong after 14. He is tall and heavy-set, with thick, curly, salt-and-pepper hair that looks a bit like a Brillo pad, and he has the nasal accent of his native Queens in New York City. Since 1996 he has been an activist in a range of cancer-survivor groups, has written a chapter for an academic book on myeloma, and has been a patient representative on an FDA advisory committee, while also working at Booz Hamilton's offices two blocks from Grand Central Terminal in Manhattan. For now, he has been able to get by with thalidomide plus a steroid, although if things get worse, he said, he might have to resort to chemotherapy or bone marrow or stem-cell transplants. Every now and then he gets a bone pain in one spot; that is how he knows the cancer has returned.

"I don't feel like I'm going to die tomorrow," he said, after explaining his disease calmly and clinically. "I have oodles of options I haven't tried yet. My financial house is in order. I have stem cells in the freezer that I harvested years ago. You can only do what you can do, and I try to enjoy the ride in the meantime."

Katz's usage of thalidomide is called off-label use: It is legal, it completely circumvents the whole point of FDA approval, it probably saves lives, and it is probably unstoppable. In fact, almost half the time drugs are prescribed in the United States, the prescription is for off-label uses, especially when it involves antipsychotics, cancer drugs, epilepsy medicine, drugs for children, and medications that have been approved only for rare conditions like narcolepsy and leprosy. This is how Paxil, Zoloft, and all the other antidepressants ended up being used by teenagers. People have been popping pills this way for decades.

The reason for this seeming contradiction is that the FDA has no authority over what doctors do. Other than what is required through the new risk management programs, remember, it is up to the doctor to decide how to prescribe. The states license doctors, but they do not regulate the way drugs are prescribed either. As long as a drug is on the market, doctors can legally prescribe it any way they see fit, for whichever patients and conditions they choose. Back in the 1960s and 1970s the FDA debated whether it should do something about unapproved uses, and Peter Barton Hutt, the patrician former counsel and de facto historian, claims credit for simply announcing, at a congressional hearing in 1972, that it was FDA policy that it had no jurisdiction.

In the example of thalidomide, Jackson of Celgene said that it has been used off-label for cancer "right from the [leprosy] launch." As of 2004, fully 92 percent of its prescriptions were for cancer, mainly multiple myeloma. Jackson will not reveal exactly how many people use thalidomide, but multiple myeloma is the second-most common form of cancer of the blood, with about 200,000 cases worldwide and 50,000 in the United States. Around 15,000 new cases are diagnosed in the United States every year. In 2002, Celgene took in $119 million in revenue from thalidomide. By contrast, only a few thousand people in the United States suffer from leprosy, and the bulk of the patients tend to live in the poorest regions of Africa, Asia, Latin America, and the Pacific islands, where they have little access to health care.

It is certainly possible to get a second FDA approval for an unofficial use, by filing a supplemental new drug application (SNDA). That gives the company a three-year extension on its patent for that particular use. Celgene, indeed, filed an SNDA for thalidomide and multiple myeloma in February 2004. Few companies bother, however. Why go through all the hassle and expense of new clinical trials and hundreds of volumes of data for something people are already taking legally?

The answer is that this is exactly the reason the Food, Drug, and Cosmetics Act and the Kefauver-Harris Amendments were enacted. Otherwise, what's the difference between off-label usage and the patent medicine quackery of the 1800s? In both cases, people are using a medicine that has never been scientifically proven to work for their condition.

"It sort of bypasses what the FDA should be approving. Ideally, you would like to have the FDA be approving drugs as physicians are using them," said Dr. Harmon Eyre, chief medical officer of the American Cancer Society—whose constituents are among the biggest users of off-label prescriptions. In an Internet poll of over 2,100 American adults conducted in May 2004 by Harris Interactive and The Wall Street Journal Online, respondents declared by a 48-to-31 percent margin that doctors "should not be allowed to prescribe a drug for diseases for which that drug has not been approved by the FDA."

True, the medicine has been tested for safety, or it would not have been approved for its on-label uses to begin with. But even that is no guarantee that the drug is safe in the secondary indication, for a whole slew of reasons. The dosage of the off-label use may be different; the off-label disease may have characteristics that alter the drug's effects; and the patient may be taking other medicines for that secondary condition that dangerously interfere with the drug's method of operation. With the antidepressants, many doctors worried that a teenager's brain is chemically different from an adult's and therefore might not be able to tolerate a medication that an adult brain could. In a six-month investigation published in the fall of 2003, the Knight-Ridder, Inc. newspaper chain found people who suddenly suffered lung damage, strokes, heart attacks, nerve damage, and even death after taking pills off-label. For instance, the newspaper chain reported, while Tammie Snyder of Michigan was pregnant with twin girls in 2002, she was given an anti-asthma drug even though she did not have asthma. It was prescribed to prevent her from going into premature labor, but it caused such damage to her heart that she was told she should not have any more children. As the newspapers wrote:

> *Doctors are giving their patients epilepsy drugs for depression and hot flashes and to help them lose weight. They use antidepressants to treat premature ejaculation and pain, and powerful antipsychotics for insomnia and attention deficit disorder. Blood-pressure pills are prescribed for headaches and anxiety; antibiotics are used to treat viruses.*

There are other concerns, too. When pills are prescribed off-label, the doctors doing the prescribing are probably trained in a medical specialty related to that off-label use, not the medical specialty for which the medication was legally approved. These doctors are unlikely to keep up with the scientific literature in the original specialty. So they might not be sensitive to all the subtleties or new information about the drug's side effects and dosages. Nor will that updated information necessarily be on the package insert. In fact, it may be just the opposite: If the manufacturer applies for an SNDA and is rejected by the FDA, the regulators by law may not disclose the test data that were submitted unless they show some unexpected safety risks. If the tests show that the drug does not work in the secondary use, no one may ever know.

But the practical fact is, doctors experiment with new approaches all the time, whenever they hear about an innovation that might help their patients. This is a large part of the way medicine develops. A drug company may not even be aware that its product could have a secondary use—and therefore could not possibly apply for the SNDA—unless it is being tried off-label by doctors. "It's in principle a good thing to allow the physicians the flexibility to use their best judgment and knowledge," said Carl Peck, the respected former head of the Center for Drugs. If Tammie Snyder's story of heart failure from a wrongly prescribed asthma drug is heart-rending, what about the other side—like Mike Katz's story of staying alive thanks to off-label thalidomide? Or Matt Sharp's story of helping AIDS victims buy thalidomide from Brazil? Or the story of Peter Barton Hutt's brother, who was dying of a brain tumor in 1967: Told that he had just days to live, the brother tried Merck's anti-inflammatory drug Decadron off-label. It shrank his tumor and gave him an extra six months.

There's more. Jack Dreyfus, the legendary founder of the giant mutual fund company that bears his name, has spent a small fortune and four decades promoting the off-label use of an anticonvulsant that he says worked wonders on his depression. Provigil is an almost miracle drug with only minor side effects that seems to be useful against fatigue, depression, attention deficit and hyperactivity disorder (ADHD), cocaine addiction, and the urge to snack; apparently it also helps boost athletic prowess, since it has been banned by the United States Olympic Committee. Some $360 million worth of Provigil pills were sold in the United States in 2004. But 90 percent of that was off-label. The drug has been approved only for three narrow sleep-related problems.

"What are you going to say?" Gilla Kaplan asked rhetorically: "'You have to wait and die of multiple myeloma because it's [thalidomide] not licensed'?"

And how about diseases that have not been formally categorized? They obviously do not have medications approved specifically for them. For years the medical community was confounded by a debilitating condition of chronic pain, sleep disturbance, fatigue, and headaches, according to a report in the *Wall Street Journal*. After brain-imaging technology made it clear that this was a discrete disease of the central nervous system, the condition was named fibromyalgia. Without any approved "fibromyalgia drugs," doctors and patients had to make do with off-label prescriptions for pain, depression, anxiety, Parkinson's disease, and sleep disorder medication, the *Journal* said. Meanwhile, in a reversal of the usual situation, adults with ADHD were taking medication approved only for children, because until the late 1990s no one thought adults could be affected by that disorder and therefore no one ran clinical trials on them.

Were the FDA to throw out Hutt's 30-year-old legal ruling and forbid secondary-use prescribing—which it may not have the power to do anyway—everyone knows that the practice would not end. If a drug were approved only for Condition A, and a physician wanted to prescribe it for a patient with Condition B, the physician would simply write Condition A as the diagnosis on the prescription pad. Suddenly, a lot of Mike Katzes would be "diagnosed" with leprosy.

"There aren't enough jail cells," scoffed Hutt, "for all the doctors who practice off-label."

Occasionally, FDA officials like Robert Temple and Mark McClellan have made comments about subjecting off-label uses to some sort of regulatory review. But as Temple testified in a 1996 legal deposition, according to Knight-Ridder, "We just don't know quite how to do it."

The only authority the FDA has over off-label prescribing is that it is illegal for a manufacturer to actively promote an unapproved use through ads, sales pitches to doctors, and the like. This is the major incentive for companies like Celgene to apply for a secondary approval, in order to openly market to a much bigger clientele. However, it is a restriction that is easily circumvented. It is an open secret, for instance, that pharmaceutical company sales representatives tout the off-label applications when they stop by physicians' offices with free samples or free lunches. Knight-Ridder reported that one Celgene sales rep went so far as to push thalidomide as a "great drug for feelings of general well-being." (John Jackson said that occurred four or five years before the articles were published, and "that guy left the company.") Drug makers also sponsor "educational" seminars where paid experts discuss the unapproved uses. Moreover, companies can legally run a type of TV commercial called "reminder" ads, which cite a medication by name without mentioning what it does (or listing side effects, for that matter). Do the commercials "remind" viewers of off-label uses or approved ones? Who's to say?

In 2000 the FDA lost one of its key weapons for controlling these promotions after a U.S. district court judge ruled, in a lawsuit brought by a conservative think tank called the Washington Legal Foundation, that pharmaceutical companies have a free-speech right to tell doctors about information in scientific journals, even if the information concerns unapproved uses. To some degree, insurance companies were thought to control the prescribing trend by paying only for approved uses. That barrier, too, may not prove very effective. In the face of a near-revolt by cancer patients, Medicare in January 2004 put off a final decision on a proposal not to cover the unauthorized uses of four drugs.

Some promotional tactics are so egregious that now and then they do get slapped down. In May 2004 Pfizer pleaded guilty to illegal off-label marketing of its epilepsy drug Neurontin and agreed to pay $430 million in civil and criminal penalties. The charges actually concerned activities by Warner-Lambert, before Pfizer bought that company in 2000. A former medical advisor to the sales staff of Warner-Lambert had accused the drug maker of illegally paying doctors consulting fees and plying them with exotic trips and fancy dinners in an attempt to peddle Neurontin for more than a dozen off-label uses. Federal prosecutors in Boston and Philadelphia, the New York State attorney general, and other law enforcement officials have investigated more companies for their promotions, including the manufacturer of Provigil. Another example: A one-time sales rep for a small California biotech called InterMune charged that her ex-employer improperly pitched its drug Actimmune, which had been approved for just two rare childhood diseases, as a treatment for a more common lung disease in adults. InterMune officials denied encouraging improper promotions. None of these cases was taken on by the FDA, however.

So if off-label prescribing cannot be stopped—and arguably should not be—the best solution is to make sure doctors get more accurate information about the drugs, all their possible uses, and their side effects, and less misleading hype. Carl Peck concluded his comment about letting doctors use their best judgment with the caveat: "I would caution that they ought to have adequate evidence."

How? Hutt suggested that the package label could include a section, prominently displayed, that cites articles in professional journals discussing the off-label uses. Two other trends in the early 2000s might also help. One was a push to make public more results from clinical trials. That could let doctors know about the dangers of some off-label uses as well as positive results. In addition, there was growing pressure to crack down on the frenzy of pharmaceutical marketing of all sorts. If approved drugs could no longer be promoted with expensive dinners and "consulting" fees to doctors, then it would certainly be harder to push the drugs for unapproved uses that way.

Alternatively, maybe the FDA could streamline the clinical trial requirements for secondary uses so that more drug companies would be willing to file an SNDA, which would essentially solve the problem. Sometimes, for instance, companies are allowed to use the original Phase I safety data for their supplemental applications. Celgene filed its multiple myeloma SNDA even before Phase III trials were completed, as cancer drugs often do under the fast-track mechanism. But if it really costs $10,000 to $30,000 per person to run a clinical trial, it is hard to imagine a balance that would provide enough scientific testing at a cost low enough to lure applicants. Some health care experts say the National Institutes of Health, the FDA, or private foundations might have to foot the bill.

In any case, neither the FDA nor all the newspaper headlines in the world will probably keep people like Mike Katz from their thalidomide, on- or off-label. The only thing that might is more and better approved drugs.

Katz said he is not concerned that he is taking medicine that has not been fully vetted for his disease. "People using it are very grateful. Because they're not dying," he said simply. And he pointed out that at the time he started on thalidomide, pretty much the only other choices of treatment were far more radical—chemotherapy or stem-cell transplants. "The incredible thing about thalidomide when it arrived was that it worked in people who were totally out of options," he said. (Since Katz was diagnosed, more options have become available. The FDA approved Velcade, an intravenous treatment for myeloma, in a speedy four months, and Celgene itself is working on another drug, Revlimid, a cousin of thalidomide without the history of birth defects.)

Of course, when Katz talks, you have to keep in mind that he is also vice president of the International Myeloma Foundation, a patient advocacy group, and, like many patient groups, it gets substantial funding from pharmaceutical manufacturers. In the IMF's case, Celgene donates a couple hundred thousand dollars a year in what both sides call educational grants. Do the corporate contributions influence the comments of advocates like Katz? Probably far less than the patients' fundamental, overwhelming desire to find a drug that could help them. (This topic is also discussed in Chapter 10.) The FDA's strict conflict-of-interest rules forced Katz to leave the advisory committee he was on, but he said he does not feel any conflict. "The notion that a person with an active disease or an incurable disease is going to either approve a drug that's a bad drug, just to help the company that's making the donation, or block approval of a competing drug because he doesn't want the company that funds his foundation to get injured—that is kind of ludicrous," he said brusquely.

And what about AIDS, the disease that brought thalidomide to the FDA to begin with? Celgene never filed for approval for that. First, the FDA wanted more data because thalidomide actually raised TNF-alpha levels initially, which is exactly the opposite of what AIDS patients need. As it turned out, the levels drop appropriately after a couple of weeks. But by the time Celgene verified those results, the breakthrough AIDS "cocktails," or combination drugs—Norvir from Abbott Laboratories, Invirase from Roche, and Crixivan from Merck—were starting to come on the market. More powerful than the earlier generation of drugs and with fewer side effects, these cocktails turned AIDS into a manageable, long-term chronic condition, rather than a short-term death sentence. Thalidomide, said Gilla Kaplan, "became a moot point."

CHAPTER 7

How Picky Is the FDA?

It is one of the nightmares that haunts anyone who has ever worked on a clinical trial: FDA inspectors are coming for an audit.

The call came to Dr. Linda Gail Bekker, head of the Infectious Diseases Clinical Research Unit at the University of Cape Town Lung Institute in South Africa, in 2003. Bekker's unit conducts clinical trials for pharmaceutical companies from around the globe. Because most of the companies naturally hope to sell their products in the huge American market, the Cape Town institute generally conducts its trials to FDA standards and is subject to FDA oversight, even though South Africa has its own Medicines Control Council that also approves drugs.

There can be a variety of reasons for an FDA audit—to check that a trial is being conducted according to the official protocol, for instance, or to make sure the results were accurately reported. In this case, the FDA was interested in the trial of a generic antifungal agent that the Cape Town scientists had done two years previously for the German pharmaceutical firm Boehringer Ingelheim. Bekker was the lead investigator on that trial, which had involved 30 patients over one year.

The lab was given six months' advance notice so it could pull together the documentation the FDA would want. "Everything would have to be opened up—all of our informed-consent procedures [which patients must sign to prove they know what they're getting into], our standard operating procedures. They're allowed to have access to anything to do with the trial," Bekker recalled. As her staff gathered the paperwork, Bekker realized she had a problem.

When researchers check on their patients, they write their notes into source documents, and the information from those documents is later transcribed into the official clinical resource forms that are sent to the drug company once a month. Because this antifungal trial had been done at a hospital—not all clinical trials are—Bekker had been concerned, as she organized the procedure, that the trial data from these checkups could accidentally be put in the hospital's ongoing patient files. So she had added an extra step to the record-keeping: Data would go from the source document to a template to the official resource form. The trouble is, she admitted later, "the more times you transcribe, the more opportunities for mistakes." Sure enough, as Bekker prepared for the audit, she discovered that in a couple of cases "we had maybe made a small mistake in transcribing data, leaving out a word or fact"—nothing significant, she quickly said. Nothing that affected the trial results. But for an FDA audit, "you had to come clean," to explain why the source document and official form were not identical. Over the next few weeks, her staff spent the equivalent of three or four days' solid working time going through the records and writing explanations of any discrepancies.

Then time was up. Two FDA inspectors arrived, stayed about two days, and were, Bekker said, pleasant, polite, and reasonable. They asked Bekker about the discrepancies, of course. But Bekker had expected far worse. "I thought that we would have to pull up more, spend more time going through detail by detail," she said, a few months after it was over. "It was more the psychological hype than the reality. Instead of reprimanding us, they knew that these things happen." The agency even had a good suggestion, to simply drop the extra template.

Now, having survived an audit, Bekker says that the whole concept is not such a bad idea. "It sharpens everyone's sense of, 'We cannot afford to be complacent.' Otherwise, human nature being what it is, standards will drop."

The companies regulated by the FDA in fact have a complicated relationship with their overseer. "Love-hate" does not quite describe it. From the industry's point of view, it is more a combination of grudging acceptance, plus fear, plus desire for a gold star that can be used in marketing, plus the natural tendency of anyone to gripe about whoever is in a position of authority over them. Sure, drug makers know they must have a seal of approval from the FDA in order to sell their food products, drugs, and medical devices in the United States. And sure, they wish the seal were easier to earn. Yet once they get it, they sure are glad that the seal stands for a rigorous vetting.

(All this concerns just the day-to-day relationship of living with the FDA's regulations—the "pickiness" part of the Type I-Type II debate. The broader questions of the industry's influence on FDA policy and decisions—the "industry pressure" part of the debate—are discussed in Chapter 8.)

In practical terms, moreover, the FDA gives the drug companies a lot of free groundwork in basic science that they would otherwise have to do themselves, like the standards it crafted in the 1960s, 1970s, and 1980s for conducting good scientific trials. The National Center for Toxicological Research in Arkansas is constantly coming up with new methodologies and running toxicity experiments on chemicals, all openly available. Anyone can take one of the transgenic "knockout mice" that the NCTR created and inject it with a chemical—say, a chemical the company hopes to use in a new drug—to see whether that causes a genetic mutation in the animal. Even more practically, the FDA, through its requirements when reviewing a trial protocol, can help improve the structure of a clinical trial.

The need goes both ways. The FDA, under tremendous public pressure, needs the pharmaceutical, medical device, and food industries to churn out a never-ending stream of miracle cures and healthful food that will not kill people as a byproduct.

In order to understand the relationship between the FDA and the companies it oversees, it is important to remember the agency's mandate: The FDA is supposed to protect the public health by making sure products are safe and effective. Unlike the case with the Department of Agriculture or the Federal Aviation Administration, it is not the FDA's job to promote the health of the industry. On the other hand, "protecting" public health does not just mean checking new drugs for side effects or recalling contaminated applesauce. It also means making sure the public has access to a wide choice of products that can keep people healthy.

What is the pharmaceutical industry's relationship with the FDA?

"It's a marriage. Just like all marriages, there are times when you feel you can't live with this other person, but then you realize you're nothing without the other person." (Howard J. Weisman, president and chief operating officer of ESP Pharma in Edison, New Jersey, a privately owned pharmaceutical marketing company.)

"I get the sense that pharmaceutical companies see it as a sort of thorn in their side. Obviously what it does is important, but it goes too far." (Dr. David Perlin, science director of the Public Health Research Institute, or PHRI, in Newark, New Jersey, and a specialist in infectious diseases who has done research for drug companies.)

"The industry is both guarded by the FDA and works pretty closely with the FDA to get drugs approved. But at the end of the day, their job is to regulate the industry. That means being the policeman." (Peter Tollman, vice president of the biopharmaceutical research and development business at the Boston Consulting Group, which has a number of large drug company clients.)

"We have the best health care system in the world, one of the safest, in large part because of the role the FDA plays in reviewing applications." (George B. Abercrombie, chief executive officer of North American pharmaceutical operations for Roche.)

"The FDA exists because the industry can't be trusted to market safe drugs." (Carl Peck, the former head of the FDA's Center for Drug Evaluation and Research.)

Behind the big criticism—the FDA is too strict and takes too long— lie the questions a reviewer asks and the information he or she requests as a drug slowly makes it way along the approval trail. The industry has four basic complaints about this barrage of questions and requests. And while the big criticism may be overdone, the companies do have some valid points in their specific complaints, as even FDA employees acknowledge:

They ask for information we already gave them. After plowing through 40,000 or so pages of a new drug application, an FDA reviewer might understandably forget what he or she had read back on page 20. So the reviewer might ask the company for data that was actually in the application. For instance, Tom Garvey, the former cardio-renal reviewer, said he would always request an analysis of a drug's impact on liver function. Even if the answer was somewhere in the NDA, it could be hard to find, he said.

Pharmaceutical company officials are not totally unsympathetic to that dilemma. "Most of the things they're looking for are in the NDA. But it's such a massive document, without really knowing it like people in the company do, it's difficult to find the answers," said Irwin Martin, the erstwhile regulatory affairs vice president at Parke-Davis who was in charge of Lipitor. This problem should largely correct itself as more companies file their NDAs electronically, making it easier to search for keywords.

They don't explain what they want. Despite all the meetings, phone calls, faxes, and e-mails during the time the drug is being prepared, the industry feels as if it still does not get enough specific guidance. "The FDA [advisory] committee does not define exactly what it takes to get a drug or device approved. It is the submitter's responsibility to demonstrate the safety and effectiveness of its innovation and to suggest how to [define standards for approval]," claimed Jeffrey B. Jump, the CEO of Xitact, a high-tech company in western Switzerland that develops robotic and simulation-based training systems for doctors.

The biggest problem: "You have to read the code," said Elma Hawkins, the regulatory affairs veteran who helped guide Antigenics at the beginning. "The FDA would say, 'Have you thought about doing a double-blind controlled study?' What they mean is, 'Do it!'" She added, with a sigh, "It would be so much better if you didn't have to read into things."

Steve Koepke, the former FDA chemistry reviewer, now at the contract research organization PharmaNet, agreed that, yes, there is a kind of code. "Words have a different meaning in regulation," he said. His colleague at both PharmaNet and the FDA, Dr. Stuart Portnoy, who spent eight years reviewing cardiac and respiratory devices, gave an example of how an application might describe the software in a new medical device. Bad wording would be: "We will prove to you that our software is working as expected." Good wording: "We will provide you results from verification and validation testing that this software is performing appropriately." The difference? "Verify" and "validate" are key words, Portnoy said.

However, others both within the FDA and outside insist that things are no worse than in any other field with its own jargon. "We endeavor to communicate as clearly and successfully as possible to require the least guessing," said Steve Galson, the acting director of the Center for Drugs. If the pharmaceutical companies believe there is some secret code, he suggested, maybe it is just an honest misunderstanding, like the classic game of Telephone. "The person communicating may think they're saying something different from what the listener is hearing. That has happened; it happens in families. We say T, U, V, W. They assumed that we meant also X, Y and Z. So they give you what they thought you asked for." Elma Hawkins agreed that this can be the case at times. Or maybe the FDA has to be a little elliptical because sometimes its analysis of one drug is based on something it knows from another application, but it cannot reveal the trade secrets in that analysis, offered Leigh Thompson, the former Lilly scientific officer.

A corollary complaint is that maybe everything would be made clear if the reviewers would just return phone calls. Linda Alexander, the president of the contract research organization Alquest, said that "many times we call them and leave three or four messages" without getting a return call. So she shortened her timeframe: If she has not heard back from the primary reviewer after two attempts, "then we'll go up the ladder till I get a call back."

PDUFA, the user fee law ought to help prod things along by requiring that certain meetings be held within set timeframes. For instance, when a sponsor requests a formal pre-IND, end-of-Phase-II, or pre-NDA meeting, it is supposed to be scheduled within 60 days. But considering the FDA's workload—in 2003 it approved 466 new and generic drugs and biologics, sent more than 500 warning letters, opened nearly 400 criminal investigations, and seized 25 illegal products—it is probably inevitable that every reviewer will overload his or her voicemail.

They keep changing the rules. By 1984 Bill Vodra had left his job as the FDA's associate chief counsel and joined Arnold & Porter, one of the nation's classiest corporate law firms. One of his clients wanted to market a cholesterol drug. Since the drug was very similar to an existing medication for triglycerides—both cholesterol and triglycerides are fats found in the blood—the FDA told the company, according to Vodra, that it would have no problem if the drug was submitted for triglycerides, too. So the company refocused its trials, the FDA approved the protocol, the company submitted its drug application in 1987, and the initial reviewer recommended approval. Then the reviewer left the agency.

For the next five years, Vodra said, the application bounced around Rockville. A new reviewer said the original study design that the FDA had approved was not acceptable. The advisory committee wanted more information on dosages. "The [supervisor] kept asking for different slices of data, arrays of data." What finally pushed the drug through, on New Year's Eve of 1993, Vodra believes, is that PDUFA was about to take effect and the FDA wanted to clear its decks.

Irwin Martin has a different horror story from his days at Parke-Davis. When one of its top-selling cardiovascular drugs (which he will not name publicly) was nearing the end of its patent protection in the early 1990s, with competition from cheaper generics looming, the company came up with a slightly modified, more convenient version that could qualify for a fresh patent. Martin concedes that the new pill was only a "modest improvement." Still, that was exactly why he figured it would be easy to get a go-ahead from the FDA. The efficacy of the two pills was virtually the same. So Martin and his coworkers met with agency officials to discuss the package label, which is usually one of the last steps before approval. "We had done everything they told us to, we spent an hour and a half discussing terms, and at the end of the meeting they handed us a nonapproval letter that had been signed before we walked in the door," he recalled with disgust. "All that we had been doing was a sham." The company appealed two levels up the chain of command before giving in.

Of course Vodra's and Martin's stories are more than a decade old. But Antigenics more recently faced something similar, if less drastic, when its review staff was replaced—twice—and it was put on clinical hold in part because the first set of replacement reviewers had not been involved in the years of planning discussions. Arguably, ImClone may have gotten mixed signals regarding its trials for the cancer drug Erbitux.

The growing number of disagreements between advisory committees and FDA staff is another illustration of the way companies cannot seem to count on anything the agency says, from silicone breast implants to the Plan B morning-after pill to food from cloned animals. *BusinessWeek* in February 2002 described the runaround faced by a heart failure drug, Natrecor, in the previous couple of years. After an advisory committee gave it a green light, FDA staff asked for trials comparing it to existing treatments—exactly what many outsiders like Dr. Angell of the *New England Journal of Medicine* want but highly unusual for the agency. The drug was finally approved in September 2001.

To some degree, inconsistency is simply inevitable in any large organization that involves a lot of human interactions, no matter how precise the law is or how well trained the staff. "Different reviewers may have somewhat different approaches to issues and different standards," noted Jay Siegel, the former official in the Biologics Center. Yet he also said that the FDA should minimize those differences, adding, "It is the job of experienced supervisors to ensure consistency across reviews." Peter Barton Hutt, the corporate lawyer and former FDA counsel, is more cynical: "Every reviewer is different. Every reviewer is a king or queen in their own realm."

If the reviewer that a company has been working with leaves the FDA, any informal arrangements that were negotiated can be thrown out the window by his or her replacement. If the primary reviewer approves the application, it can still be knocked out by the supervisor or the division director.

On top of all that, different divisions have reputations for being tougher or easier to deal with. Even Steve Galson conceded this point. Industry and FDA insiders say that CDER's gastrointestinal division is more likely to clamp a clinical hold on an application than cardio-renal, while the cardiovascular and orthopedics units tend to provide more explicit guidance. And of course the three big Centers—Drugs, Biologics, and Devices—all have their distinct personalities, stemming from history and the different intrinsic qualities of their products. CDER, the Center for Drugs, clearly the first among equals, is the businessman of the bunch, efficient, careful to follow the rules, and good at meeting its user-fee deadlines. CBER, the Center for Biologics, is more like the tweedy academic, staffed by scientists who have been doing their own cutting-edge genomics and proteomics research and who still look a little askance at the idea of medicine as a business. (More can be found on the CDER-CBER tension in Chapter 12.) CDRH, the Center for Devices, has a "cowboy" image, with the most lenient approval requirements, the smallest trials, the fastest reviews. CDRH is the only center, said David Feigal, its ex-director, where MDs might be supervised by PhDs, and PhDs by people with only a bachelor's or a master's degree—a breach of hierarchy that would never be found at a university.

If a product overlaps jurisdictions, the bureaucratic-cultural differences can create some crossed wires. Back in 2001 when Stuart Portnoy was still reviewing devices at the FDA, a company showed up with something called a drug-eluting stent. (Portnoy will not reveal the name of the company, but around that time both Johnson & Johnson and Boston Scientific were developing exactly that sort of product.) A stent is a tiny mesh scaffolding that is used to prop open a clogged artery after it has been cleared, and it is particularly effective when coated with a drug that can prevent scar tissue from forming. Because this stent in 2001 combined a device and a drug, both the Drugs and Devices Centers got involved in the review. In one meeting soon after the preclinical trials, Portnoy said, the company described how it had tested its stent on some 20 animals for one to three months. As Portnoy recalled the scene: "For Devices, we were very comfortable with that level of data. However, some guy from Drugs said, 'I want to see you test this in 200 animals.' I saw the look of horror on the face of the company." The upshot: The Drugs representative never showed up again, and the Devices people quietly told the company that its 20 animals were good enough.

The FDA has undertaken some efforts to coordinate all these far-flung parts of itself. Jay Siegel said that he and his counterpart on the Drugs side, Bob Temple, "met and talked and e-mailed frequently to ensure consistency in our interpretations of regulations, review standards, and policy." There are also many regular meetings of CBER-CDER staff and committees that cover the same topics—for instance, the two centers' clinical hold committees. The agency revamped its Office of Combination Products in 2002 and issued a proposed rule to help determine which center would have primary responsibility for a product that crosses jurisdictions, like the drug-coated stent or orthopedic implants with genetically engineered human proteins. (If there really is no clear-cut "primary mode of action," then it goes to the center that regulates similar products or, failing that, to the one with the most relevant expertise.)

Then again, maybe the industry should be careful what it wishes for. Consistency may not always be such a virtue. For instance, Steve Galson noted that different divisions of CDER have historically had their own policies for communicating with industry; some let a pharmaceutical official pick up the phone and call anyone, while others insist on having all contact go through a single FDA liaison. Galson said he was going to scrap that approach and develop a consistent policy for all divisions—the most restrictive policy. All contact must go through a single liaison. This is nice and consistent, but it gives industry fewer people to talk to.

In yet another ironic and inconsistent twist, exactly the opposite has happened at the Devices Center. There, David Feigal noted proudly that companies have a lot more points of access than when he first came in 1999. In the olden days "only the consumer safety officer could talk to a company. Our statistician couldn't talk to their statistician."

They don't understand the real world. By and large, most pharmaceutical executives say the FDA staff are smart and dedicated and certainly understand science in an academic way. Probably no other government agency, with the exception of the National Institutes of Health and the Centers for Disease Control, has such a high percentage of PhDs and MDs. What the FDA's scientists do not understand, critics say, is the real world of business—the hassle and cost of developing a successful drug, and the pressures from Wall Street.

As an example, Russ Herndon of Antigenics recalled the meeting where the FDA reviewers put his firm on clinical hold but would not provide a copy of their prepared statement until it had gone through all the steps of the agency's inner bureaucracy. Antigenics could not wait; this was a material event that the company had to report to shareholders immediately. "They don't understand what it means to be a public company. They don't understand SEC regulations or materiality," Herndon protested.

His colleague Taylor Burtis saw the attitude from the inside when she worked at the Biologics Center's Office of Compliance and Biologics Quality from 1991 to 1996—she was an inspector of inspectors, as she puts it. Before and after that, Burtis has had an eclectic career, focused mainly on issues to do with transplants, at Brigham and Women's Hospital in Boston, Memorial Sloan-Kettering Cancer Center in New York, Yale University, Duke University, the American Red Cross, and, finally, Genentech in California, where she clearly transplanted her own heart. She left Genentech only because she had to come back to Massachusetts for family reasons, Burtis said, which is how she ended up at Antigenics. Husky and blonde, she shares with Renu Gupta the main responsibility for Antigencs' relations with the FDA.

Burtis said her fellow staffers at the FDA simply did not grasp the dollars-and-cents of running a company or of drug development. They would scoff if drug firms cited cost as the justification for seeking to have clinical trials smaller than the agency wanted. "Can you believe they'd try to get it by us by claiming poverty?" her coworkers would say. Or, "I see they posted a $1.4 billion profit. What do they mean they don't have the money to put back into research?"

Not understanding the real world is, of course, a complaint that industry often levies against "ivory tower" academia and government bureaucrats. For that matter, the food industry says the same thing about the FDA's Center for Food Safety and Applied Nutrition. Steven Grover, a lobbyist for the National Restaurant Association, claims that state and local health departments are more attuned to what it is like to really run a restaurant because they are the ones actually doing the inspections, not just writing some pie-in-the-sky FDA model code. "Folks that we deal with at the state agencies, they have to walk in and look people in the eye and explain why they do things," he said.

FDA officials from Acting Commissioner Lester Crawford on down insist that they do have a sense of the real world. The industry could hardly phrase things more sympathetically than Dr. Jesse Goodman, the director of CBER, did: "I don't want to give the impression that we can underestimate how important the economics are in all of this. People are going to have to make it a reasonable investment. The incentives that are needed to get drugs developed are not always there." The agency is so sensitive to the workings of the business world that it tries to wait until after 6:00 PM Eastern time—that is, after the stock market has closed—before announcing approvals, Steve Galson pointed out.

All those complaints are basically logistical. The industry's more sweeping criticism is that from the get-go, in everything big and small, the FDA demands too much ridiculous paperwork and backup data, which then bogs down drug development and hikes costs.

The best way to gauge the truth of those claims is to ask the scientists who actually conduct the clinical trials. Even more than the pharmaceutical companies that hire them, these scientists are the ones who have to collect all the records, fill out all the forms, and dot all the i's before data can be submitted for a drug application. Moreover, they can compare the FDA's red tape with the requirements when doing a study for the NIH, universities, or other independent research institutions.

The quick answer is that working with the FDA definitely means piling up the paperwork. David Perlin of the PHRI in New Jersey likened it to the extra bookkeeping a person might do to prepare for a tax audit.

But the longer answer is, it's not that big a deal.

The PHRI does a lot of DNA sequencing in its study of the mechanics of molecular reactions to drugs. Normally, the scientists will store the data—tens of thousands of sequences—electronically in order to save on paperwork. But when he is running FDA-related molecular sequencing for drug companies, which usually involves post-market studies of antifungal drugs, Perlin said, he has to churn out actual printouts of the sequences and match-ups, which can double the time spent on the project. Perlin seems to have mixed feelings about the FDA requirements. At one point he said that "there's a little bit more scrutiny in terms of detailing information, signing [record] books. That's probably not a bad thing. It probably makes us think a little more." However, in talking about the printouts of the molecular sequencing, he said, "That's not an efficient use of time. If you're building something, you can build it very simply and functionally, or you can build it so it has lots and lots of bells and whistles and safeties that are not critical to the ultimate goal. I feel like when we're involved with the FDA, we're creating a lot of excess work." Luckily, he does not do much FDA work.

At Mount Sinai School of Medicine in New York, Dr. Jeffrey Silverstein, an associate professor of anesthesiology and an assistant professor in two other disciplines, has been conducting trials under the auspices of both the FDA and the NIH since the late 1980s in an eclectic mix of medical areas—anesthesia, blood substitutes, beta blockers, and more. "There's a degree of stringency to what the [FDA] paperwork looks like, another order of magnitude higher," he said. He gave an example that sounds like a caricature of bureaucracy: Let's say that in taking notes on a patient's condition for a clinical trial, he had written down that the hemoglobin level before an operation was 9.1, and later discovered that he should have written 9.2. That kind of minor mistake happens "a lot," Silverstein admitted. "With the NIH, I can cross it out. If I did the same thing on an FDA trial, I would have to put a single line through it, date it, initial it, and put a little note explaining why it happened."

To take a different example: Consider how Silverstein might go about double-checking the accuracy of data in a patient's chart. When it is for a study overseen by the NIH, Silverstein and his staff will spend a couple of hours every two weeks or so double-checking. For an FDA trial, by contrast, the company manufacturing the drug will send a monitor to check the records for two or three patients at a time. The monitor "sits here all day long and looks for a source for every little piece of information."

Altogether, Silverstein figured that complying with FDA oversight takes his staff maybe one or two hours extra per patient, compared with doing a trial for the NIH. Yet in the most important ways, he said, "It's not that different." One of the biggest pieces of bureaucracy in any research is the "informed consent" form that patients must sign. It is a legal requirement that applies whether or not the FDA is involved.

Gilla Kaplan, the immunologist who studied thalidomide in leprosy, tuberculosis, and AIDS patients, now works at the PHRI with David Perlin, but she does not appear to be as troubled by the FDA's rules as he is. One example she cited was that, if she is using experimental drugs on patients, "I do have to report any toxicity at the time of toxicity." Considering the ethics of testing on human beings, she thinks that this is reasonable, and not much of a burden anyway. "There's a standard process you would follow that would pretty much meet the FDA requirements. You have to keep good records."

In fact, plenty of scientists and pharmaceutical veterans are glad the FDA is so demanding. They feel that the questions that reviewers ask and the requirements that the agency imposes are generally smart and fair. They say the staff will listen to reasoned arguments and explain their own reasoning. There are even people, like Linda Gail Bekker in South Africa, who assert that the paperwork and the rechecking they are asked to do have actually helped them improve their operations or produce better drugs; even David Perlin said as much. After all, that is the role the FDA sees itself playing, as the greybeard science advisor, starting in the 1970s when it pioneered the use of double-blind, randomized dose-response trials instead of an empirical approach.

If there was a subtle problem with a heart irregularity in patients during a trial, and the company missed the signs, it is far better to have the FDA catch it during the approval process than to go out on the market and have your customers start getting serious heart palpitations. By the same token, if the FDA sends the company back to check what looks like a spate of side effects, and it turns out that it was only one patient with a history of heart troubles unrelated to the drug, then that is an extra level of assurance for the company as well as the FDA, which the company can certainly parlay to good advantage in its marketing. ("This drug has not been found to cause…") "What the agency does is call from you an enormous level of analysis—they call from you excellence," said Boyd Clarke, the former Merck executive who now runs the Philadelphia-area biotech Neose.

The story of Eli Lilly's Axid, a histamine blocker for ulcers and heartburn, shows not only how FDA intervention can improve a clinical trial, but also how no one else but the FDA could do it. Lilly was ready to start its trials of Axid in 1985, recalled Leigh Thompson, when two of the FDA's top reviewers "suggested a radical change in protocol." Instead of running a standard double-blind study using the drug and a placebo for eight weeks straight, the reviewers proposed limiting the initial test to four weeks, then randomly reshuffling the patients for the remaining four weeks so that some of the people originally on the drug would now have the placebo, and vice versa. That way, Thompson said, "we were able to track how many [patients] had ulcers go away on the drug and come back on the placebo. The drug acted faster than we expected and wore off faster than we realized. We got much better data, and it didn't cost us more." The FDA reviewers had based their suggestion on something only they could have known: the trial results from other, similar drugs.

Similarly, the FDA once requested that Gilla Kaplan alter a trial in which she was trying to see if injecting recombinant molecules would stimulate a better immune response from leprosy patients. (This was separate from her work on thalidomide.) While Kaplan had wanted to test 50 people, the FDA limited the trial to 24 because it was experimental. So Kaplan tested 24, then had to reapply to test the next group of 24. But that actually turned out to be a good idea, she said, because "you have an opportunity to evaluate the data and redesign your next question."

Another Lilly scientist is Dr. Maida Taylor, an obstetrician-gynecologist in San Francisco who started overseeing clinical trials at Lilly in the early 2000s, after more than two decades in private practice. The first year that she had to write an annual product report, "it was a good exercise for me because I was new—like finger exercises on the piano. I enjoyed the opportunity to review everything." Taylor admitted that the task might get a little routine in subsequent years, but it will also grow easier. Alternatively, "someone junior to me will have to do it."

The key to dealing with the FDA, many pharmaceutical executives say, is simply to overcompensate. Provide much more data than you think the reviewers could possibly ask for.

"You can answer them short or long. If you answer too short, the agency will come back with questions," advised Ken Moch, the CEO of the New Jersey biotech Alteon that is studying glucose-protein links. Leigh Thompson recalled that when Prozac first came out, Lilly's European affiliates would fax the U.S. office a copy of every article they saw on the drug's side effects. "We would immediately fax it to the FDA," Thompson said. "We didn't want them to be blindsided by a reporter's questions."

"The FDA is not the villain that everyone portrays it to be. These are reasonable people," summed up Garo Armen of Antigenics. Of course, he felt that the new set of reviewers back in September 2003 should have given his company a chance to file the missing Oncophage data instead of immediately putting the vaccine trial on clinical hold. He is also annoyed that the agency sometimes takes a long time to respond to submissions. But, he said, "We have never been in a situation where we have not been able to reason with them based on scientific facts."

O r are pharmaceutical officials just too scared to voice their real complaints?

Like Irwin Martin and his colleagues at Parke-Davis with the modified version of their cardiovascular drug, companies are reluctant to push appeals all the way up the FDA ladder. They try not to make pests of themselves by calling too often (at least, as they define "often"). Several refused to be quoted by name for this book. And for good reason: A thumbs-down from the FDA can mean that 12 years and tens of millions of dollars' worth of work on a drug are on hold, or even out the window. The merest hint that the FDA may have serious questions can prompt Wall Street to flee the stock, as Antigenics learned when it was placed on clinical hold. "The FDA makes or breaks them. That's their livelihood," said David Perlin.

So people working for a drug company are going to be very, very careful about what they say in public.

Because of the FDA's impact, "if you get a 301-area code phone call"—that's the area code for Rockville—"late on a Friday afternoon, it is always something you take with a certain amount of trepidation," said Boyd Clarke.

Do pharmaceutical executives really think that if they utter some criticism of the FDA in public, the agency's reviewers would retaliate by rejecting their drug? "It is not so much that there is a real fear that if you say something that is unpalatable, that there would be a retribution. But the thought of that is resident enough in the base of your mind," one biotech executive explained (anonymously, of course). He compared the risk of talking about the FDA to the way a baseball player or manager would feel if asked to give his opinion of an umpire: "You may have no reason to believe they'll shrink the strike zone, you may not have any evidence that they ever have, but the impact of tightened requirements is so damaging."

People on both sides describe a relationship that can be capricious on the FDA's part and almost obsequious on the company's. "If they say, 'run Study X,' and Study X is one of the stupidest ideas," said Hutt, the patrician lawyer, "I advise the client to do it anyway." If a reviewer asks for something, don't argue that you have already provided it; don't complain that the FDA told you last year that you would not need to have the data.

Across the divide, from his vantage point as a one-time FDA reviewer, Tom Garvey can see how an executive would jump at his slightest command. For instance, Garvey might request an analysis of liver abnormalities in three of a company's studies. "[The company] would say, 'I'll have it to you later this afternoon. Whatever you say, sir.' And they would have it." What did it feel like, to have all that power? "Like nothing," Garvey said. He just wanted to know about those liver abnormalities.

But if the FDA's requirements are so onerous, no one, not even the free-market critics who wanted to drastically revamp the FDA in the 1990s, has calculated the actual cost of complying with them. This is partly because it is impossible to say how much testing for safety and efficacy the pharmaceutical industry would do if the FDA did not exist. (Everyone concedes that companies would have to run some trials—enough, at least, to avoid mass poisoning and class-action lawsuits.) Moreover, the cost of compliance cannot be calculated because there is no agreement on how much companies spend to create a drug to begin with.

The industry in the early 2000s usually claimed it cost around $802 million to develop the average new drug, including the earliest molecular screenings, animal trials, clinical trials, overhead, and regulatory steps. That estimate was based largely on research done by Joseph A. DiMasi of Tufts University's Center for the Study of Drug Development and published in 2001. DiMasi came up with his total by analyzing 68 drugs that he chose at random from Tufts' comprehensive data base of drugs in development, then asking the manufacturers how much they spent per year to develop those 68.

However, DiMasi's figure was hotly disputed for a variety of reasons: The industry has never publicly revealed any of the numbers backing up its R&D spending claims. DiMasi's calculations did not subtract certain freebies that offset the expenditures, such as federal tax credits for research and development or the billions of dollars' worth of basic research that drug companies get from the NIH. There were accusations of bias, because 65 percent of the Tufts Center's funding comes from the industry. Most controversial, nearly half the $802 million consisted of opportunity costs, or the profit a company could have made by investing its cash in other ways, rather than actual expenditures on research. DiMasi defended his methodology as standard economic practice and said he was not influenced by the industry funding that Tufts receives. The opportunity costs were high, he said, because the companies are forgoing investment returns for as long as 12 or 15 years while they conduct tests and research.

Using an entirely different system, Boston Consulting produced a similar estimate of $880 million to develop a new drug. First, it asked several dozen of its pharmaceutical clients to walk through the process of drug development, step by step. Then it analyzed each step in order to estimate the cost of each. An even bigger price tag came in 2003 from the consulting firm Bain & Co., which added in marketing expenses to bring the average per-drug total to an astounding $1.7 billion. In 2004, Pfizer made eyes pop by promising to spend nearly $800 million just on one set of clinical trials for an anticholesterol medication with a radically new approach.

Consumer groups, meanwhile, tended to knock the development tab down to a couple hundred million or even less. Some of their numbers were based on real-life but narrow examples. For instance, they looked at the tax credits that companies claim when they manufacture drugs for rare diseases. In some cases, the organizations interviewed consultants, contract research organizations, or former pharmaceutical employees for cost estimates from their own experience.

Assuming that $800 million per drug is in the ballpark, Peter Tollman, the Boston Consulting vice president, and Henry Miller, the author and former FDA official who is one of the agency's harshest critics, both estimated in separate interviews that FDA requirements eat up fully half of a company's total R&D cost. But one health care expert at a major consulting firm gave me a very different rough guess: a bit more than ten percent of company spending.

The research scientists' personal experiences are just as wildly varying. At the PHRI, David Perlin estimated that printing out the molecular sequencing doubles his workload, while Gilla Kaplan said she might need to hire another research assistant to help with all the reporting. Silverstein of Mount Sinai puts in one or two hours extra per patient to do his paperwork.

Anyway, many in the industry acknowledge that there really is no choice. The FDA has to be tough, said Taylor Burtis of Antigenics, because "people do cut corners."

They also manipulate, exaggerate, push the exemptions to the limit, and lie. Sometimes the mistakes are unintentional: Small, new biotechs may not know how to put together a drug application. "They have good people, but they have never done it before. The NDAs are written terribly, or they don't have good data," Leigh Thompson pointed out. And sometimes there is downright fraud. Ann Campbell, an Alabama research scientist who had worked on a clinical trial of an antibiotic for what was then Aventis Pharma, Inc., pleaded guilty in October 2003 to providing false data on the number of people participating in the trial. Tom Garvey, who is now an industry consultant, told me he actually has to warn his clients not to try to hide problems like the number of people who had side effects. No wonder CDER spends over $45 million a year on drug safety (including post-market studies).

"There are ways to frame something," explained Nancy Roach, a survivor of cervical cancer and an occasional patient representative on one of the FDA advisory committees. With cancer, for instance, a commonly used endpoint is "time to progression"—the measurement of how much a tumor has grown after specified amounts of time. Roach claimed that companies will use longer intervals than they are supposed to between measurements, "so it might look like the tumor is growing slower."

In public opinion polls, how a question is phrased can make all the difference. The same is true in a clinical trial. Dr. Anne Peters Harmel, an endocrinologist and director of the clinical diabetes programs at the University of Southern California, participated in several studies of a diabetes drug that would ultimately be sold as Glucophage by Bristol-Myers Squibb. She said the number of reported side effects could vary by nearly 90 percent from site to site merely because different researchers used different words in asking if someone had diarrhea or cramps. "I think I asked in more detail. Rather than asking whether a person had any intestinal problems, I asked how many stools they were having per day, if their stool was softer, more watery etc.," Harmel said.

What could the FDA do about Nancy Roach's long counts and Anne Harmel's uneven comparisons? A vigilant reviewer would notice that there were too many months between measurements in Roach's case and ask for revised data using the correct checkpoints. He or she might wonder at the huge discrepancies between sites in Harmel's study and ask for the actual case reports and source documents.

The long string of recalls and withdrawals in the late 1990s and early 2000s provides plenty of proof of what happens when drugs with dangerous side effects slip past the FDA's review, whether through fraud, carelessness, misplaced confidence, or some other reason. The *Los Angeles Times* won a Pulitzer Prize in 2001 for a series investigating some of them. Take Posicor, the blood pressure drug made by Roche (and one of the cases where an advisory committee member had a conflict of interest). According to the *Times* and other published reports, Roche submitted the drug for approval even while the cause of more than 200 deaths during clinical trials was unresolved. There were also questions about how the drug might interact with other medications. After heavy debate at the FDA, Posicor was approved in June 1997—and withdrawn almost exactly a year later, amid reports of dangerously lowered heart rates, severe interactions with over two dozen drugs, and approximately 100 more deaths.

Janet Woodcock, who was then the head of CBER, first claimed the problems were "unexpected" but later admitted to the *Times* that some of the serious adverse reactions in connection with one other particular drug "perhaps could have been anticipated."

Propulsid, a heartburn medicine made by a subsidiary of Johnson & Johnson, might also have been caught by a more alert FDA. In clinical trials, a small number of patients experienced some heart rate and rhythm disorders, and eight children died. The FDA nevertheless approved the drug in 1993 based on the recommendations of its gastrointestinal experts, who said the deaths were attributable to other causes. However, according to the *Times*, the FDA never checked with its own cardiac division, the specialists in the kind of heart-rate problems that the patients had experienced. "By not tapping their expertise," the *Times* wrote, "FDA officials failed to notice what should have been another warning flag: Electrocardiograms showed that Propulsid prolonged patients' 'QT interval,' the time during which the heart's main pumping chambers contract and then relax"—which can lead to sudden death. The label that the FDA OKed for the drug merely mentioned "rare cases" of increased heartbeats and said Propulsid's role in that symptom "was not clear." Over the next seven years the label would be changed five times, each time with tougher warnings, until in 2000 the drug was taken off the market except as a last, closely monitored resort for patients who have tried every other treatment. Janet Woodcock told the *Times*: "We have to sort of walk that line: Where do we inform and where do we intervene by removing a drug from the market? That is a very draconian step...And so, we do try to avoid that."

The story of Merck's arthritis blockbuster Vioxx is more tangled. At the time the FDA approved it, in the spring of 1999, there had never been the slightest hint—publicly—of any serious cardiovascular side effects. Within less than a year, however, researchers began to notice that patients on the drug seemed to experience an unusual number of problems like strokes and heart attacks. The FDA sternly criticized Merck for promoting the drug without making those risks clear and ordered a tougher warning label in April 2002. Merck finally took the drug off the market in September 2004.

Just another case where serious side effects did not become apparent until after the drug was in use? Maybe not. The *Wall Street Journal* subsequently reported that scientists at Merck had actually pinpointed potential cardiovascular problems more than two years before the FDA approval. And the company kept downplaying the subsequent studies hinting at cardio

risks. (Merck officials said that the company "acted responsibly and appropriately as it developed and marketed Vioxx.")

Aha—a case where a manufacturer misled the FDA? Well, maybe that's
not the whole truth either. One of the FDA reviewers working on the original Vioxx application actually did raise the question of a "theoretical" risk
of blood clots, based on the clinical trial data, according to another *Journal*
article. But the risk wasn't clear, and the drug was approved. Then, in
August 2004, more than a month before Merck pulled the pill, a different
FDA reviewer—one who is known to be particularly aggressive in pursuing safety questions—wrote a preliminary, in-house report bluntly warning about the dangers of strong doses of Vioxx, based on an analysis of a
large patient database. Higher-ups in the agency, he claimed, tried to delay
or water down his report. He later hired a lawyer who specializes in protecting "whistle-blowers" and said he was afraid of being fired in retalia-
tion for his accusations.

So who was guarding the henhouse? The respected British medical
journal *The Lancet* soon afterwards came out with an editorial lambasting
the FDA's oversight of Vioxx, and two congressional committees launched
investigations. "The agency must address what looks like systemic problems when it comes to putting public health and safety first and public
relations second," growled Senator Charles Grassley of Iowa, chairman
of one of those committees, who was already furious at the FDA over
teenage use of antidepressants. FDA officials retorted that what looked
like a cover-up was simply normal, collegial back-and-forth. They argued
that they took the reviewer's warnings seriously but they never had definitive data, and ordering a drug pulled is, as Janet Woodcook noted with
Propulsid, an extreme measure. Still, the agency announced that it was
revamping its internal appeals process and hiring the top federal scientific
review board to analyze the way it reviews drugs for safety after they're on
the market. It also began a review of drugs like Vioxx.

Cop. Thorn. Jailer. Spouse. Gold standard. And now, with the "critical
path" initiative, business partner, too.

The FDA is all of these to the industry. It can be arbitrary, nitpicky,
contradictory, and sometimes seemingly impossible to please. But let's not
kid ourselves: The industry is not exactly helpless.

CHAPTER **8**

How Powerful
Is Industry?

The interview was just winding down in Bill Vodra's surprisingly small office four blocks from the White House. Blonde-wood bookshelves fill almost one wall of the office, a window fills another, and a third wall is decorated with framed Civil War memorabilia like the wartime flags of Maryland and a poster of Gettysburg. Vodra, tall and craggy-featured, with a white goatee, grey mustache, and tweed jacket—he's the former FDA lawyer who now represents pharmaceutical companies at the prestigious firm of Arnold & Porter—had already gotten up from his desk in front of the bookshelves, heading out for another meeting. Casually, as I shut my notebook and stood up across from him, he said, Of course drug companies will get members of Congress to call the FDA commissioner, to ask why it's taking so long to approve a particular drug.

I sat back down and yanked open my notebook.

Vodra went on: "The Washington representatives of drug companies have told me, 'We've got So-and-So [member of Congress] primed to call [the FDA] if we need him. We've met with Congressman So-and-So, he's offered to help us.' They know their congressman, the people who are interested in their disease. You can find out easily in this town which members of Congress have an interest in a disease." A congressman or senator might care about a certain drug the FDA is reviewing because the company that makes the drug is headquartered in the city or state the lawmaker repre-

143

sents. Or a family member might suffer from the disease the drug treats. So, as the drug wends its way through the FDA's review, for six months or more, a top official from that company might call the interested lawmaker to mention that a promising cure has been sitting around at the FDA for a long time going nowhere. And then, Vodra continued, that lawmaker might ring up the FDA commissioner and say, "This company is in my district, you've had the application for 90 days—is this some sort of bureaucratic hustle?"

Yes, the pressure behind the scenes can be that heavy-handed. Yes, the drug companies carry that much clout. Lester Crawford, the veteran FDA official and acting commissioner in the early 2000s, estimated that the agency gets 200 to 300 letters a year from members of Congress, some of them along the lines Vodra described. Other FDA staffers say that a congressional phone call of this ilk comes in about once every six months— to the commissioner, to another high-level official such as the director of the Center for Drugs, or maybe to a midlevel manager who supervises the scientist reviewing the drug. Typically, the calls and letters come because of a delaying action that has been taken, like a clinical hold, or because no action has been taken and the drug is still waiting for approval. Sometimes the caller might have questions about some miracle drug that does not actually exist. Whatever the exact motivation, the calls and letters are almost always complaining. They will ask, invariably: Why is this drug's approval taking so long?

To appreciate the full significance of these calls and letters, you have to remember that Congress controls the FDA's budget, and therefore, to FDA employees, a member of Congress carries the approximate authority of a god on Mount Olympus. For a reviewer to get a phone call from a member of Congress inquiring as to why a drug has not been approved yet is more or less like a mechanic in a company's auto pool getting a query from the chairman of the board as to whether his car is ready. You bet it is.

This is not a topic the FDA cares to talk about. The FDA prefers to claim that it is above both politics and pressure from industry, that its decisions are based solely on science. Jesse Goodman, the head of the Biologics center—after dancing back and forth as to whether he does or does not get calls from Congress—summed up the official view: "That doesn't affect our work. The central thing is, the scientific process, does it proceed with integrity? And I think it does."

"I think we've always been pro-consumer," said Steve Galson, Goodman's acting counterpart at Drugs. "A Republican administration hasn't had much of an impact on the consumer focus of the agency. We're not going to consider politics in our drug review decisions."

By and large, what Goodman and Galson assert is true. But the FDA is also an arm of the government, overseeing products in some of the most controversial areas of modern society, overseeing at least one-fourth of the economy, headquartered just a half-hour's Metro ride from the White House and the Capitol—in other words, operating right in the bull's eye of political pressure.

And in politics, the pharmaceutical industry that the FDA regulates, known as Big Pharma, carries outsized clout. It has enough lobbyists to put a shadow on each member of Congress. Its trade organization, the Pharmaceutical Research and Manufacturers of America, or PhRMA, spends some $150 million a year in lobbying, including nearly $5 million just to lobby the FDA. In most years that total has been the biggest political wallop of any American industry, according to the consumer group Public Citizen. It is not hard to see why Big Pharma devotes so many resources, because the stakes it is lobbying for are also huge. Drug companies, after all, claim they spend more than $800 million, on average, to develop a drug. If the FDA gives its imprimatur, the most successful products could bring in over $500 million in sales apiece each year.

So the pharmaceutical industry throws its weight around where it can, and everyone knows it. For years the industry used its clout to keep Congress from adding prescription drug coverage to Medicare, the health insurance plan for the elderly, because the manufacturers feared that would mean government price controls. When public outrage finally forced the drug makers to give in on the basic principle of Medicare coverage, in the early 2000s, they still managed to persuade the Republican-controlled Congress to ban any government-negotiated price caps. Drug companies have also persuaded politicians to prevent Americans from buying lower-priced medicines from Canada, to allow prescription drugs to be advertised on TV, and to limit developing countries' access to cheaper generic versions of drugs still under patent. Their power even reached all the way across the globe: In 2004, the United States negotiated a free trade agreement that allowed the drug companies to challenge Australia's prescription insurance system.

After the Republicans also took control of the White House in 2001, Big Pharma's muscle grew stronger yet. Several ex-pharmaceutical executives and allies were appointed to key federal posts, most notably the FDA's new chief counsel, Daniel E. Troy. A former law clerk for the conservative icon Robert Bork, Troy had spent his career suing the FDA and other government agencies on behalf of various business clients, including drug companies. He was the lawyer who had represented the Washington Legal Foundation against the FDA in the crucial 2000 case regarding marketing of off-label drugs, in which a U.S. district court told the FDA that it could not stop pharmaceutical sales reps from informing doctors about articles in scientific journals that talked about off-label uses. Troy was so controversial that in 2004 the House of Representatives even approved a measure by Democratic Congressman Maurice Hinchey of New York to strip $500,000 from the counsel's office and transfer it to the arm of the Center for Drugs that oversees drug ads; Hinchey specifically cited "unprecedented activity on the part of Chief Counsel Daniel Troy that runs contrary to the FDA's mission of protecting the public." (Troy resigned soon after the 2004 elections.) Meanwhile, it was industry opposition that kept Alastair Wood, the Vanderbilt University professor, from being named FDA commissioner in 2002.

Tossing out years of government policy, the Bush White House began intervening in court cases to argue that patients and their families had no right to sue manufacturers of drugs and devices that had been approved by the FDA, because this would be "to second-guess the FDA's scientific judgment," as the administration put it in one instance. Should the judges in those trials agree, it would mean that if the FDA ever made a mistake—if it ever approved another Bjork-Shiley artificial heart valve or Posicor or Vioxx—families might have no way to get any compensation for their suffering, loss of income, or medical expenses. The manufacturers would be safe from any punishment.

And since the FDA oversees so much of the corporate world, the pharmaceutical companies are hardly the only ones that make their presence felt in Rockville. The food business may be even more influential than its drug counterpart, though much less famous. Then there are the industries like tobacco and dietary supplements, which use their clout in Congress to make sure the FDA never gets jurisdiction over them.

Still, it is one thing for companies to lobby Congress or even the FDA commissioner over broad policies like Medicare drug coverage. That happens with every industry, at every level of government, every day. Business executives also talk with regulators all the time about practical issues, like how many patients to include in a Phase III trial. Consumer groups may grouse, but all that is an understood part of the game. Nor is it surprising when politicians take a public stand about a medical condition that affects their families. Nancy Reagan, the widow of former President Reagan, became an outspoken advocate for using human embryonic stem cells in scientific research, possibly to develop new treatments for the Alzheimer's disease that her husband suffered from. Peter Deutsch, who was then a congressman from Florida and who is genetically at risk for skin cancer, testified at an FDA advisory committee meeting on a skin cancer drug in May 2004. Of course, people like Nancy Reagan and Peter Deutsch want to see faster cures. (Reagan's activism made headlines because of the type of research she supported—using stem cells from human embryos, which many religious conservatives oppose—not because she advocated research on Alzheimer's disease itself.)

But what Bill Vodra was so casually talking about, in his office with its bookshelves and Civil War flags, is something much less well known and far more controversial than all these other interactions. It is exactly what consumer activists warn about: undue industry influence on the way medicines get to market. The FDA's record in holding its own against this influence is decidedly mixed—actually better on the pharmaceutical side than most consumers assume, worse on the food side than most realize, and too weak as a general rule.

Until the 1970s, the FDA and the drug companies barely spoke to each other. The FDA did not give any guidance on organizing clinical trials or compiling an application. As Bob Temple, the associate director of medical policy, wrote in a textbook he coauthored in 1995, "There was, in fact, an explicit concern that too much participation by FDA staff in the development process would leave the Agency unable to be appropriately neutral and analytical when the resulting data were submitted as part of an NDA." By the same token, the agency did not get all those phone calls from Congress. Bill Vodra said that when he was associate chief counsel in the late 1970s, "a drug company wouldn't have a congressional strategy as part of drug development."

Things slowly changed, in part spurred by the constant complaints that the FDA was taking too long to approve new drugs. Agency officials decided that during the trial process, neutrality did not have to mean silence. If there were standards for safety and efficacy that new drugs needed to meet, and if the FDA had recommendations on how to meet those standards, then telling the drug companies what those standards and recommendations were would not be some sort of unethical collusion that would cause unsafe drugs to be slipped onto the pharmacy shelves. On the contrary, more communication could help ensure that the drugs that reached the FDA had in fact followed the best procedures for ensuring safety and efficacy. The bigger problem would actually be if the companies *did not* know what the FDA's standards were.

So, over the years, the FDA began publicizing more and more of its requirements, starting with its first definition of "adequate and well-controlled." It issued the various guidance documents described in Chapter 5 on dosages, on testing on women and the elderly, even the nitty-gritty details about how to format the NDA or put page numbers on documents. The agency Web site is widely praised for the amount of information it includes to help companies put together a drug application. And as the crew at Antigenics learned, FDA staffers will walk applicants through the years and years of drug development. Janet Woodcock said that the biggest change she had seen since coming to the agency in 1986 is that "the review process has become more open and transparent." (She started out in CBER as a midlevel manager overseeing vaccines and allergy drugs before moving up the ranks to head of CDER in 1994 and acting deputy commissioner for operations in 2004.) Clearly, pharmaceutical executives say, there is a lot more communication than they get from European regulators. While a certain amount of this is basic industry schmoozing and soft lobbying, like faxing the reviewers an article from a medical journal with positive data on a drug trial, this sort of communication is generally seen as good for both sides and for the public.

The FDA-industry communication gets a little more controversial once the new drug application is actually filed. After all, what need is there to talk now? The clinical trials are already designed and done; it is too late for any advice. Industry officials even concede that calling too often at this point and bothering the staff could backfire.

Yet they do call. "Every 20 minutes," Tom Garvey, the former cardio-renal reviewer, griped, only partly joking. Actually, it might be more like every 168 hours: Irwin Martin, the manager who oversaw Lipitor at Parke-Davis, said that when he was handling regulatory issues he would phone the agency once a week "during the active review stage," which he defined as after the submission of the NDA. Yes, that means once a week for at least six months. "Of course I was constantly on the phone with the FDA. That's what regulatory affairs is," he snapped.

Mainly, Martin would talk to the project manager, who is the official FDA liaison, rather than the reviewer. He would ask if the agency had any questions, or if there was anything he could do to help speed things along. Martin said he did it because "you want to pull the questions as they're going through the review so you can answer, so you don't have questions at the time of the approvable letter [at the end]." Dr. Susan Alpert, vice president of regulatory affairs and compliance at Medtronic, Inc., the big Minneapolis-based devices maker, has a bit more relaxed schedule. Since a priority device is supposed to be reviewed in 180 days, she said, Medtronic will call if "we haven't heard anything and it's well beyond 100 days. We anticipate that around that time we're going to be getting some questions."

People like Martin and Alpert may say they are merely anticipating the FDA's need for more information. (And Alpert presumably knows what the reviewers want, because she was director of the FDA's Office of Device Evaluation from 1993 to 1999.) Occasionally, there may be some genuine news to impart, like a report in a scientific journal. But the real translation of a pharmaceutical official's conversation at this stage, as both sides know, is: "Why haven't I heard from you?"

Companies contact the FDA now for two main reasons: To satisfy their own impatience—or to pressure the reviewers. Alpert admitted that after 100 days of silence, she starts to wonder, "Are they even reviewing it?"

For that matter, since the FDA is never really supposed to stop reviewing—remember all the audits of trial sites and the call to keep studying drugs after they are on the market—the industry never stops pushing to influence it. The *Wall Street Journal* in July 2004 reported on persistent efforts by Medtronic to tone down an FDA warning about its device for treating aneurysms, which are bulges in the main artery leading to the heart that can be fatal if they rupture. As some problems became apparent, two years after the device had been approved, the FDA wanted to compare the safety of the device (known as an AneuRx stent graft) with surgery, the main alternative. Medtronic sent two teams of experts to argue that earlier drafts of the warning unfairly compared the device to hospitals with the best surgical records, the newspaper said. Ultimately, the FDA did weaken its warning.

Industry critics suspected that Vioxx was another example of invidious Big Pharma influence. Why else would the FDA want to block its own reviewer's warning of the drug's cardiovascular dangers? Still, there was little evidence of pressure from Merck, other than a couple of references in e-mail messages from a midlevel FDA manager. Those messages seemed to say that the FDA had a deal to let Merck know in advance of any agency publication relating to any Merck product. FDA officials, for their part, argued that they were simply being careful, as they always are, before doing anything as drastic as ordering a drug off the market.

Another controversial intersection between the FDA and industry occurs at the exit—at the revolving door that exists at every regulatory agency and even in Congress and the White House. With the FDA's relatively low salaries and generous retirement incentives, many reviewers leave after 20 years, and the obvious move is to work at or consult to a big drug company. This is what Tom Garvey did in setting up his own consulting firm, and Susan Alpert did in going to Medtronic. So did Steve Koepke and Stuart Portnoy, who joined the contract research organization PharmaNet. Jay Siegel now runs research and development at Centocor, after leaving the Center for Biologics. Michael Friedman, the acting commissioner during the tumult of the late 1990s, became a senior-level executive at G.D. Searle & Company, then at Pharmacia Corporation when the latter bought Searle's parent Monsanto Company in 2000. He also did special work on preparedness for PhRMA, the industry trade group, after the September 11, 2001, terrorist attacks. Members of the advisory committees, too, frequently consult for the industry, as in the cases of Posicor and Lotronex.

Every government agency sets up rules to try and minimize the conflicts of interest that inevitably accompany these career moves. Usually the emphasis is on making sure that regulatory officials, while they are still in government, do not make decisions that could affect their future employers, and that ex-officials do not come back to lobby until a decent interval has passed. FDA advisory committee members are supposed to abstain from voting on products where there might be a question of bias (but they can still join the discussions, as happened with Posicor, when the chairman had ties to the manufacturer). Friedman said that "from the first moment that it crossed my mind [to work at Searle], I immediately went to [the lawyer for] HHS and disclosed that information. I was careful to recuse myself. So there could not even be the perception of conflict of interest. When I went to Searle, I never set foot in the FDA, never appeared before an advisory committee, never ever did anything that could be interpreted as influencing a decision."

But the rules can only really kick in when the job negotiations are solid enough that the employee feels comfortable telling the FDA brass. The problem is that the potential for conflict may start years earlier, while a reviewer is mulling over taking a job in industry some time in the future. Consumer advocates worry that FDA staffers and advisory committee members are afraid to be too hard on the companies where they soon hope to be sending their résumés.

With the FDA's "critical path" report in 2004 and its promise to help industry use cutting-edge science to develop new drugs more quickly, the ties between the two sides are likely to grow even closer. Now the agency and the industry could work together, for instance, to come up with techniques for spotting the risks in gene therapy or create new surrogate markers as measurement points in clinical trials.

Jesse Goodman gave an example of how his staff at the Biologics center has already cooperated with industry on blood screening tests, almost like a joint venture partner. Goodman is a virologist, specializing in oncology, infectious diseases, and internal medicine, with wavy grey hair, thick eyebrows, and a slow, gravely voice. He has an air of the absent-minded scientist and is famous for talking endlessly, but his slow, rambling speech can disguise a careful search for the most diplomatic word. When he started at the FDA in 1998, he was working directly with the commissioner (at that time, Michael Friedman), running an interagency task force on antimicrobial resistance. Then he took on a variety of projects at CBER. He became head of the center in December 2002 after his controversial predecessor, Dr. Kathryn C. Zoon, angrily quit over the agency's restructuring.

In late 2002, as cases of West Nile virus were erupting in the United States, the FDA became worried that the virus might infect the blood supply. So the agency brought together the Centers for Disease Control, the blood banking industry, and diagnostic-test makers to discuss the possibility of creating a test that could screen donated blood for the virus. "We think there is a market there," Goodman said the FDA told the group. "CDC and FDA provided samples and research to facilitate standardization of assays" and also held a workshop for potential test developers. Eight months later, the nation's blood supply was being screened with kits from Gen-Probe Incorporated of San Diego and the Roche Molecular Systems unit of Roche, even while their formal applications were under review. Goodman bragged that at least 1,000 tainted units of blood were detected.

He added, "People here are very happy when a product is approved."

PDUFA, the law establishing user fees, piled another controversy onto the question of whether industry exerts too much influence. In the beginning, it was actually the pharmaceutical companies, along with conservative politicians, that opposed the idea of forking over extra money to pay for what was supposed to be paid already by their taxes. "Philosophically and conceptually, it couldn't be more wrong, more destructive of good government," said Peter Barton Hutt, the corporate attorney. C. Boyden Gray, who was President George Bush's counsel, claimed that the problem at the FDA was bureaucratic inertia, not lack of resources, so user fees would not help. Small companies were especially upset. According to an industry lawyer, one British manufacturer complained that the annual fee was bigger than its U.S. sales: The fee was $50,000 when the law was first passed, plus $6,000 a year for each product already on the market and $100,000 for each new application. By 2001 all three rates had approximately tripled. When a similar system was proposed for the medical devices industry, where the typical manufacturer is far smaller than the typical drug maker, "they looked at the pharmaceutical industry, and they were scared to death that the amounts that would be charged would be overwhelming," Susan Alpert of Medtronic said. (In 1997, as part of the FDA Modernization Act, a Medical Devices User Fee Act, or MDUFA, was passed with a lower fee scale.)

As the years went by, however, opinions shifted. The math seemed to work in industry's favor. Each time the law was renewed, in 1997 and 2002, the deadlines for the FDA to finish its approval tightened. For fiscal year 1994, the goal was to "review and act upon" 55 percent of all new drug and biological submissions within 12 months; by fiscal 2003, that goal had been slashed to 10 months for nonpriority submissions. (Of course, the FDA did not always meet its PDUFA goals, but the actual amount of time spent on reviews steadily shrank.) Although fees were increasing, the profits that could be gained from getting to market faster more than made up for that. Taking the industry's claim that it costs over $800 million to develop a new drug, then "if you pay $500,000 in user fees and get your NDA approved one month earlier, you make money," calculated Peter Hutt. That was enough to change his view of PDUFA: By 2003, he was calling it "one of the few examples of paying the government an outrageous amount of money and you get back more than you pay."

Now it was consumer advocates who worried that PDUFA gave the drug manufacturers too much influence. The fear was that the FDA had come to rely too much on industry largesse, so that when the two sides sat down to talk about setting future review deadlines, requirements for post-approval testing, and other issues, Big Pharma would threaten to oppose the next PDUFA renewal and pull its funding unless the FDA did what it demanded. As the cliché goes, who pays the piper calls the tune. An unlikely coalition of unions, big employers, insurers, and consumer groups concerned about health care costs, called Rx Health Value, protested loudly about some of the new deadlines and other provisions in the 2002 renewal. "Where you have a regulatory agency that's being funded to a great extent by the group that it's regulating, that just does create a lot of potential for the funding entity to put a lot of pressure to speed up the process—the potential to create conflict of interest," warned Dee Mahan, senior policy analyst at Families USA, a Washington, D.C.-based consumer group that focuses on the cost of drugs for the elderly.

Congressman Bart Stupak, a Democrat from Michigan, told me he would be willing to appropriate more money to the FDA's budget from tax dollars in order to eliminate the user fees. "We should get away from this thing where drug companies pay a fee to have their drugs approved quickly. It just gives the appearance of a conflict. Why don't we fund the FDA, do it publicly? Are we concerned about money or safety?" Stupak is the exact opposite of the politicians who try to do favors for drug makers: He has been a particular critic of FDA-industry ties ever since his 17-year-old son B.J. killed himself in 2000 while taking Accutane, the acne medicine from Roche that has been linked to suicide, birth defects, depression, and other horrific side effects. Among other criticisms, Stupak claimed that the FDA and Roche have been hiding information about the dangers of the drug (which both deny).

Nevertheless, critics mostly folded up their protests after 2002—until the Vioxx recall in 2004. Practically speaking, since 217 other members of the House of Representatives, 51 senators, and the president are unlikely to agree with Congressman Stupak to eliminate user fees and raise the FDA's budget instead, consumer advocates concede that it is hard to see how else the agency could get enough money to be an effective regulator. "I don't know how much I would fault the agency for [not lobbying for a bigger budget]," Dee Mahan said.

What about those phone calls and letters from Congress?

Here is the authorized version of what happens when a call comes in, according to Janet Woodcock: "We listen sympathetically, [then say to the caller], 'We'll tell you the answer when we tell everyone.' We basically shield the review people from these totally." In other words, Woodcock or another high-level manager brushes the congressmen off, and the calls do not impact the review process. Woodcock added, "They have the right to contact their government. They're citizens, too."

Similarly, Lester Crawford said that when one of those hundreds of congressional letters arrives, "the letter goes to the Office of Legislation [the FDA's political office], which prepares a response for my signature or the center director's signature or the office director's signature." Only if the FDA official needs more information would he or she call the staffer who is actually reviewing the drug.

But in fact, the political calls sometimes do hit the drug reviewer directly. It happened to Steve Koepke three times in his nine years as a reviewing chemist and midlevel manager at the FDA, from 1992 to 2001.

Koepke is the husky chemist who looks like a farmer, now with PharmaNet. All three times that he faced drug company pressure, he said, he was called into the commissioner's office and hooked up to a conference call with a congressional aide. The first time, when Koepke was a reviewer, his supervisor came as well. As Koepke recounted it, the congressional aide always said something like, "This guy [pharmaceutical executive] is a good member of my district. Why are you beating up on this drug?" Like virtually everyone else who was even willing to discuss this topic, Koepke would not reveal which drugs, members of Congress, or companies were involved, but the commissioner in all of his examples happened to be Michael Friedman, he said.

Under the gun, Koepke was scared. "Just going in front of the commissioner had me in such a state—you don't go in front of the commissioner very often. You have to be sure you're right. You have to put it in terms that a layman can understand." Luckily, Koepke said, he did have the facts, and the congressional aide accepted his explanation each time. In one case, the FDA had said that a particular company had changed its method of manufacturing a drug while the company insisted it had not. Well, the way the drug reacted to high temperatures—a standard method of testing whether a medication will remain stable during a long shelf life—showed that it was being manufactured differently, Koepke told the aide. Nor did Friedman pressure him; "Friedman was only the moderator."

So I asked Friedman about this sort of congressional communication in general, though not about Koepke in particular. He replied: "I do not recall getting any such calls about a drug under review." He added that "if there had been a call, you simply respond with whatever information is publicly available, [saying something like] 'The product is under review.' Nobody gets more than that." Would he have contacted the lower-level reviewer directly? Yes, if there had been a question he could not answer himself, such as a question about the drug's status. He would not tell the reviewer why he wanted to know. But such a query from him, as commissioner, would not be a big deal, Friedman claimed. "I called and asked questions all the time."

Another midlevel official, who would not let his name be used because the topic is so sensitive, stammered a bit as he described the conditions under which he would pass a congressional call on to a reviewer. "I would only do that, most likely, if the person [from Congress] I'm talking to tells me they [the reviewer] seem to be doing something that's not consistent with our policies, then I would talk to the reviewer." Or, he added, he and the reviewer "may chat in an informal sense, 'Oh, So-and-So called.'" Could that make the reviewer feel under pressure? The manager quickly backed off: "I'm doing that less and less as time goes on. It's not even worth talking about. If it happened to be something that's a fairly controversial topic and a highly publicized topic. They should just know that there's extreme interest in the topic."

Once the reviewer learns of the politician's phone call, he or she will usually have one of three reactions, Koepke said. "One is, they become very cowed. One is, they let it roll off their back. One is, every application that comes in from that company is looked at very closely—that is, the reviewer overcompensates by becoming more demanding." In his case, Koepke claimed, the three congressional calls did not prompt him to go especially easy or tough on the applications. "We were already upset at one company anyway," he shrugged.

Tom Garvey said he chose the let-it-roll-off-his-back route. When he was a first- and second-level reviewer, he said, his division director used to tell him about occasional calls, more in the way of gossip. They might be having lunch, Garvey said, and the director would mention, "'That asshole So-and-So called.' We'd laugh about it. There's a certain set of legislators who always call. They can't influence anything. They very rarely have any concept of what they're talking about." For that matter, sometimes the politicians themselves do not seem to take their lobbying all that seriously. Jere Goyan, the commissioner appointed by Jimmy Carter and fired by Ronald Reagan, recounted one episode that he termed "amusing." First, someone from the drug company came to him to complain about whatever the agency was doing (or not doing; Goyan did not remember exactly). After that the congressman called and merely said, "I'm going to write a very strong letter about it—which you can ignore." Goyan said he does not know whether the drug was ever approved.

However, Jay Siegel was not so blasé the one time it happened to him, when he was the director of CBER's Office of Therapeutics Research and Review. In fact, he was shocked. A high-level FDA official said to him, almost offhandedly, "Things would go well on a certain legislative issue if this approval happened." Siegel, too, will not reveal what drug, what legislative issue, or which FDA official was involved, and he said he rejected the drug for other reasons.

To many consumer advocates, and especially to victims of drugs that caused severe side effects, it seems obvious that there must be many more instances of reviewers being cowed than those who let industry pressure roll off their back. The congressional phone calls and letters, the user fees, the nudgings from pharmaceutical officials like Irwin Martin every week after the NDA is filed, the revolving door, and the general Big Pharma lobbying all must be having some effect. Otherwise, why would the FDA let companies sell dangerous drugs? Look at how Medtronic persuaded the FDA to weaken its criticism of the aneurysm device. Look at Vioxx, Posicor, and Propulsid.

At the advisory committee meeting on antidepressants, parent after parent cited the drug companies' campaign contributions, Dan Troy's appointment as chief counsel, and Commissioner McClellan's brother in the White House, as they asked why the powerful drugs were still being prescribed for teenagers. "They all have financial ties" to Big Pharma, Lisa Van Syckel said to me, referring to the advisory committee. Her 15-year-old daughter twice attempted suicide while on Paxil.

Of course, FDA and pharmaceutical officials insist that the industry pressure does not influence agency decisions. (At least, that is what the industry claims publicly; whatever achievements the lobbyists may brag about privately to their Big Pharma clients is another matter.) FDA staffers are candid about their willingness to communicate with industry while clinical trials are under way and the protocols are still being written, but as soon as the NDA is in their hands, they say, the camaraderie has to stop cold. "Once it has been submitted for approval, it becomes more formal. We really are not at liberty to discuss too much until we have made a decision," said Phil Noguchi, the supervisor who worked on Antigenics' application. Noguchi said he understands the companies' impatience and curiosity. After all, with potential sales of half a billion dollars or more at stake, time is money. But the only thing he or his reviewers can really tell pharmaceutical officials if they call is, "We're working on it."

Look, added Steve Koepke—speaking now from his nine years inside the FDA, not as an industry consultant at PharmaNet—there is no point bugging the reviewers. If it is not a breakthrough drug, it has to wait in line behind the priority reviews. And "if it's a very high-profile drug, maybe for cancer, then the FDA will light a fire under *you*."

The most that Bill Vodra will admit is that "White House or congressional pressure makes them [reviewers] move faster." The pressure will not, he asserted, persuade the FDA to approve a bad drug. But that begs the question of whether moving faster causes reviewers to miss danger signals in a trial result.

Obviously, the industry tries its hardest to make its opinions known in Rockville. But how well does it really succeed?

A number of academic researchers have pored over years of data, correlating drug approvals with the FDA budget, the budgets of various lobbying groups, the number of times a disease is mentioned in the news, the number of people who have a particular disease, the number of congressional hearings on the disease, the order in which drugs come onto the market, the number of other drugs a manufacturer has ever taken for review to the FDA, and other factors, to try to figure out what drives the FDA. Several studies in particular have received a lot of attention, all with different implications for Big Pharma's power.

In a paper published in the *American Journal of Political Science* in July 2002, Daniel P. Carpenter, who is now a professor of government at Harvard University, studied 450 drugs reviewed by the FDA between 1977 and 2000. His conclusion: The biggest influences were the number of times a disease was mentioned in the *Washington Post* (but not on TV news broadcasts), the budget of the Center for Drugs, and the budgets of patient advocacy groups. An increase of 290 stories per year over four years in the *Post*, Carpenter calculated, could reduce expected approval time by 10 to 22 months, while adding 100 full-time staffers to CDER could cut the timeframe by three to five months. (Carpenter speculated that the *Post* has such outsized influence because "FDA personnel...probably pay more attention to 'authoritative' news sources such as the *Post* and the *New York Times* than they do to TV news." Also, he noted, "disease mentions on the nightly newscasts of the major networks are few and far between.") In other words, what spurs FDA approvals is a combination of public pressure to make drugs available, and the resources available to the FDA to do the reviews.

One problem with that study was that it did not factor in direct lobbying by pharmaceutical companies. As Carpenter conceded, "While firm political strategies are not the primary concern here, firm attributes undoubtedly sway the FDA's decision making in drug approval cases." Some of their clout could be seen in the influence of the patient advocacy groups, since drug makers often provide the patient groups with substantial funding, as in the case of Mike Katz's myeloma foundation.

In another paper, written with three colleagues from Michigan and published in *Health Affairs* in December 2003, Carpenter looked a bit more at corporate lobbying and influence—and did not discern much impact. In this case, the academics studied user fees, analyzing 843 new drugs submitted to the FDA from 1977 to 2000 (including 320 that were not approved). "We find that neither PDUFA nor CDER staffing accelerated drug reviews for firms with higher sales, . . . more lobbying activity, . . . or number of NDA submissions," they wrote.

Nine years earlier, in 1994, David Dranove of Northwestern University's Kellogg School of Management and David Meltzer of Brigham and Women's Hospital, looking back at some 700 breakthrough drugs approved since 1950, came up with a result that showed a lot more industry influence. They determined that the FDA seemed to approve drugs with big potential sales faster than it approved those that were major scientific innovations. The pair measured approval times against sales figures and also, as a proxy for scientific importance, against the number of times a drug was cited in medical journals, medical textbooks, and subsequent patent applications. "This suggested that the companies were able to do quite a good job of influencing the approval process. We were surprised that the FDA was as responsive to the needs of the market over the needs of science," Dranove said when I interviewed him, nearly 10 years after the study was published. However, Dranove went on to point out that the analysis was done before PDUFA kicked in. And since the user fee system has drastically revamped the review process, and Dranove had done no follow-up and planned none, he conceded that his conclusions could be completely out of date.

Then let's consider the user fees. Industry wants drugs reviewed faster, and it is certainly indisputable that review times have been squeezed dramatically since user fees were instituted—from almost three years to a little over half a year for priority drugs. There are two main reasons.

The FDA prefers the benign one: Thanks to the fees, it now has the money to hire more staffers (which also fits in with Carpenter's research showing that CDER funding is one of the three major factors behind the speed of drug approvals). With the 2002 PDUFA renewal, the Drugs and Biologics Centers would now get more than $200 million a year from these fees. "Instead of having one physician regulating, we would put two or even four on," said David Feigal, who was a director of drug evaluation at CDER when the law first passed, before moving over to the Devices Center. The new Devices user fee, he added, would allow that Center to replace the 150 inspectors, reviewers, project managers, and outside experts that it had lost to budget cuts over nearly a decade.

The less benign explanation has to do with the fact that PDUFA sets ever-tighter deadlines for completing reviews. Almost everyone admits that those deadlines inevitably put pressure on the reviewers. It is also an open secret that industry representatives negotiated the deadlines with the FDA for the law's second renewal. What worries critics is whether the deadline pressure is so unreasonable that it pushes reviewers to make sloppy or bad decisions, perhaps sending dangerous drugs out to the market, because the scientists do not have the time to go over the applications as thoroughly as they should. There is also the larger question that consumer advocates raise: Does controlling the purse strings give the industry too much influence in setting those deadlines and otherwise breathing down reviewers' necks?

Exhibit A is the wave of drugs that were recalled in the late 1990s and early 2000s, almost all of them approved after PDUFA was passed. Never before had so many dangerous drugs been pulled off the market in such a short period of time. The Pulitzer Prize–winning series in the *Los Angeles Times* in 2000, analyzing eight of those drugs in detail, described some of the user fee pressure but never quite came out and said that this could have led the agency to approve drugs that it should not have approved. The newspaper cited an agency publication in which Janet Woodcock, the CDER director at that time, said that the law's performance goals and a heavy workload "create a sweatshop environment that's causing high staffing turnover." (Woodcock similarly told me, three years afterwards, that she wanted "to allow the staff some breathing room. We're really in a sweatshop environment," although she did not relate her comments specifically to PDUFA.) When the consumer group Public Citizen surveyed medical officers—those are the ones who are in charge of the first stage of drug reviews—in 1998, 34 of the 53 who responded said that the pressure to approve new drugs was "much greater" or "somewhat greater" than it had been before the user fee law. Nineteen said there were more than two dozen new drugs that they had reviewed and that had been given a go-ahead that they felt should not have been allowed on the market. Nine also reported what they considered "inappropriate" phone calls about a drug under review, usually from the manufacturer.

Comments by some industry officials confirm the consumer groups' and victims' worst fears. A typical example comes from my interview with Jerome Halperin, president and chief executive of a trade group called the Food and Drug Law Institute in Washington, D.C. The institute was founded by law professors in 1949, with backing from the FDA commissioner, to offer fellowships for the study of food laws; it now provides training of various sorts for lawyers and executives from the food and drug industries. Halperin lavished praise on the way the user fee legislation has transformed the relationship between companies and the FDA, saying, "When the industry pays multimillions of dollars a year, for PDUFA and MDUFA, it forces a closer communication. Among the give-and-take in the negotiations on the bill, the industry said, 'If we're going to put all this money up, we want to know that we have the ability to communicate.'"

In fact, the consumer groups are probably right. PDUFA, with the power implicit in controlling the purse strings as well as the tighter deadlines, has undoubtedly given the industry increased influence over the FDA. But that is also not the whole story.

For one thing, Carpenter's studies show that it is the simple fact of how much funding CDER has, not where the money comes from, that makes the biggest difference. Indeed, in the December 2003 paper, Carpenter and his coauthors found that funding had already increased and review times had already dropped even before PDUFA was passed. And health care ethicists at The Hastings Center, a respected think tank on the Hudson River north of Manhattan, point out that matters could be a lot worse. Under the law, the industry payments are made automatically, whether or not a drug is approved. Imagine if the fees were on a contingency fee basis, as a lawyer might charge, so that the FDA got paid more if a drug got approved. Talk about pressure then!

The truth is, the FDA is constantly on a seesaw, pushed at one end and then the other by a range of forces. In the early 1990s, the long approval times led to a public consensus that drugs had to get out faster; so Congress passed PDUFA. Then the spate of recalls in the late 1990s and early 2000s got the public nervous that the FDA was rushing too fast, so the seesaw tipped the other way, approvals were delayed while the FDA tightened its reviews, and the number of recalls shrank. The increasing complexity of new drugs also slows things down. So does the lack of a commissioner, because staff may be reluctant to take a chance on a brand-new kind of mechanism. All of this has very little to do with pharmaceutical company clout.

PDUFA can even backfire on the industry. Because staffers are so stressed out trying to meet the deadlines, many do not have time for the companies' constant phone calls.

At any rate, the FDA brass do not seem to think user fees from industry are a major problem. As the Center for Veterinary Medicine was considering its version of PDUFA in 2003, Stephen Sundlof, the director, recalled, "I asked Janet Woodcock at one point, 'If you had it to do over again, would you do it?'

"She said, 'Oh, there's no question that this was the best thing that ever happened.'"

If Big Pharma as a whole has a mixed record of influence, however, some companies certainly seem to be more equal than others.

Judy Tenenbaum is president of Meetings in Medicine, a New York City–based firm that arranges public events for drug companies, such as luncheons to tell physicians about new products. Companies want to hold these meetings as soon as their drugs are approved, so that doctors can start writing prescriptions without delay. But it takes time to make the arrangements. Typically, there will be simultaneous lunches in 26 to 60 big cities, all hooked up by satellite to the main location, which means Tenenbaum needs to find enough sites that are large and attractive, with good satellite communication ability, yet with no mirrors or windows (which can interfere with satellite reception). Then invitations must be printed and mailed, and audiovisual equipment must be rented. So there is a real premium on getting word from the FDA as fast as possible—even before the approval is announced. And some manufacturers seem to get the word faster.

"Half the companies won't do anything until they have the letter [of approval] in hand," Tenenbaum said. In the rest of the cases, "someone has connections to someone at the FDA, [who tells them] 'we think you'll get approved tomorrow.'" Those well-connected clients tell Tenenbaum to go ahead and book luncheon sites.

Sure, their advance tips may be wrong. In 1988, Tenenbaum needed hotel rooms in 200 cities to announce the launch of a rheumatoid arthritis drug, Rheumatrex, by Lederle Pharmaceuticals (owned by Wyeth). If she really pushed, she could get everything arranged in eight days. The company gave her advance word a week before it expected to receive approval. But a week later, it changed the date. Three days later, still no approval letter. Tenenbaum had to cancel her arrangements three times before the letter finally came.

But why shouldn't some companies be favored, if they have proved that they are reliable, Steve Koepke asked—or, more accurately, why shouldn't those that have not proved their reliability be given a more careful once-over? "A company that recently had a $500 million fine would be looked at very closely for everything," he said, referring with very large winks and nods to Schering-Plough, which in 2002 had been ordered to pay a record fine of exactly that amount. The fine was for repeated problems at four of its factories, including the one in Puerto Rico that made the corticosteroid with the mysterious black particles and the one that made the faulty asthma inhalers. European-based firms have a reputation for being a little casual about the composition of their basic drug chemical, Koepke continued, so he might demand more records of their manufacturing process. On the other extreme, until the Vioxx debacle, Merck was held up as a model for getting through the FDA, because it had never had a drug recalled for safety reasons.

There is one type of favoritism that almost everyone will concede publicly: It is harder for small new biotechs to get through the process than it is for big manufacturers that have been submitting drugs for years and can afford huge staffs like Irwin Martin's, dedicated to nothing but communicating with the government. "Very experienced large companies like Pfizer, Merck, they've been doing this for decades, they know what's expected. The smaller companies, the newer companies, the biotechs, they're just going through this," said Steve Galson of CDER. If the small firms' applications take longer to review or are sent "not approvable" letters, he added, "one possibility is that the application is lousy, it's missing some major things." Some executives of those biotechs say the FDA seems to be trying to even the balance. Boyd Clarke—who has been an executive at both small and large companies—praised the agency for its willingness to take extra time to work with small newcomers.

Daniel Carpenter of Harvard has studied this issue, too, analyzing 766 drugs submitted to the FDA from 1979 to 2000. Along with Marc Turenne of the University of Michigan, he looked at review times, drug companies' political contributions, the ownership of drug companies, and the budgets and membership size of patient advocacy groups, among other criteria. In a paper presented at a Harvard-Massachusetts Institute of Technology workshop in March of 2001, the pair gave their conclusion: First, large firms get their drugs through the process faster. For instance, after 15 months of review, over 40 percent of drugs from large firms but only 15 percent of those from small firms had been approved. But second, the authors went on, that is mainly because of "the greater regulator familiarity that large firms enjoy." Two other significant factors, as in Carpenter's other studies, are pressure from patient advocacy groups and mentions in the press. When Carpenter and Turenne correlated Big Pharma's lobbying efforts with approvals, however, they found "inconsistent results that disappear once other covariates are added to estimates." The authors summed up: "We find no consistent support for . . . 'political clout' explanations."

Pharmaceutical companies' outsized influence finally failed when it came to the biggest medical-political issue of the new century, the cost of prescription drugs. Even Republican senators and representatives abandoned Big Pharma. But the FDA stayed faithfully by the industry's side.

Public anger had built rapidly, as consumers saw their bills for prescription drugs rising at double-digit rates year after year for half a decade, far faster than the consumer price index. Now the Baby Boomers were about to push that tab into the stratosphere as they started reaching the age of arthritis, osteoporosis, and sexual slowdown—76 million potential prescriptions for Celebrex, Fosamax, and Viagra. And the burden was hitting harder than ever because insurers and employers were shunting more and more of the cost onto employees. In the 2000 elections, drug costs had been a campaign issue in Senate, congressional, and gubernatorial races from Maine to California. Four years later, all the leading Democratic candidates—the presidential and vice presidential nominees, Senators John Kerry and John Edwards, along with former Vermont governor Howard Dean—campaigned against the drug industry in one way or another.

Many consumers and politicians found a logical solution: Buy medications in Canada, where government regulation kept prices some 70 percent lower than in the United States. Although technically this practice, known as reimportation, was illegal, the FDA had never interfered when individuals crossed the border to pick up a few prescriptions for their own use. But by 2004, thanks to soaring drug prices and the ease of purchasing over the Internet, the cross-border trickle had turned into a billion-dollar deluge. Now even people living in Florida or New Mexico could get Canadian drugs without driving a thousand miles.

The pharmaceutical companies bitterly opposed reimportation, because every bottle that sold for $60 in Canada instead of $90 or $110 in the United States was a bite out of their profits. Several of them threatened to curtail supplies to Canadian distributors that resold their stock to Americans. The FDA also leaped into battle against the practice, arguing that it could not guarantee the safety or purity of drugs that had not gone through its approval and inspection process.

At first, consumer groups and business were divided on the issue, debating cost versus safety. For instance, the Rx Health Value coalition of employers, unions, and insurers never took a stand, because its members could not agree. To the extent that people saw a villain, it was Big Pharma, not the FDA.

Gradually, however, the tide began to swing more strongly in favor of reimportation, even crossing party lines. The Republican-controlled House of Representatives attached a provision to the 2003 Medicare prescription drug bill, legalizing the cross-border drug-buying practice. (Under tremendous pressure from the Bush White House and with the promise of further study, the reimportation section was eventually removed before the Medicare bill passed, but two similar measures were promptly introduced by senators from both parties the next year.) Defying the FDA, governors and mayors started purchasing drugs for their own employees via the Canadian pipeline and set up Web sites to help local residents do the same. Vermont even vowed to sue the FDA for trying to block it.

More and more, reimportation was seen as a price issue, especially for the elderly. The FDA's supposed safety concerns seemed like a red herring. After all, the various bills in Congress would subject reimported drugs to FDA oversight, and the FDA already inspected manufacturing plants throughout the world and was clamping down on counterfeiting. This was *Canada*, for heaven's sake—you didn't see Canadians dropping dead by the dozens from poisoned hypertension pills. Cross-border trade of this sort was routine in Europe. "Every year about 6,000 Americans die in hospitals because they're getting the wrong dosage or the wrong medicine," declared Minnesota congressman Gil Gutknecht, the Republican sponsor of the reimportation provision that had been attached to the Medicare bill. "And how many Americans have died from taking drugs from Canada?" Gutknecht held up a thumb and finger to form a big zero. (Ironically, he said this in an interview on the very day in February 2004 that the FDA announced its new bar code system designed to eliminate the hospital mistakes.)

Indeed, to most politicians and patient groups, it was puzzling that the FDA they had always admired, which was supposed to be protecting consumers, now was apparently siding against them. And what had happened to Commissioner Mark McClellan's vaunted political savvy? "They're reading different polls than we are," Congressman Gutknecht scoffed. The Republican governor of Minnesota, Tim Pawlenty, who had set up a Web site to facilitate cross-border purchasing, called the warnings he kept getting from the FDA "snotty-grams." Yet McClellan and other top FDA officials continued to speak out forcefully against reimportation. In fact, critics charged that during the debate over the Medicare bill, the agency's buttonholing on Capitol Hill came close to violating a ban on lobbying by federal employees.

In the fall of 2003, Donald McLearn, a Washington, D.C. publicist who spent 17 years handling public affairs at the FDA in the 1980s and 1990s—and who knows something about molding a public image—phoned his old colleagues to warn them about the PR black eye they were getting. "Most consumers see them as sold out to the pharmaceutical industry," he said to me.

As cynics viewed it, McClellan was just dancing to the pharmaceutical industry's tune, or at least he was dancing to the White House's tune under George W. Bush and the White House was kowtowing to the industry. But why? Had the FDA's independence been corrupted by the user fees and the revolving door? Had all the phone calls over the years made the agency too cozy with Big Pharma? "I think they've [the FDA] been encouraged by industry and by sympathetic legislators," said Alastair Wood, the nominee for FDA commissioner who had been blocked by the drug companies. He added, "I'm less impressed with the danger of Canadian drugs than Mark [McClellan] appears to be. It's hard for me to believe that Pfizer is selling drugs that are less safe in Canada." If Wood had been appointed instead of McClellan, it was clear, Americans might already be getting their supplies from Ontario.

But to FDA old-timers like McLearn, who remembered the panic over poisoned Tylenol, the agency's stated concern about drug purity was perfectly consistent. In fact, it had been consistent under Democratic as well as Republican administrations. As if to prove the FDA's point, several

Canadian pharmacies, pinched by the sudden spurt in demand and the drug manufacturers' cutoff of supplies, began reimporting drugs themselves from other countries—presumably ones with reliable regulation, like Australia, Israel, Chile, and New Zealand, but still, this was stretching the supply line further and further out. The small staff in the FDA's Office of Criminal Investigation was at one point in 2004 probing 100 Internet drug sites for possibly selling unapproved imports and even counterfeit drugs. So old-timers figured the FDA's reputation would bounce back. "All it'll take [to erase consumers' skepticism about the FDA's motivation] is a hundred people dying of [reimported drugs] that come in," McLearn said soon after warning his colleagues.

Janet Woodcock also insisted that she was sure the agency's reputation would survive. "The public has a high opinion of the FDA. I think they're going to blame the [Bush] administration."

What finally budged McClellan—slightly—toward the pro-reimportation side was the threat that the Senate might delay his appointment to the Medicare job in protest against his stand. So in late February 2004 the Health and Human Services Department announced the formation of a task force "to advise and assist HHS in determining how drug importation might be conducted safely." McClellan claimed that this was simply carrying out the new Medicare law, which required HHS to make recommendations on the issue of reimportation by early December 2004. Speaking at an industry conference on Medicare at around the time of the HHS announcement, McClellan implied that he did not have any problem if Americans went to Canada in person for their drugs. "That's very different from buying drugs on the Internet or storefronts," he said. He also told senators that he would work with Congress to try to find ways to assure the safety of drugs imported from Canada—and then turned that offer, with consummate political skill, into a plug for a budget increase for the FDA. Four days later, the Senate confirmed him for his new job. And even though the anti-reimportation George W. Bush won the presidential election eight months after that, the industry had lost the battle of public opinion.

If the pharmaceutical world has clout, the food business has something even better: clout plus looser regulations.

The dietary supplement makers proved their power by getting Congress in 1994 to block the FDA from regulating their products. Ditto for the meat processing and pet food industries, which pressured the FDA during the mad cow scare in Europe in the mid-1990s not to get too tough in its restrictions on cattle feed. Seven years later, after the disease showed up in the United States, the FDA took steps to tighten the rules, but consumer activists complained that industry pressure still won out. The agency considered—then ultimately watered down—even stronger prohibitions against letting cows eat possibly dangerous cattle blood or chicken waste.

Meanwhile, the meat industry has always had a good friend in the Agriculture Department, which limits what the FDA can do. As for restaurants, the Model Code is only advisory. And when it came to the one thing restaurateurs fear most—being required to list the nutritional content of their offerings on their menus, the way they are listed on packaged foods—the FDA backed off.

With an ever-growing specialization of American eating habits, there was definite demand for this sort of information. A vegetarian meal is distinctively different from a vegan or organic one. Moreover, an estimated 3.5 percent of Americans have some sort of food allergy, according to the Jaffe Food Allergy Institute at Mount Sinai School of Medicine in New York. As well, the burgeoning of traditional religious practices, plus immigration from a wider range of countries, meant that more people were trying to follow kosher, halal, and Jain diets. All of this required restaurant customers to know to the onion flake what was in their meals. And, this was at a time when two-thirds of the nation was either overweight or obese, and thus at risk for heart disease and diabetes, with people filing lawsuits against fast-food chains for not warning them about how fattening their food was. So health officials saw restaurant labeling as a way to help Americans count calories. Sixty-two percent of the people polled by the Harvard School of Public Health in May 2003 said that nutritional information should be required on menus.

Chains such as McDonald's and Burger King had been listing ingredients, calories, and the like since the early 1990s, though usually on wall posters or throw-away paper tray liners. Higher-class restaurants, however, claimed that such labeling would be impossible for them, because they do not have a standardized menu. They constantly add specials, and their gourmet chefs may change recipes at the spur of the moment. And where would they put the information—on their linen tablecloths? On a Post-it note stuck on the menu? "That sucker [the menu] is crowded as it is. You will end up with something you've got to read with a magnifying glass," scoffed Chet England, who is the senior director of product safety and regulatory affairs at Burger King Corporation but who sympathizes with the fancier restaurants on this issue. Besides, he does not want any government regulation of what his company does on its own.

The FDA in 2004, after a big study of the issue, declined to require any listing of information. It simply called on restaurants to provide information voluntarily and customers to ask for it. Bob Brackett, the head of the Center for Foods, did not dispute the virtues of making ingredients public. He simply predicted that market pressures would force the industry to act, "if consumers are expecting and want to see this information."

True, nutritional listing is mandatory on packaged food, but that had required congressional action in 1990, while Kellogg touted the wondrous properties of its All-Bran cereal and other manufacturers publicized similar supposed health benefits in their products. And a decade after the 1990 law, loopholes were popping out all over the label. "Serving size," for instance, had become meaningless, if not misleading, because people were eating bigger portions than they had 10 years earlier. Consider the 20-ounce plastic Coke or Pepsi bottle ubiquitous in vending machines. One person almost always drinks a whole bottle. By the FDA's decade-old definition, however, that bottle contained two and a half servings of eight ounces each. Therefore, manufacturers could legally claim on the label that a "serving" of Coke had only 100 calories—which most consumers took to mean that the whole bottle had only 100 calories, not the actual 250. Similarly, a standard muffin had ballooned from a nugget two inches in diameter into something the size of a baseball.

Carbohydrates were another area of confusion in the Wild Wild West of FDA food regulation. As carbohydrates replaced fat as the bogeyman of dieters in the early 2000s, manufacturers wanted to jump on the bandwagon by labeling their food low in carbs. The Agriculture Department and the Alcohol, Tobacco, Tax, and Trade Bureau in the Treasury Department managed to define "low carbohydrates" for meat, poultry, and beer. But the FDA had no definition of the term. There are healthier, high-fiber carbohydrates that are digested more slowly (the kind found in whole grains and fruit) and unhealthy ones that cause blood sugar to spike rapidly (the kind found in potatoes and processed cookies). Even the same types of carbohydrate can increase blood sugar levels more quickly, depending on what foods they are found in or even how they are processed. Should they all be counted the same? To make matters worse, in the original nutrition labels, the FDA had played up fat content, with a special listing for "calories from fat," not carbohydrates.

In 2001 the FDA and the food industry worked out a concept of "net carbs," which essentially allowed food makers to subtract the "better" ones—fiber and sugar replacements—from the total count for labeling purposes. However, this compromise came under attack for keeping consumers in ignorance of what they were truly eating. Meanwhile, without any clear rules, hundreds of new food labels appeared touting themselves as "low carb," "carb counting," and "smarter carb" anyway. As the FDA still dallied in 2004, consumers lost interest in carb-counting and the sales boom in low-carb receded.

The swarm of misleading and missing nutritional information meant that people were undoubtedly chowing down far more calories than they realized. This of course meant that they were probably buying more Cokes and muffins than they would have had they known just how many calories the food truly contained—which contributed to the food makers' profits as well as the national epidemic of obesity.

Starting in the summer of 2003, the FDA issued a contradictory flurry of new labeling proposals that both toughened and loosened the rules. It also created a special Obesity Working Group to study what the agency might do to reverse the national trend.

On the pro-consumer side of demanding more informative labeling, the agency declared that makers of cookies, crackers, chicken pot pie, and the like would have to specifically show the amount of trans fat in their product, not just general "fat." Trans fat is particularly dangerous because it raises the level of "bad" cholesterol and lowers the level of "good" cholesterol. Score one point for consumers.

After the Obesity Working Group issued its recommendations in 2004, the FDA moved slowly to update the rules on serving size, but it still was not clear whether those would be voluntary or mandatory. The regulators also promised to consider making the calorie count more prominent on food labels and to come up with some definition of low carbohydrates before the end of the year. So give the agency the benefit of the doubt, and give consumers another point for those efforts combined.

Another new, pro-consumer requirement for packaged food labels in 2004 was that the ingredients that cause the vast majority of food allergies (milk, eggs, fish, crustacean shellfish, tree nuts, peanuts, wheat, and soybeans) would have to be listed in plain English. However, that order came from Congress, not the FDA.

Meanwhile—on the pro-industry side—the FDA relaxed its hard-fought requirement, stemming from the 1990 law, about what sort of health benefits could go on a packaged food label. It was that law that the FDA and the Department of Agriculture had fought about, that had gone all the way to President George H. W. Bush to resolve, that David Kessler had been ready to resign over. Originally, the measure had required that any health claims for food must be supported by "significant scientific agreement." Now the agency was allowing a weaker labeling called a "qualified health claim." Under this rubric, food processors could make claims that were backed by less solid scientific evidence, as long as they could demonstrate, "based on a fair review by scientific experts of the totality of information available, that the 'weight of the scientific evidence' supports the proposed claim," according to the FDA's new rules. The first claim the agency approved was for walnuts, stating that "supportive but not conclusive research shows that eating 1.5 oz. of walnuts per day, as part of a low saturated fat and low cholesterol diet. . . may reduce the risk of coronary heart disease." Next came similar claims for fish containing omega-3 fatty acids and for olive oil.

This was something the food manufacturers had tried unsuccessfully to get the first time around. The Grocery Manufacturers of America pressed again in 2003 after seeing the kinds of generous (or outright wild) claims that dietary supplements were getting away with, and this time it found a receptive economist's ear in Mark McClellan. The FDA now asserted that a U.S. Court of Appeals ruling in 1999 striking down its restrictions on health claims for dietary supplements forced it also to allow more generous claims on food. Anyway, the agency argued, it was just giving Americans more information.

But consumer groups retorted that it was misleading information. "I saw it as one of the fantasy things that economists do, seeing people as economically rational actors," said Carol Tucker Foreman, director of the Food Policy Institute at the Consumer Federation of America and a dean of the consumer movement. "The FDA did no research to learn, if I see a 'qualified health claim,' do I understand that that is less information and less of an assurance than the old-fashioned claim?" Jerry Mande, Kessler's one-time executive assistant, outright called the new labeling "a complete cave to the food industry." Perhaps he was taking it personally, since he had been a key author of the original nutrition labels—in fact, a framed poster of the labels is one of only three decorations on the white walls of his small office, just off Yale's stunning, balconied historic library.

What made it especially troubling, Mande continued, was that "food package claims that consumers can trust are an important legacy of the first Bush administration. It is a shame that the current Bush administration is taking that away from consumers with policies such as qualified claims." This time, a point for the industry.

In rethinking its approach to labeling fat, the FDA took a related step. It began allowing some foods, like almonds and hazel nuts, to make health claims about their benefits in reducing the risk of heart disease even though they have high fat content.

And the list goes on. The fat substitute olestra, made by Procter & Gamble Company, had been touted as a great way to let people have their potato chips and their diets, too: Added to snack food, it contained zero fat and calories. The catch was that it could cause loose stools and cramps, and it inhibited the body's absorption of vitamins A, D, E, and K. When the FDA approved the additive in 1996, it required a warning about the side effects. Food manufacturers hated the warning. Seven years later, the FDA quietly removed it. Two points.

Nutrition experts were simply stunned in January 2004 when Tommy Thompson, the secretary of Health and Human Services, the FDA's parent agency, sent a long letter to the World Health Organization (WHO) protesting that organization's call for people to eat more vegetables and less sugar and fatty food. How could anyone—let alone the nation's top health official—be against vegetables and in favor of too much dessert? And especially at a time when the FDA was launching a campaign against obesity? Well, industry lobbyists such as the Sugar Association had objected to the WHO recommendation. Another point for industry.

(Bob Brackett professed not to be familiar with Thompson's letter. When I told him about it, he said it did not contradict the FDA's anti-obesity campaign, because obesity "is not just one thing. There's no such thing as a good food or a bad; it's the proportion you consume." He went on to note that when he had raced bikes, years earlier, "it was nothing for me to lose weight on 3,500 calories," which is an extraordinarily high-calorie diet. It is also a fairly irrelevant example, since most people don't get that much exercise.)

One of the weirdest and most obscure examples of the food industry's power has to do with oysters. Like other shellfish taken from the Gulf of Mexico during warm weather, oysters are often contaminated with *Vibrio vulnificus* bacteria, which can cause a severe type of blood infection that is fatal half the time. There are typically around 50 serious cases of illness each year. "Many consumers were saying you should ban raw oysters being harvested from the Gulf in warm weather. Microbiologically, I agree," said Joe Madden, the former strategic manager for microbiology at the Foods Center. But the FDA has not banned the oyster catch; in fact, it has set no safety rules at all.

This is because, since 1982, the FDA has let something called the Interstate Shellfish Sanitation Conference (ISSC) essentially regulate the harvest. "They make the rules, what could be sold or not, what temperature to hold the oysters at and how long," Madden said. The conference consists mainly of representatives of the shellfish industry and of states that rely on this $40 million business. Of the 20 voting members on the executive board, the industry and what the ISSC calls "producing states" have 16 seats; the FDA has exactly one.

From the late 1980s through the early 2000s, the ISSC debated proposals to try to control the bacteria, according to the Center for Science in the Public Interest. The proposals kept being weakened, from a complete ban on selling raw oysters during warm months, to letting oysters be sold but requiring that they be kept refrigerated longer, to mere "goals" of reducing illness from oysters. Even so, most of the attempts failed. Madden said he spoke to the ISSC every other year (which was when it met) until he retired in 1997, urging it to take stronger stands. "That was frustrating. They would say something like, 'The oysters that are consumed were mishandled.'" In other words, if consumers were being killed, it was the fault of the stores where they bought the oysters, or the restaurants where they ate—but certainly not the shellfish industry.

Maybe the most sweeping issue to face the food regulators was bioengineering, or altering the DNA of crops and animals. Beginning in the 1980s, scientists found that they could take a plant or animal, then insert a gene from another organism or change the coding of an existing gene, to produce a characteristic not naturally found in that plant or animal. At a small California company called Calgene, researchers reversed the DNA of the gene that controls the process that makes tomatoes rot. Now there was a tomato that could last longer in transit and on the shelves. They called it the Flavr Savr. Because this was food, the FDA would have to regulate the products.

Or would it? The key issue was whether foods like the Flavr Savr— usually known as genetically modified, or GM, food—were new products or simply new ways of making an existing product. Were the added genes technically "additives," which would require very strict testing for safety?

Or was the Flavr Savr just a tomato? If that was the case, no big deal—Americans had been eating tomatoes longer than there had been an FDA.

Some FDA scientists as well as consumer groups argued that the FDA needed to treat these genetic modifications as additives, which would mean testing, regulating, and approving them. These were powerful forces that were being manipulated here—the basic coding of DNA. Who could be sure what impact this manipulation might have over the long term on the humans who ate the food or the environment the plant was grown in? Could pollen from GM plants be accidentally carried to other crops? Could GM food affect human DNA? "I have argued that if you've added a new gene to the product, it is by definition a food additive," said Foreman of the Consumers Union.

But Presidents Ronald Reagan and the first George Bush were not eager to expand government regulation or impose expensive mandates on businesses of any kind. The GM industry pointed out that if it had to wade through an FDA inspection process before putting its products on the world market, the United States could lose its big technological lead. So the U.S. government declared that a tomato was just a tomato. As long as the end result was identifiably a food that already existed, and the food's nutritional composition was substantially unchanged, it would be, in the FDA's definition, GRAS—"generally regarded as safe"—and no new special tests or labels would be required. The Bush administration finalized the rules in 1992. The commissioner at the time, David Kessler, went along with the laissez-faire approach—yes, the same David Kessler who did not hesitate to tear after orange juice labels and tobacco.

At that point, the biotech industry still wore a halo in the public mind. Genetic modification was seen almost as a miracle technology, a way to ease hunger in the developing world while reducing the use of chemical pesticides that harmed the environment. Corn and cotton got new genes with insect-fighting powers, in essence producing their own natural pesticides. Genes from a daffodil and a bacterium, inserted into rice, produced "golden rice" with an infusion of beta-carotene, which looked like it could save millions of children in the developing world from going blind. For picky consumers in the wealthier nations, GM held out the promise of perfect fruits and vegetables year-round. The United Nations Food and Agricultural Organization, the WHO, and the Organization for Economic Cooperation and Development (a group of developed nations that focuses on economic and social policy) all supported the Reagan-Bush policy. "The public wasn't against those foods," said Gregory Jaffe, director of the

CSPI's biotechnology project. So there was no political pressure on Kessler or the FDA to get tough on the industry.

A decade later, the industry's image had shifted dramatically in Europe and, to a lesser degree, in the United States—and in large part it was precisely because the products had never gone through a rigorous FDA vetting. Tales of damage from GM food began to spread. In a well-publicized test at Cornell University in New York in 1999, nearly half the monarch butterfly larvae that were fed pollen from genetically modified corn died, and the rest were just 50 percent of their normal weight. Grains of StarLink, a modified corn approved only for animals, somehow were jumbled with corn for human consumption in 2000; the corn went into taco shells throughout the United States, and 17 people reported allergic reactions after eating the contaminated shells. Britain's Prince Charles joined the debate, protesting that "This kind of genetic engineering takes mankind into realms that belong to God, and to God alone." The evil of bioengineering was even the theme of two novels in the early 2000s: *All Over Creation*, by Ruth Ozeki, in which an odd assortment of protagonists fight a corporation that wants to market genetically engineered potatoes, and Margaret Atwood's futuristic *Oryx and Crake*, which lays out a dystopia where people re-engineer everything from their own skin and organs, to weird animal hybrids and an entirely new human species. In the remake of the movie *The Manchurian Candidate* in 2004, the brain implants that are used to manipulate the main character stem from the GM technology behind a tomato much like the Flavr Savr.

Europeans—spooked by mad cow disease, furious at the way McDonald's had taken over their countries' cuisines, and generally concerned about environmental issues—were ready to pounce on the potential threat of food that had been scientifically altered by big American multinational companies. In 1998 the European Union placed a moratorium on virtually all new bioengineered crops. Although the moratorium was lifted in 2004, and a couple of types of genetically engineered corn were soon approved, the EU imposed strict labeling requirements. Any food with as little as 0.9 percent genetically modified ingredients would have to be labeled—effectively a scarlet "A" (or "G," in this case).

The moratorium strained relations with the United States, which was pushing to open more markets for its GM farmers. Over 80 percent of the U.S. soy crop and 40 percent of its corn were genetically modified, with nearly 100 million acres of farmland devoted to bioengineered crops. Washington filed a case with the World Trade Organization charging that the EU's moratorium was really an illegal trade barrier. The second Bush administration even blamed Europe for contributing to world hunger, saying that the moratorium discouraged farmers in poor countries from planting bioengineered crops with higher yields.

Elsewhere in the world, public attitudes toward this new type of agriculture were mixed. By the early twenty-first century, GM canola, corn, cotton, and soybeans were firmly rooted, especially in Argentina, Canada, China, South Africa, and (illegally but openly) Brazil—and the acreage was growing steadily. However, bioengineered potatoes, lettuce, and wheat never took off, and there were only small markets for GM papaya and squash. Monsanto—the biggest backhoe in the business—halted efforts to grow GM potatoes, wheat, and crops that would make pharmaceuticals; it bought Calgene and then killed off the Flavr Savr. A number of countries in South America and Africa forbade or restricted the imports.

The GM controversy also spread to cows. About one-third of the U.S. dairy herd is injected with a genetically engineered growth hormone, recombinant bovine somatotropin (RBST), to stimulate milk production. The FDA approved this in 1993, using the same argument as with plants: the end product, milk, was no different from milk that came from untreated cows. Consumer groups, however, said that the milk from RBST cows showed elevated levels of a growth factor that has been linked to an increased risk of cancer. Canada and Europe outright banned the hormone. The consumer backlash against RBST milk grew so strong that states like Maine and Vermont required special labels, and dairies began falling over each other to proclaim themselves "hormone-free." The FDA then warned some dairies about that wording. For its part, Monsanto (which markets RBST) sued one of the biggest dairies in Maine over a different issue of anti-hormone labeling.

Meanwhile, the FDA stuck to its policy: Genes are not additives, so GM foods do not have to be tested or labeled. Companies can voluntarily show the FDA their data on toxicity, allergens, and side effects, but they do not need FDA approval to sell the products. As the journalist Peter Pringle wrote in his 2003 book about the GM industry, *Food, Inc.*:

> . . . *from the start the FDA and the EPA had passed the research buck to the companies. The regulatory policy for GM foods created under President Ronald Reagan and continued under presidents Bush and Clinton was to let the companies do the research: if they found anything wrong, they would tell us. The policy had ultimately caused a steady decline in the public trust in biotech science.*

Even Greg Jaffe of the CSPI conceded that it would be tough for the FDA now to turn around and say that genes are additives, after insisting for a decade that they are not. A report in mid-2004 by a special panel of scientists convened by the FDA, the EPA, and the Department of Agriculture came out more or less on both sides of the issue, though slightly more favorable to the FDA view. It said that GM crops pose no inherent extra health risks and did not recommend any changes in the FDA's basic procedures; but at the same time, it called for tighter screening and more information about the food that was created from these crops. Jaffe said the FDA should at least look more closely at the data that the industry submitted voluntarily. The CSPI did so, and it found inconsistencies, "obvious scientific mistakes," and failure to follow up when the FDA asked for more information.

Speaking of the agency in general, Jaffe's colleague, Caroline Smith DeWaal, said brusquely, "They don't regulate the food industry. They respond when there is an outbreak."

Of course, it is the CSPI's mission to push federal regulators to do more to protect consumers (no matter how much the regulators are doing already). Food industry executives would never say the FDA goes easy on them. Still, it is a sign of the FDA's tilt that the food industry's complaints are much milder than those from consumers, even allowing for the natural diplomacy of any industry toward its regulators.

Steven Grover, the vice president for health, safety, and regulatory affairs at the National Restaurant Association, heads a staff of three that spends $100,000 to $200,000 a year lobbying the FDA on behalf of 300,000 member restaurants. He said that the greatest disagreements arise when his group feels the FDA is pushing for perfection over practicality. "The science might say one thing, they may be perfect from a theoretical public health point of view, but they just don't work when you come to the street level." He figured his trade association has had only a half-dozen major areas of dispute with the agency, over issues like nutritional labeling on menus, or the temperature to be maintained at buffet steam tables. "As we tell them, in a 400-page document"—the Model Code—"that's not much."

If the FDA is more lenient on food makers than on pharmaceuticals, in part it is because that is the way the law is written: Food products do not have to go through three phases of clinical tests to prove safety and efficacy. The FDA does not inspect food before it goes on the market.

But some of the differences in regulatory approach come from differences in the FDA's basic attitude toward the two industries. In the winter of 2004, I asked Bob Brackett the same question I would ask Steve Galson of the Center for Drugs two days later: What did he think of a recent article in the *New York Times* that said that the FDA was coming out with some surprisingly pro-consumer rulings, even in a Republican administration? Unlike Galson, Brackett did not leap to reply that of course the agency was pro-consumer—to assume, in other words, that being pro-consumer is a good thing. He said: "Everybody that I have dealt with has public health as their sole priority and keeping the science in it. It's unfortunate that if it happens to be the regulated industry's desire to do it, you are labeled pro-industry." As the official regulator sees it, then, the food companies are good guys, so why do people jump on the FDA when it takes the companies' side?

CHAPTER 9

Case Study:
The Death of
Monica George

By the mid-1990s, Monica George was embarking on a whole new life. She had become a grandmother for the first time at age 64, then gained a second grandchild a year later. She retired from her job as a registered nurse, although she continued working part-time at a nursing home in Rockville, Maryland, not far from the FDA headquarters. That still left plenty of spare hours for traveling to elder hostels in Italy and Scandinavia, attending art lectures at the Smithsonian Institution museums in Washington, D.C., and reading. Recently she had become engrossed by Daniel Jonah Goldhagen's book *Hitler's Willing Executioners*, about how the German people cooperated in the Holocaust. It hit Monica personally because her grandfather had emigrated from Germany in the 1880s, and she felt there was a lot of anti-Semitism in the German-American community where she had grown up near Harrisburg, Pennsylvania.

Best of all, "she had this new love of her life," a divorcé named Ron, whom she had met at a dance, said her youngest daughter, Donna Storey. Monica had not had things easy when it came to romance. Her first husband was killed by a drunk driver in the mid-1950s, leaving her with two young daughters. She remarried and gave birth to Donna, and then her second husband died. The mother and daughters grew close, moving around from Elizabethtown, Pennsylvania; to Pittsburgh; then to Albany, New York; and finally to Rockville.

Monica's health was good for a woman in her late sixties. That was not surprising, since both of her parents had lived into their nineties and all five of her older siblings were still alive in their seventies and eighties. She had slightly elevated blood sugar, which made her a borderline diabetic—again, hardly a surprise, because both her father and youngest brother had diabetes—but she controlled it with diet and exercise. As a nurse, after all, she knew how to take care of herself. Her only other health concerns were high cholesterol, for which she took the drug Zocor, and some cardiovascular blockage that she discovered after finding herself short of breath during a trip to Montana in 1994. She underwent an angioplasty, a procedure in which a catheter with a balloon attached to the tip was threaded into the artery, and the balloon was then inflated and deflated repeatedly to distend the artery and reduce the blockage. "She was not a person who would whine or complain," said Donna, a writer and teacher of Japanese literature who lives in Berkeley, California, with her husband and two sons.

Mainly, Donna added, her mother "was a very friendly, outgoing person. She would always be the life of the party. She had a lot to live for."

After the angioplasty, a specialist recommended that Monica try to bring her slightly elevated blood sugar down to normal, because blood sugar affects circulation and the elevated level could cause more cardiovascular problems. In the fall of 1997, her general practitioner—not a specialist—started her on a terrific new diabetes drug he had heard of that had just been approved by the FDA that past January. It employed a different method than existing medications to help the body more efficiently use insulin to process blood sugar, and it was the only one that could be taken just once a day. The drug, made by the Parke-Davis division of Warner-Lambert, was called Rezulin.

Meanwhile, Monica and her new boyfriend Ron went dancing and traveling, and Donna thinks they may have considered marriage. In the summer of 1998, they took a cruise to the Caribbean. Monica noticed that her skin seemed darker, but she figured it was just a suntan. However, when Donna called her after they returned from the cruise, "she sounded really terrible," Donna said. Monica told Donna that she was tired; her doctor had diagnosed a thyroid disorder.

Over the next couple of weeks, Donna's sisters, who lived fairly near their mother, reported that Monica was spending virtually all her time in bed and gaining too much weight. Finally, at the end of July, Monica tried another doctor. After one look, he diagnosed her skin color as a classic symptom of jaundice—a liver malfunction that hinders blood circulation—and took her off Rezulin. At that point, half a dozen patients who had been taking Rezulin had died of liver failure, and the FDA had ordered changes in the drug's label to warn of possible liver problems and to advise doctors to monitor their patients regularly. Great Britain had banned the drug. But by then it was too late for Monica.

Her liver was shot. She was sent to Johns Hopkins Hospital to await a liver transplant, and a week later Donna's eldest sister called to say that Donna had better get back to Maryland right away. Donna, her husband, and their young son took the next overnight flight. Matter-of-factly, Donna described her first view of her mother: "She was this mass of swollen yellow. Her eyes were like egg-yolk yellow. She couldn't move; she lay in bed moaning. They were drawing blood all the time, so her arms were black with bruises." Monica told Donna, "I hope I can live to see my grandchildren's graduation from kindergarten." Her grandsons were then three and four years old.

Monica tried to fight back. "She said, 'I'm going to show them. I'm going to get better,'" Donna recalled. She went on a salt-free diet and transferred to the University of Virginia Health System, which had a shorter waiting list for a transplant. Her condition only worsened, however. By the end, according to Donna, Monica's skin itched so badly—an allergic reaction to one of the drugs she was given—that she was pulling at her feeding tubes and catheter until she had to be tied to the bed, "moaning and yelling, 'Lord have mercy.'" She died on September 28, 1998.

Rezulin was pulled from the U.S. market a year and a half later, after 63 deaths—including Monica George's—were officially tied to the drug. Eventually, it would be implicated in about 100 cases of liver failure or death, and thousands of lawsuits would be filed against Warner-Lambert and Pfizer, which acquired Warner-Lambert in 2000. Altogether, during Rezulin's three years of sale, the FDA changed the warning label four times.

I see that as a great success of the system," said Michael Friedman, who was the acting FDA commissioner for nearly two years while Rezulin was on the market and the reports of liver failures were trickling in.

Friedman is not being as callous as it sounds in talking about Rezulin, along with the spate of other drugs that were withdrawn from 1997 to 2000. As he and virtually everyone involved in any aspect of pharmaceutical development and regulation constantly point out, there will always be some harmful drugs that get on the market, because it is not practical to catch every dangerous side effect during the clinical trials. Even if a drug is tested on several thousand people—which is standard—it may have a serious side effect that shows up in only one or two of the patients in those trials. Even if a drug is tested over the six years it typically takes to get through Phases I, II and III, it may have long-term effects that do not become apparent for a decade or more. In the case of silicone-filled breast implants, for instance, one manufacturer said that only 1.2 percent ruptured over a two-year period; however, looking at a 12-year span, FDA data showed that one-fourth ruptured, on average.

The testing that goes on now costs (so the industry claims) hundreds of million dollars. The cost to test seven or eight times as many people over 12 times as many years—that is, 20,000 or more people over a lifetime—would be prohibitive. And it still would not guarantee 100 percent safety

Every drug has some side effects. Even the most uncontroversial, the most widely used, the oldest, and the "safest" do. These are powerful chemicals whose purpose is to change a particular human biological function, and it would be absurd to think that they would glide through the body without impacting more functions on their way.

So, in the opinion of Friedman and FDA officialdom, the stories of Rezulin and all the other drugs that were recalled from 1997 to 2000 simply prove that the system worked. Doctors who were prescribing Rezulin started noticing liver problems. They told the FDA, the agency saw a pattern, it warned doctors, and finally it pulled the drug before too many people were hurt. "The goal is to learn more information about new products as they're used, until sufficient new information becomes available to allow you to make a judgment quickly about any concern about one group or another," Friedman said. "There have to always be recalls. You can't know everything about a new drug when it's approved for marketing. I'm not in any way saying side effects are acceptable in a cavalier way. The value of an active FDA is to be able, if you find new information, to take advantage of that and move swiftly." Monica George was just one of the unlucky few.

By and large, the medical community—and even consumer advocates and health care ethicists—agree with this as a basic philosophy in most cases. Critics may argue that more side effects could be rooted out earlier if the FDA required tougher tests before approval, or more drugs ought to be recalled sooner based on stricter standards of acceptable levels of side effects.

But the drugs of the 1997–2000 era are a special case, and Rezulin most of all. Many people say that the FDA knew Rezulin was potentially dangerous even while the drug was going through the approval process—indeed, that the agency muzzled the reviewer who was raising red flags. They say the story of Rezulin proves that the FDA is overly influenced by drug companies. It may also be a precursor of what would happen with Vioxx, four and a half years later.

And there is yet a third group of people—employees of Warner-Lambert, the manufacturer, and its Parke-Davis division, of course, but also independent doctors and patients—who believe Rezulin was a great drug that should have been kept on the market. They say the FDA caved, not to the drug company, but to panicky consumer activists.

If thalidomide is a prime example of the good that can result when the FDA pushes aggressively to approve a drug, Rezulin is perhaps a key example of the opposite.

The man at the center of the Rezulin story lives in a modest split-level house with a thickly wooded backyard three miles from FDA headquarters. Inside, the house is dark and crowded with family photos and Native American–style blankets, reeking faintly of cigar smoke.

Dr. John L. Gueriguian is a small man with a trim snow-white beard, white hair, dark eyebrows, and a faint polyglot accent. Like Garo Armen of Antigenics, he comes from an Armenian family that survived the Turkish massacres; his parents fled to Alexandria, Egypt, where Gueriguian grew up speaking French, Egyptian, and English. He has an impressive background that spans a number of medical specialties, with an MD in internal medicine and endocrinology, additional training in chemistry, and a stint teaching pharmacology, plus 20 years reviewing drugs at the FDA, starting in 1978. "I am not a subjective person," he said. "I've always been a scientist: Analyze data, discuss it with peers, come to a conclusion." Over the course of a two-hour interview at his house, plus phone calls and e-mails throughout several months, he was variously charming, businesslike, patiently patronizing, and quick to get annoyed, and he scattered conspiracy theories like chicken feed.

Depending on who is telling the story, Gueriguian is either the courageous whistle-blower who realized early on that Rezulin was dangerous and refused to be bamboozled by Warner-Lambert, or else a hot-tempered, unreliable crank whose reviews were always careless.

Here is how Gueriguian told it to me:

He had questions about Rezulin starting back when Warner-Lambert first filed its investigational new drug application in order to launch human tests. For one thing, "the chemical molecule was very quickly absorbed [in the bloodstream] and it stays a long time in the body." That could make the drug quite effective, of course, but it also increased the danger if it was toxic. In addition, of the other drugs in the same pharmaceutical class that Gueriguian had seen, "every single one of them that had been tested in animals had very serious cardiovascular problems and liver problems." Indeed, liver problems can be a fairly common side effect of diabetes drugs. Gueriguian discussed these questions with Warner-Lambert, and "they promised to address the issues, and they never did. They were never cooperative except in words.

"When I have an IND, I constantly follow up on everything that comes in. I expressed my concerns to the company time and time again. The [FDA] pharmacologist who had the file of animal testing, he was constantly coming to me and expressing his concern. I have never had a behavior like that from any company." During the years of testing and preliminary review, Gueriguian added, he heard no complaints about his work from his colleagues or supervisors at the FDA: "I always discuss the drugs I am reviewing with other medical officers. You don't want to be subjective. Everyone agreed with my conclusions." Finally, in the summer of 1996, the new drug application for Rezulin was formally submitted under the agency's accelerated approval program for innovative drugs, which meant the agency was supposed to make its decision within six months. Practically speaking, when all the bureaucracy of higher levels of reviews was factored in, Gueriguian said, that gave him just four months to analyze the application.

He asked Warner-Lambert for all of its data relating to liver tests. First, he said, "the company sent some sort of summary, nothing even close to the entire liver safety database." He asked again. Then it offered testimonials from experts, which are not considered acceptable evidence by the FDA. By then Gueriguian was also having doubts about another aspect of the drug—whether it worked significantly better than other products already on the market. As the first-stage reviewer, he did not have authority to recommend approval or rejection, but he wrote up all his concerns in a report. He met with Mary E. Taylor, the liaison from Warner-

Lambert's regulatory affairs office—the office headed by Irwin Martin. Then on September 25, 1996, Taylor came to see Gueriguian again.

"You have to understand the context. These people had been promising to address the issue for six years and they hadn't done that. I had developed data during those six years of all the liver problems. Now I had received an NDA and it had to be approved in a very short while because it was accelerated. The deadline was coming down. I was supposed to do my review without having any data. So here is some person"—Mary Taylor—"who comes to me and asks, 'What do you think of this drug?'" And Gueriguian retorted with the fateful words: "To quote President Johnson, 'You can't shine shit.' This drug is shit."

Gueriguian claimed that he does not remember what happened right after that, what he and Taylor did or whether they kept on talking, but he said she did not storm out of his office in any reaction to his saying "shit." The next day he sent her an apology for his language in a memo that went through his supervisor, Dr. G. Alexander Fleming. He said he was not reprimanded. Then he went off on vacation to France for two weeks.

In the middle of this urgent and stressful review?

Gueriguian was clearly annoyed at my question, as he snapped out his justification for taking a vacation: "The draft review was almost done. They hadn't given me the data." But by the time he came back from France, Gueriguian had been pulled from the Rezulin review. Fleming took over, and Gueriguian was hauled in for a disciplinary hearing regarding his use of the word "shit." Eventually he was issued a formal reprimand, but Gueriguian denied that he was fired or pressured to retire, as some rumors have it. "I stayed there another two years. I retired after 20 years, which is what I planned from Day One"—and which, in fact, is a common retirement plan among FDA long-termers. During his last two years, Gueriguian added, smiling, "they sent me only good drugs to review, safe and effective drugs," including another diabetes treatment for which he recommended accelerated approval. Meanwhile, Rezulin was approved in January 1997.

So that is Gueriguian's story. There are several controversial postscripts concerning some unusually cozy interactions between the FDA and Warner-Lambert, and some questionable behavior by Warner-Lambert, according to published reports, court records from a lawsuit that Monica George's family filed against Pfizer, and my own interviews. The FDA supervisor who took over Gueriguian's review, "Zan" Fleming, supposedly did unusual favors for Warner-Lambert and Irwin Martin, like letting them propose revisions to Gueriguian's negative report. Then the report was removed from the official Rezulin file altogether and not shown to the FDA advisory committee, according to news accounts. Fleming and Martin went out to dinner at least once, in September 1998—albeit after Fleming had left the FDA, and they split the check. In an internal Warner-Lambert memo back on August 7, 1995, while Warner-Lambert and the FDA were still discussing the company's plans for clinical trials, and Gueriguian was the reviewer, Mary Taylor reported that Fleming "offered that if our discussion did not go well, he would ease Dr. Gueriguian out." When the drug finally came before the advisory committee, Warner-Lambert asserted that there were far fewer instances of liver damage than was actually the case.

Of course, there are other versions of this story. Irwin Martin would not talk publicly about Rezulin because lawsuits are still pending. Zan Fleming first agreed to an interview, then failed to reply to repeated e-mails to try to arrange it. A Warner-Lambert official who was involved with the drug (and who would not let his name be used, also because of the lawsuits) claimed that when Gueriguian cited liver problems, he was simply misreading the drug application. In one case, this official said, Gueriguian pounced on a number that was mistyped in a chart. "He found a nine that should have been a zero. If he had read the text, he would have seen it was a zero." Warner-Lambert officials also argued that Gueriguian was biased against Rezuin and was unpardonably rude to Mary Taylor by calling the drug "shit." Moreover, Gueriguian's personality and the quality of his reviews have a mixed reputation among his former colleagues.

So maybe it would have been hard to catch the problems before Rezulin was approved. Maybe Gueriguian's warnings were overblown. Still, once the drug was being used and people started dying, why didn't the FDA act faster to order it withdrawn? While the agency toughened the warning labels, there is widespread skepticism about whether doctors ever read these labels on any drug, especially for a drug they have already become accustomed to prescribing. As time went on, more and more midlevel FDA managers began turning against Rezulin. However, Janet Woodcock and her deputy at CDER, Dr. Murray M. Lumpkin, held on. Why?

The answer—as with Propulsid and Posicor in the late 1990s, as with Vioxx—is that withdrawal is a major step. Every drug has side effects, and before possibly overreacting by yanking a medication that may be helping people, the FDA wants to be sure that the problems are actually caused by the drug, are persistent, and outweigh the benefits. Woodcock told the *Los Angeles Times* that in the case of Rezulin, she held off asking for it to be withdrawn because she wanted to see if a couple of similar drugs, approved two years after Rezulin, would be less toxic to the liver and could thus be substituted. Speaking of all the recalls of that era, she also said to me, "Those critics are very irresponsible with their data. You never find everything when a drug is approved. We took stuff off [the market] promptly." In some of the cases, she added, the technology to pinpoint side effects, such as side effects from interactions between two drugs, did not even exist when the medications were first approved, so the problems could not have been caught. "We've improved our pharmaceutical system, we built a new computer system, we developed screening techniques to look at liver metabolism."

Out in Arkansas, Daniel Casciano said the FDA's National Center for Toxicological Research is trying to learn from the long line of withdrawals in order to improve the screening even further. His center is studying some of the recalled drugs, under its mandate to evaluate the safety of chemicals in drugs that have been approved but have led to adverse events. Casciano would not reveal exactly which drugs are being analyzed, only that they are in the class of glitazones and are being evaluated for liver and cardiovascular toxicity—which definitely describes Rezulin. "It is not a negative evaluation of the industry," he went on. "The systems were not as sensitive at the time [when the drugs were approved]. The mechanism of the metabolism was not known at the time. Research is a dynamic process." In its "critical path" program to help industry develop new drugs, the FDA specifically notes that new methods are needed for gauging liver toxicity in drugs.

Woodcock and the FDA brass have their defenders. John D. Golenski is a child psychologist, head of the Institute for Ethics and Health Policy in Berkeley, California, and founder of Rx Health Value, the union-employer-insurer-consumer group that focused on health care costs in the late 1990s. He also worked with insurance companies on a committee that chose which drugs would go on the insurance formularies, or approved lists. As reports about liver problems with Rezulin trickled in, he said, "the FDA was quite rapid in picking that up and acting on it." His committee did not remove Rezulin from its formularies until a few weeks before the FDA banned it.

One more plot twist: It is sometimes hard to remember that stories like Monica George's, horrible as they are, were actually the exception. Many people felt that Rezulin worked well for them, and they did not want to lose it.

"I loved Rezulin, because it was a neat drug," said Anne Peters Harmel, the endocrinologist at the University of Southern California who analyzed the different ways people can be asked about side effects. Back in the mid-1990s she was a relatively junior clinical researcher conducting some of the Rezulin trials at Cedars-Sinai Medical Center. (That means she was paid by Warner-Lambert to conduct research, although she has no connection with the company now.) Harmel had seen that the eight existing diabetes products were not doing enough to get blood sugar down in her patients. "We needed additional drugs," she said. "This was a totally different class, an insulin sensitizer." She recognized that Rezulin could lead to liver problems, "but I knew to monitor the liver trials. My patients all did really well because they were monitored." She even testified in favor of the drug at an early FDA advisory committee hearing.

Other testimonials: Stuart Portnoy (the former FDA chemistry reviewer who now works for PharmaNet) said Rezulin was "marvelous" for his uncle. Howard Weisman of ESP Pharma also had relatives who took the drug successfully. Irwin Martin's father was on the drug for over two years, until it was recalled. Okay, so it was Martin's job to push Rezulin, and Weisman had a vested interest as director of new products and senior director of diabetes marketing at Parke-Davis during the Rezulin era. But would they risk their relatives' lives?

In the opinion of some of these people, the FDA gave up too easily. "A poorly led FDA let the media take control of an issue that the media didn't understand, forcing the FDA's hand," Weisman said impatiently. He added, "I still get calls from doctors who say they haven't been able to treat patients effectively since."

More than four years after the last Rezulin pill was legally sold, the number of diabetes cases in the United States has surged. The National Institutes of Health in 2003 estimated that 17 million Americans have the disease, with 16 million more at risk. Most of the major pharmaceutical companies are trying to develop diabetes drugs. Merck, for instance, had to cut off research on one product in late-stage testing in the fall of 2003 because of unexpected tumors in mice, but it had a couple of others in the pipeline. It was also developing a third with Bristol-Myers Squibb that used a mechanism similar to Rezulin.

Fleming and Gueriguian both left the FDA to do consulting work—yes, Gueriguian has pharmaceutical company clients, although Pfizer is not among them—while Martin was squeezed out of Warner-Lambert when that company was acquired by Pfizer in 2000.

Monica George's daughters sued Pfizer for $1.8 million in compensatory damages plus $10 million in punitive. The trial started in January 2002 and ran for five weeks. Donna said they turned down two settlement offers from the company, including one of over one million dollars. But after just 45 minutes of deliberation, the jury ruled in Pfizer's favor. The jurors offered various explanations, according to Donna: "No drug company would put a bad drug on the market." "Companies misrepresent data all the time." "Drug companies are trying to help people."

"I felt," she said, "like my mother had been tortured all over again."

CHAPTER 10

When Consumers
Get Angry

When people talk about consumers storming the FDA, they could mean consumers like Laurie Girand. Or they could mean consumers like Abbey Meyers.

Laurie Girand is clearly used to making methodical decisions. With degrees in electrical engineering and computer science from Princeton University and an MBA from Stanford University, she ran a Silicon Valley consulting and recruiting firm that helped launch several Internet companies; at its peak, her company was logging $450,000 in sales. She applied the same sort of careful oversight to feeding her daughter, Anna McGregor: strict limits on sweets and fast food. Lots of fruits, vegetables, yogurt, and milk. And organic fruit juice, "which we assumed was safer, because it had no pesticides."

In the fall of 1996, Girand and her husband, Scott McGregor, president and CEO of Philips Semiconductors, went off on a week-long vacation to Fiji, leaving three-year-old Anna with Girand's mother. Grandma figured she was sticking to the regimen by giving Anna apple juice from Odwalla, Inc., a locally based company that advertised itself as socially responsible and its products as natural.

Then Anna began to have stomach cramps and diarrhea. The doctor thought it might be flu or food poisoning. But the diarrhea went on for six days. The little girl was not eating, barely drinking water, and her blood and kidney tests were abnormal. She was admitted to the hospital. Girand wondered if they were overreacting, so when she was told a name for her daughter's problem, she looked it up on the Internet. It was HUS, or hemolytic-uremic syndrome, a condition (most often found in children) in which red blood cells are destroyed and the kidneys stop working properly. It is generally caused by *E. coli* 0157:H7 bacteria from under-cooked hamburgers, contaminated water (such as that in lakes), and unpasteurized milk. Or, sometimes, roadside apple juice.

After a brief improvement, Anna only seemed to get worse. Her body puffed up with fluids from her IV feedings, so her intake had to be re-stricted; parched with thirst, she begged her parents for water. Her color grew ashen. Even two blood transfusions did not improve her red blood count, and a measurement of her wastes rose to dangerous levels. Also, a friend heard on the radio that Odwalla apple juice was being recalled in Washington State for causing an *E. coli* outbreak. Another Northern California child was hospitalized with serious kidney trouble and put on dialysis.

Deep inside, Girand felt a chill. Would Anna ever be able to leave the hospital? How much worse could it get?

By the thirteenth day—Halloween—things finally started picking up for Anna. Her blood signs were improving, thanks to the transfusions, and she was allowed more fluids. She returned home two days after that. But she had lost a lot of weight, and she will have to worry about kidney damage for the rest of her life. Altogether, 70 people became sick from drinking Odwalla juice that fall, including one child who died from HUS. The company was fined $1.5 million—the largest penalty the FDA had ever levied in a food industry case—for selling unsafe food.

Nevertheless, Odwalla won praise from business observers for acknowl-edging the problem publicly and quickly, and it promised to "flash-pasteurize" its juice to kill off any *E. coli* bacteria. This went well beyond what the FDA required. Not only did juice not have to be pasteurized, under FDA regulations, but unpasteurized juice did not even have to carry warnings of the dangers of bacterial contamination.

That might have been the end of the story for Anna McGregor and her parents. But in mid-December Girand happened to read in a newspaper article that the FDA had recently convened an advisory committee meet-ing with juice manufacturers to discuss pasteurization and HUS. That got her thinking about the FDA and its regulatory role, and why Odwalla had been allowed to sell unsafe juice. How come the industry had been invited to Rockville while victims like her family had not? Was the FDA now going to require pasteurization, or at least warnings on juice bottles? How could little girls like Anna be protected in the future? What really galled Girand was that one industry executive was quoted as saying a person would be more likely to get hit by a car on the way to the store to buy apple juice, than to get ill from drinking the juice. "I went through the roof," Girand recalled. "I couldn't believe the industry was getting away with saying something like that." She looked up the telephone number for the FDA's Center for Food Safety and tried to call the director at the time, Dr. Fred R. Shank.

She didn't get through, of course. But she learned some disturbing things. No victims had been at the advisory committee meeting. She could submit public comments about the meeting, but the comments were due in two weeks. And when would the transcript of the meeting be available so that she could know what had taken place in order to comment on it? In about two weeks.

"I barely managed to get out a strangled 'good-bye,'" Girand recalled.

Despite several attempts, Girand never did make contact with Shank before he transferred to another FDA job in January 1998. However, after hooking up with consumer organizations like the Center for Science in the Public Interest and STOP (the group founded in 1993 after an outbreak of food poisoning from Jack in the Box hamburgers), she got the comment period extended by one month. That was only the first step in her real goal, to persuade the FDA to add a warning label to unpasteurized juice, or even ban it outright.

She began calling the agency, every month or two, for the next four years. Now she got through. She talked to Shank's successor, Joe Levitt, and his deputy, Janice Oliver, as well as other staffers. The FDA "seemed to be genuinely interested in being conscientious, kick butt and move the world to a better place. If I called, I got put with the right person. They were always enthusiastic to speak to me."

Girand had some powerful advantages. Coincidentally, President Bill Clinton had called for a food safety initiative, so she got the attention of people like Jerry Mande, Commissioner David Kessler's executive assistant. Handing off more and more of her Silicon Valley business to consultants, she was able to work 20 hours a week on food safety, traveling to Washington and Sacramento, writing letters, and meeting with government officials. She also became copresident of STOP, which provided another platform. In 1999 the FDA gave her an award for her efforts.

Even with all that support, it took until January 2001 to get a label, and the final version was not as strong as Girand had wanted. Following government procedures, the FDA first had to issue a preliminary statement of proposed regulations, allowing time for comments. The powerful orange juice lobby fought back. Then the federal Office of Management and Budget had to approve.

Today most juice processors must use a set of principles called Hazard Analysis and Critical Control Point (HACCP) to examine their manufacturing systems for potential microbial, chemical, and physical dangers. However, juice sold at roadside stands or juice bars is not included because, as with restaurants, the FDA has no jurisdiction. Unpasteurized juice is required to carry a warning label that says: "WARNING: This product has not been pasteurized and therefore, may contain harmful bacteria that can cause serious illness in children, the elderly, and persons with weakened immune systems." Every now and then there are still outbreaks of what the FDA calls foodborne illnesses probably caused by this sort of juice.

To some degree, Girand sympathizes with the FDA, hamstrung by regulations, political pressure, and limited resources. But her experience has also taken some of the glow off her opinion of the agency. Before Anna's illness, Girand said, "I had the impression that the government was largely protecting me from things that shouldn't happen, like car tires exploding. Or you go on a roller coaster and you assume it's been checked. I didn't think much about it." And now? "The FDA should have been on top earlier—this is the thing that's so depressing. The FDA doesn't tend to act till something rears its head more than once."

Abbey S. Meyers, too, is a mother who does not sit back when her child is ill.

In 1970 her son (whose name she will not reveal publicly) was two years old and suffering from a hereditary neurological disorder called Tourette's syndrome, which is characterized by severe motor and vocal tics. Although the little boy had been doing well on the experimental drug pimozide, the manufacturer was planning to discontinue production because there were not enough customers with the condition to make the effort profitable. It took a few years before Meyers could find another medication that worked as well.

If she was having so much trouble getting medicine for her child, Meyers wondered if she wasn't the only one. So she proceeded to organize an assortment of nonprofit health care groups, all of which focused on often-ignored conditions that affect relatively few people, into a federation called the National Organization for Rare Disorders, Inc., or NORD. Then Meyers and NORD, along with other patient groups, lobbied Congress in 1983 to pass the Orphan Drug Act, which tries to encourage pharmaceutical companies to make drugs for these small markets by offering some tax credits and exclusive marketing rights for seven years. (Antigenics would later take advantage of those inducements in developing its cancer vaccine.) Even before the law was passed, the FDA set up a special Office of Orphan Products Development, which Meyers praises because "we finally had one place in the FDA we could go to."

Still, Meyers soon realized that the Orphan Drug Act and the Orphan Products office did not necessarily mean that the pharmaceutical industry or the FDA would whisk new drugs—or even old ones—down the racetrack.

In the mid-1990s, according to Meyers, FDA inspectors showed up for one of their periodic inspections at a plant run by Armour Laboratories that made Acthar Gel. That medication, derived from pig glands, was the main treatment for the rare disease West syndrome, a form of epilepsy that affects infants. (It has also been approved by the FDA for a range of other conditions, including multiple sclerosis.) Armour had been manufacturing Acthar Gel since 1952, and the FDA, Meyers said, was aghast at the decades-old technology still being employed. The inspectors ordered Armour to update the technology, Meyers said. Instead, Armour said it would shut down the line.

Like Laurie Girand, but from the opposite direction, Meyers can sympathize with the FDA just so far. She recognizes that the agency wanted to be scrupulous in regulating a product made from animal parts. "They didn't trust the manufacturer. They're trained to look for rat hairs in factories. You're dealing with mad cow disease, you're dealing with things from animals you can't trust." But by focusing only on the safety of the drug-making process, she argued, the FDA was missing its bigger health and safety mission—making sure drugs were produced to begin with, so that patients could maintain their health. Meyers' constituents had to have the Acthar Gel, and they didn't care if it was being made in outdated facilities. "People who needed it were calling us—parents, doctors," Meyers continued. "They [FDA] don't understand, with some drugs you can't go in and close the place down. Let's find a way to fix the problem. Don't just say, 'Don't make this drug.' We told both the company and the FDA that this was unacceptable."

When the FDA and Armour sat down for a discussion in Rockville, Meyers said she "barged into the meeting" and threatened to take the story to the reporters on "60 Minutes" unless production resumed. "We'll put those babies on television," she warned.

Eventually, the FDA halfway agreed to Meyers' demand. It would let Armour continue making Acthar but insisted on inspecting each lot of the drug. That, of course, slowed the output to a trickle, enough for just 1,600 people per year. So the FDA asked the Rare Disorders group to ration the limited supply. Highest priority went to children and those who had been taking it for multiple sclerosis for years; way down the list were people with nonfatal ailments like rheumatoid arthritis. Luckily, after four years of rationing, Questcor Pharmaceuticals, Inc., of Union City, California, acquired the worldwide rights in 2001. It updated the technology and began churning out enough for 5,000 more people, and the rationing and fury ended.

American history began with a rebellion against authority and has continued to be defined by waves of consumer and populist activism—the abolitionist and Progressive movements of the mid- and late nineteenth century, women's suffrage and Prohibition in the early twentieth century, the civil rights movement and Vietnam War protests of the 1960s. In the 1970s came a range of concerns about pollution, nuclear proliferation, patients' rights, and the safety of consumer products. In the 1980s activism turned more inward, as aging Baby Boomers started worrying about their health, diet, and fitness. The Internet put consumer groups on steroids; now they could organize in minutes and dig up the newest information from around the world. "People are more and more inclined to demand what they think is theirs, rather than be told. It's probably true of almost everything in America," not just food and drugs, said Jere Goyan, the FDA commissioner under President Carter.

Especially starting in the 1970s, modern consumers wanted to know just what was in the emissions coming out of the local factory and in the food going into their stomach They went toe to toe with the experts and refused to blindly accept the word of their doctors (or stockbrokers or local merchants). One result of this demand for information and control was a flurry of self-help books and online chat rooms. Another was the creation of federal agencies meant to protect Americans' health, safety, and pocketbooks, including the Environmental Protection Agency and the Consumer Product Safety Commission. The FDA flexed its muscles, too, as it implemented the Kefauver-Harris Amendments, set standards for clinical trials, and developed nutrition labels for food.

However, even into the early 1980s, patients and other consumers were not really seen as a constituency that the FDA had to answer to; doctors were. "Medicine was one of those things where the patient was very passive. The FDA for the most part focused on the intermediary, the physician," explained Jerome Halperin of the Food and Drug Law Institute in Washington, D.C. Drug companies marketed their wares only to doctors, after all, and patients were expected to obey their physician's word without question. Many prescriptions were still even written in Latin.

"Patient activism" back then meant Jerry Lewis hosting telethons to raise money for muscular dystrophy research. "It was a pity thing," said Eileen Crowley, a publicist specializing in health care. "It was done in a very passive way. It wasn't about what a drug or treatment could actually do to prolong the life of someone." Or there were fringe groups like the Church of Scientology, which attacked Eli Lilly for making Prozac, on the general principle of being against personality-altering medication.

AIDS changed all that. As it started killing people by the hundreds and thousands, activist groups blocked traffic on Wall Street, trashed pharmaceutical company displays at conferences, and marched on the FDA headquarters in Rockville demanding that the agency give them new drugs faster. "It was the first time the agency had to deal with an active, intelligent group of people that made demands," explained Ira S. Loss, a financial analyst specializing in health care at the Washington, D.C.–based firm Washington Analysis.

A lot of people were angry at the AIDS community's tactics. Gerry Meyer, the former deputy director of the Center for Drugs—the one who scoffed at David Kessler's moves on orange juice and tobacco—called the activists unprofessional and unreasonable. Still, even he does not deny that in some ways their methods worked. Their impact on the FDA's approval process has been widely reported: They spurred the creation of treatment INDs and parallel track programs to speed up access to lifesaving drugs, and by the mid-1990s the two sides were working together instead of fighting. At the same time, other groups of patients with serious conditions, watching the AIDS activists' success, began rethinking their own approaches. Rather than play up their helplessness and need, these patients began to wonder, what if we, too, play up our strength?

Eileen Crowley described the new strategy: "When we would be doing PR campaigns, we would look for more of a complete picture. There has to be a tiered effect, with funding for research, and look at how managed care puts things on the formulary, and then you had to put a face on a condition, and also show that there is hope. Who is the patient that this drug is targeting? How can you help tell the story pre-approval to the [FDA] advisory committee? You have to have patients demanding it in the physician's office, you have to have physicians demanding it from managed care."

On the food side, advocates also became savvier, said Bob Brackett, head of the Center for Food Safety. They learned to "go straight to the top" and contact him (or his predecessors) directly, as Laurie Girand did.

Patients' official roles in the drug approval process grew over the years as well. At least one patient or consumer representative must be appointed to each advisory committee. In a sign of the times, Matt Sharp—the AIDS activist and dancer from Oklahoma who protested at the big demonstration at FDA headquarters in 1988—was appointed to the Antiviral Drugs Advisory Committee in April 2003. He now praises the FDA members' knowledge and competence. There is also a patient consultant program, in which the FDA selects and trains patient representatives who "will provide advice to the FDA and to the drug sponsor on topics such as clinical trial design, endpoint determination, expanded access protocol development, and clinical trial patient recruitment strategies" earlier in the application process, according to the FDA's official description. The idea is to add the patient's point of view to all the other considerations of dosage, safety, effectiveness, and scientific validity. Often, this means reminding the scientists and bureaucrats that live human beings are being tested, and tests can hurt. For instance, Mike Katz of the International Myeloma Foundation sat in on a meeting in the late 1990s where some regulators and drug company researchers were discussing how to conduct bone marrow biopsies, in order to check patients' responses to a cancer medication. These biopsies are painful procedures in which a tool Katz calls a "harpoon" is inserted to suction out bone marrow cells from the pelvis, Katz explained. The FDA and the company, he continued, were proposing three biopsies per person: The company would run one test before the drug was taken and another afterwards, and then an independent party would do its own test to confirm the results. It would spare the patients a lot of pain, Katz suggested, if they could drop the company's "after" test and let the independent test fill that role.

Another patient consultant is Nancy Roach (the one who explained how companies can fudge their measurement of disease progression). A former systems analyst from Oregon who was diagnosed with cervical cancer in 2001, Roach now works with a small cancer-patient advocacy group based in Northern California called the Marti Nelson Cancer Foundation. One time she had a suggestion for redesigning the test of an injectable colorectal cancer drug. Rather than test the drug only in conjunction with a pump, she said, could the manufacturer also test it in use with a new oral medication, which patients prefer to the pump?

Okay, skeptics might say, so the FDA occasionally lets real people have a word at meetings. But how warmly does the agency really welcome these advocates and their suggestions? Scientists are not known for their eagerness to take advice on technical topics from nonscientists who lack a collection of graduate degrees. And remember how industry executives— and even some FDA officials—often complain that consumer representatives on the advisory committees lack the necessary educational grounding to know what they're talking about. Roach admitted that they have a point: "There's a lot of unevenness among the advocates. There are advocates who sit there and don't say a word the whole damn meeting. There are advocates who are hitting an agenda."

In the end, the way the FDA views its patient constituency is probably not that much different from the way any business views comments from the peanut gallery. Sometimes there is annoyance or disdain. And sometimes the commentary proves helpful.

After the final advisory committee hearing on methylmercury in fish, Doug Archer, the former deputy director of the Food Center and also a member of that committee, groused a bit about the consumer groups that "tend to speak in absolutes. If the level is set at 0.1, someone will say 0.12 is dangerous. No it's not. You can't draw a line in the sand." Mike Katz has encountered "a few [FDA] folks who have been aloof and condescending." The regulators did not accept Roach's idea about testing the colorectal cancer drug in conjunction with oral medication, and Katz did not know what happened to his suggestion on the bone marrow trials.

Still, Roach and Katz insisted that the FDA staff and committee members usually act respectfully toward them. Doug Archer, for all his complaining, also said that the very fact that the patient advocates are not scientific experts is what makes their perspective valuable. "A lot of times it's very easy to get your mindset locked into something that only makes sense because of the science. Consumer groups make regulators stop and think about other aspects of a problem, human aspects."

The FDA has a special problem coping with the American public, however. Unlike most other businesses, institutions, and government agencies, the FDA faces two different sets of consumer groups, both of which can call on a tradition of populism and the speedy information potential of the Internet.

There are the Laurie Girands, whose main concern is making sure that consumers are not harmed by drugs and food. These are the parents who showed up at the advisory committee meeting on antidepressants and similar sessions on the acne drug Accutane. They make their influence felt through public interest groups like the Center for Science in the Public Interest, Public Citizen, and STOP, and they often work on a range of health care, environmental, or consumer issues. Learning of outbreaks of food poisonings, dread diseases, suspicious clusters of cancer, side effects from new drugs, and the like, they demand that the FDA pull dangerous products off the shelf or at least issue tougher warnings. With so many choices of treatment often available for a particular ailment, they say, it is not worth putting even a small percentage of people at risk for horrible side effects or death from the umpteenth new drug.

And there are the Abbey Meyers, who want people to have access to as many different treatments as possible. These consumers are usually organized by disease—Meyers' NORD, Mike Katz's International Myeloma Foundation, Nancy Roach's Marti Nelson Cancer Foundation, the American Cancer Society, the militant AIDS group ACT-UP (an acronym for AIDS Coalition To Unleash Power). They hear about compounds in the earliest stages of clinical trials, alternative medicines, or drugs on the market in other countries, and they demand that the FDA make those treatments available immediately.

Many consumers from the first group scoff that the second group is just a front for industry, since drug companies keep in close contact with and often provide funding to organizations representing people who have the diseases that the companies' drugs treat. It is a time-honored tactic among lobbyists on any issue. Since a cause will always have more credibility if it seems to be backed by ordinary folk rather than big business, industry lobbyists try to find (or create) a "grass-roots" group that will agree with their agenda.

Meyers' National Organization for Rare Diseases gets several hundred thousand dollars from drug and biotech companies, mainly by way of its annual banquet, with much of the proceeds dedicated to a program that makes drugs available to people without insurance. The American Cancer Society draws seven to eight million dollars, or about one percent of its total revenue, from pharmaceutical companies. The International Melanoma Foundation receives its $200,000 (more or less) each year from Celgene, the maker of thalidomide. As for the Marti Nelson foundation, fully half of its funding comes from industry.

Antigenics, said Russ Herndon, the chief operating officer, visits the American Cancer Society "all the time." In February 2004, eight of Antigenics' top officials hosted three Cancer Society guests for lunch— catered sandwiches—in the Lexington, Massachusetts plant. "Those are the major constituencies—patients, advocacy groups, payers [such as insurance companies], physicians," Herndon said.

Perhaps the most famous example of industry-consumer collaboration was the way the British drug maker AstraZeneca used patient groups to push its innovative lung-cancer drug Iressa. The drug had generated a lot of excitement because it took a new tack in fighting cancer that held out the hope of fewer side effects. Rather than bombard the cells (and the patient) with radiation or chemotherapy, it homed in on a crucial molecule on the surface of cancer cells, called epidermal growth factor receptor, that functions as a kind of switch in helping the cells pursue their unchecked, deadly process of division. By blocking the receptor, Iressa could slow the process. However, there were also doubts about Iressa because the formal application to the FDA was based on just two small trials, neither using a control group, that showed that tumors shrank substantially in only 10 percent of the patients. Two larger studies, moreover, did not demonstrate that the drug kept patients alive any longer than chemotherapy alone. As Iressa came up for FDA review, the staff found "several bothersome issues." But meanwhile, AstraZeneca had been supplying more than 18,000 cancer patients with the drug through a "compassionate use" program. So, when the FDA advisory committee met in late September 2002, members of patient advocacy groups showed up pleading for their drug. The committee recommended approval of Iressa, and the FDA made it official the following spring.

The various patient organizations, of course, insist that the money they get from pharmaceutical companies does not make them mouthpieces for the donors. At NORD, Meyers noted that "we are one of the most outspoken critics of the drug industry"—which is true; she frequently lights into Big Pharma for not doing enough for orphan diseases and focusing too much on pleasing Wall Street. "So obviously," she went on, "their donations have had no influence on our policies." Katz has spoken about how absurd it would be for him to block a drug that might help him, solely because it was made by a rival of Celgene.

"There are times when industry wants advocates' help because we can put political pressure," admitted Nancy Roach, who chairs the Marti Nelson foundation's treatment intervention committee. But she said that she will challenge the hand that feeds her. "They'll put advocates in a room. They'll say, 'Look at this data, the FDA is holding [a drug] up.' But you're only seeing part of the story. Let me see the application; let me see all the data."

The two types of consumer groups simply reflect the conflicting pressures that FDA insiders and outsiders alike constantly talk about, the difference between Type I and Type II mistakes. If the FDA lets a drug through without double-checking the data, it may be allowing the next dangerous Rezulin on the market. If it is too stringent in demanding more tests and more answers, it may delay the next AZT for AIDS. "The American public expects two things simultaneously that are very difficult if not impossible to deliver: They want everything as soon as possible, and everything as safe as possible," sighed former acting commissioner Michael Friedman. "But you have to try, because that's what you're charged with doing."

Conventional wisdom holds that it's the Laurie Girands, the consumer activists who advocate for safety issues, who wield the most influence, in the same way that the FDA has tended to fear Type I errors (approving new drugs that later cause harm) more than Type II (failing to approve new drugs that could have benefits). A look at the headlines in 2003 and 2004 would seem to bear out that analysis. In most of the big controversies—the ones regarding Vioxx, silicone-filled breast implants, methylmercury in fish, Accutane, antidepressants, mad cow disease, and the diet supplement ephedra—the letters, protests, and people crowding into advisory committee meetings were mainly of the "don't let this dangerous product on the market" variety.

But there are some strong reasons to argue that the other type of consumer is just as powerful, if not more so. Daniel Carpenter, the Harvard government professor, said there was an "explosion" of new consumer groups of the Abbey Meyers variety in the 1970s and 1980s, dedicated to advocating faster approvals of drugs for their own particular disease. Writing in the January–February 2004 issue of the journal *Health Affairs*, he said his researchers counted more than 3,100 "disease-specific advocacy groups with at least some involvement in political issues," and added, "The rise in patient advocacy has led to a balancing of the visibility of Type II versus Type I errors... To a degree never before witnessed, disease-specific lobbies now press Congress for medical research funding, insurers and state governments for favorable coverage rulings, and the FDA for quick approvals." No wonder that in his July 2002 paper in the *American Journal of Political Science* Carpenter found that patient advocacy groups were one of the three biggest influences on the FDA.

This second kind of consumer activism fits right in with several social and political trends. Baby Boomers may have worried about the safety of ingesting chemicals or preservatives in the 1960s and 1970s, when they were in their twenties, but by the time they started hitting their fifties in the 1990s and 2000s, what they wanted was more chemicals—Celebrex, Fosamax, Botox, Viagra, Propecia, and any other new miracle drugs that might keep them feeling like they were still 20. Moreover, the Republican Party had captured Congress and the presidency repeatedly since 1980 on a platform inveighing against government regulation of all sorts. Less regulation by the FDA would probably mean letting more drugs on the market faster.

One biotech executive from the Northeast noted that there are probably a lot more voters who are cancer patients and organized in groups to press for new drugs, than voters in organized groups worried about drugs already on the market with scary side effects. "A commissioner [of the FDA]," he said, "is going to be responding to patient advocacy groups, industry advocacy groups, and politicians saying, 'We've got a lot of cancer patients out there and they vote, and there's a lot of new products out there. You've got to find a way to shake up the bureaucracy so we can get things going faster.'" Jere Goyan, the former commissioner, also thinks that the consumers pushing for faster approval have more influence now than in his day, because people are simply more aware of the drugs in the pipeline.

However, Fred Smith sees a limitation in the supposed clout of these advocates. Smith should be their natural ally: He is one of the most persistent critics of the FDA from a Type II viewpoint, as president of the Competitive Enterprise Institute (CEI), a Washington, D.C.–based think tank—funded with a lot of drug and tobacco company money—that specializes in studying risk and regulation from a libertarian point of view. The problem, as Smith sees it, is that the advocates do not change the mindset of the FDA; they merely move their own particular drug along. "If it [a disease] becomes politically salient like AIDS, or some cancers, it puts them in front of the line of other drugs." So then some other drug that is not as well connected politically is delayed.

For both Type I and Type II activists, the key is how well they can grab public attention. It works just like any other political or marketing campaign.

Breast cancer survivors were the first big Type II group to follow the path carved by the AIDS activists. They never were quite as aggressive; they did not go around trashing booths at industry conferences or stringing up the FDA commissioner in effigy. "Cancer advocates tend to be a little more polite," demurred Nancy Roach. Still, sheer numbers made them a formidable force. Breast cancer is one of the four most common types of cancer, and 182,000 women are diagnosed each year, according to the National Breast Cancer Foundation, Inc. The activists learned to push the FDA, the National Institutes of Health, and Congress for more trials of potential treatments, at one point in 2004, there were fully 300 breast cancer trials under way. Probably most important, they lobbied for a declaration that mammograms should be part of regular check-ups for women over 40, which is the only way insurance would cover the cost. With their pink ribbons and their fund-raising Making Strides Against Breast Cancer walks, "they were able to place this condition high up there as the Number One health care concern of women," said Eileen Crowley, the publicist—even though breast cancer is not, in fact, the Number One killer of women. (Heart disease is.)

So breast cancer had clout because of its savvy use of publicity and its numbers. As Carpenter of Harvard pointed out, however, size does not always matter. Consider asthma versus arthritis. "By just about any measure of public health," he wrote in the same *Health Affairs* piece, "asthma is a more severe problem in the United States than arthritis." Nine times as many people died of asthma and related illnesses than died of arthritis in the 1990s, he reported. Yet Carpenter clocked nearly twice as many stories about arthritis as asthma in the *Washington Post* and on the TV news—and, not coincidentally, he claimed, the FDA typically approved arthritis drugs one-third faster. He did not speculate on the reason arthritis gets so much disproportionate attention, but one factor may be that it is a big concern for aging Baby Boomers who want to continue their workouts.

In his *American Journal of Political Science* article, Carpenter even argued that having a lot of victims may not help if that leads to the formation of too many uncoordinated and competing advocacy organizations for the same disease. "Lobbying the FDA for quicker approvals requires collective action among groups. The greater the number of groups, the more difficult such cooperation becomes," he said.

The pharmaceutical companies have their own priorities, which determine which drugs they develop and, to some degree, which patient advocates they pay the most attention to. Start with the fact that they want products that will bring in at least $500 million a year apiece in sales. They will naturally focus on diseases that affect a wide number of people, especially chronic conditions that require customers to keep buying their products day after day for the rest of their lives. With an eye on 76 million greying Baby Boomers, the manufacturers are also looking at drugs to treat the ailments of old age. Hence, they pay special attention to conditions like diabetes, Alzheimer's disease, high cholesterol, high blood pressure, depression, anxiety, allergies, obesity, osteoporosis, and arthritis.

When a medical condition affects a celebrity or someone else with wealth and influence, it opens up several paths to drug development. The celebrity may testify in front of Congress, putting pressure on lawmakers to boost funding for the National Institutes of Health for research into that condition. Since the drug makers often rely on the NIH for the basic science that jump-starts their clinical trials, they are likely to pursue the diseases that the NIH is pursuing. In addition, wealthy patrons sometimes create private foundations to study their disease, and that can lead to partnerships with struggling biotechs. Thus, it became a lot easier for Parkinson's disease advocates to capture attention and funding once actor Michael J. Fox went public about his condition in 1998. The next year Jay Monahan, the husband of "Today" show co-anchor Katie Couric, died of colon cancer. Couric went on to testify to Congress, have her own colon screening televised, and help launch the National Colorectal Cancer Research Alliance, which in turn has developed a new screening test and is researching a genetic cause for the cancer. As far back as the late 1960s and early 1970s, Mary Lasker, the wealthy widow of an advertising executive who died of cancer, marshaled politicians, researchers, government medical officials, patients, and the American Cancer Society to prod President Richard Nixon to declare an official War on Cancer.

Of course, consumer groups' influence is not limited to medicine. It was the clout of tens of thousands of health-food store shoppers, flooding Congress with letters, that blocked the FDA from regulating herbal remedies and dietary supplements in 1994. Similarly, in 1977, diet soda drinkers pressured the FDA to keep saccharin on the market.

On the Type I side, one of the most enduring, if surprising, consumer lobbies seems to be cell phone users worried that the phones cause brain cancer—probably another example of the power of the mass market. The phones operate in a frequency range that produces a kind of radiation called non-ionizing radiofrequency energy, or RF. At high levels, RF can heat living tissue enough to cause biological damage; in microwave ovens, it cooks food. But the levels produced by cell phones are very low, and most studies over the years have found no link between those levels and cancer. A Florida man lost a lawsuit claiming that a cell phone was responsible for his wife's death from brain cancer.

Still, a few hints of a possible cell phone–cancer connection have cropped up. According to the FDA, Australian mice that were genetically altered to be predisposed to lymphoma developed twice as many cases of cancer when exposed to RF energy as mice that were not exposed. In a test published in 1999 of over 200 people in Sweden with brain tumors, mobile phone users with certain types of tumors said they kept their phone on the side of the head where they developed the tumor. Then "Larry King Live" did a segment on cell phones and cancer in August 2000 in which an epidemiologist warned that there was "plenty of reason for concern," and panic swept through the airwaves. The FDA announced that it would participate in studies with the World Health Organization and the Cellular Telecommunications Industry Association.

David Feigal, the head of the FDA's Center for Devices at that time, seemed resigned to the ongoing controversy. "Somebody will find something. When you go back to look, you don't find it again. Cell phones is one issue that we're asked to have ongoing studies of," he said. In fact, scientists grouse that skeptics will be impossible to satisfy on this issue because they are demanding that the FDA prove a negative: How many studies showing no relationship will it take to persuade consumers that no more studies are needed? Anyway, if people are concerned, they can just use headsets where the antenna is not right next to their head. But with millions of cell phone users in the United States, the controversy will not disappear.

Then there's the story of Lotronex. It breaks all the rules of Type I and II.

Lotronex is the GlaxoSmithKline drug for irritable bowel syndrome, or IBS—a gastrointestinal condition, more common in women than men, that causes abdominal pain, diarrhea, and constipation. In November 2000, less than 10 months after it was approved, Lotronex was taken off the market because it was linked to five deaths and scores more cases of potentially fatal colitis, severe constipation, hospitalization, and bowel surgeries. For that reason, it was among the drugs profiled in the Pulitzer Prize–winning *Los Angeles Times* series about the spate of FDA withdrawals. This was also one of the cases where a member of an advisory committee had a controversial relationship with the drug sponsor. So it's a classic Type I, a clear-cut case where a drug caused side effects worse than the condition it treated, and with some industry hanky-panky to boot. The withdrawal in November 2000 should have been the end of the story.

Yet one and a half years later, flooded with letters, e-mails, and phone calls from thousands of patients demanding the drug, the FDA let Lotronex back on the market. The agency added some requirements before prescriptions could be filled, similar to the kind levied on thalidomide and Accutane—doctors must get special training from the manufacturer, explain the risks to patients, and report serious adverse effects to either the FDA or GlaxoSmithKline. Also, all prescriptions must have special stickers. But the agency rejected the protests of the watchdog group Public Citizen that the new safeguards were not strong enough. The IBS patients insisted that Lotronex was the only treatment that worked for them, side effects or not. And they won.

CHAPTER 11

A Political Pawn

It would be bad enough if the only political pressures that the FDA had to withstand were from powerful drug and food companies with multimillion-dollar lobbying budgets, consumer groups that pounce every time a drug shows serious side effects, and consumer groups that want drugs for their disease approved *now*. But there is more. As a federal agency, run by a commissioner who must be confirmed by the Senate, who must go to Congress every year for money, and who must report to another political appointee (the secretary of Health and Human Services), the FDA also has to live in the hardcore world of Democrats and Republicans, Congress and the White House—the world of pure politics.

That means the agency can get caught up in fights that have almost nothing to do with diseases, cures, foods, and side effects. In the mid-1990s, for instance, when congressional Republicans tried to strip the FDA of much of its power to review drugs, it was only partly because of what they saw as the agency's dawdling; the FDA was also just a pawn in the Republicans' broader goal of cutting government down to size. Similarly, the George W. Bush administration's new policy of preventing patients from taking drug makers to court was tied in with its larger campaign against trial lawyers and multimillion-dollar court awards.

Or, the FDA may hit political hot wires because the drug, device, or food that it is considering intersects with a major public concern. As David Feigal of the Center for Devices saw it, that's what happened during the controversy over silicone-filled breast implants: His Center got 22,000 e-mails about the implants, mostly urging rejection. "You can't take the FDA in isolation. There was the [injured] patient reaction, there was the press reaction, there was the [satisfied] implants' users reaction. And then the problem you get into is that it's all caught up—you see the public reaction to the Super Bowl ad." (These words were spoken three days after the notorious half-time show at the 2004 Super Bowl, when the singer Janet Jackson's breast was briefly flashed on TV, prompting a flurry of outraged comments, a congressional hearing, and an equal flurry of televised instant replays.) In other words, Feigal implied, the American public has difficulty dealing with anything that has to do with female breasts. Thus, something that should have been a discussion of a medical procedure became tangled in social attitudes toward sexuality, women's self-image, pornography, and TV censorship.

According to Dr. Arthur Caplan, an ethicist who specializes in health care and also director of the Center for Bioethics at the University of Pennsylvania, anti-abortion members of Congress are constantly asking the FDA to investigate loaded topics like the safety of equipment used in abortions, or whether abortions increase the risk of breast cancer. "The FDA keeps saying, 'There's no evidence of this.' The FDA is being pushed by Congress," he said. Lester Crawford said he did not recall any congressional pressure specifically about abortion while he was either the acting or deputy commissioner but added that "I would not be surprised."

The political pressure can come from Republicans and Democrats alike. Considering the scope of its jurisdiction, from birth control to the purchase of Canadian drugs to genetically engineered tomatoes, how can the FDA avoid bumping up against a minefield now and then? And political views are inevitably part of the mix when the president selects an FDA commissioner—as is the case with any major presidential appointment. For instance, Massachusetts Senator John Kerry, the Democratic nominee for president in 2004, supported reimportation from Canada in his campaign, so it was a good bet he would not have appointed an anti-reimportation FDA chief had he won.

Heavy as the politics has been over the years, however, things took a leap into another dimension when George W. Bush came to Washington, D.C. in 2001.

First, it is important to understand what has historically been taboo in terms of politicking of and by the FDA. Appointments to the advisory committees, for one, are supposed to be based solely on scientific credentials. Only in rare cases, committee members say, were they ever asked about their political leanings or given a litmus tests on controversial issues.

Charles O'Brien was one of those exceptions. O'Brien, the founder of the University of Pennsylvania drug-treatment clinic, said that a staffer from the Health and Human Services Department called him during the Reagan administration to invite him to join an FDA advisory committee. There was just one question, the staffer said: Was O'Brien a Democrat or Republican?

A Democrat, O'Brien confessed.

"That's too bad, doctor," the staffer replied, according to O'Brien. "I have to have a Republican. Do you know any Republican scientists?"

(This was not, O'Brien added, a joke in the way President Reagan quipped to his hospital emergency room team, after he was shot in 1981, "Please tell me that you're all Republicans.")

Lobbying is another area where the FDA theoretically stays above politics. Officially, as a federal agency, it is not supposed to lobby Congress. However—again, as with any agency—there is plenty of seepage at the edges. The FDA openly runs a sizable Office of Legislation that is tasked with answering congressional requests for information, and the line between answering and lobbying can be nearly invisible. "The first few days of a new session of Congress, 300 bills are introduced to amend the Food and Drug Act. It and the tax code are the two most involved sets of regulations," said Gerry Meyer, the former deputy director of the Center for Drugs, who headed the legislative affairs office in the early 1970s, overseeing about two dozen employees. The assistant commissioner for legislation appointed by the Bush administration in 2004, Patrick Ronan, came with years of political experience on the staffs of four Republican representatives and the Republican majority on the House Energy and Commerce Committee.

In addition, nothing stops FDA employees from buttonholing colleagues in other parts of the executive branch or meeting with lobbyists from any outside organization. During the unsuccessful campaign to regulate tobacco in the 1990s, then-Commissioner Kessler had a policy of, as he put it in his book, "surrounding the President with advocates for our initiative," bypassing the standard chain of command through HHS. He sent Jerry Mande to sound out Mande's old boss, Vice President Al Gore; sent another emissary to Dick Morris, one of President Bill Clinton's top political advisors; and even asked a staff attorney to get in touch with a childhood friend who had become a speechwriter for First Lady Hillary Rodham Clinton. After the Supreme Court blocked the FDA's bid for jurisdiction, several members of Congress in 2003 and 2004 introduced bills that would allow the FDA to regulate tobacco. Lester Crawford, who was either the deputy or acting commissioner at the time, insisted that the FDA did not get involved in discussing these bills with Congress—that it couldn't, by law. But FDA personnel did talk to the legislative affairs staff of the American Cancer Society, according to Harmon Eyre, the Cancer Society's chief medical officer, and Wendy Selig, its vice president for legislative affairs. Then the Cancer Society went out and lobbied members of Congress. The Senate ultimately passed one of the measures in July 2004, but it died in the House.

The FDA has apparently skirted even closer to the lobbying line on at least two other occasions. David Theno, the senior vice president who handles regulatory issues for Jack in the Box, said that "we've certainly stood next to them [the FDA] in congresspeople's offices and chatted with aides" to push for regulations that would require testing for the highly dangerous *Listeria monocytogenes* bacteria in food processing plants. The *Listeria* bacteria, which may be found in a wide range of food—meat, seafood, milk, raw vegetables, and dairy products—can infect almost any organ of the body, causing meningitis, eye infections, and death, as well as miscarriages in pregnant women. So fighting *Listeria* clearly seems a worthy cause. But unless the FDA personnel standing next to Theno back in 2000 were silent or were answering factual questions only, those congressional visits sound an awful lot like lobbying. And then in July 2003, according to published reports, Mark McClellan and staffers from the FDA's legislative office spent a week telephoning and meeting with members of the House of Representatives to argue that it would be a bad idea to let Americans reimport cheaper medications from Canada. This was just before the House was due to vote on reimportation.

One of the most popular venues for Washington, D.C. grandstanding is the congressional hearing room. Sooner or later, any government agency that handles any topic of strong public interest can expect to be hauled in front of a congressional committee, whether it's because consumers want to keep diet supplements easily available or because they want the acne drug Accutane to be less available. That comes with the U.S. Treasury paycheck. The FDA, which oversees so much terrain, has a lot of chances to be hauled.

Sometimes the congressional staff really do their digging and the hearings reveal wrongdoing or unheralded information that will help Congress do its job better. And sometimes the hearings just make headlines that help get the lawmakers reelected.

Peter Barton Hutt, the former chief counsel, said he testified in front of Congress 80 times in four years. There have been hearings on Accutane, on Vioxx, on silicone-filled breast implants, on ImClone and the cancer drug Erbitux of Martha Stewart fame, and on the Republican proposals to cut back the FDA's regulatory authority in 1996. Tobacco alone rated three sessions, and a House subcommittee held two separate hearings on the issue of antidepressants and teenage suicide in September 2004 after learning about the staff report that the FDA had kept from its advisory committee.

"It's not fun," said Doug Archer, the erstwhile deputy director of the Center for Food Safety.

He should know. Back in the early 1990s, he was the lead witness at a one-day congressional hearing on the diet supplement L-tryptophan.

In 1990 the FDA began to hear about cases of a very rare problem called eosinophilia-mylagia syndrome, a condition of elevated white blood cells that causes severe muscle pain, nerve damage, swelling, and fatigue. "The New Mexico health department was the first one to warn us that something was going on. They had three cases in one hospital, which was unusual," Archer recalled. Next came reports from Minnesota, Washington, and Oregon.

The first task was for epidemiologists to figure out what the victims had in common. They thought the symptoms might indicate trichinosis; however, few of the victims had eaten pork, which causes that disease.

Then it turned out that everyone affected had taken L-tryptophan, an amino acid that supposedly works as a "natural" tranquilizer. Thousands of people in the United States swore by it for stress, premenstrual syndrome, and sleep problems. But that discovery led to a new dilemma: The patients had used a wide range of brands of these supplements. Did the brands have anything in common?

"I was down in the FDA labs with our chemists every day. The hard part was, each of the brands may have been buying the amino acids from a different chemical supplier, so then it came down to which of the chemical suppliers had been having this problem. We had to ask each manufacturer where you get ingredients from. It got more complicated because they may buy the ingredients from one supplier one month, then switch another month." Using lot numbers from the victims' opened bottles, among other clues, researchers from the FDA, the CDC, and the NIH finally traced the problem back to a supplier in Japan that had recently started using a genetically modified strain of bacteria.

So then yet another debate began: Was the problem just this one supplier, or all versions of the supplement? Many people argued that it was just the one supplier, but the FDA eventually levied a total ban, in part because related problems had arisen with a similar chemical, Archer said. Ultimately, about 1,500 people would be injured by the supplement, and nearly 40 would die.

In light of the deaths, the popularity of the supplement, and the controversy over the ban, it was hardly surprising that Congress decided to investigate. Archer spent a day prepping for the hearing, trying to anticipate the questions he might be hit with. As he remembered a few years later, he was asked, "How did you let this happen?" "Why hadn't you done safety studies?" "Why didn't you keep this off the market?" Victims were there, too. "The best you can hope to do is break even," Archer said afterwards. By "break even," he did not mean that he hoped to change his questioners' minds; he merely meant, "not look foolish, not look like you totally didn't do your job."

Did he succeed? He said he doesn't know. "You think you're explaining something, and they don't seem to be hearing it. We did make the point that we had limitations in our statutory authority." Even then— before the 1994 law restricting the FDA's jurisdiction—supplements were rarely regulated, and if they were, it was under the looser rules of food additives, not drugs.

(In 1992 the FDA would find itself grappling with L-tryptophan again, in a PR disaster, when it raided a clinic in Washington state that was selling the supplement along with other illegal devices and substances. One of the sheriff's deputies that went to the clinic with the FDA inspectors overreacted and drew his gun. Local activists videotaped it, and soon the raid was all over the news, combined with rumors that a contingent of gun-toting FDA agents was trying to take away consumers' vitamins.)

Michael Friedman laughed when I asked him about testifying at congressional hearings, as the acting commissioner. "I'm not sure," he said, "that respect from Congress is something that any public servant should seek or expect."

The change in the political winds blowing on Rockville started less than a week after Inauguration Day 2001, when George W. Bush fired Jane Henney as FDA commissioner and announced that his administration would review her approval of RU-486, the "abortion pill. " It was widely assumed that Henney was fired at the behest of ultraconservative religious groups, for having approved the pill. Bush had spoken against the approval while he was a presidential candidate. Subsequently, when Alastair Wood was being interviewed for the commissioner's position, he was asked his opinion of RU-486.

In any case, Wood did not get the job, and Mark McClellan did. For the supposedly pure-science, above-politics FDA, McClellan seemed the perfect candidate. With his MD from Harvard, PhD in economics from the Massachusetts Institute of Technology, and stints teaching both disciplines at Stanford University, he had brains and credentials that were unassailable. He clearly knew his science. Both industry and consumer groups approved of him. He was charming and charismatic, yet unpretentious. And talk about being apolitical: He had worked in the Treasury Department for Democratic President Bill Clinton.

Of course, McClellan was not apolitical at all. He was, in fact, probably the most political commissioner the FDA had ever seen. No other commissioner had ever had a close relative working right in the White House (McClellan's younger brother Scott, the presidential press secretary). No other commissioner also had a close relative who had been elected to a statewide office and was likely to run for governor (McClellan's mother, Texas state comptroller Carol Keeton Strayhorn). No other commissioner had ever gone out and campaigned for a presidential initiative that was not related to the FDA. Yes, David Kessler had certainly lobbied everyone he could find regarding tobacco, but tobacco had been his own project and it was specifically about FDA jurisdiction. By contrast, months before he was named to head the Medicare-Medicaid office, McClellan was giving speeches touting the Bush plan to add prescription drugs to Medicare, something that did not fall in his bailiwick as the FDA commissioner. He was also one of the last loyal soldiers to back the White House on the debate over reimporting drugs from Canada, even after many Republican legislators and governors pulled away. "One of his objectives is to help the president," Peter Barton Hutt said bluntly.

In his State of the Union speech in January 2004, Bush called for a crackdown on the use of steroids by athletes. Right on cue, less than two months later, McClellan's FDA announced that it was sending warning letters to 23 companies that make products containing androstenedione, or andro, a substance that acts like a steroid.

After he moved to the Medicare-Medicaid office, McClellan continued his political work. During the 2004 election campaign, he used ostensibly nonpartisan announcements about rural health care and federal payments for oncologists to plug the GOP ticket in the battleground state of Iowa and also a Republican House candidate in Georgia. To reassure the public about supplies of the flu vaccine, he just happened to schedule his reassurances in two more battleground states, Ohio and Pennsylvania. Not surprisingly, he was on everyone's short list to be promoted to secretary of Health and Human Services, an outright political appointment, even before Tommy Thompson resigned in December 2004. He was passed over only because the White House decided it needed him more where he already was, to oversee the new Medicare prescription drug benefit.

Increasingly, hot-button political considerations related to sex or reproduction—issues like abortion, teenage promiscuity, and stem-cell research—began to seep into FDA decisions. In the fall of 2002 an official at the Center for Biologics asked Dr. Thomas H. Murray if he would be interested in being on the Center's Biological Response Modifiers Advisory Committee. Murray would certainly seem to have the qualifications: He is a PhD with expertise in gene transfer research, reproductive technology, and genomics. In addition, he is also president of The Hastings Center, the think tank specializing in health care ethics run out of a 150-year-old converted boys' school an hour and a half north of Manhattan. Murray said yes, he would like to join the FDA committee. Several other nominees were approved, but not Murray. When he asked why, he says he got an "uninformative" reply.

There were clues, however. During the Clinton Administration, Murray had been a member of a panel on human embryo research for the National Institutes of Health. That panel had written a report recommending that the government help pay for medical research using stem cells from human embryos. Even more controversial was the recommendation that federal funds be spent on cloning human embryos specifically for research purposes, a process known as therapeutic cloning.

Murray could hardly have waded into topics more likely to light up the switchboard at the White House. In August 2001, George W. Bush, in his very first televised speech since Inauguration Day, had announced a policy tightly restricting taxpayer funding of research using human embryonic stem cells: Stem cells, which exist only in very early embryos, ultimately specialize and give rise to all other cells and tissues in the body. Scientists believe they could be used to help treat Parkinson's disease, spinal-cord paralysis, diabetes, and possibly Alzheimer's disease and some forms of blindness. Under Bush's new policy, however, federal money could be allocated only for work on the limited number of stem cell lines that already existed, not for research on any new lines that might be created from that day forward. In addition, a Council on Bioethics appointed by Bush issued a paper condemning all human cloning, whether for reproduction or for research.

To many of the political and religious conservatives who form a crucial bloc in the Republican Party, embryonic stem cell research and therapeutic cloning are akin to abortion, because they involve the intentional destruction of a human embryo. And abortion, to these critics, is akin to murder. Other people in both parties do not object to embryonic stem cell research but draw the line at research cloning, which they see as going too far in playing God with human DNA and opening the door to cloning for the purpose of reproduction. Virtually no one in mainstream science or politics advocates reproductive cloning.

So maybe, Murray thought, he had been rejected for the FDA committee because of his work on the NIH panel. Or maybe it was just the stigma of having been a Clinton appointee. Or maybe it was an article he had written in *The American Prospect* in September 2001 criticizing Bush's decision on stem cells.

Meanwhile, the Bush administration was eager to make a different appointment to another FDA advisory committee. It wanted to seat Dr. W. David Hager, a controversial Kentucky obstetrician-gynecologist, professor, and Christian fundamentalist, as chairman of the Reproductive Health Drugs committee—the panel that, among other things, had recommended approving RU-486. Hager had helped the Christian Medical Association compose a petition objecting to the pill. He had also written a couple of books—one of them entitled *As Jesus Cared for Women: Restoring Women Then and Now*—that advocate Bible reading and prayer as remedies for conditions like headaches and premenstrual syndrome. Reportedly, he refused to prescribe contraceptives for women patients who were not married. As word of this potential appointment leaked out in autumn 2002 and a number of public interest groups protested, including Planned Parenthood and the National Organization for Women, the White House backtracked a little. It named Hager as a committee member but not chairman.

A year later, the reproductive health committee, along with the Nonprescription Drugs Advisory Committee, would take up one of the most political issues ever to hit the FDA—the morning-after pill known as Plan B. If taken within three days of intercourse, the pill enables women to avoid becoming pregnant, probably by interfering with ovulation (though no one is quite sure exactly how it works). While the drug had been available by prescription since 1999, now the committee was considering whether women should be able to get it over the counter, without going to a doctor first.

About three dozen people showed up to testify at a public hearing at the Hilton hotel in Gaithersburg, Maryland, in December 2003, and it was clear from the tension and the questions that this was no ordinary advisory committee meeting—not even an ordinarily controversial, crowded, and heated meeting. Opponents like Hager worried that making Plan B so easily available would encourage teenage sex. There were also concerns that the way it worked was too much like abortion. One speaker fretted that if no prescription were required, a nine-year-old could go to the drugstore and buy the pill.

Yes, a supporter replied, but nine-year-olds do not usually menstruate or get pregnant.

"What we heard about today," Hager said, "was frequently about individuals who did not want to take responsibility for their actions and wanted a medication to relieve those consequences."

The problem is, all those are political and sociological arguments. And advisory committee deliberations are supposed to be about science; after all, the FDA has taken the stand that it makes its decisions only on scientific factors—not cost, not ethics, not political trends.

According to the FDA's usual standards, the first considerations for approving a drug are always safety and efficacy. Those obviously were not at issue with Plan B, whose safety and efficacy had presumably been established when it was approved for sale by prescription. So then, in deciding to make a medication available over the counter, the key factor typically is whether the drug is safe enough for a patient to use without a doctor's supervision. Is the medical condition something the patient can self-diagnose? Are the risks and directions clearly spelled out on the label? Can patients medicate themselves without a doctor's help or any special training? Supporters argued that not only were those conditions met, but that a drug with a 72-hour deadline like Plan B by definition needs to be available on the spot, without the delay engendered by waiting until the doctor has time to make an appointment and write a prescription.

The two panels ultimately voted to recommend approval of the non-prescription sale by an overwhelming margin of 23 to 4, and the issue went to the FDA staff for a final decision. That should have led to official approval within a couple of months, because the agency normally follows an advisory committee's lead. In fact, many of the professional staff were ready to approve the application. The main organizations representing obstetricians and gynecologists also backed the over-the-counter use, saying that all the scientific issues had been satisfactorily resolved. But in mid-February the FDA announced that it was delaying a decision for three months, saying it wanted more data about the potential use among teenagers. And in early May the agency said no.

The given reason was that "the sponsor's application contained no data in subjects under 14 years of age and very limited data in adolescents 14 to 16 years old." Therefore, the FDA could not be sure that young girls would understand how to use the pill without a doctor's help—in other words, that the application did not meet the scientific criteria for approving over-the-counter use. The FDA offered the manufacturer, Barr Pharmaceuticals, Inc., two options for resubmitting its application: Either do a new study proving that younger teenagers could understand the labeling, or figure out a way to limit over-the-counter sales to women 16 and older. (About five months later, Barr formally submitted a new application taking the latter route.) "It was a scientific decision," insisted Lester Crawford. Added Janet Woodcock, "We don't base our decisions on pressure."

Almost no one believed that. During the months leading up to the ruling, the FDA had been hit by a barrage of political lobbying simply unprecedented in its history. It wasn't just that interest groups showed up at the advisory committee meeting—that's to be expected. But even after the committee had voted, missives from politicians, religious and social conservatives, and antiabortion activists flooded Woodcock's office, and 49 Republican members of Congress sent a letter to Bush opposing over-the-counter sale. Almost always, they hit on the social and political angle of discouraging teenage sex, not the science. Crawford pointed out that supporters of reproductive rights also lobbied the White House and FDA urging approval; however, they did not lobby nearly as hard. Moreover, in rejecting Plan B, the FDA's top brass overruled its own staff's recommendation—something so rare that officials could dredge up only one other example in the past decade. Coincidentally or not, the announcement came on the same day that Bush spoke at an annual National Day of Prayer ceremony in the White House, attended mainly by evangelical Christians.

Feeding the controversy was the question of just where the buck stopped. Officially it was Steve Galson, the acting head of CDER, who made the decision to overrule the staff. Lester Crawford told me that "I could have overturned Galson" and didn't. But that was a pretty momentous decision for a career bureaucrat like Galson, who had been at the FDA barely three years and was only the "acting" director of CDER, not the permanent one. Before coming to the FDA in May 2001, Galson had worked in a variety of areas at the Environmental Protection Agency, the U.S. Department of Energy, the National Institute for Occupational Safety and Health, and the New York State Health Department, making his way up the Public Health Service to the rank of rear admiral. His specialties had ranged from children's health to refugee emergencies to pesticides and toxic substances, but there was nothing, at least in his résumé, pertaining to reproductive health issues. Personally, too, Galson seems an unlikely sort to make waves—friendly and boyish-looking, with blue eyes and a crop of brown curls that is just starting to thin on top.

So if Galson was only a figurehead (or scapegoat), then who really made the decision—if it was made at the FDA at all? Mark McClellan, the former commissioner, was safely gone by the time of the final announcement, but he was certainly a strong force at the agency during most of the months of deliberations. According to the *Wall Street Journal*, he participated in at least one staff meeting where he spoke out against approval and supported an age restriction. Or Crawford could have played a bigger role than he admits to. Like Galson, he was only "acting" in his job, and he seems the image of a cautious bureaucrat in the way he carefully chooses his words. A native of a small Alabama town, he had run the FDA's Center for Veterinary Medicine for most of the years between 1978 and 1985, then moved on to stints at the Agriculture Department, a trade group for food processors, an association of veterinary colleges, and an independent organization on food policy before returning to the FDA in 2002. Again, there was nothing in his background remotely connected with Washington politics or hot-button issues of abortion and birth control. Still, Crawford is a good enough political player to have been a serious contender for permanent commissioner at least once. (More on that later in this chapter.)

Perhaps the decision was really made at the White House—if not the Bush campaign headquarters. After all, this was a presidential election year, and the Republicans needed to shore up their restive conservative base, which felt Bush had not been sufficiently vocal in opposing gay marriage or abortion, among other things. If this was the case, the FDA was only the messenger.

Michael Greene, the Harvard reproductive biology professor and a "special consultant" with voting rights on the reproductive health committee, told friends about what he called a "surreal" conversation with an FDA staffer, who phoned to alert him about the Plan B decision just before the news broke. As Greene relayed it, in part:

> FDA: We made this decision due to concern for the implications of OTC [over-the-counter] availability of Plan B on the sexual behavior of 14-year-old girls.
>
> Greene: Is this based upon some data?
>
> FDA: No, it's based on the lack of data addressing this issue. There is no "actual use" data to address this issue.
>
> Greene: Can you imagine the response if the sponsor said that they wanted to obtain that data by making Plan B readily available to 14-year-old girls?
>
> FDA: Yes, we realize that there would be some methodological difficulties in trying to obtain that data. But that's not our problem.
>
> Greene: It is likely that Plan B will sell for about $30 per dose. Where do you imagine 14-year-old girls getting the kind of money that it would take to buy repeated doses of Plan B?

FDA: We are not allowed to consider price in our approval decision.

Greene: But you told me that your main concern regards behavioral changes in 14-year-olds. Don't you think that the price of the product will affect behavior?

The reactions to the agency's rejection were as heated as the lobbying. Even before the final announcement came out, when the FDA had merely postponed its decision, Greene, Alastair Wood (the would-be commissioner and a member of the reproductive health panel), and Dr. Jeffrey M. Drazen, editor-in-chief of the super-prestigious *New England Journal of Medicine*, wrote an editorial in the *Journal* in April 2004 warning that the action so far "suggests that the FDA's decision-making process is being influenced by political considerations." "This is the first time in anybody's memory that a delay on a decision was prompted by a political consideration," Greene snapped to me in an interview. After the announcement, 37 members of Congress, including Democrats, Republicans, and one Independent, sent the FDA a letter condemning its move as "clearly based on right-wing ideology rather than sound science." An editorial in the official journal of the American College of Obstetricians and Gynecologists joined the chorus of criticism. Adding further support to those who favored the application, the Canadian government less than two weeks later declared that it intended to allow the sale over-the-counter. By apparently giving in to politics, "we've simply squandered the trust we have built in the process," Wood said to me. "That trust will be hard to rebuild."

It wasn't just abortion, and it wasn't just the FDA that felt the new, more partisan White House hammer. The political considerations that had ended Jane Henney's tenure so abruptly began to infect what had previously been strictly scientific decisions throughout the government.

In February 2004, a group of 60 prominent scientists—including 20 Nobel laureates plus former government officials from both parties—accused the Bush administration of politicizing scientific research on issues ranging from global warming to arms control to condom use. The scientists claimed the administration censored reports it did not like, manipulated the membership of scientific panels, misrepresented the finding of mainstream scientists, gave business undue influence on advisory committees, and ignored outside experts. As they wrote in a 38-page paper, "the Bush administration has suppressed or distorted the scientific analyses of federal agencies to bring these results in line with administration policy." The report was issued by an advocacy organization, the Union of Concerned Scientists, that generally takes up liberal causes and had long criticized Bush's policies. The White House science adviser, Dr. John H. Marburger III, dismissed the criticisms as "inaccurate" and in some cases "preposterous."

But more examples cropped up. A prominent cell biologist claimed she was kicked off the President's Council on Bioethics for disagreeing with some of its stands, particularly the issue of whether adult stem cells—which abortion opponents don't object to—can be as useful as those from embryos. Several groups of health professionals protested that the administration put inaccurate information about birth control and AIDS on government Web sites and in sex education programs. In July the Union of Concerned Scientists came out with a follow-up report charging that nominees for NIH advisory panels were vetted for political reasons—including being asked whether they had voted for Bush. A biologist resigned from the National Marine Fisheries Service after his recommendations on saving endangered salmon were ignored, saying that "this administration has considerably set back the public's understanding of science." The National Academy of Sciences even held an all-day hearing on how politics was getting dragged into the previously off-limits realm of advisory committee appointments.

All this was in addition to the more traditional political influence wielded by the pharmaceutical industry and described in Chapter 8, which tends to be stronger when Republicans control Congress or the White House. There, too, politics was reaching unprecedented heights. As the *New York Times* put it, "Some analysts argue that the Bush administration has introduced rules favoring industry with a dedication unmatched in modern times."

By 2004, the politicization of science in general, and stem cell research in particular, had even become an issue in the presidential campaign. At the Democratic convention that summer, President Reagan's son Ron crossed party lines to speak in favor of stem cell research, Senator Kerry, the nominee, talked in his acceptance speech about needing "a president who believes in science, so we can unleash the wonders of discovery like stem cell research to treat illness and save millions of lives."

The most famous example of how politics and drug industry clout may have influenced FDA decisions is the case of the innovative cancer drug Erbitux, its manufacturer ImClone Systems, and Martha Stewart.

Separating the rumors from the truth in this complex story is not easy. Most attention has focused on the first half of the story, the FDA's initial rejection of the drug. But the real mystery—and significance—actually lie in the second half, the FDA's about-face.

From the start, Erbitux drew a lot of notice. That was partly because of the star-studded connections of Samuel D. Waksal, the CEO of ImClone, who had pals in politics, on Wall Street, and in the arts, including Stewart. Moreover, Erbitux was seen as the pioneer in a whole new approach to treating cancer. Traditional treatments like chemotherapy and radiation hurl a torrent of powerful ammunition that ends up hitting both healthy and malignant cells, causing severe side effects such as nausea and hair loss. Erbitux, however, homes in on a narrow target, blocking a molecule on the surface of some cancer cells that spurs the cells to divide. (Iressa—the cancer drug that AstraZeneca gave to thousands of patients who then lobbied the FDA for approval—takes a similar approach, but it was about a year behind Erbitux in development.)

Erbitux does not "cure" colon or rectal cancer; it did not even extend patients' lives significantly in clinical trials. Oncology drugs rarely do. But measured by the yardstick generally used for cancer treatments—how well they shrink tumors—Erbitux seemed promising. ImClone applied to the FDA based mainly on a trial of 120 patients in advanced stages of cancer that showed that Erbitux, when taken along with chemotherapy, shrank tumors by at least half their size in 22.5 percent of the participants. The FDA gave it the fast-track approval status typically granted to cancer and other life-saving drugs. Sam Waksal talked its promise up to investors, and Bristol-Myers Squibb Company, which had been a pioneer in cancer research, signed a deal to pay $2 billion, in stages, for approximately 20 percent of ImClone.

Then in December 2001 the FDA refused to accept the drug application, saying that important safety and efficacy data were missing, the trials were too small to be meaningful, and ImClone had not done enough of the standard Phase III comparisons involving chemotherapy alone, Erbitux alone, and Erbitux and chemotherapy combined. Even worse, the FDA said it had repeatedly warned ImClone about that last point (a contention that ImClone denied). And the FDA gave the firm the bad news in an extraordinarily long, nine-page refusal-to-file letter. Tipped off ahead of time about the pending refusal, Waksal tried to dump all his stock and advised his father and daughter to do the same, before the news became public and the stock price inevitably fell. Soon after, Martha Stewart sold nearly 4,000 shares.

Over the next two years, ImClone went back to its German partner Merck KGaA (no relation to the U.S. Merck), conducted new and larger trials with control groups, dug up some of the missing data, and resubmitted the application. The test results were virtually the same as before; tumors shrank in 22.9 percent of patients on the Erbitux-chemo regimen. In February 2004, the FDA gave the application a green light. Meanwhile, Waksal pleaded guilty to insider trading and went to prison. Martha Stewart was convicted of lying to investigators about her own stock sales and also went to prison.

So what changed over the two years to justify denying patients the treatment and ordering Waksal and Stewart into the slammer? Clearly, not the drug itself. Nevertheless, FDA officials insist that they had no choice but to reject Erbitux the first time, and that both their rejection and then approval were based purely on scientific data. In the original application, "they [ImClone] already knew that the studies they were submitting might not be acceptable. The response [in the clinical trial results] wasn't verifiable," said Bob Temple, the FDA's associate director of medical policy. Only with the second application, he continued, "you had actual evidence that it worked."

"We're required by law to have evidence that the drug works. We can't start filing or approving drugs that don't meet the standards, or people will get hurt," Janet Woodcock noted, in a separate interview.

Other drug companies by and large have backed the FDA's position regarding data, and almost no one defends ImClone's methodology. Even an executive from Bristol-Myers Squibb told a congressional hearing in 2002 that the FDA was justified in rejecting the first application. As one biotech CEO—who is not working on cancer treatment—said to me, "Every scientific person believed the drug was active. There was a tremendous amount of enthusiasm. The problem was, they rolled a Phase II [trial] and tried to make it into a Phase III. If the FDA lowers their standards for ImClone on what the trial design looks like, do they have to lower it for everyone else?"

But many members of Congress angrily faulted the FDA for mishandling the application and misleading ImClone. Did the agency give ImClone sufficient advance warning? Why did it grant fast-track status if the plans for Phase III trials were so lousy and too small? The House of Representatives' Subcommittee on Oversight and Investigations held two hearings on the topic in 2002.

However clumsy or not the initial rejection may have been, there may have been more at work than pure science in the final acceptance.

When Erbitux first came to the FDA, it was assigned to the Center for Biologics because it is a genetically engineered version of a mouse antibody—that is, a biological product, rather than a chemical. At CBER, it was placed in the Office of Therapeutics Research and Review, which handled so-called therapeutic proteins, or biological drugs (as opposed to, say, vaccines or tissue products).

With the FDA under tremendous pressure from Congress and drug makers to push approvals faster, Biologics has traditionally been considered slower and less friendly to industry than Drugs. (To give a couple of examples: According to FDA statistics, in 2003 the median review time for priority products at Biologics was over a year, compared with just 7.7 months at Drugs. The Drugs Center managed to maintain that pace, moreover, while also churning out a lot more approvals annually—66 NDAs in 2001, 78 in 2002, and 72 in 2003, compared with 16, 21, and 22 biologics license applications, respectively, for CBER. Jesse Goodman, CBER's director, bristles at those sorts of comparisons, arguing that "we deal with a lot of very challenging products never found before.")

By the time Erbitux returned to the FDA for its second try, almost the entire office of therapeutic proteins and its roughly 200 reviewers—that is, the heart and soul of biologic drug review—had been moved to the more industry-friendly terrain of Drugs.

The head of the Drugs Center's Division of Oncology Drug Products was Richard Pazdur. He has a mixed reputation, considered a first-class scientist though often abrasive. But the key thing to remember is that he is not an ordinary bureaucrat.

During the long interregnum after Jane Henney was fired, Pazdur had been under consideration by the Bush White House to be appointed FDA commissioner. Moreover, it was Pazdur who in December 2001 alerted a lawyer-lobbyist for Bristol-Myers that the FDA was not going to accept the Erbitux application. According to press reports, that lobbyist told three Bristol-Myers executives, who told Sam Waksal's brother, Harlan, who then told Sam, thus presumably setting in motion the inside trading.

Pazdur is probably best known for advocating faster drug reviews. After Erbitux was first turned down, he testified in front of the House Oversight and Investigations subcommittee on June 13, 2002, about "a high degree of inconsistency" in the way CBER and CDER operate, especially the way they communicate with drug companies—strongly implying that his Center's approach was more sensitive to companies' public reputations. For instance, he said, if his reviewers saw that an application was so badly flawed that it could not even be reviewed—like Erbitux's—they might call up the manufacturer to give it a chance to withdraw the application quietly, rather than be handed a formal refusal-to-file letter.

On top of all that, Pazdur had been a professor and administrator at the M. D. Anderson Cancer Center from 1988 to 1999. That might not seem surprising, since the Anderson Center is a prestigious cancer research facility. (Antigenics, in fact, conducted some of its clinical trials there.) But what makes this part of Pazdur's history significant in some people's eyes is that both Erbitux and the Bush family also have important connections with the Anderson center—and it was George W. Bush who would decide whether Pazdur became FDA commissioner. The Bushes' ties to M. D. Anderson are deep and long-standing: Former President George H.W. Bush and his wife Barbara have been on the advisory Board of Visitors since 1977. Bush was chairman from 2001 to 2003. The couple funded a $1.35 million endowment for research. A special clinic for children and adolescents is named for their daughter Robin, who died of leukemia. The former president even celebrated his eightieth birthday with a $50 million fundraising drive at the center in 2004. In addition, at least two members of the first Bush Cabinet, James A. Baker III and Robert A. Mosbacher Sr., have been on the Anderson board. Meanwhile, Dr. John Mendelsohn, the physician who did the original molecular research that led to Erbitux, became president of M. D. Anderson in 1996, in yet another overlap with Pazdur.

And throw one more consideration into the mix—ordinary Big Pharma influence. Even in an industry famous for its campaign contributions and lobbying prowess, ImClone's partner Bristol-Myers stood out. In 2001, the year the Erbitux application was submitted, Bristol-Myers employed more lobbyists than any other pharmaceutical company except Pfizer, according to Public Citizen. In the election cycle just before that, the Center for Responsive Politics listed Bristol-Myers as the industry's second-biggest donor to political action committees, again trailing Pfizer. Sam Waksal, with his wide-ranging friendships, was no slouch either.

Put together all these political and industry cross-connections, CBER's reputation for slowness as compared to CDER, Pazdur's sympathy toward drug companies and faster approvals, the congressional criticism over the way CBER had handled the rejection of Erbitux—and where does it lead? To most observers, it sure looked as though the FDA had caved in to pressure to put Erbitux into the friendlier hands of CDER, then tried to disguise the motivation—or, more generously, make approval easier for future biologic drugs—by transferring the entire category of therapeutic proteins out of the Biologics side. Virtually all the skeptics assumed that the pressure came from the pharmaceutical or biotech industries, although some people also wondered about possible Bush family influence. In one of our interviews, Ira Loss, the financial analyst, described the CBER-CDER transfer as "a political maneuver caused by Erbitux and pressure from Congress." At a House subcommittee hearing on October 10, 2002, then-Congressman Peter Deutsch of Florida outright said to Lester Crawford, "It's widely alleged that the decision to transfer the review of most biological drugs from the Center for Biologics to the Center for Drugs was not originated from either center, but rather was imposed by the department at the behest of the biotech drug industry."

Later, in an e-mail interview, Deutsch declared, "Given the testimony we'd heard, it seemed like Erbitux was the catalyst."

Crawford's role stirs more spice into the mix. He was in charge of the FDA during the time when Erbitux was reconsidered and the decision to transfer therapeutic proteins was made, and he has said the transfer decision was his alone. But he was also a bit player on the political scene. In late 2001 the scuttlebutt was that he would be named FDA commissioner, thus apparently beating out Richard Pazdur. His would-be boss, Health and Human Services Secretary Tommy Thompson, publicly backed him for the job. However, Crawford, like Pazdur, failed to get the nod. The main theories circulating in Washington and Rockville are that administration brass were annoyed with Thompson for being too hasty in pushing Crawford before getting formal White House approval, or that the White House wanted an MD while Crawford is "only" a veterinarian. In addition, some consumer groups were worried about his ties to the food-processing industry. So Crawford became acting commissioner until Mark McClellan was appointed, then deputy commissioner, and then, after McClellan left to run Medicare and Medicaid, acting commissioner again—and once more, rumored as a top contender for the permanent job.

At the subcommittee hearing in October 2002, Crawford admitted that he and some FDA staffers at various times discussed the transfer idea, or "the importance of achieving consistency at FDA," with industry officials and other unspecified "outside organizations."

However, Crawford and other top FDA officials deny on the record that politics, industry pressure, or Erbitux had anything to do with the transfer of therapeutic proteins. As Crawford explained things in our interview, he decided to shift the therapeutic proteins unit because that fit in with his overall plan to consolidate agency operations. Having biologic and chemical drugs together makes sense, he continued, because their similarities are so much stronger than their differences—that is, the fact that they are all drugs is more important than the fact that some of those drugs are biologically based and some are chemical. "I look at the functions, how they perform. It is immaterial to me where they come from. You would review something as an antibiotic, not a chemical antibiotic or a biological antibiotic. The tests are the same." Reinforcing that argument, in July 2004, two months after our interview, he announced plans to create a single Office of Oncology Drug Products that would bring together all drugs and therapeutic biologics "used to diagnose, treat, and prevent cancer" and, in the process, raise oncology's status in the FDA bureaucracy. The reason he put all the chemical and biologic drugs into the Drugs center rather than Biologics, Crawford added, is that CDER "had more people, more experience with reviewing these drugs, more expertise."

There are certainly reasonable arguments to be made for assigning Erbitux-type drugs to either jurisdiction. On the pro-drugs side, as Crawford said, it makes sense for all drugs to be housed together by disease, not method of manufacture, because that is how drug companies and patients see them. If some cancer treatments are in CDER and others are in CBER, "there's an inconsistency that totally confounded drug companies, which often have products in both Centers," said Carl Peck, the former head of the Drugs Center.

However, you could just as well argue that all biologic drugs should be kept under one jurisdiction, no matter what disease they treat, because biologics are similar to each other and very different from chemical drugs in the way they are manufactured and in their composition. Their manufacturing process is much more complex, and their composition is much more volatile. A biologic cancer drug, in other words, has more in common with its cousins from the biologic side—such as cell and gene therapy, which stayed in CBER—than its cancer cousins. As Robert Essner, the chief executive of the big drug company Wyeth, described biologics in one interview: "Like live organisms, they mutate and evolve in ways that are not always predictable." It is therefore more important to have biologic cancer drugs overseen by reviewers who understand biologic processes, even if they are not experts in cancer. Moreover, the FDA had tried before to combine Biologics and Drugs, and the oil and water had never mixed.

And if the transfer was supposed to make drug reviews more efficient, it may have backfired in the case of Antigenics. This was the reorganization, after all, that swept away the reviewers who had handled Antigenics' vaccine Oncophage, while leaving the vaccine itself behind in CBER, forcing Antigenics to start from scratch with a new crop of reviewers and possibly triggering the clinical hold.

Crawford just smiled when I sketched the argument about political influence and the Pazdur-Bush-Anderson suspicions. He pointed out that he was not at the FDA when Erbitux was first turned away and said he had never met Pazdur until a couple of years later. (Those statements may be true, but they are both irrelevant to the controversy. The accusations of political and industry pressure do not concern the first rejection of Erbitux, but rather, Crawford's subsequent decision to transfer jurisdiction over therapeutic proteins. Furthermore, Crawford did not have to know Pazdur personally in order to feel that pressure.) Anyway, it's a pretty big stretch to connect a drug approval to the far-from-earth-shattering coincidence that a cancer specialist and a Texas political family both have ties to a major cancer center in Texas.

"The Bush family," Crawford added, in his conversation with me, "I'm sure has other things to worry about."

Beyond the industry influence, beyond the possible connections to Erbitux or the Bush family, the transfer of the biologics unit was controversial also because of the abrupt and somewhat mysterious way in which it was done—which only fed the rumor mill even more. In the summer of 2002, six months after Erbitux was first rejected, Crawford asked Kathy Zoon, then the head of CBER, whether biological therapeutics ought to be regulated by the Drugs Center. Zoon wrote a memo outlining why she thought the transfer was a bad idea, turned it in, and, she said, never heard back. When Jay Siegel, the head of the therapeutics drug office, returned from a long vacation in the south of Spain, Zoon informed him about the memo, and he, too, thought that "it sounded like a dead issue." A few weeks later, Zoon said, "I was called into a meeting and told there was the decision." The biological therapeutic drugs would be transferred the following June.

Zoon spoke out publicly against the decision, but all she succeeded in doing was burning her own career bridges. In December 2002 she announced her resignation from the FDA and moved to a job as principal deputy director of the Center for Cancer Research at the NIH, where she had begun her career nearly 30 years before. More quietly, Siegel took his 20-year pension and headed to Centocor in Pennsylvania. The rest of the CBER staff were just as anxious. They were also furious at Pazdur for airing the agency's turf battles in public. Many of them even rang up congressional offices, which is an extraordinary step for a lower-level bureaucrat to take. By one informal employee survey, nearly three-quarters of the reviewers affected by the transfer considered quitting the agency in the first days after the decision was announced, although most were partly reassured after Janet Woodcock came to speak with them, and in the end only about one-quarter left. (No one has calculated exactly how many people the agency lost as a result of the move, because some staffers switched to other offices within Biologics, some went to other branches of the FDA, some quit due to unrelated factors, and some were still job-hunting a year later.)

"The reason for the transfer was not made clear or justified based on the performance of CBER or what we accomplished," Zoon declared, as I interviewed her in her new office, a year after she left. "I'm not saying it's bad. Without understanding why this was done, I had problems accepting that it was the right thing to do. I try to keep their spirits up [among the people still at the center]. When you have people who love you, when you tear people apart, it's not very good." Her face reddened and her eyes started to tear—for the third time in a one-hour interview. "It's difficult. I don't want to speak badly of anyone."

The story of Erbitux, then, is a lot more than the story of an innovative drug. It is even more than the story of how Martha Stewart went to prison, or how the drug industry influences the FDA. There is yet a fourth installment to the saga. The next chapter goes into it in more detail, but the upshot is this: If Erbitux was in fact the reason for the interdepartmental shuffle, then all the tussle over the drug may hurt the FDA's ability to keep up with exploding changes in science—which means, ironically, that Erbitux will actually impede the FDA's ability to approve future Erbituxes.

CHAPTER 12

FDA and DNA

It takes about ten minutes to drive through the National Institutes of Health campus in Bethesda, Maryland. As you meander past towering red-brick buildings of varying architectural styles, spreading lawns, clumps of trees, and an occasional building of concrete or brown brick, it is impossible to tell at first glance which structures are for the NIH and which are for the FDA's Center for Biologics Evaluation and Research. That is hardly surprising. Until 1972, the biological products regulated by CBER, including vaccines, serums, and blood, were part of the NIH. In many staffers' minds, CBER still is.

"There's been this friction between Biologics and Drugs from time immemorial," said Tom Garvey, the former cardio-renal reviewer (who worked in Drugs). If the pharmaceutical industry complains that Biologics reviewers are slower and less cooperative than their counterparts in Drugs, many Biologics scientists have traditionally seen themselves as a higher, purer breed. Their mandate is older, dating back to the 1902 Biologics Control Act, four years before the FDA's 1906 Food and Drug Act. Their products, made from living sources like microorganisms or human cells, tend to be more individualized and finicky, subject to unexpected variations during production, compared with the assembly-line manufacture of chemical drugs. (That became dramatically apparent in the fall of 2004, when the British factory making flu vaccine had to be shut down because of contamination.) Their office was always less hierarchical and more open to people without medical degrees. What is now CBER started out as the Division of Biological Standards in the NIH, and because of that history Biologics staff considered themselves scientists, not paper-pushers; they did original work at the NIH alongside some of the leading minds in biology, rather than merely putting check marks in the boxes on some drug company's application. They worked, moreover, in real labs, not in the notoriously stifling "rabbit warrens" of CDER reviewers. "They saw the drug people as not the same caliber of scientist," said Gerry Meyer, the former deputy CDER director.

CBER's self-image is epitomized by the almost iconic figures of Dr. Henry M. Meyer Jr. and Dr. Paul D. Parkman, two Biologics scientists who in the 1960s developed a rubella (German measles) vaccine from monkey cells that would be widely used in the United States and credited with nearly eliminating the disease. Biologics employees did not just review other people's drugs; they created their own.

Unfortunately, creating products that you are also supposed to be regulating can lead to conflicts of interest. In the mid-1960s the Division of Biological Standards approved the Meyer-Parkman vaccine, which was then marketed by Merck, and rejected a competing vaccine made from human cell lines that supposedly had fewer side effects and that was used in Europe. It was partly because of the controversy that ensued that Biological Standards was transferred out of the NIH and into the FDA in 1972 to become the Bureau of Biologics (inadvertently transferring college intern Phil Noguchi, who would later oversee Antigenics' vaccine application).

The transfer was more theoretical than real, however. "They didn't want to come," Lester Crawford said. Most of the Biologics staff stayed on the NIH campus and continued conducting research, while FDA head-quarters and the Bureau of Drugs were based in the Rockville building a few miles away.

One way to make sure Biologics was firmly implanted into the FDA would be to coordinate it more closely with Drugs. The FDA first tried to do that in 1982, but old-timers say it was less for philosophical reasons and more because the agency could not find anyone to run the Bureau of Drugs. So the two specialties were combined into a new FDA National Center for Drugs and Biologics under the aegis of Henry Meyer—the same Meyer who had helped create the controversial rubella vaccine. The Drugs-Biologics combination lasted only a few years, however. The two divisions stayed physically, psychologically, and even functionally separate. During factory inspections, for instance, one set of field officers did the job for drugs and devices, while Biologics sent its own team. As the AIDS crisis started to overwhelm the FDA, Commissioner Frank Young finally annulled the shotgun marriage in 1987 and separated the two functions again, creating two units with yet a new set of names—the current CDER and CBER. Carl Peck, the first director of the new drugs unit, said he was "thrilled" at the separation because "I knew these cultures were so fundamentally different."

The most important difference would prove to be their approach to research.

When Kathy Zoon arrived at what was then the FDA's Bureau of Biologics as a staff fellow in 1980, "the bureau had a nice program of research and review," carried over from its days at the NIH. At the peak, she said, there were about 250 reviewer-researchers spending half their time analyzing biologic product applications and half-time doing their own research. In addition, several hundred staffers worked solely on applications.

Petite and perky, with a blonde page-boy haircut and glasses, Zoon could pass for the shorter, thinner sister of the actress Meg Ryan. After earning a PhD in biochemistry from Johns Hopkins University, she spent five years doing postdoctoral research on a type of human interferon at the NIH before switching to the FDA. It was almost as though she had never changed jobs: At the FDA she continued her research on interferon, a highly touted protein that, because of its ability to inhibit viral growth, has been used in treatments for Hepatitis C and several forms of cancer. As Zoon sees it, her story shows the value of letting Biologics staff do hands-on research at the FDA. Her work sequencing interferon, she said, "was instrumental in developing guidance to manufacturers."

It also shows the depth of CBER staffers' feelings about their research. The discussion of CBER's scientific tradition was one of several points in our interview when Zoon had to stop, when her face got red, her eyes teared up, and she looked at me with a twisted smile, but she did not quite cry. "To a certain degree, we've tried to preserve that culture, but financially it's hard to do. The ability to really regulate new products of technology and vaccines requires an understanding of the science. I don't think that's valued as much by the FDA today."

In science there are two main types of research. Basic or pure research delves into questions of the fundamental mechanism of whatever is being studied, without necessarily having a goal in mind, while applied research is usually more narrowly focused, seeking a practical result. Take AIDS, for example: A university professor doing basic research might investigate the structure of the HIV virus that causes AIDS. A drug company bench scientist doing applied research would take that basic research and look for a means to block the virus.

So in talking about whether the FDA does or should conduct research, it is important to distinguish between the types. Contrary to what many Americans think, FDA staffers do not actually discover drugs (Meyer and Parkman excepted). However, they do undertake a regulatory form of applied research fairly often, at CDER as well as CBER. To continue with the HIV/AIDS example, the agency might develop standards for testing the sensitivity and specificity of HIV diagnostic kits, then use those standards in reviewing kits that were submitted for approval. What Biologics uniquely brought with it from the NIH was a tradition of doing the other kind of research.

Another fundamental aspect of science also has to be kept in mind. Drugs and medical research are getting ever more complex. Back in the 1970s, most medicines were derived from natural microorganisms, discovered by painstakingly analyzing, testing and tweaking samples of soil, sludge, mold, ground-up plants, and other exotic bits of nature. The resulting drugs were mass market products, one-size-fits-all drugs for all people with high cholesterol or all people with arthritis. They were aimed at the broadest possible audience in order to bring in the drug companies' goal of $500 million or more in sales each year. But the advent of genetic engineering in the 1980s, the decoding of the human genome in 2000, and other advanced techniques of biotechnology opened the door to much more complicated and finely targeted molecules, both chemical and biological. In theory, the new disciplines of genomics and proteomics (the study of proteins) could draw a veritable road map to the causes of disease. By comparing the genetic sequences in patients who have a particular disease with those who do not, so the assumption goes, researchers can look for the precise mutation that marks the presence of the disease. Then they can craft a molecule that will latch onto a receptor on the trouble-making cell, fiddle with its function, and halt the progress of the disease— or, alternatively, spur a cell to churn out more of a beneficial protein. They should even be able to target their molecules to the smallest subset of patients with a particular strain of the disease—a torrent of Erbituxes and Iressas and Oncophages. And if the traditional Big Pharma companies were too bureaucratic to move quickly to take advantage of the new scientific discoveries, or if the targeted subsets of patients were too small to be a profitable market, a horde of versatile biotech firms would spring up to fill the vacuum.

In light of these changes in the drugs that the FDA will be reviewing, many people—in the industry as well as at CBER—say that it is more important than ever for Biologics staffers to maintain their tradition of research. For starters, they say it helps in attracting top scientists who will also be courted by higher-paying drug companies and universities. Then, because they understand the science, the reviewer-researchers can move faster in evaluating applications for innovative drugs and will be more willing to take risks. "You have people who are doing basic and applied research on the mechanisms of drug action, the biology of drug effectiveness, the toxicology—who can step away from their lab bench and feel confident that they not only are knowledgeable of what industry is doing, but are doing equivalent things," said Mark Novitch, the FDA's acting commissioner in the early 1980s. Boyd Clarke, the CEO of the biotech Neose, spoke eagerly about how "one is more likely to attract and retain high-quality staff in the reviewers' office of CBER if they have the opportunity to do at least some basic research. Reviewers that are doing their own work on the cutting edge of science are also more likely to be responsive to the science of innovative products." It was the same feeling of doing real science that persuaded Phil Noguchi to stay at the FDA even after his internship ended. After all, it is the Center for Biologics Evaluation and *Research*. The "R" in its name should mean something, shouldn't it?

Not only that, but to make sure the staffers are not wasting their time on ivory-tower speculation, "each researcher is required, annually, to describe how each major effort contributes to the FDA mission," noted Jay Siegel, the erstwhile director of therapeutic proteins review under Zoon. The information is evaluated by both senior managers and outside experts, he continued. "Some of the research may seem more basic, some more directly product-related, but all are deemed critical to mission."

As the senior director of regulatory affairs at Antigenics, Taylor Burtis has seen the difference that a reviewer with research experience can make. One such time was in 1998, when she was doing some follow-up studies at Genentech on a monoclonal antibody product that had been on the market for a year. Normally, she explained, she might have used 14 assays, or lab tests, in her studies. But she was able to persuade her CBER reviewer that only seven were necessary in that particular case because "the other seven were either redundant or didn't produce information." She estimated that this shortcut saved Genentech "well over" $2,700 a year. And the reason the CBER reviewer could understand her point, Burtis said, is that he had done his own research on cell immunology.

By contrast, Burtis went on, "When I'm dealing with people who haven't run assays, they may not know to ask the proper questions. It's going to make people [reviewers] cautious about putting their name on a product. There's going to be more box-checking. They're not going to have the science to say 'okay.'"

Jay Siegel gave another example. In the mid-1990s there was a flurry of interest in xenotransplantation, or transplanting of animal cells and organs into humans as possible replacement parts. Researchers in industry and private labs were using a specially bred type of pig because the organs were the right size and the animals would not be too expensive. But when they began experiments with liver and pancreatic cells, they discovered a porcine virus that could infect human cells. Luckily, an expert on this virus was working at CBER. With her guidance, the Biologics Center was able to analyze samples from patients who had been in the trials. "We looked at what human cells could be endangered, what conditions, what would allow that transfer. We put a moratorium on it. Then we put together a collaboration with industry to develop state-of-the-art assays for the products." This is the kind of work—investigating problems in a clinical trial, analyzing cellular function—that a drug company or a research lab would usually do, not the FDA. But because CBER had the scientific expertise, it was able to work with the companies. That inside track into the process would help later if a product ever came up for review. "Industry needs scientists [at the FDA] who understand, instead of going by rote rules that were written five years ago—people who won't say 'no' automatically because they don't know what the risks are," Siegel said.

Not everyone in the worlds of drugs or government agrees that this research tradition is quite so valuable. The hours that the reviewers are spending at the lab bench are hours they could otherwise be devoting to pushing drugs through the review process. Someone also has to pay for all those test tubes, beakers, batches of vaccine, reagents, and other tools. Zoon calculated that it takes $30,000 to $50,000 to keep a lab in supplies for a year, plus the cost of rent and salaries. (The reviewers probably make between $40,000 and $150,000, depending on their rank in the government bureaucracy.) The money could come from only two places: general federal revenue or industry user fees under PDUFA. For all his enthusiasm about the advantages of reviewers who keep up with cutting-edge science, Boyd Clarke noted that "some people in the industry felt that wasn't such a good idea, because what they were supposed to be paying for out of PDUFA was approval in the fastest way. They weren't paying for people to do research."

Other skeptics wonder whether doing research really helps reviewers be more efficient in their day jobs. "What you review at the FDA is clinical data showing safety and efficacy. That's largely statistical. It doesn't have anything to do with understanding how a molecule is created," scoffed one long-time government observer of FDA decision-making who didn't want to be named.

"This is a law enforcement agency. It's not the NIH," Peter Barton Hutt, the FDA counsel-turned-corporate attorney, said dismissively. "With virtually every commissioner in the last 40 years, I have at one point or another had to remind them that it's not a science agency. Its job is not to do research. Its job is to review applications. If you want to win Nobel Prizes, you don't go to the FDA." As for the CBER tradition, he added, "you'll see everybody walking around in a white coat, pretending they're scientists. Nobody else at FDA wore white coats."

Over the years, the FDA has alternately questioned the value of the researcher-reviewer concept and considered expanding it. For instance, in 1974 the agency was accused of caving in to industry pressure. Eleven cardiorenal reviewers who were considered too pro-consumer had been transferred out of their jobs, and Senator Edward Kennedy of Massachusetts chaired a dramatic set of hearings that August. Afterwards, the government commissioned a report by an outside expert, Norman Dorsen of New York University Law School. Among other things, the report called for the FDA to increase its research capability, and the FDA staff followed up with a recommendation to create a National Center of Clinical Pharmacology, Mark Novitch recalled. At one point, the agency even started building some labs. But money was always a problem, and nothing came of it. In any case, none of the other arms of the FDA ever did the kind of scientific work that CBER did, except for a bit of radiological research at Devices.

The fact that Drugs and Biologics take different approaches to research may stem from more than tradition. Arguably, Drugs staffers do not have as great a need to do research, since the small-molecule chemicals they handle are better known and less complicated and volatile. "Because biologics are complex, their mechanism may not always be understood. They tend to be very process-driven. So one needs to understand the product as much as possible and the process by which it is made," Zoon said.

Whatever the reason, because Drugs did not do research, inevitably research was looked on a bit askance. As one former FDA official put it, "The attitude [throughout the agency] was generally that CDER was doing a really good job of making everyone happy with the speed of approvals, and CBER was not. CDER was the flagship. They [CDER] weren't doing research, so why should anyone?"

The upshot is that more than 30 years after Biologics joined the FDA, research remains a major dividing line between it and its sister center. Wistfully, Novitch said, "[Biologics] was a science agency that wasn't averse to regulation. They turned out to have over time what was really a mix of regulatory capability and scientific orientation. I've always admired the way Biologics does that."

In transferring the Office of Therapeutics Research and Review over to Drugs—whatever the real reason, however well or poorly handled—Lester Crawford was also in effect making another effort at melding Biologics into the FDA. In fact, he told me that he actually considered merging CDER and CBER completely but dropped the idea because "it didn't work before." A year later, the new Office of Oncology Drug Products would try to integrate the transferred unit even more closely.

By and large, the biotech industry whose products were most affected by the transfer supported it, at least publicly, hoping that the switch to CDER would magically speed up their drug reviews. Garo Armen of Antigenics said he noticed—happily—that "things are being tightened up. [Under the old system] we were getting one type of formal message from higher-ups, another type of informal message from people we were dealing with. Now it seems like they're speaking with one voice. We prefer that because we know exactly where we stand."

The FDA vowed that this time it would do things right and fully integrate the Biologics employees into CDER, unlike what happened in the patched-together merger of 1982. So the therapeutics staff moved to one of the buildings that housed Drugs, and Steve Galson and Janet Woodcock even gave up their offices to make room. Biotech executives, watching anxiously as Zoon, Siegel, and the flurry of reviewers left, worried about a brain drain. So did some members of Congress, whose offices were barraged with phone calls from anxious CBER staffers. There were, of course, all the inevitable bruised egos and mismatched computer systems that come with any merger and loss of turf. Reviewers who remained at CBER muttered that proportionately too many support staff had been moved along with the therapeutics scientists. Even a year and a half after the transfer, Peter Deutsch, the former congressman who had questioned Lester Crawford at the Erbitux hearing, told me that "I remain concerned that in the course of altering the composition of the agency, they may have reduced its efficacy."

But the biggest potential disruption, and what could hurt the biotech industry most of all, is the future of CBER's tradition of research. Will the former Biologics staff still be encouraged to do research in their new home in CDER, which does not share that tradition? Steve Galson declared, six months after the transfer, that "we have committed to CBER folks that nothing is going to change over a five-year period." Judging from his conversations with former colleagues who were shifted, Jay Siegel warily backed up that assessment, saying, "CDER has been continuing to support their efforts. They are, as they have been for some time, endangered [by tight budgets], but they haven't been dismantled." Phil Noguchi, before he switched out of CBER, said he was able to hire some staff to split their time between research and review, although "it's not very easy" to do the shared job.

However, a big question mark is what will happen in 2010, when all the far-flung staff of Drugs and Biologics, along with the Devices and Veterinary centers and the commissioner's office, are scheduled to move to the huge complex that the FDA is constructing on a 130-acre wooded site in another part of Maryland. David Kessler first tried to centralize the staff in a single location 10 years earlier, and clearly the consolidation will make it more efficient and convenient for most of the agency to collaborate. (The only ones missing will be the Center for Food Safety and Applied Nutrition, which is ensconced in brand-new offices in a nearby city; the Center for Toxicological Research in Arkansas; and various district offices and labs throughout the country.) Crawford said the new site will actually give CBER and CDER a bit more lab space as a percentage of total footage. But Siegel wondered how much his former colleagues will lose by not being able to schmooze easily with the scientists at NIH, who will then be some 15 miles away, rather than 15 yards.

(That is not the sole problem with the new headquarters, by the way. The site is 15 minutes from the nearest Metro stop. By contrast, the Rockville headquarters is just a few blocks from the Metro, and some of the other soon-to-be-abandoned offices are fairly accessible to mass transit as well. So staffers without cars have been fretting over how they would manage their new commute.)

If it does survive, FDA research looks likely to tilt more and more toward the practical, "regulatory" type, such as developing standards for AIDS test kits, rather than the fundamental research that has been Biologics' glory. That, at least, is what came through from interviews with the top people who will probably be making the decisions.

Crawford certainly made his preference clear. "FDA is not a research organization," he said flatly. "At CBER, there were some people there that were trying to do that, trying to discover the meaning of life. They weren't supposed to do that." He praised the agency's applied work but said that when it comes to questions of basic science, "traditionally, we've always gone to the NIH." It was obvious that the rivalry between the two big government health bureaucracies has not diminished much since the Biologics unit was dragged out of NIH in 1972, as Crawford went on, referring to the NIH's $27 billion annual research budget, "With $27 billion, there's no known issue they can't research."

Janet Woodcock, for her part, turned a question about continuing CBER's brand of research into a pitch for a longtime cause of hers, an office of applied—not basic—research in which staffers would conduct studies on biological and chemical processes that could help speed up drug development and reviews. This would go along with the FDA's new, professed "critical path" program to collaborate with the industry in getting drugs to market; it could also, she said, help attract good scientists. Woodcock has clearly done a lot of thinking about this office: There would be about 50 people at a time, each staying six months to a year. They might develop better models for predicting drug toxicity by analyzing the data from previous trials. Or they could try to come up with new yardsticks for measuring whether a drug really works.

Jesse Goodman, who should be the main defender of his own Center—and who never quite seems to answer a question without meandering a few times around the garden—started out by saying "I am very supportive of that [CBER's tradition of research] and proud of it and it is a good tradition that we want to maintain. It is an investment that will pay off in the long run. We're less likely to make mistakes in either direction"—that is, Type I or Type II mistakes. "Within CBER we have not made significant cuts or changes in research within the last year." But as he went on, his support became more qualified. "I don't think every reviewer needs to be a researcher. There's many ways to have scientific expertise. It's not just lab expertise; it could be clinical [like practicing physicians], statistical, epidemiological expertise. I'm not even sure we need more [research]. What we're trying to do is continue to improve it, targeting toward issues that will really impact product development. Budgets have generally been tight, and our first priority has to be excellence and timeliness of the review process." As an example of ongoing research, he offered a kind of applied research that would certainly be timely eight months later, when the flu vaccine manufacturer would be shut down—working with the NIH and the Centers for Disease Control to investigate "how do we make sure cell cultures for vaccines or cell treatments are free of contaminating agents?"

So no doubt all this sort of practical exposure is useful. But the problem is that it does not help the FDA stay on top of the revolution that is happening in science the way basic research does.

For the immediate years after the departmental transfer, keeping up would not be an urgent problem, because there were not that many drugs to keep up with. The great promises of genomics and proteomics—the road map to the genetic causes of human diseases, the personalized drugs, the cornucopia of Erbituxes and Iressas—were turning out to be more difficult to achieve than most people had expected. The road maps were not that clear, and the genes were not that easy to manipulate. The same thing had happened in the 1980s, the first time biotech was heralded. In fact, this time the mapping of the human genome had actually flooded pharmaceutical labs with too many potential targets to plow through quickly. On top of that, it always takes a while to adjust to new technology. And the diseases that drug companies were now tackling, most notably cancer and central nervous system disorders, are much more complex than previous targets like high cholesterol or hypertension.

Accordingly, the industry scaled back its hype and was now predicting that marketable results would not be seen until 2010. Even some of the pioneers in biotechnology, like Human Genome Sciences, Inc. and PPL Therapeutics in Scotland—the company that helped create Dolly, the first cloned mammal—were laying off people or liquidating entirely. The venture capitalists who financed most of the new firms, nervous about backing early-stage speculative research, were focusing on drugs further along in development.

But eventually the breakthroughs would come. The FDA had merely been granted some breathing room. As Jesse Goodman noted, "A lot of the really new science, like proteomics and genomics, is still in the process of discovery and the early stages of validation. A lot of the positive impact is potential. What we need to be is scientifically prepared for that."

The FDA had not, of course, been sitting blindfolded in a dark corner, oblivious to the changes in pharmaceutical labs. CBER research aside, for some years the agency had been adjusting its requirements for approving drugs to prepare for the new products, most notably its system of surrogate endpoints. Traditionally, a drug application had to show some concrete health benefit, such as increased life expectancy. But for the kinds of life-threatening, long-term, or complex diseases, such as cancer, that companies were increasingly targeting, a drug might be able to get approval using yardsticks that merely measured progress toward the goal. That might mean proof that a tumor had shrunk or that it was taking longer for polyps to recur. Similarly, AIDS drugs did not need to demonstrate long-term survival in order to be approved, as long as they could prove an increase in the amount of immune-system cells in the blood. The manufacturers would, however, just have to continue tracking patients after the drug was on the market. And companies with life-saving products might be able to submit their application with only one Phase III trial rather than the normal two, as Antigenics hoped to do eventually.

Another big concern had to do with personalized drugs. During the course of clinical trials, companies might collect a lot of specific genetic data on the trial subjects, especially if they hoped to target their drug to submarkets of patients with certain genetic mutations. How much of this data would they have to turn in to the FDA, and—even worse—what would the agency do with that information? "Their nervousness is that we will use the information against them [to reject an application], that we will take information and find some very small safety question," Steve Galson acknowledged. To reassure the companies, the FDA in the fall of 2003 issued a set of proposed guidelines saying that, essentially, the information would be required only if it was directly relevant to the drug application—for instance, if companies employ genetic testing in selecting patients for clinical trials, or if statistics from the tests are used in marketing. As for other test data, the agency would like companies to submit those voluntarily, as background, but the information would not be considered as part of the review. "Even if it doesn't support an application, we would like to see it anyway because we want to see what kind of data can better define a drug review process," Galson explained. "We will keep it in a separate reviewer route, unless there's an indication that there's a safety consideration."

All that was fine, but drug makers and patient groups were pushing the FDA for more flexibility, especially when it came to personalized drugs. These products, they claimed, should not be judged according to the FDA's classic assumptions about risk, benefits, and proof, because they would be used only by a very small group of people with precise genetic qualities. Normally, the FDA demands that a drug show a fairly high level of benefit to make up for the inevitable side effects. If a cancer drug keeps people alive for an extra six months but causes fatal heart attacks in one-tenth of those who take it, the benefit is simply not worth the risk. But the personalized drugs theoretically eliminated a lot of the risk on both ends. They should help a far higher percentage of patients and cause far fewer side effects.

And pharmaceutical companies wanted more surrogate markers—ones even further removed from proof of survival, ones that might not even measure progress in the disease but merely indicated that the drug had had an impact on a bodily process that was believed to affect the disease. Look at Alzheimer's disease, suggested Garo Armen. It is fairly well accepted that this condition is connected with the buildup of plaque in the brain, formed by a protein called beta-amyloid. If a reduction in that buildup could be accepted someday as a surrogate marker, that would be a lot easier than trying to prove that a drug had halted the patient's mental deterioration. Other possibilities might involve using gene chips to show that certain crucial genes had been turned on or off by a drug, or advanced imaging techniques to demonstrate that a drug had bonded to the protein it had targeted.

Furthermore, the new science was even upending the time-honored structure of clinical trials. Some researchers were effectively adding an efficacy test to Phase I, which traditionally looked only at safety, by gauging the drug's impact on biomarkers like gene chips. Some were using people instead of animals for the very first safety tests, on the theory that this would catch ineffective drugs far earlier. The FDA had to approve these protocols, of course, and there were scientists who raised ethical concerns. But Lawrence J. Leskin, director of the agency's office of clinical pharmacology and biopharmaceutics, told the *New York Times* that the new approaches "don't seem to be overly burdensome and invasive."

So drug makers and the FDA pondered the implications of the new science. How much benefit was good enough for a drug to be approved?

How much proof? If Iressa could be approved after helping just 10 percent of the trial population, how about a drug that helped eight percent? Five percent? If it was not necessary for a cancer drug to show five-year survival rates, would one year be enough? How about a drug that kept people alive an extra six months? One month? A drug in Phase III was traditionally tested on several thousand people. If the entire market for a personalized drug was hardly any bigger than that, then obviously the universe for its Phase III trial had to be smaller. How small? Could a drug be approved after being tested on only 50 people, if it showed effectiveness in 48 of those 50?

Garo Armen settled back in a blue-grey swivel chair in his small, corner office in Rockefeller Center, to lay out his philosophy toward the FDA approval process:

"Because of where we are in terms of drug development and discovery, there are both challenges and innovations that will make the FDA, the way it functions or it has functioned historically, obsolete. Presumably, the science is taking us to another level of safety and efficacy, which will be a quantum jump from where we have been. It won't require the convoluted process we have had to endure.

"If a product"—a traditional drug in a clinical trial—"works in 20 percent of subjects, and the control works in 10 percent, you need a large study, carefully designed, to capture that small difference in benefit. But if a product works in 90 percent"—which, in theory, a targeted drug could do—"you're going to see that in a very small trial. And if it's targeted to work on a very specific pathway that's relevant to your disease, by definition there will not be interactions with other pathways that do other things.

"We're not there yet," Armen conceded. "It is my strong conviction that we will be there in the next five to 10 years." Logically then, he said, the FDA could base its approval on trials that involved as few as 10 or a dozen people, or on fewer trials. Conveniently, of course, basing approvals on smaller trials would make drug development a lot more feasible for a new biotech—like, say, Antigenics—that could not afford large trials.

Testing the limits of what the FDA will allow, two small biotech companies in the spring of 2004 submitted separate applications for cancer drugs with only minimal or fuzzy results. In one case, trial data seemed to show that the drug Genasense, when taken in conjunction with a chemotherapy treatment, typically delayed the worsening of skin cancer by less than a month. In the other case, a still-unnamed drug that was supposed to make radiation therapy more effective did not improve survival overall, although the manufacturer argued that in one narrow subset of patients it did. The FDA rejected both drugs, saying that the claims were not strong enough to outweigh the risks to patients. The two manufacturers vowed to return with new and more convincing trials. Meanwhile, the baseline seemed to be that a drug's impact on patients has to last at least a month.

In our interview in his office a few months before those rejections, Jesse Goodman agreed that the FDA has to keep rethinking the way it approves drugs and biologics, including the use of smaller trials and different endpoints. "We need to be open to study designs and development plans that incorporate new theories, and I think we are," he said. "We approach them [by asking], What do we need to know about this product? We've tried to be very open and not prescriptive, thinking about what is the data we really need to understand whether something really works." So, he continued, "in some cases that could be smaller trials. To the extent that you can target treatment, if you can define upfront the people who are more likely to benefit, you can do smaller trials. Another is the validation of surrogate endpoints where they are useful. At the same time our job is to protect people."

As science galloped on, the FDA would be confronted by an array of products even more advanced and controversial than personalized Erbitux-style drugs.

Although the Bush White House had blocked federal funding for work on new stem cell lines from human embryos, investigations into that promising medical area would not be stopped. California voters in November 2004 authorized their state to spend up to $3 billion over 10 years on stem cell research, going outside the federal rules. Also in 2004, New Jersey used state and private funding to launch a $50 million stem cell research institute. Harvard had a much smaller, $5 million institute and was trying to raise $95 million more in private funds. Stanford University was doing likewise, and Columbia University Medical Center had drawn in $23 million to set up 40 labs. In Israel, a group of scientists had successfully used human embryonic stem cells in an experiment that reduced symptoms of Parkinson's disease in rats. Most famously: In the winter of 2004, South Korean researchers announced that they had cloned human embryos and extracted stem cells. A British group soon began a similar project.

Genetic engineering, meanwhile, was working its way beyond drugs and the few types of food that had already tied the FDA in knots. GM animals were the next frontier, to be engineered for food, preclinical trials, and as drug factories. For instance, researchers were trying to see if cows could be engineered to produce milk with less lactose, less water, or more of a naturally occurring, antimicrobial enzyme that increases shelf life. Other scientists were attempting to create fish with more of the healthful omega-3 fatty acid, or to manufacture therapeutic human proteins in the milk of animals like sheep. The first to actually hit the agency for approval were fish. Two kinds of fish, to be exact: a tiny zebra fish that glows under ultraviolet light, and salmon that grow superfast.

The zebra fish, renamed the GloFish and marketed by a small company from Austin, Texas, called Yorktown Technologies, is essentially an expensive bauble for the aquarium owner who has everything. It is created by injecting zebra fish embryos with a sea coral's gene for fluorescence. Meanwhile, another company, Aqua Bounty Technologies of Waltham, Massachusetts, had genetically engineered a fish hormone gene into Atlantic salmon, enabling the salmon to use food more efficiently. As a result, the GM salmon could reach market weight in 18 months, versus 24 to 30 months for the unmodified variety. Aqua Bounty promised to distribute only females that had been sterilized, so that they could not reproduce, and provide them only to fish farms that would keep them carefully contained. The salmon would then be sold for food.

The issue before the FDA's Center for Veterinary Medicine in both cases was not just the critter itself, but its effect on the environment. What would happen if a GM fish escaped from its aquarium or fish farm into the wild? Would it breed with natural zebra fish or salmon—or even, in the case of the salmon, with a closely related trout species—and mess up the genetic pool? Would it beat out the unmodified varieties for food? Would it prey on other creatures that were not the species' natural prey? And as for the salmon, how would it affect people who ate it?

"We're constantly rethinking our policies. Probably the most complicated question is the whole issue of the environmental impact," Stephen Sundlof, the Veterinary Center's director, told me. A report from the National Research Council of the National Academy of Sciences, released in January 2004, warned that with current technology, it would be difficult to completely prevent bioengineered plants and animals from having some unintended environmental impact.

If someone invented GM chickens or pigs, that would not be such a problem, Sundlof mused aloud, because "chickens and pigs are not feral animals. If they escaped out of their pen, that would pretty much be it for them"—that is, they would be so helpless that they would get eaten by wild predators before they could have a chance to affect the environment. On the other hand, "wild animals such as fish, there the environment issue becomes very complex. Our assumption going in is that if these animals were allowed to escape into the environment, there is a relatively good likelihood that they could cause environmental destruction.

"Can anything be done to mitigate that to our satisfaction? The only way to prevent a gene from becoming established is to make sure those animals don't reproduce." That means either sterilizing each and every fish, or else creating just a single gender, as Aqua Bounty had pledged. "But I read *Jurassic Park*," Sundlof laughed, "so I'm a little bit concerned." (The scientists in that novel claimed to have prevented their cloned dinosaurs from breeding by creating only females. But some of the females were able to spontaneously change into males, thanks to a fragment of frog DNA that had been used to connect their dinosaur DNA, and the animals started breeding in the wild.)

"The more complicated answer is, how sure are you?" Sundlof continued. "Ninety-nine-point-nine percent sterile, is that good enough? Probably not."

So then could the FDA ever be assured that a GM animal is safe?

"Right now those are some of the discussions that are taking place."

As of the time this book was written, the FDA still had not made a decision on the salmon, but it gave the GloFish the go-ahead—or rather, it said that there was nothing to regulate. Zebra fish are not consumed, the agency declared, so they were not GM food. And they would be confined in an aquarium, so there was no risk of breeding in the wild. "We talked to the Fish and Wildlife Service, and they basically told us they weren't concerned about it. They are the ones who are responsible for an invasive species," Sundlof explained. Yorktown Technologies was free to sell the fish to pet stores.

But by ducking the question, protested Gregory Jaffe of the Center for Science in the Public Interest, the FDA missed an opportunity to start laying out some parameters for the bioengineered animals it would undoubtedly face in the future. Besides, the GloFish may not be as safe as the agency assumed. While it might start out in a secure aquarium, the owner could get sick of the fish and flush it down the toilet, Jaffe pointed out. Or it could be kept as a pet in a pond. From there—well, as the mathematician Ian Malcolm of *Jurassic Park* might say, "life finds a way."

To be fair, even if they are not doing original NIH-style research, many FDA staffers get extra training to prepare for the next advances in science, and that has been on the increase in recent years. Spending on staff training at the Center for Drugs, for instance, gradually rose from $1.25 million in 1999 to $1.86 million in 2002 and then took a big leap to $2.7 million in 2003. According to Steve Galson, it was financed out of the user fees that industry pays to speed up drug approvals. "We can use it for training that's related to the new-drug review process," he explained.

The training occurs in a variety of ways. Reviewers go to professional meetings, and guest lecturers come to the FDA. Professors from three local colleges even teach a for-credit class at the Center for Devices' suburban Maryland office.

One FDA guest lecturer, in the summer of 2003, was Josh Wolfe, a managing partner in the New York City venture capital firm Lux Capital. Lux invests in fledgling companies working in nanotechnology, which is the science of using the tiniest of molecular building blocks to make functioning devices such as semiconductor circuits. While this technology has been used mainly in electronics, the FDA was interested in how companies might employ biological nanotechnology—using bodily processes to deliver drugs. An associate FDA commissioner happened to be in the audience when Wolfe gave a talk as part of the federal government's National Nanotechnology Initiative in February 2003, and he invited Wolfe to come to the FDA that summer for an all-day session on the new science. As the associate commissioner e-mailed to Wolfe: "FDA reviewers are very naïve regarding nanotech. However, we're very concerned because the FDA regulates such a large portion of the types of products that the nano community envisions."

In fact, Wolfe was impressed with the curiosity and competence of the 200 or so staffers he spoke to. Even the size of the audience was a good sign that people were interested, he felt. He talked for over an hour, on topics ranging from the basics of nanobiology to "some of the changes going on in academic labs, how quickly this is being developed, some technology that's being developed that could lead to some health breakthroughs." The questions from the audience, he added, showed "a fair mix [of sophistication]. Most people had kind of read about nanotechnology and were trying to understand how it might change the way they do their job."

According to Jesse Goodman, CBER lets reviewers take time off for teaching and clinical practice, even helping staffers find these opportunities by listing them in a data bank. Goodman himself still sees patients at Walter Reed Army Medical Center and the NIH, where he consults on infectious diseases. And every week one or two Drugs reviewers come to Carl Peck's Center for Drug Development Science at Georgetown University, to teach or participate in work on clinical trial development, data analysis, and pharmacology. It is also official FDA policy to encourage staff to publish papers in academic journals.

Still, this training is not enough to keep current with cutting-edge science, and it does not make up for any reduction in CBER-style research. While the lectures on nanotechnology and the like are a good start, the best way to learn is by actually doing. Yet a lot of the doing that is going on at the FDA is not research—it is the clinical work that Jesse Goodman encourages, which may involve fairly routine patient care.

Not everyone has to be doing research, but the FDA needs a core that does. In the long run, putting all the agency's resources into faster reviews rather than allocating some to research will not make the reviews go faster—not if the staff do not have an up-to-date understanding of what they are reviewing. There really is no substitute for sitting down with a test tube, a petri dish, and a solution. (They can do without the white lab coats that Peter Barton Hutt makes fun of, however.)

As Kathy Zoon put it, "When the products are cutting-edge science, there's not a history. If you're not at the forefront of the science, you're not going to understand the technology you're reviewing."

CHAPTER 13

The FDA Meets Madison Avenue

On the TV screen, a man and woman are getting ready for bed. The woman, sitting at her bedroom dressing table in a silky negligee, cheerfully recalls the details of the party they attended that evening. But the man only pretends. He can't chat; he's in the bathroom, in terrible pain. Indigestion. Heartburn. Or something really serious called acid reflux (whatever that is). He needs a powerful medicine. And the answer is right there on his doctor's prescription pad—a brand-new purple pill from AstraZeneca called Nexium.

Every year AstraZeneca and its fellow pharmaceutical makers together spend over $3 billion—and growing—to bombard the public with television commercials and magazine ads like the one for Nexium. The advertisements have soft-focus photography and catchy music, attractive men and women lolling on a hammock and going for a swim, self-confident grey-haired women mowing lawns, and warm-hearted grandpas hugging their grandsons. Sports stars extol drugs for high cholesterol and arthritis. Bob Dole, the Republican candidate for president in 1996, famously endorsed the impotence drug Viagra. In a different ad for Viagra, a blonde woman, laughing, wearing what could be a nightgown or slip, wraps her arm around a smiling dark-haired man. Cialis, a rival impotence drug, runs a TV commercial in which a brunette couple link hands at a restaurant while exchanging meaningful looks, and two other couples also flirt and fondle. The advertisements openly sell sex, youth, celebrity, and family togetherness. Like any other ad.

And it's all because of the FDA.

To pharmaceutical industry executives, some doctors, some consumer groups, and the FDA officialdom, this is just an example of the government doing its job and trying to educate the public. The commercials provide information so that patients can make their own decisions about their own bodies. But to most doctors, many consumer groups, and other critics, this is salesmanship, not education, and something as serious as medicine—something that can have horrible side effects, that can save lives if used properly or kill people if something goes wrong—should not be pitched like toothpaste.

Critics wonder why in the world the FDA ever allowed these ads to happen, back in August 1997.

The FDA says it had no choice. Times were changing, and all it could do was try to throw a weak little lasso on the tornado.

Maybe. But when an opportunity came six and a half years later to exercise a bit more control, the FDA wimped out.

In fact, the advertising of drugs to the general public, along with controversy and attempts to curtail it, is decades older than the FDA itself. The phony patent medicines of the nineteenth century were spread by hyperactive newspaper ads touting their supposedly miraculous powers. According to the writer Paul Starr in his book *The Social Transformation of American Medicine*, the American Medical Association (AMA) in 1900 attempted to put a halt to this marketing by demanding that manufacturers end all public advertising, urging medical journals not to accept ads from drugs that also "advertised directly to the laity," and promising to stop publishing patent medicine ads in its own *Journal* as soon as existing contracts expired. Even after the first Food and Drug Act was passed in 1906, the AMA was far more aggressive than the Bureau of Chemistry (the FDA's predecessor) in clamping down on drug promotions. For instance, the AMA established a special office to try to persuade newspapers to cease running patent medicine ads, Starr writes.

Starr points out that the doctors' opposition to advertising did not arise only from concern that patent medicine makers were hawking dangerous stuff. "The logic of the 1906 [Food and Drug] law," he says, "was to improve the functioning of the market by making consumer information more accurate. The logic of the AMA's regulatory system was to withhold information from consumers and rechannel drug purchasing through physicians." In other words, the AMA established a philosophy that prescription drugs were too specialized, powerful, and complicated for laypeople to understand without the intervention of their doctor. These dangerous products should be promoted only via sober listings (presumably in small type) in professional journals read by people with medical degrees. It was a philosophy that would hold for nearly a century.

However, by the end of the twentieth century, as the modern consumer movement took off in all directions, that philosophy of protecting the patient began to give way. Throughout society, ordinary people were taking on jobs that professionals used to handle. Decreeing that Americans had a right to know what was in the food they were eating, Congress had ordered the nutrition listings that the FDA put on packaged foods starting in 1992. Employers were turning over to their workers the responsibility for their entire financial security after age 65, by replacing pensions with 401(k) accounts. People were writing their own wills, negotiating their own divorces, and investing their own money in the stock market. Not all of this was the consumers' choice, most notably the switch to 401(k) retirement plans, which was usually a decision initiated by companies to save money. And too often, especially when it came to investing those 401(k)s, the consumers lacked the necessary training. Still, for better or worse, American society was undoubtedly going through a shift to consumer control. So why should medicine be any different? Why shouldn't people at least know what substances they were putting in their bodies, along with the risks and reasons? Why should they simply accept their doctor's word?

At the same time, courts were throwing out traditional restrictions on advertising by other professions, such as lawyers. "It used to be considered bad medical or legal etiquette to advertise. But there was a trend that advertising is a form of free speech," explained Daniel Callahan, a cofounder of The Hastings Center, the think tank north of New York City that specializes in health care ethics. The U.S. Supreme Court in 1976 agreed with the Ralph Nader–affiliated Virginia Citizens Consumer Council, in a suit against the Virginia State Board of Pharmacy, that state laws that banned pharmacies from advertising their prescription drug prices violated the public's right to information.

Veterans of that era at the FDA say it was not clear whether advertising prescription medicine to the public—known today as direct-to-consumer, or DTC, advertising—was either legal or illegal. The Kefauver-Harris

Amendments had said only that if drugs were advertised, there had to be a thorough description of the risks. "The law just didn't envision [TV ads]," said Louis A. Morris, a social scientist who spent 23 years at the FDA, helping devise its first DTC rules and researching the impact of communication on consumers.

Alert to the changing social attitudes, the pharmaceutical industry began probing the FDA, gauging how far it could go. In May 1983 the British firm Boots Pharmaceuticals ran what is considered the first consumer TV drug commercial, to promote its ibuprofen pain reliever Rufen (which is similar to brands like Advil and Motrin). As Morris and other veterans recalled, the ad merely consisted of a picture of the company's U.S. chief executive and a blackboard, with a list of side effects. But it was enough to shake up Arthur Hull Hayes, then the FDA commissioner. "He said, 'This is something we need to be really careful about,'" Morris said. Mainly, Hayes wondered whether the public could really register all the facts about side effects as they scrolled down the screen. The FDA asked the industry to agree to a temporary moratorium while it tried to figure out what to do.

Today, Morris lives on a tree-lined street of thick green lawns in Long Island, New York, working as an independent consultant advising drug companies and agencies on how to design ads to meet the very FDA rules he helped devise. He is portly and balding, with a small, grey, walrus-style mustache and a tonsure of grey hair. He went to the FDA almost straight from earning his PhD in social psychology at Tulane University in 1974, mainly because he saw it as a place where he could continue his research; then, like so many others, he left when he had stayed long enough to qualify for a good retirement package. Although his voice is usually soft, he can get snippy and impatient.

During the advertising moratorium, Morris ran a study to analyze whether commercials could adequately communicate a drug's risks to the public. An outside ad agency created various sample spots, which Morris screened in front of test audiences in a half-dozen cities. One was a general ad that just said, "Ask your doctor." Other samples specifically listed a drug's risks and side effects. "We didn't know," explained Mark Novitch, who was, alternately, the deputy and acting commissioner during that period and who helped put the moratorium in place. "How could you get fair balance [a listing of risks] into a 30-second commercial or even in a print ad? Were you going to put the same material that was in *The New England Journal of Medicine*?" As it turned out, people saw the more general type of ad in Morris's study as a reassurance rather than a warning. Apparently, they needed to be shown a specific list of side effects.

So the FDA came out with a ruling that consumer ads, whether in print or on TV, had to follow more or less the same rules as those in professional medical journals. If an ad was touting a drug for a particular condition and enumerating the wonderful things the drug did, it had to list all the side effects, instructions, conditions, and warnings exactly as they appeared on the package insert, or label, that came with every drug. (This requirement is known, with unintended irony, as the "brief summary.") That was theoretically doable in a magazine or newspaper ad, although it would be expensive to buy the necessary space and would clutter up the page with lines and lines of ugly, tiny "mice type." But it seemed impossible on TV unless the commercial ran for about two solid—and costly— minutes or the announcer spoke faster than the speed of sound. Alternatively, companies could run "reminder ads," which mention a product by name without saying specifically what the product does, in which case the list of side effects could be omitted on TV. "The assumption," Morris said, "was that the requirement effectively prohibited ads being on TV."

That compromise quickly foundered. Industry veteran Robert Ehrlich explained some of what followed. (As a marketer, Ehrlich helped launch the cholesterol blockbuster Lipitor at Parke-Davis and is now the chairman of a New Jersey–based consulting firm, DTC Perspectives Inc., that publishes a magazine and online column and runs conferences, focusing on consumer drug ads.) Manufacturers tried advertising in magazines, to the tune of perhaps $500 million to $600 million. The problem was that "print ads by themselves are ineffective and slow. You can't find three magazines that everyone reads." Then there were a few spots on cable TV, where time was cheaper than on networks. "But no one wants to spend 90 seconds of your two minutes scrolling through fair balance." For that matter, Lou Morris said dismissively, "the only people who ever read [the list of side effects] were FDA people."

The industry kept pushing the limits. "People didn't know what the FDA would allow. They were dealing with things on a one-off basis; they were almost at a loss for what to do. A lot of people just took chances," recalled Michael Myers, executive vice president of Palio Communications, an ad agency in Saratoga Springs, New York that has worked with such pharmaceutical giants as Schering-Plough, GlaxoSmithKline,

Pfizer, and Roche, as well as nonpharmaceutical clients in publishing and plastics.

Most worrisome of all, the drug makers were simply bypassing the whole issue of side effects by increasingly turning to reminder ads. That meant a batch of fuzzy, vague mood spots with no specifics about any-thing—disease, benefits, or side effects. "It was ridiculous, the industry running ads without saying what it was for. Doctors were getting requests for drugs that weren't appropriate because no one knew what they were for. The FDA was under pressure," Ehrlich said.

"There was tremendous pressure for ads to occur," agreed Janet Woodcock, who headed the Drugs Center at the time. "It was clear that that was going to happen, in light of consumer expectations and the judi-cial attitude on commercial speech."

And the FDA opened up the floodgates.

On August 12, 1997, it issued a revised set of guidelines that allowed TV and radio commercials to pitch prescription drugs by name, while also saying what medical conditions they treated, without the full, long list of side effects that ran in print ads. Broadcast ads still had to provide some level of warning to consumers, but the new requirements were a lot easier to comply with in 30 or 60 seconds. Commercials needed to men-tion only the major risks, limitations, and cautions about who should not take the drug—in "consumer-friendly language"—rather than the com-plete details from the package label. (This is what Novitch referred to with the term "fair balance.") In addition, ads must let consumers know where to get all the details that are omitted, which usually means provid-ing a toll-free phone number, a Web site address, and the names of some magazines where print ads are running. The commercials must say that the drug is available only by prescription. And, in a vestige of the olden days when doctors knew best, they have to tell viewers to—as the com-mercials always put it—"ask your doctor."

Woodcock argues that the FDA could hardly have done otherwise—certainly not by forbidding the ads altogether. "The legal framework was there. What we did was provide a way that the brief summary could be met with the broadcast ad," she said. The industry was pressing. The courts were ruling against government restrictions on commercial speech. Consumers were getting incomplete information. The old rules were being strained. "How can they stop it? It's free speech," said Michael Myers.

Besides, most FDA officials say, what's so terrible about these ads anyway?

The argument in favor of DTC advertising begins with the consumer movement and people's right to have more control over their lives. Sure, a 30-second TV commercial with a sports star or a sexy blonde does not provide all that much in the way of detailed medical information. But even from the skimpiest of commercials, patients pick up some genuine facts about symptoms and possible treatments. Just the statement to "ask your doctor" is important, because so many people with serious conditions—especially diabetes, depression, and impotence—are not getting treatment. For instance, the National Diabetes Institute estimated in 2003 that there were nearly six million Americans with diabetes who had not been diagnosed. And once people start getting medical care, the commercials can be a valuable reminder to take their pills. So, thanks to DTC, Americans are paying more attention to their health, noticing warning signs they used to ignore or consider embarrassing, and discussing these warning signs with their doctors. All of that is a lot better than passively accepting every word out of the physician's mouth, maybe months after the symptoms begin. Pointing to Bob Dole's commercials for Viagra, Jerome Halperin of the Food and Drug Law Institute said that because of DTC, "something that was snickers and embarrassing now is a health issue."

Anyway, the argument goes on, it is not as though someone can run out to the drug store and buy a pound of Nexium after seeing the commercial with the man and woman getting ready for bed. Patients still must have a physician's signature on the prescription form. So it is not just rhetoric when the commercials say, "ask your doctor." Trained professionals still control the use of prescription drugs.

This line of reasoning gets support from some public interest organizations and doctors, not just the pharmaceutical industry. Back when unions, consumer groups, insurers, and employers were organizing Rx Health Value to battle soaring drug costs, said John Golenski, the founder and former executive director, the issue of DTC split the coalition. "A lot of consumer groups were saying, 'That's how we get our information [from TV].' They find the commercials helpful. It lets them know what medicines are out there because their doctors don't tell them." Jere

Goyan, who headed the FDA in the days before DTC, said he initially opposed the concept but subsequently changed his mind. "Advertising is another way of educating the patient," he said. Agreed Michael Friedman, who was the FDA's acting commissioner during that fateful August 1997, "I feel pretty strongly about DTC ads because I think that patients ought to be empowered and want to have options to exercise their autonomy, and one way to do that is by having information out there."

No other country except New Zealand permits DTC ads, and in many places drug companies are not even allowed to provide information to consumers via telephone or the Internet. To log onto a company's Web site, users often must have a password that is given only to physicians. But the same force of consumer power that swept across the United States is apparently starting to erode those restrictions. Patients who speak English have long managed to skirt the Internet ban by simply logging on to Web sites that are supposed to be for U.S residents, and Switzerland finally eliminated the password requirement in 2004. One European manufacturer of birth control pills skirted the ad ban by sending monthly "public service" e-mails to women who agreed to receive the messages, reminding them to take their pills. By 2004, European regulators were talking about easing their regulations a bit to allow drug makers, in conjunction with governments and patient groups, to publicize general information.

So, it would seem, consumers everywhere want information about drugs, even if it comes via commercials. And information will find a way to get out to them.

Critics of DTC do not oppose the concept of giving consumers more information or control. Their argument is that DTC ads are not the way to do it.

The decision about whether to take a medication and which one to take should involve sober considerations of symptoms, diagnostic test results, family history, general state of health, possible interactions with other medicines, lifestyle, insurance coverage, and cost. There are a lot of ways patients could get this data, even if they do not feel qualified to tackle professional journals. They could read articles in consumer health magazines or consumer-oriented reference books like *The Merck Manual*, seek a second opinion from another physician, surf the Internet, and talk with friends and relatives who have the same medical condition.

But no TV commercial could possibly cover the real issues in 30 or 60 seconds. That is not what advertising is designed for. Advertising is not meant to be a serious analysis of complex issues. Advertising is meant to persuade. It is meant to be eye-catching, to appeal to emotions, to sell a product. The pitches for drugs use the same persuasive techniques and implied messages as those for toothpaste and toilet paper—even the same Madison Avenue agencies. You can skate like Olympic star Dorothy Hamill if you use Vioxx for your arthritis. If you want a gorgeous blonde to caress you, just take Viagra.

It is telling that in a prepared statement to the FDA in 2003, during a formal review of the DTC guidelines, lawyers for Pfizer wrote: "One has only to watch a laundry detergent ad to realize that the vendor does not have to disclose the stains that the detergent cannot remove in addition to the ones that it can." Pfizer apparently saw no reason why ads for its powerful, life-saving medicines should be any different than ads for something as innocuous as laundry detergent.

But what's the danger? What terrible thing could these catchy, heart-warming, sexy, celebrity-laden DTC commercials persuade viewers to do? After all, they're not pushing poison, illegal drugs, or cigarettes. They are pitching therapeutic, FDA-approved, safe and effective medicine.

Well, yes. But first of all, not every viewer needs these wonderful medicines. Yet people who are not at risk can be easily manipulated by powerful images. If they have ever had any symptoms that resemble the ones in the ad, they may blow that experience out of proportion and imagine that they have a terrible, chronic condition that they do not really have. Or, if they genuinely have a condition that needs treatment, they may be persuaded that the miraculous new version of patent medicine on the TV screen will completely and immediately cure them, when they might do just as well with a less expensive generic or over-the-counter medication—or even something as simple as a change in diet. In either case, "people come in with information that is partial or mistaken, and they think they're being deprived if the drug isn't prescribed," said John Golenski—repeating the complaints of the other half of his RxValue Coalition.

Furthermore, the medicines that are advertised are inevitably the newest ones, which are almost always the priciest options. In a study released in November 2001, the National Institute for Health Care Management (NIHCM), a nonprofit group heavily funded by the insurance industry, found that the 50 most advertised drugs in 2000 included a slew of the pharmaceutical industry's expensive new blockbusters, but no generics.

Number one on the list, for instance, was the arthritis and pain medication Vioxx from Merck, with nearly $161 million worth of DTC spending—later yanked off the market because of serious cardiovascular risks. Number seven, at over $78 million, was a similar pill, Celebrex, from Pfizer—which also was later linked to an increased risk of heart attacks, at high doses. (When the news was announced in December 2004, the FDA issued an unusual warning to doctors that it "advises evaluating alternative therapies." Pfizer insisted it would keep Celebrex on the market but cancelled all its ads.) Even before Vioxx and the Celebrex ads were withdrawn, these drugs were highly controversial, with critics charging that they were no better at relieving pain than much cheaper over-the-counter ibuprofens like Motrin or Advil.

Or take Nexium, the purple pill for the poor husband with indigestion. Nexium is actually half of the molecule that makes up another purple pill for heartburn, Prilosec, marketed by the same company, AstraZeneca, and there is some debate as to whether the two drugs are significantly different. For its part, Prilosec was once the top-selling drug in the United States. AstraZeneca dedicated more than $107 million to advertising it in 2000, the second-highest amount of DTC spending for a prescription drug that year, according to the NIHCM. But the next year, Prilosec's patent was about to expire, which meant that other companies could sell generic versions at far lower prices. AstraZeneca abruptly dumped its one-time favorite. Instead, it poured four times as much—$478 million—into advertising the brand-new Nexium, which it could continue selling at a premium price. In 2003, those sales came to $3.1 billion.

So it is not that TV viewers watch commercials and are inspired to sit down with their doctors for an in-depth conversation about current medical thinking. Rather, they head for the doctor's office and demand the newest, most expensive cure. Period. "They think it's got to be better if it's new. And it's hard to convince them otherwise," said Dr. Susan Hendrix, a gynecologist in Detroit who frequently consults for major drug companies. Patients do not want to be told that the new medicine has not been shown to help with their condition, or that they should try cutting out dessert and spicy food first.

But of course, from the drug companies' point of view, that is exactly why they should run the commercials. The ads work.

Over and over, surveys show that people are paying attention to the ads and taking that information to their physicians—and physicians are writing prescriptions for the drugs that are advertised. When *Prevention* magazine queried 1,222 Americans in June 2000, 32 percent of those who had seen a DTC spot said they talked with their doctor about the advertised medicine, 26 percent proceeded to ask for a prescription, and 71 percent of the ones who asked got the prescription they wanted. A year and a half later, the Henry J. Kaiser Family Foundation came out with a survey of over 2,500 people in which 30 percent had spoken to a doctor about a specific advertised medicine and 44 percent got a prescription. From 2002 to 2004, Ipsos Group—a market research firm that specializes in health care, consumer products, technology, and financial services—repeatedly found that around 20 percent of consumers called or visited their physician to discuss a prescription drug they saw advertised. While these numbers vary somewhat, they are all substantial.

Susan Hendrix frequently encounters the influence of TV commercials when women of menopause age arrive for a check-up and promptly ask for a pill for osteoporosis, or severe loss of bone mass. "Just because you have bone-mass loss doesn't mean you're going to develop a fracture. Bone-mass loss is normal to a point," she noted. Whether a woman needs a drug to help halt the process or replace lost bone mass depends on risk factors such as family history and the degree of loss. But "everyone wants a magic bullet because it is difficult to go back to what we know works," like diet and exercise.

"You have people walking in to doctors saying 'I want Celebrex.' For a lot of people, you could try generic ibuprofen first, it's a lot less expensive," Dr. Ira Bloomfield, a longtime internist and emergency room physician, now chief medical information officer of a physician-hospital network in North Carolina, told me when I interviewed him in 2002 for a previous book.

True, the surveys also show that plenty of doctors did not succumb to their patients' pleas. They prescribed a different medicine, or suggested a change in diet, or maybe told the patient to take two aspirin and call back in the morning. But the real question is whether the doctors who gave the patients what they asked for would have prescribed the advertised medicine anyway. Did the ads, and the demands from patients, pressure physicians to agree to a treatment they really did not think was very good? Are DTC commercials perhaps dangerous?

The only survey that comes close to answering that is a poll of 642 physicians across the nation by Massachusetts General Hospital's Institute for Health Policy in 2003. These doctors said they prescribed an advertised drug 39 percent of the time that patients requested it. And five percent said they did so even if they believed a different treatment was more effective.

What do Ira Bloomfield's doctors do when patients ask for Celebrex unnecessarily? "If doctors think it's medically reasonable, they will often bend to the patient's wishes."

In light of the commercials' powers of persuasion, it is simply wrong as a policy, critics say, to peddle prescription drugs so cavalierly. "Medicines aren't like shampoo or perfume. They're things people need to maintain health, not discretionary products a person can use or throw away on a whim," wrote Dr. Erin N. Marcus, an internist and professor at the University of Miami School of Medicine, in an op-ed article in the *New York Times* in January 2003.

But since the ads do exist, the debate now turns on what they should look like. How far can the entertainment overwhelm the information? Clashes are almost inevitable because two completely different value systems are at work.

Consider the self-evident fact that most drugs are for people who are elderly, incapacitated, or ill, not gorgeous young models. Yet who wants to see a commercial full of sickly, frail, or wrinkled people? So producers try to find the best-looking old or sick people they can. Merck's osteoporosis medicine Fosamax, for the bone-mass loss that can begin at menopause, showcases women in their fifties pushing lawn mowers, not women in their eighties pushing walkers. The Viagra ads may have started with the septuagenarian Bob Dole speaking about the physical changes that occur as men age, but they soon switched to a baseball star, a race car driver, and the sexy blonde wife, focusing on the fun you can have while you're still young. The brunette couple in the Cialis spot cannot possibly be over 45. (Pfizer, fearing that the Cialis ads were making Viagra look too stodgy, proceeded to spice up its marketing for Viagra with the campaign slogan "Get back to mischief.")

Unlike the case with the drugs themselves, the FDA does not have the authority to approve or reject drug ads before they go on the market. Companies merely have to give the agency a copy of every spot at the time it is aired or published. If the agency finds that the ad has violated the law, it can send warning letters, demand corrections, or go to court (but not issue fines). In fact, companies usually do submit their plans in advance, because they do not want the PR black eye of a warning letter. But often they go ahead and air the commercial while they wait for the FDA's review—and by the time the regulators have finished analyzing the ad and sent their letter or a judge has ruled, the ad may have been broadcast for weeks, even months; it may have even finished its scheduled run and be off the air. Meanwhile, the public has been inundated with the misleading message.

What might prompt an FDA warning letter or lawsuit? Everything from style to substance. An animated Lamisil tablet was too quick and thorough in eradicating a little yellow cartoon toenail fungus called Digger the Dermatophyte, in a spot Novartis ran in 2003, because the drug in real life does not work that powerfully. GlaxoSmithKline's 2004 commercial for Paxil CR (a new version of the controversial antidepressant) wrongly implied that it had been approved for broader uses than it actually had and "fails clearly to communicate the major risks." A Pfizer "Get back to mischief" spot for Viagra finally went too far in its mischiefmaking, and the FDA in November 2004 protested that the commercial—which featured a man staring at sexy, black, women's underwear in a store window, among other things—implied more potency for Viagra than clinical trials had ever proved. Another problem was that the ad was positioned as a "reminder ad," meaning that it would not say what Viagra does, and therefore did not need to list the side effects. The FDA retorted that the implications of what Viagra does were so strong that it breeched the definition of reminder ad.

One of the earliest crackdowns hit an ad for Lipitor, the cholesterol blockbuster. According to Bob Ehrlich, the industry consultant, who was in charge of Lipitor marketing for Parke-Davis at that time, the FDA rejected a pitch showing a car driving fast past lovely scenes of nature. There was too much music, too much distracting action, and too many happy people walking by while the side effects were being read, Ehrlich said the FDA told Parke-Davis.

Indeed, the enumeration of side effects is one of the requirements that annoys the ad world the most. Precious seconds have to be taken up reciting information that will not sell the product—that in fact might discourage potential customers. By most accounts, a company may well have to double the amount of air time or print pages it purchases to accommodate the "fair balance." Loretta Lurie, an executive at the Manhattan agency Lowe Worldwide, said that fully 13 seconds of the 30-second spots she did for the allergy drug Nasonex in the late 1990s consisted of listing side effects. And the recitation must be in the same tone of voice as the rest of the ad—no fast-talking auctioneers' spiels—without the kind of distracting music or images that the FDA cited in the Lipitor spot.

"They protect the consumer far more than the consumer needs protecting. They make you tell the consumer things the doctor should be telling them, including side effects," Lurie asserted. A collection of marketing-industry trade associations calling itself the Coalition for Healthcare Communication filed a report with the FDA in early 2004 arguing that putting too many details in DTC ads could backfire. Consumers, the group said, would not absorb the mass of information and might be scared off from going to the doctor.

The Paxil CR ad is an example of another common issue—what kind of claims an ad can make. Certainly any claim must be supported by valid data from well-controlled clinical trials. That seems obvious enough. An advertiser cannot just invent a fake trial. And apples have to be compared with apples, or livers with livers. One time a cardiovascular drug cited results from two separate studies, each of which used a different methodology, in the same commercial. The FDA ordered it to drop one of the data sets because the ad seemed to imply that the same methodology was used for both studies. You cannot say that Drug A starts working to relieve the symptoms of hay fever in just 30 minutes, based on a trial of 500 people in Pennsylvania, and also say its relief keeps working for 24 hours, based on a trial of 250 people in Texas, without explaining that these are two different test groups. Otherwise, it sounds like a single group of hay fever sufferers got relief that began 30 minutes after taking the pill and lasted for 24 hours. In the case of the cardiovascular drug with two studies, the ad designer conceded that the FDA's criticism was reasonable.

However, sometimes—so pharmaceutical and advertising officials complain—the nuances of when an ad has misstated a drug's safety or effectiveness can be downright Talmudic. Even drug companies and their ad agencies can't always agree. Landor Associates, a San Francisco–based branding and design firm owned by the British communications conglomerate WPP Group, wanted to say that a certain product could "slow" the progress of a disease. Nope, said the cautious pharmaceutical client. The ad should only say "impact" the progress. What's the difference? Julia Beardwood, who was then Landor's executive director, just shook her head. (Well, "impact" is more vague than "slow," so maybe the drug company thought it was safer not to be specific.) Bob Ehrlich, in one of his weekly online columns, called the FDA's complaints about Novartis's Digger the Dermatophyte spot a case of "stretching their interpretation of the law too far to find violations." He said it was obvious that the toe fungus takes months, not 60 seconds, to clear up.

"In a consumer [nondrug] ad you can make wild allusions to a guy driving a car through space. The FDA doesn't want that. 'This implies that cars can fly. It is unsafe for people to drive their cars off a cliff'—I swear that's what you'd get back," Michael Myers, the Saratoga Springs advertising executive, said contemptuously.

By virtually all accounts, there were far more clashes between industry and the FDA in the early years. Starting in 2001, the number of warning letters began to plummet. Congressman Henry Waxman of California issued a report in October 2002 noting that "FDA enforcement actions for false and misleading drug advertising dropped significantly in the first two years of the [Bush] administration"—that is, 2001 and 2002. Waxman gave the new commissioner, Mark McClellan, a year to settle in, then produced a follow-up report in January 2004. The findings: Even fewer warning letters were going out now. While the average number of new promotional pieces reviewed by the FDA each month increased by about six percent from 2002 to 2003, the number of enforcement letters fell 15 percent. In 1999 and 2000, the FDA had sent an average of 95 enforcement letters annually; by 2003, that was down to just 24.

As consumer advocates saw it, those statistics showed that the FDA was not keeping up with the industry's false advertising. One problem was that the agency's budget had not risen in line with the ever-growing amount of money spent on ads, which had more than doubled since the barrage began in 1997. Nor can the FDA tap its income from user fees, since by law those funds may be spent only to review the first ads for a new drug launch. Critics also blamed a Bush administration policy that required the chief counsel—that is, the controversial former industry lawyer Dan Troy—to sign off on all DTC warnings. That was one reason Congressman Maurice Hinchey had introduced his amendment to shift $500,000 out of Troy's office and into advertising enforcement.

People in the industry, however, asserted that Waxman's data simply proved that there were fewer "bad" ads, because advertisers had come to understand the guidelines better (despite all their grumbling about unclear definitions and the rest). The FDA seemed a lot pickier and mysterious in the first couple of years, Bob Ehrlich said, but now drug companies "feel pretty good that the rules are fairly well established. They know what they can and can't do."

Advertising agencies say they know to give their pharmaceutical clients lots of alternative ads, in order to have enough backups should the FDA shoot the first ones down. "You'll take three different campaigns to the client to approve, each with two or three concepts," Lurie said. Those versions are then run past the drug company's review committee, consisting of staffers from the medical, marketing, and legal or regulatory departments. Of course, all the layers of bureaucracy inflates development costs, perhaps by 10 to 15 percent, experts say.

Typically, the ad agencies want to be more daring than their pharmaceutical clients feel comfortable with. For instance, it is not unusual for them to shoot a spot with relatively young and healthy models, and then be told by the client to go find a new set of actors who look just pale or overweight or old enough to need the medicine, without turning off viewers.

"Everyone interprets what you need to do with respect to the FDA in a unique manner," Michael Myers said. "Some people will read it as the law. Some will look for precedents. I've seen some pharmaceutical companies where the legal people are told, 'We should never get a warning letter.' And some clients try and push it right to the edge."

There are also pharmaceutical marketers who say they appreciate the difference between ads for drugs and for toothpaste, and they don't mind doing a limited amount of fair balance. They realize that the side effects that must be spelled out can be serious and painful ones. Liver problems, like the type that killed Monica George on Rezulin. Heart attack or stroke, such as Vioxx may cause. A drop in blood pressure. Weight gain. Diarrhea. Impotence. "There is an ethical aspect to health care products and health care marketing that is necessarily different from making potato chips," said Julia Beardwood of Landor.

Of course, it is a far cry from Boots Pharmaceuticals' long scroll of side effects to Dorothy Hamill on ice skates, Digger the Dermatophyte, and a sexy blonde in a nightgown. But when it gave the go-ahead for Boots-type ads back in 1997, the FDA should have seen what was coming. No other commercials on TV are straightforward discussions of facts. Why would drug commercials be any different?

Many former FDA officials say they did in fact realize what they were getting into. "I thought it would open the floodgates. Television conveys certain emotions you don't get in print," Lou Morris conceded. Gerry Meyers, who was the deputy and acting director of CDER during some of the early debate over DTC, recalled that "we thought that was a risk," that the ads would become flashy. "The industry assured us that wouldn't happen." Did he believe the industry? He gave a little smile. "Partly, I suppose."

However, others claim they had no idea where things would lead. "I'm not sure I had a good sense of what industry would do, what would be a good way" to advertise to consumers, Michael Friedman said. He added, "I wish drug companies would use more of the DTC time for learning, for educational moments, and less about specific medications."

Well, in that case, why doesn't the FDA just make them do that?

In 2003, the agency announced that it was going to thoroughly analyze and rethink the whole controversial topic of DTC. Public hearings were held, op-ed pieces were published. The industry nervously braced for a clampdown. There was speculation that the FDA would make it a formal mandate that TV spots be approved in advance, or even order companies to run new ads correcting any misleading ones. And then in February 2004, the FDA coughed up a mouse.

The main change in the new guidelines was that print ads, instead of having to repeat all the risk and efficacy information from the package insert in a page of small type in the "brief summary," could substitute a genuine summary of just the most important risks. The risks would have to be written in "language easily understood by the average consumer," perhaps highlighted by being placed in a box with bullet points. The justification for this change, which virtually no one disputed, was that people do not read the tiny print, but they might actually look at the shorter, catchier version. (The FDA was also working on making the package insert itself easier to understand.)

As for the controversy over television marketing—whether claims are exaggerated, whether music is too distracting, whether commercials should be approved in advance—the only thing the FDA had to say involved a type of commercial known as a "bookend." This consists of a "reminder" ad that mentions a drug without saying what disease it treats—then a commercial for some entirely different product—immediately followed by a "help-seeking" spot from the same company as the "reminder" ad, this one naming the disease that was never disclosed in the first ad but not saying the name of the drug. This type of pitch is rarely used and generally frowned on even by the pharmaceutical industry itself. Only Roche and Merck are known to have tried the tactic. So it was hardly trend-setting or brave of the FDA to mildly note that it "is concerned that they are understood by consumers as product claim advertisements, without the inclusion of proper disclosure of required risk information."

And that was all. The paltry guidelines might be seen as yet more proof of the pharmaceutical industry's huge influence on decision making in Washington, D.C., except that they were even weaker than the industry had dreamed of. "I was surprised how minor they were compared to my expectations," Bob Ehrlich wrote in his weekly online column on February 6. Mike Myers opined that "they hit us not as hard as I thought they would. It was reasonable. It was almost like they jumped across the table"—that is, made an extra effort to accept DTC. Indeed, not only did drug companies avoid any tough new restrictions, but they might also save money under the new guidelines: If they followed the suggestion to replace the full reprinting of side effects with a smaller box listing only the highlights, they would need to buy one-third to one-half less space, Myers estimated.

Lester Crawford, who was deputy commissioner when the guidelines came out, explained that the agency did not take any other action because "that would be sort of bureaucratizing to death. We're trying to facilitate." And Janet Woodcock claimed that tougher rules were not needed for TV commercials because most companies prescreen voluntarily. The FDA's major concern, she added, "was to try and get the brief summary into a form that will inform the people of something." Otherwise, "we think the ads are congruent with current law."

Certainly, the FDA never considered banning DTC outright. Beyond the legal question as to whether the government could forbid a form of free speech, it is simply too late. "You can't put that one back in the bottle," Mark Novitch, who helped launch DTC as acting commissioner in the 1980s, said—with a grimace.

Yet there was so much more the FDA could have done to curb the glitz and give consumers real information.

Start with print ads. If the FDA could design a standardized way for packaged food to list ingredients and compare them to some average daily allowance, why can't it do the equivalent for medicine? *BusinessWeek* magazine suggested that drug ads could include a table, using actual data from clinical trials, that would show the advertised drug's benefits and risks and also compare that with the data for other brand-name drugs and generics.

Something similar, albeit simpler, could even be run on TV. A spot for a diabetes drug might include the advice: "This medicine may not be necessary for everyone who is at risk for diabetes. Studies have shown that diet and exercise can reduce the risk of developing Type II diabetes." John Edwards, then a senator from North Carolina, twice introduced bills along this line while he was running for president in 2003 and 2004, one of them cosponsored by Senator Tom Harkin of Iowa, although neither measure passed. He brought the topic up again after he became the Democratic vice presidential nominee. The basic idea of this sort of proposal would be for commercials to hold the drug up against alternative treatments— including over-the-counter products, generics, older brand-name drugs, and changes in lifestyle—and to give equal time to the risks and benefits.

Another possibility is that, for every DTC ad a company broadcast, it would also have to run a public service announcement about good health practices that do not involve prescriptions, or a "help-seeking" type of ad about a disease without mentioning particular products. Even an industry insider like Bob Ehrlich urged the FDA to "consider mandating disease education ads as a percent of total DTC spending." Actually, a drug maker might not find these public service spots such a burden, since they would undoubtedly inspire some people to start thinking about their health and wonder if they need a prescription.

A lot of consumer advocates would not mind if TV commercials reverted to the boring Boots model that started the whole mess. Instead of trying to peer at each frame to decide whether this particular bar of music is too loud while the risks are being recited or this specific cartoon figure is too distracting, why not insist that the ads be exactly what the industry claims they are—educational? "No loud music or beautiful scenes of skiing while listing the side effects. Put a lot of those side effects in plain English," said Dee Mahan of Families USA, the advocacy group that focuses on drug prices and the elderly. Most FDA officials reply that the agency does not have the power to order anything like this, because that would be close to censorship. "If they felt an ad should only say the name of the drug, Congress would have to say that," Woodcock commented. Michael Friedman said that when he issued the original 1997 rules, he did not try to restrict the glitz because "now you're talking about the artistic impression of something. To say there's no music or it's got to be classical music, that's ludicrous." But since the FDA already rejects ad pictures and music that it considers distracting, clearly it does feel it can legally regulate "artistic impression" to some degree. Moreover, the courts have consistently allowed government to set stricter limitations on commercial speech than on other kinds of speech.

Perhaps technology will eventually solve the problem. By the early 2000s, companies of all sorts were beginning to wonder whether there was any point running commercials on TV because TiVo and other devices let viewers just zap the ads when they recorded shows.

But ad-free TV is still in the future. Meanwhile, as drug prices soared and Americans headed to Canada for their prescription shopping, DTC spots joined the hated pharmaceutical companies as a convenient political target in the 2004 elections. Senator Edwards had his proposals about promoting other treatments, and another leading (if unsuccessful) Democratic candidate for president, former governor Howard Dean of Vermont—who is also a physician—called for an outright ban on DTC "except for situations where there is a compelling public health justification." Yet amazingly, the FDA, which had made the ads possible to begin with and refused to tighten the rules now, largely maintained its public halo. Dean criticized the Bush administration in general and "the drug industry's massive campaign contributions to the Republican party," but not the FDA.

Sean Brandle is a consultant at The Segal Company in New York City, advising big corporations on what sorts of prescription benefits to provide for their employees and how to keep expenses under control. The rising cost of drugs is thus a big issue for his clients, and they know that DTC ads contribute to that cost. "It naturally comes back to the drug companies because they do the advertising," he said. "I don't know that they tie it back to the FDA."

CHAPTER 14

Frivolous Drugs?

In the early 2000s, the FDA publicly fretted that it was getting fewer and fewer applications for truly innovative new drugs. That was, agency officials said, one of the reasons they were going to work more closely with industry through the "critical path" initiative to try and push drug development along faster. In 1996 the regulators had approved 53 of the most innovative type of drug, known as new molecular entities (NMEs), or compounds that had never before been sold in the United States. By 2003, that number had fallen to 21. In the 1990s, innovative compounds constituted 36 percent of all new drugs approved. By 2003, they represented just 30 percent.

Then what were all those other applications that were keeping the FDA's reviewers busy? Sometimes a company will alter a drug to make it more effective or convenient. For instance, Merck's original osteoporosis product Fosamax had to be taken every day; then Merck came up with a once-a-week version and got a new patent. And there are the supplemental new drug applications that a manufacturer files if it decides to seek formal approval for a secondary use rather than counting on off-label sales, as Celgene did with thalidomide for multiple myeloma. All those are fair enough and certainly helpful to the public, if not always dramatic.

But many applications involve just a minor modification, or a combination of two existing drugs, or a drug similar to half a dozen already on the market. For that matter, even the NMEs are not always important

273

treatments for serious, life-threatening diseases. NME designation is not the same thing as qualifying for fast track, priority review, or accelerated approval; it simply means that the drug is an innovative new formulation.

So the FDA has approved:

- Humatrope, Eli Lilly's genetically engineered growth hormone. This had been sold since 1987 for one specialized use, for children with a particular hormone deficiency. In July 2003 the FDA gave it the go-ahead for children who have no hormonal deficiency but are simply a little shorter than average.

- Crestor, a drug for high cholesterol made by AstraZeneca. By the time it was approved in August 2003, patients with cholesterol problems already had a choice of five other, very similar brand-name drugs, plus generics, in the category called statins. But the problem wasn't merely that Crestor might be redundant: The consumer advocacy group Public Citizen charged that it actually caused worse side effects than the other statins, including kidney damage and severe muscle deterioration, and called for it to be banned. During dramatic testimony in front of Congress in November 2004, David Graham—the controversial FDA safety reviewer who had raised the red flag on Vioxx—included Crestor among five questionable drugs whose safety problems, he said, should be "seriously looked at."

- Botox, the famous paralyzing drug injected by movie stars and TV news anchors to banish their wrinkles. Derived from a toxin that can cause botulism—"the most potent poisons known," according to *The Merck Manual*—the drug was first approved for a rare disorder of the eye muscles. The FDA opened the door to vanity use in 2002 by allowing it for forehead wrinkles. The following year, the agency OKed another drug for smoothing facial wrinkles, Restylane. A third drug, Sculptra, which took a different approach to helping faces look youthful, was also in line. In that case, the FDA granted approval for a genuine medical purpose (facial wasting connected with AIDS) and then helped the French pharmaceutical giant Aventis design clinical trials to test it for purely cosmetic uses.

- Clarinex, Schering-Plough's second-generation allergy medicine. The patent on the company's innovative and phenomenally successful allergy pill Claritin was due to run out in 2002, which meant that people would be able to buy much cheaper generic copies from other companies. Schering-Plough would suddenly lose a golden goose that had been laying as much as $3 billion a year in sales. So the manufacturer dug up a second patent that it had obtained years earlier, this one on the molecule, or metabolite, that Claritin turns into once it is in the body. Schering-Plough named that molecule Clarinex and got the FDA's green light in December 2001. True, Clarinex was also approved for a usage (year-round indoor allergies) that Claritin does not cover, but since the two pills are virtually the same thing, perhaps Schering-Plough could have just gotten a secondary indication for Claritin. Of course, the patent extension on a secondary indication would have been more limited than the patent on the "new" drug Clarinex. In all, patenting Clarinex was akin to eating your dinner, then pumping your stomach and selling what emerged as a fresh meal—at almost the same price as the original dinner. (As it happened, Claritin ended up becoming an over-the-counter drug, so no generic versions ever came out.)

- Two generic versions of the powerful and controversial painkiller OxyContin. Drug officials (of both the FDA and the illegal-drug type) had been worried for a long time about how easily OxyContin was being abused, even while it was still on patent and thus expensive. It is supposed to be taken pill by pill, over many hours, so that its slow-release chemical is gradually absorbed into the body. Instead, abusers grind a bunch of pills together and snort or inject the powdered mixture all at once to get an instant, powerful high. A federal study in 2002 found that nearly two million people had used OxyContin without a genuine medical need. What made this drug more worrisome than other time-release pills was that it had managed to pack more hours' worth of doses into its formula. So by letting cheap generic copies onto the market, in March 2004, the FDA was acting like a drug pusher declaring a half-price sale. The agency acknowledged the "potential for abuse, misuse, and diversion," in an unusual press release accompanying the approval. It noted that the generic manufacturers had promised to include some sort of risk-management safeguards, but nothing specific was spelled out. Eight months later, the FDA announced a pilot project to use special labels with tiny radio-frequency electronic tags on bottles of OxyContin and a few other drugs, in order to track shipments from the factory and prevent theft and counterfeiting.

However, that would not stop people with legitimate prescriptions from abusing the pills or selling them via underground networks— among other tactics.

• Cialis, the third of the highly advertised impotence drugs, approved in November 2003. When Pfizer launched Viagra, in 1998, it insisted that the drug was aimed at older men suffering from a diagnosed medical condition called erectile dysfunction. But as the ads with beautiful blondes and hulking sports stars make clear, that strategy was quickly abandoned, and now all three brands are basically pitched to younger men like expensive sex toys. Indeed, the fastest-growing group of Viagra users from 1998 to 2002 was men aged 18 to 45, according to a survey by the pharmacy benefits manager Express Scripts, Inc. (A pharmacy benefits manager is a company that administers health insurance programs.) And the San Francisco Department of Public Health, citing a trend of "recreational Viagra use," in August 2004 asked the FDA to require stricter labels that would warn that "Viagra use may increase the risk for sexually transmitted diseases and HIV infection." What if Viagra and another competitor, Levitra, are not powerful enough for this active younger market? Try Cialis—which, manufacturers Lilly and Icos Corporation brag, is effective for up to 36 hours.

In other words, a significant percentage of the drugs the FDA spends time on are arguably unnecessary, trivial, and possibly even dangerous: Botox, Propecia (for baldness), and Humatrope to save Baby Boomers and their kids from the horrors of looking anything other than perfect. Clarinex to stretch out a pharmaceutical maker's monopoly beyond what the patent system actually intended. The umpteenth version of a cholesterol drug that may actually be worse than the others already available.

The industry churns these drugs out largely because they're profitable. Schering-Plough produces Clarinex, because fiddling with an existing Claritin is so much faster and cheaper than spending 12 years and $800 million developing a totally new drug. AstraZeneca produces Crestor because it is relatively easy to follow a scientific path and a market that have already been established. Allergan Inc. makes Botox, and Lilly and Icos make Cialis because there is a huge population of Boomers.

This sort of roster is often Exhibit A in criticisms of Big Pharma by politicians, consumer groups, and crusading journalists. "Schering-Plough's

Clarinex illustrates the industry's increasingly common practice of developing drugs that offer only marginal improvements over existing products," asserted Families USA in its 2002 booklet *Profiting from Pain: Where Prescription Drug Dollars Go.* "We think most experts would agree that there is little or no rationale for having four or more me-too drugs," wrote Arnold S. Relman and Marcia Angell, both former editors of *The New England Journal of Medicine*, in *The New Republic*, also in 2002, specifically mentioning statins like Crestor. Tacitly agreeing that these products are of questionable value, insurance company formularies often make patients pay higher than usual copayments for second-generation drugs like Clarinex or lifestyle drugs like Viagra, or they may even refuse to cover such drugs at all.

Underlying the criticisms is the argument that products like Clarinex, Crestor, and Botox waste resources, keep drug spending high, and distract the industry from doing really important work. In a ridiculously vicious circle, the high prices forked over by patients for Clarinex and the other drugs go to pay for the three billion dollars' worth of DTC advertising that the companies promulgate in order to persuade us to keep on buying high-priced new drugs like Clarinex that we don't really need. Meanwhile, all the brainpower that is devoted to tweaking Claritin or developing Botox could have been used to cure cancer.

On the other side of the debate, the drug makers point out that no company in any industry can come up with significant innovations day after day. Everyone needs some workhorse products to provide the cash flow for the truly innovative R&D. "Copycats are what we used to call competition," scoffed Fred Smith of the Competitive Enterprise Institute, the libertarian think tank.

And who gave the critics the right to tell people what drugs they do or do not need? Crestor is not totally identical to Lipitor, Zocor, and the other statins, and some patients do better on one brand than on the others. I know people whom I respect—intelligent people, some of them doctors—who swear that Nexium works where almost-identical Prilosec doesn't, or that Vioxx, used sporadically, was more effective than the similar painkiller Celebrex or Ibuprofen. As for Botox, Propecia, and Viagra, well, there's obviously a public demand for having no wrinkles, a headful of hair, and great sex. Is being short just a cosmetic problem, if you spend your life being bullied and teased? If it keeps you from a becoming a firefighter? James Love is one of the most vocal critics of the drug industry and its prices, as director of the Consumer Project on Technology, a group founded by

Ralph Nader, yet he shied away from criticizing the decision to pursue a Botox or Propecia. "I don't know how judgmental I want to be about these things. If I was a woman and I had a lot of facial hair, I would want a product. It's not as high a priority maybe as a product for cancer, but nobody condemns people who make Nike sneakers because they don't cure cancer."

For that matter, maybe these drugs are not as frivolous as they seem. Botox started out as a medication for a serious eye condition. By relaxing muscles and easing pain, it later showed some promising results in clinical trials as a treatment for such disparate—and nonfrivolous—problems as carpal tunnel syndrome, facial tics, incontinence, lower back pain, migraine headaches, stroke paralysis, stuttering, tennis elbow, and writer's cramp. In 2004 it was approved for severe underarm sweating, which is in fact a medical condition known as severe primary axillary hyperhidrosis. Pfizer is seeking FDA approval for Viagra for a rare but life-threatening lung disease called pulmonary hypertension.

So there is a genuine debate to be had on the question of what constitutes a frivolous waste of prescription dollars. Yet a key player that should be part of this debate has been deliberately missing in action: the FDA.

There's no doubt that the FDA has a stake in this debate. These are issues of public health that the agency is supposed to protect. Its staff and money are possibly wasted in reviewing applications for Botox, Crestor, and the like. Can't the FDA do something to encourage more innovative drugs for serious medical needs? Why can't it just reject some of the silly ones?

It's the law, Janet Woodcock said. "We adhere to a statutory requirement for what we're supposed to do. We're looking at the clinical data, whether the drug works in a certain case. Also the safety. We aren't making value judgments about different uses."

Safety and efficacy. If a drug is brought to the FDA, and the clinical trial data show that it is safe and it works, then the agency must approve it— silly or not, needed or not. "They wake up every day and say, 'Safety and efficacy. Efficacy and safety. Here's as far as we go, this is our track, and we go on this track,'" commented Arthur Caplan, the health care ethicist from the University of Pennsylvania, who worked directly with FDA officials from 1997 to 2001 as chair of the Blood Products Advisory Committee.

The debate over "frivolous" drugs goes back to the dispute over whether to test new drugs against placebos or against existing drugs. As

Bob Temple wrote in the September 19, 2000, issue of *Annals of Internal Medicine*, "under law, a drug need not be superior to or even as good as other therapy to be approved." It can be less potent, take longer to kick in, and have worse side effects, as long as those side effects are not too severe. So Crestor may be worse on the kidneys than Zocor or Lipitor, but it still gets on the pharmacy shelves. "It is not their [FDA] only job to approve breakthrough champions," said Kevin DeStefino, a consultant with the giant firm of Watson Wyatt Worldwide, defining "champion" as "a drug that absolutely does a superior job."

Instead, in the FDA's view, market forces will make the comparisons. Presumably, if a new medication has no noticeable advantages over its rivals, doctors and patients will do what the FDA cannot, and shun it. By the same token, manufacturers voluntarily test certain drugs against rivals when they expect to see favorable comparisons that they can use in marketing. The only way the FDA gets involved in distinguishing frivolous drugs from breakthroughs is to help the latter get to market faster by granting them fast-track, priority review, accelerated approval, and treatment investigational new drug designations.

In December 2004 an FDA advisory committee recommended against a drug from Procter & Gamble Co. dubbed "the female Viagra"—a hormone patch that was supposed to increase sexual desire and satisfaction among postmenopausal women. No doubt the patch, like the original Viagra, would have been used off-label as a sex toy by those without a demonstrated medical need. But it's not clear that the advisory committee's action was some kind of statement against lifestyle drugs. The main issues raised by both staff and the committee had to do with basic efficacy and safety. They said the clinical trial data didn't show a significant increase in sexual satisfaction. And with serious questions already being raised about the risks of hormone replacement therapy for postmenopausal women— on top of the barrage of criticism of the FDA for allegedly missing the dangers of Vioxx—the FDA was in no mood to blithely approve another female hormone treatment.

Senators John Edwards and Tom Harkin, in their 2003 bill on drug advertising, took a shot at trying to spur innovation by changing the FDA approval process. Their measure would require drug companies to prove that a new drug is easier to use, safer, or more effective than what is already on the market, not just safe and effective in itself. But the two Democrats' measure went nowhere in the Republican-controlled Congress. Edwards also talked about drug choices in his unsuccessful vice presidential campaign, calling for more research that would compare prescription drugs to over-the-counter alternatives. *BusinessWeek* had a similar idea in its proposal for comparative data in drug ads.

To Marcia Angell, the former *New England Journal of Medicine* editor, requiring the FDA to evaluate new drug applications against existing drugs, as part of the approval process, is "the single most important change that should be made" to spur real innovation and bring prices down.

It might seem that the patent laws would give the FDA some leverage. After all, a patent is supposed to be granted only for something that is useful, novel, and not obvious. The sixth version of a cholesterol drug hardly seems novel or not obvious, and a generic form of an easily abused painkiller hardly seems useful. If drug makers knew they could not get a patent on ridiculous stuff, maybe they would spend more time developing real innovations.

However, the FDA does not grant patents; the U.S. Patent and Trademark Office does. The FDA claims it is merely a stenographer, recording drug patents in what is known colloquially as the "Orange Book" because the title was traditionally printed in orange (the official name is *Approved Drug Products with Therapeutic Equivalence Evaluations*). Nor are the standards for winning a patent considered very tough. Schering-Plough got one for the Clarinex metabolite, and AstraZeneca got one for Nexium, which is simply half the Prilosec molecule. Astra-Zeneca also had 11 separate patents for Prilosec listed in the Orange Book. Drug companies patent just about everything except the water you swallow the pill with—the pill, the method of manufacturing the pill, the metabolite produced in the body, the coating on the pill, the subcoating between layers of the pill, and different dosage forms of the pill. "What you're really asking is a patent legal policy question," Steve Galson, the acting head of the Center for Drugs, replied when I asked him why the FDA let the drug makers get away with what seemed like repetitive and nonsensical patents. "It's not something CDER gets involved in. The Patent Office makes judgments on whether to patent."

Galson did note one exception: "We get dragged in sometimes if the claims are purely scientific for a new patent, such as patenting a metabolite." So why doesn't the FDA at least block that kind of application, by saying that it is not based on any true scientific innovation? "If it's not, we'll say it's not. We've always felt like we've been tough," Galson asserted, although he could not come up with any examples of cases where the FDA had said a claim was not scientifically original. In fact, when Bristol-Myers Squibb in 2000 tried to fend off generic versions of its anti-anxiety medication BuSpar by filing for a patent on swallowing one of the pill's main metabolites—that's right, a patent on swallowing, which the company described as a method of administering the drug—it was a federal court, not the FDA, that finally threw the case out. The FDA accepted the patent that had been issued by the Patent Office and agreed to delay the generics.

(Maybe the drug makers will try to patent water after all.)

Still, even if the occasional patent is rather ridiculous, the patent system is supposed to encourage innovation by setting a limit on how long a company is permitted to maintain a monopoly on its invention. Once the patent monopoly ends, rivals can undercut the original manufacturer with identical but lower-priced generic copies—as Schering-Plough anticipated with Claritin. Supposedly, customers will flock to the cheaper alternative, and the brand-name drug company will then focus on creating another innovative drug. It will reap the monopoly profits from that second drug as long as it can, and when that patent expires, turn to the next innovation in its lab. And on and on.

That's the theory, anyway. In reality, federal laws have regularly given drug makers more and more ways to extend their patents. First came the Hatch-Waxman Act in 1984, which tried to balance the demands of generic and brand-name drugs. For the generic companies, it granted "bio-equivalency," letting them obtain FDA approval if they just showed that the active ingredient in their drug was released and absorbed into the body at about the same rate as the active ingredient in the original. Thus, generic companies did not have to repeat all the clinical trials that had been conducted for the first NDA. These companies also were allowed to file their applications and get tentative approval in advance, so that they could jump right into the market the day the patent expired. In return, the brand-name companies got a patent extension of five years, plus three more years for any secondary usage that was approved and— this was crucial—30 months if they challenged a generic. Subsequently, to conform to the rules of the General Agreement on Tariffs and Trade and the World Trade Organization, the United States in 1994 changed the term of its patents to 20 years from the date of application, versus the previous limit of 17 years from the date it was granted—which, depending on the circumstances, might mean a longer effective monopoly in the market. In 1997 the FDA Modernization Act let drug makers tack on an additional six months of patent exclusivity when they tested the drug on children.

If all that was not enough time, the drug industry found ways within the law to stretch the government's generosity even further. Patenting qualities like coatings and metabolites was just one tactic. Companies filed what are called citizens' petitions against generics, challenging whether the generics really were safe or bioequivalent. They bought off the generic makers, paying them millions of dollars to delay marketing their copycat drugs. Or, they sued generic makers repeatedly, which automatically activated one 30-month extension after another under Hatch-Waxman. All this fiddling had three major consequences that might have been handy for the drug companies but were lousy for society in general. The FDA actually took longer to approve the typical generic—even though it was a copy of an already approved drug—than a new NDA. Drug prices stayed high, because there was less generic competition. And as long as the companies could live off the fat of their old patents, they felt no urgency to research new drugs.

Whatever opposition there might be to these patent-delaying tactics was usually led by generic companies, patients seeking access to generic versions, or other government agencies—not the FDA. Consumer groups sued GlaxoSmithKline in 2003, charging that it tried to illegally extend a patent on its anti-inflammatory drug Relafen by hiding information; both sides settled in 2004 for $75 million. Eli Lilly's patent on the schizophrenia medication Zyprexa was challenged in federal court in 2004 by two generics makers that argued that data from animal trials were flawed. Meanwhile, the Federal Trade Commission in 2002 launched a study and filed civil charges against several brand-name drug companies for payoffs to generic companies.

The main way the FDA got involved in any of these challenges was in scrutinizing the big pharmaceutical companies' citizens' petitions. Four-fifths of the time it rejected the main charges in the petitions, but that usually took six months—which was all the delay the drug companies expected anyway.

By 2002, the manipulation of the patent laws had gotten so egregious that even several big pharmaceutical makers such as Merck were publicly condemning it, and the Senate by an overwhelming 78-to-21 margin voted to restrict the companies to just one Hatch-Waxman lawsuit with one 30-month extension. Although the one-lawsuit limit never passed the full Congress, the Bush administration, sensing the public pressure, declared that the FDA would issue regulations to the same effect. Not only that, but when the final regulations came out, they also included a ban on some of the silliest types of patents, like patents on packaging. In other words, the FDA could have clamped down all along, without a change in the law.

"Congress has sent us a mini-signal that we need to be a little more careful, a little more aggressive," conceded Lester Crawford, who is usually not one to get out in front of an issue. And that signal applied, he added, not just to the Hatch-Waxman lawsuits but also to other patent issues.

So did that mean that if the signal had been sent before Schering-Plough put in for its patent on Clarinex, the FDA would have rejected the patent?

"I doubt it," Crawford replied.

The FDA has made other efforts to help generics get to market faster. For instance, it told generics manufacturers they could introduce a product just different enough from the original to merit its own patent but similar enough to use the first drug's trial data to prove efficacy and safety. So the regulators gave a company from India named Dr. Reddy's Laboratories Ltd. the go-ahead to make such a version of Pfizer's blockbuster blood-pressure pill Norvasc in November 2003. Unfortunately, as soon as this happened, Pfizer filed suit, and the FDA promised to reconsider. Meanwhile, the White House grandly announced that it wanted to give the agency an extra $13 million to hire more reviewers devoted to generics, but that figure got whittled nearly in half by the time the federal budget was done.

The FDA spent much of 2003 and 2004 trying to figure out whether it was possible to produce certifiable generic versions of biologic drugs. Traditional chemical drugs can be copied fairly easily because they are based on active ingredients and processes that are relatively well-understood and straightforward to analyze. Biologics, however, are considered much harder to duplicate, thanks to the complicated way they are made and the quirky nature of the proteins they are usually made from. Indeed, this is a problem even in manufacturing the original drugs. The same proteins made from different cell lines or in different factories can act differently when put in a pill. The consistency of any vaccine varies because each batch has to be grown in a separate cell culture.

For years, the whole concept of a generic biologic drug thus seemed impossible. It also was moot, since the innovative biotech drugs were new and largely still under patent. And because most biologics do not fall under the 1906 Food and Drug Act or the Hatch-Waxman Act—they date back to the Biologics Control Act of 1902—the FDA had the ready excuse that its hands were tied unless Congress untied them by passing a law specifically about generic biologics. In summer 2004 the regulators told Novartis' generic unit Sandoz that they simply could not make any decision on its application for a generic recombinant-DNA human growth hormone Omnitrope because of "uncertainty regarding scientific and legal issues."

However, Mark McClellan and Janet Woodcock made it a priority to develop guidelines for the few biologics that, by a legal quirk, were subject to Hatch-Waxman—and that, fortunately, were the simpler and older products that would lose their patent protection first. While the FDA brass did not see any chance of creating completely identical generics, they were hopeful that they could devise some tests for proving that a generic was similar enough to the original that the approval process could be streamlined. Then, the generics could use the same alternative route that the FDA had originally allowed for Dr. Reddy's.

"Some people believe the FDA should leave this alone until Congress acts. But new developments are going on all over the world. It's important for FDA to play a leading role in this area," McClellan told a small pharmaceutical industry convention in November 2003. Ira Loss, the Washington, D.C. health care analyst, suggested that the idea of generic biologics appealed to both of McClellan's areas of expertise—the science of copying something difficult, and the economics of getting prices down.

Theoretically, if the FDA could figure out a way to certify biologic copies, the generics makers would apply the same kind of pressure on biotech companies that they supposedly applied to traditional drug manufacturers, forcing the big guys to go back to their labs and start finding new molecules. Of course, the brand-name biotechs might just as easily find the same loopholes.

CHAPTER 15

The Next 100 Years

As if the FDA weren't busy enough doing its regular work—analyzing new drug and device applications, looking out for contaminated foods, tracking any suspicious spurt of side effects among drugs already approved, scrambling to keep up with the way science is changing, policing drug ads on TV—it is also staring at a pantry full of fresh demands. Some are responsibilities it has eagerly sought, while others have been shoved onto its shelves. Some are first-time issues, prompted by new science, new health problems, and new social pressures; some are reruns that the FDA thought it had already settled. Waiting in the wings, moreover, are controversies the agency has managed to avoid so far, but somebody is going to have to tackle them, and the FDA is probably the most qualified to do so.

Taking on these tasks will not only enlarge the FDA beyond its already huge mandate. In some cases, the new duties could also drastically change the way medicine is practiced, the way government is viewed, and the way Americans live.

THE COST OF MEDICINE

In his short stint as commissioner, Mark McClellan was a whirlwind of activity, seeming to publish a different pronouncement every week. Most of them were at least within the range of the FDA's normal jurisdiction, topics like getting more women into clinical trials, speeding up approval of generic drugs, or requiring bar code labels on drugs and blood products. Then in September 2003, in a speech to pharmaceutical industry executives in Cancún, Mexico, he startled all sides of the health care world by talking about the cost of drugs.

Specifically, McClellan complained that Americans were paying far more for their medicine than people in other well-off countries where the governments either controlled prices or negotiated big discounts for national insurance programs. Canadians, for instance, typically paid 70 percent less than Americans, a fact the fight over reimportation highlighted. Those prescription dollars were presumably being used by industry to finance new research. But the United States could not carry the oversized load alone forever. So unless some other nations were willing to chip in more, pharmaceutical companies would not have the $802 million they supposedly needed to bring a drug to market. "If we do not find better ways to share the burden of developing new drugs," McClellan warned, "all of us will suffer." He repeated his message in a slew of speeches that fall and brought it up during trade talks with Australia. The next year, the United States and Australia negotiated a trade pact giving the industry unprecedented power to challenge the prescription prices authorized by Australia's Pharmaceutical Benefits Scheme.

Perhaps it was no wonder that the FDA commissioner plunged his agency into the arena of drug costs, because this was becoming a bigger and bigger problem and a hotter and hotter political potato. Two major consumer groups, AARP (formerly known as the American Association of Retired Persons) and Families USA, issued separate reports showing that prices for the most popular name-brand medications had risen at roughly three to four times the rate of inflation between 2000 and 2004. Some of the amazing new targeted cancer drugs also had amazing price tags. Erbitux plus chemotherapy ran a whopping $161,000 a year, according to an article in *The New England Journal of Medicine* in July 2004. Iressa cost $1,700 a month, and Avastin for colon cancer was $4,400. Public fury at the bill for prescriptions had prompted a huge backlash, forcing Congress to add drug coverage to Medicare and pushing it to the brink of legalizing reimportation from Canada, while the major Democratic candidates for president in 2004 all denounced the soaring cost of prescriptions. Sooner or later, someone in the federal government was clearly going to have to face this problem.

Still, McClellan's speeches marked the first time any FDA commissioner had taken on drug prices as a specific, official issue, and for many people—whatever they thought of drug prices—the move stretched the agency's authority just too far beyond its traditional one-fourth of the U.S. economy. Nor was it clear whether the agency could tackle prices along the lines McClellan was talking about without specific congressional authorization. "It's not part of their mandate. Certainly regulation of drug prices in other countries is not within their mandate," said Alastair Wood, the Vanderbilt professor who was almost named commissioner before McClellan. At Families USA, where the main issue is the affordability of prescription drugs for the elderly, senior policy analyst Dee Mahan hesitated. "I was a little surprised—pleasantly surprised—to hear him say rich countries should pay more, poor countries pay less," she said. Yet she worried that the overworked FDA staffers would have less time to review drugs if they also had to start looking at price. Other people pointed out that the agency's scientists and reviewers were not trained in economics. "Don't make this plate bigger than we can handle," warned Don McLearn, the former FDA public relations official, now a public relations executive in Washington, D.C.

Estes Kefauver tried to delve into drug costs, high markups, and anticompetitive pricing in 1959 and 1960, but he found little interest and was ultimately diverted by the thalidomide scandal. Even David Kessler demurred at taking on prices. During his confirmation hearing as FDA commissioner, he was asked by Al Gore, then a senator from Tennessee, "As more spectacular drugs are developed and the cost of health care continues to spiral upward, can we afford a drug pricing policy whose bottom line is whatever the market will bear?"

Replied Kessler: "I have my hands full enforcing the Food, Drug, and Cosmetic Act. That act tells me to worry about safety and effectiveness."

So when McClellan raised the price issue, no one was sure just how seriously to take it. Lester Crawford, who temporarily moved into the 14th-floor commissioner's office after McClellan left to run Medicare, claimed that his predecessor pretty much got into the topic by accident, as a spin-off from the debate over importing inexpensive drugs from Canada. "Congress asked the FDA, 'Can you give us some figures on [the cost differences between the two countries]?" Crawford said. "He [McClellan] was trying to point out that the issue of Canadian drugs is not what people think. It's because Canada has cost controls, and we have a free market economy." Things simply grew from there, according to

Crawford. However, many observers suggested that McClellan's interest was genuine, if mainly intellectual, stemming from the fact that he is an economist as well as a doctor—in fact, probably an economist first and foremost. "All of his mentors at Harvard Medical School say he takes things first like an economist, then like a doctor," said Peter Barton Hutt, the former FDA counsel.

More cynically, Hutt and others speculated that McClellan latched on to the cost issue—or was forced to—for political reasons, to deflect public anger at the White House's opposition to reimporting drugs from Canada. "He didn't do it voluntarily. Kicking and screaming, they have been dragged into this debate," insisted Congressman Gil Gutknecht, one of the leaders of the Canadian importation effort.

For that matter, McClellan was not exactly arguing the populist case against the Big Bad Pharmaceutical Industry. Yes, he was sympathizing with American consumers, but he was also taking mostly at face value the drug companies' claim that they needed high prices to pay for R&D. Consumer groups dispute that argument, pointing out that a big chunk of the drug makers' income goes to advertising, management, and profit margins that historically are far higher than at any other industry. Families USA, for instance, published analyses in 2000 and 2002 showing that most big companies spent more than twice as much on marketing and administration as they did on research. So maybe McClellan's price campaign was actually just another example of Big Pharma's power over the FDA and Washington, D.C. in general. "If I were commissioner," Gutknecht scoffed, "I would want to find out why drugs are cheaper in Switzerland, rather than say the Swiss have to pay more." In any case, once McClellan left the FDA, the cause left with him. "We don't do drug prices," Crawford told me flatly.

The irony is that Crawford is wrong. The FDA often "does" pricing issues; however, it gets at them from under, over, and around the side, rather than head-on.

As McClellan himself pointed out in many of his speeches, anything the agency can do to move generics to market faster or to certify biologic generics would give patients access to drugs that cost less than name-brand prescriptions. Also, he argued, by pushing approvals along faster and working with companies on the "critical path" program to expedite their R&D, the FDA should help industry save time and money, which supposedly would translate to lower prices.

That's not all. In regulating drug ads, the FDA sometimes has to consider pricing claims, according to Peter J. Neumann, an associate professor of policy and decision science at the Harvard School of Public Health. When he and four other academics studied 2,144 prescription drug ads in six leading professional journals from 1990 to 1999, they found that 11.1 percent used some sort of economic assertion. It might be that the drug was "less expensive" or "costs less" than a rival, or that it provides "value" or "savings." Well, as Neumann and his colleagues wrote in the journal *Medical Care* in 2002, "FDA officials have noted that economic claims could be misleading for various reasons—for example, if they contained unsupported claims of equivalence in the effectiveness or safety of a medication, or if they made claims of cost savings when there were additional costs which are unmentioned." Neumann told me, when I interviewed him about his research, that five percent of the FDA's warning letters for drug ads cite these sorts of economic violations.

When poisoned Tylenol capsules were found for a second time, in 1986, the FDA faced a direct conflict between price and safety—and it sided with price. Congress had passed a law mandating tamper-resistant packaging after the first Tylenol scare, in 1982, when seven people died from poisoned capsules. That law was supposed to protect over-the-counter pills from any meddling. Nevertheless, in February 1986 a 23-year-old woman in New York took two Extra Strength Tylenol capsules and died within minutes. Another tainted bottle was found elsewhere in New York state. Johnson & Johnson, the manufacturer, considered a recall. The FDA debated whether to require a second layer of tamper-resistant packaging; drug companies warned that it would cost $1 billion to revamp their production lines or subcontract the manufacturing. "The FDA looked at it and said, 'It's not worth it,'" said Bill Vodra, the former associate chief counsel. In other words, the supposed regulator of safety and efficacy made a decision that $1 billion was too high a price to pay for an extra measure of safety, based on classic cost-benefit analysis. Presumably, the extra $1 billion would have been shifted to consumers in the form of higher drug prices.

Thus, the agency can never completely avoid dealing with the cost of the products it regulates. And there is a more important overlap that almost no one, not even McClellan, has considered publicly, a question that gets to the core of the FDA's mission. Al Gore came close at Kessler's confirmation hearing. As Jerry Mande, the former aide to both men, put it, "If patients can't afford a new cancer drug, can that drug be said to be truly effective? And if not, is the FDA fulfilling its mandate to make sure drugs are effective?" "If people can die because they can't afford drugs, why isn't that as bad as the fact that people may die because some drugs are unsafe?" asked Dan Callahan of the Hastings Institute.

"That's a very good point," Lester Crawford conceded in our interview. But, "it's not our job."

If not the FDA, then whose job is it? The Centers for Medicare and Medicaid Services would seem the obvious candidate, now that the federal government was going to be paying for drugs through Medicare, and in fact in 2004 that agency launched an Internet listing that compared prices of some commonly used drugs. But the Republican majority in Congress wrote the new Medicare law to specifically forbid the CMS from negotiating prices with drug companies.

So let's consider what would happen if the FDA did take on some price regulation. First, it could conduct a cost-effectiveness analysis as part of the approval process, comparing new drug applications to existing drugs—essentially abandoning its insistence on placebo comparisons. Here is how it might have worked with Clarinex:

The FDA would have compared Clarinex to Claritin, which was about to be sold over the counter. Both drugs claim to help relieve the symptoms of seasonal outdoor allergies without causing drowsiness, but Clarinex was also seeking approval for year-round indoor allergies. So, the FDA might ask, how much more powerful is Clarinex? How much did Schering-Plough anticipate charging for the two drugs? What alternatives are available?

Under this proposal, the FDA would not be able to reject a drug based solely on cost, the way health maintenance organization formulary committees do. Nor should it. Let consumers have plenty of choices. However, the FDA could give buyers more information about comparative price effectiveness, to help them juggle all the choices and decide whether an expensive new medication was really worth the cost. It's only fair, after all: In 1997 the FDA paved the way for patients to get bombarded by glitzy, incomplete, and manipulative drug ads on TV, so now it should make sure they also have real information.

Going to Congress would open up more possibilities. James Love of the Consumer Project on Technology would like to see mandatory disclosure about the R&D process as part of any new drug application. Companies would have to provide information regarding the types of clinical trials that were done and the real cost of doing them. Pharmaceutical makers are famously secretive about this, which is one reason the $802 million-per-drug claim is so disputed. The Tufts University researchers who came up with that figure had access to proprietary information from a database of prescription drugs they have been maintaining since 1972, but even they do not have a complete data set. They are missing about 10 percent of the drugs in development, and most of the early-stage numbers are aggregated, not specified drug by drug. "It would be good if we had more information. That would allow us to make more rational decisions" about policies like tax credits, Love said. He pointed out that regulated utilities traditionally have had to reveal detailed information on their costs and profits.

PERFECT BODIES

When it comes to vanity drugs, Botox, Propecia, and Humatrope are just the beginning. Looking ahead, experts imagine all sorts of ways that genetic engineering, neuropharmacology, stem cell therapy, and other forms of biotechnology could be harnessed to the medicine cabinet. Pills that would boost memory, to help students taking tests. Or pills that would erase memory, so that rape victims could forget their trauma. A Prozac without any side effects whatsoever to make us all calm and happy. A completely safe "designer" steroid to make us star athletes. Pills that stop bone-mass loss, keep joints flexible, erase wrinkles, and reduce the buildup of amyloid plaque connected with Alzheimer's disease—in other words, pills that hide all the signs that we are getting old. Or that delay old age indefinitely. Pills that eliminate all the seven deadly sins, all aggression, all social unease, even an anti-smoking vaccine. Just about everything short of *soma*, the narcotic that the people in *Brave New World* constantly take to escape from the slightest hint of unpleasantness.

Some of this is already under way. Human growth hormone, which first was prescribed only for a rare hormone deficiency, then for short kids in general, is increasingly being provided to adults who want to hold off the symptoms of aging, because it seems to build up muscle and reduce fat. A researcher at Case Western Reserve University gave Aricept, an Alzheimer's medication from Pfizer, to nine healthy, middle-aged aircraft pilots every day for 30 days in 2002—pilots with no apparent symptoms of Alzheimer's. Compared with a group on placebos, the pilots did measurably better on complex flight simulators. Scientists have found a gene that, if switched off, dramatically extends the lifespan of worms and mice.

Another scientist won a prize for keeping a mutant mouse alive the equivalent of 180 human years on a low-calorie diet, while yet a different group used gene therapy to make mice more muscular.

As soon as a pharmaceutical company wants to test on humans any new pills that might be derived from the mouse experiments, it will have to get approval from the FDA. It will also need approval to sell that pill. But approval of what?

Is it sufficient for the FDA to evaluate such controversial, revolutionary, even humanity-altering drugs only for their safety and efficacy? What worries many people is not that these drugs wouldn't work—in fact, the problem is just the opposite. The real fear is that they will work as intended, and thus change human nature, turning us all into beatifically calm zombies with Superman pecs.

"In wanting to improve our bodies and our minds using new tools to enhance their performance, we risk making our bodies and minds little different from our tools, in the process also compromising the distinctly human character of our agency and activity," warned the President's Council on Bioethics in a report in the fall of 2003. And in another section: "By providing quick solutions for short-term problems or prompt fulfillment of easily satisfied desires, the character of human longing itself could be altered, with large aspirations for long-term flourishing giving way before the immediate gratification of smaller desires." The report pointed to everything from everyday drugs like Ritalin (to calm hyperactive kids) and Rogaine (to grow hair), to an imaginary "Memorase" or "Eroticor."

Would an Einstein on super-Prozac have had the curiosity and drive to delve into the relationship between energy and matter, and thus revolutionize our understanding of physics? But maybe if he had had a memory-enhancing pill he could have produced the grand unified theory of physics, interweaving all the forces of nature, that he spent three decades unsuccessfully trying to construct. Is it so terrible to want human beings to have better mental ability, be more physically fit, live longer and healthier lives, and be happy?

"Suppose a drug without side effects could reduce aggression," mused the veteran journalist Gregg Easterbrook in *The New Republic*. "It might cut down on crime and bad driving, but might we also lose the aggressive desire to excel and to create?" Then imagine all of society on these memory-enhancing, body-building, depression-busting drugs.

These are not flippant questions. Yet they cannot be answered only by looking at the FDA's mantra of safety and efficacy. "Somebody's got to ask the question of, what's the impact on cultural values? If we decide to put implants in our heads, does that change humanity?" asked Arthur Caplan of the University of Pennsylvania's Center for Bioethics.

Maybe, said Lester Crawford, but again, that somebody is not the FDA. "We don't have any authority to do that at this time. That's for Congress to address." Would he like Congress to give the FDA some guidance? First, Crawford answered that "there is no administration bill" to that effect. Okay, but personally, would he like some guidance? "I don't do personal," he replied.

Crawford has a point. Issues this crucial to the very existence of the species should not be decided casually or behind closed doors as an offshoot of a drug application by a group of technocrats. Ideally, experts like the Council on Bioethics would come up with some thoughtful recommendations, which Congress would then debate. For instance, Congress has already been considering various types of bans on human cloning.

If that is the way to go, there are a lot of official bodies that might lay claim to helping set the policy—the Council on Bioethics and the National Institutes of Health, most obviously. But the FDA needs to participate in the debate, too. Caplan suggested that it could set up special advisory committees on ethical issues such as designer drugs, xenotransplanting (transplanting of animal organs and cells into humans), and stem cell research. Only the FDA has the on-the-ground expertise to know just what products are coming down the pike, and what is scientifically feasible at any point. The Bioethics Council is merely an ad hoc advisory board with a two-year lifespan created by George W. Bush in 2001. Future presidents could expand its mandate—or eliminate it.

What also makes the FDA a logical choice to cope with these ethical questions is that it has actually been doing so for years.

It is almost impossible to approve drugs like Humatrope for short kids, antidepressants, or even the big precursor of the abortion debate—the birth control pill in 1960—without thinking about the ethical and social implications. This is true even if the FDA ends up insisting that it cannot take ethics into consideration in its approval decisions. Moreover, in agreeing to some of the new clinical trial protocols that skip animal testing, the agency has had to weigh the ethics of turning humans into guinea pigs—almost literally. And what else was the original, controversial compromise on silicone-filled breast implants except a value judgment? The implants are no more or less dangerous when used by women who have had breast cancer than by women who want a sexier figure. Nevertheless, the FDA decided that women who do the procedure for purely cosmetic reasons do not have the right to the more attractive but riskier silicone implants. For all the scientific window-dressing, it is also pretty clear that the decision on Plan B, the over-the-counter emergency contraceptive, involved the bioethical judgment that the agency should not do anything that would encourage teenagers to have sex. Both the silicone implants and Plan B drew heavy lobbying by outside groups, which is hardly uncommon, except that in the case of Plan B a lot of the lobbying came from religious groups raising ethical issues, rather than the usual coterie of patients who suffered horrible side effects versus patients who need the drug.

Even Crawford noted that the FDA took an ethics-based stand back in the early 1980s, when some state governments asked it to evaluate the safety and efficacy of the lethal injections they were using to execute prisoners on death row. "Most of the [FDA] leadership were medical doctors who had taken the Hippocratic Oath. They couldn't approve [the injections]"—that is, doctors who had taken a vow to save lives felt they could not approve a drug whose sole purpose was to kill, Crawford explained. The agency told the states to use their own regulatory discretion. So the FDA officialdom refused to carry out its most basic legal duty, to rule on the safety and efficacy of a legal drug, because of qualms about whether the drug was ethical.

Those instances of bioethical decision making are, admittedly, rare. The next tests could come in 2 294005.

One involves Gardasil, Merck's vaccine for human papillomavirus (HPV), which the company expected the FDA to approve by the end of the year. What makes this so controversial is that HPV—the leading cause of cervical cancer—is spread mainly through sexual contact. And Merck was seeking approval for a target market of girls and women aged nine to 24. Thus, if the FDA approved the application as filed, it would essentially be telling parents: Your nine-year-old daughter might need this because she could be having sex in the near future. In light of their multiple victories in the 2004 elections, religious conservatives were guaranteed to storm the FDA on that one. They wouldn't be arguing that the vaccine was unsafe or ineffective—in fact, clinical trials had shown that it was stunningly effective at preventing HPV infection. They would be arguing, as with Plan B, the ethics of "facilitating" teenage sex.

The other looming ethics test involved a California biotech called Geron Corporation, which planned to ask the FDA to approve its protocol for clinical trials of a treatment for spinal cord injuries using cells derived from human embryonic stem cells. Crawford, who is not one to get out in front of an issue, said the FDA would not ask Geron if the stem cell work was done with federal money, or if the cells came from the limited number of cell lines allowed by the White House policy on federal funding for stem cell research. Those are not questions of safety and efficacy. The FDA would simply evaluate the protocol as it would any other proposal for a clinical trial. But of course the world would not see this as just another clinical trial. Like it or not, the FDA would be plunged into the political-religious maelstrom. If it approved the trial protocol, it would be denounced for letting drug companies kill babies in order to use their stems cells. If it rejected the protocol, it would be denounced for succumbing to political pressure from religious extremists.

THE WAY WE LIVE

The FDA has traditionally regulated *what*, not *how*. It makes sure that the ingredients of the foods we eat are safe, not whether we eat too much of them. It approves the drugs that doctors prescribe, not the way doctors prescribe them or to whom. That is the basis of the whole debate over off-label prescribing—taking a drug that has been approved only for Condition A and prescribing it, legally, for Condition B. It is because the FDA does not regulate the way doctors prescribe that Mike Katz is able to get thalidomide for conditions other than leprosy, and teenagers are using antidepressants that have never been approved for people under age 18.

By the same token, the FDA regulates merely the medicine we take to cure a disease, not what caused the disease. This is why so many people criticize CBER for doing research into the basics of human biology or molecular structure. None of the FDA's business, they say.

The only way the FDA might get into "how" is in giving warnings about the side effects of the drugs it approves and who should not use them (typically, pregnant women, the elderly, children, or people with weakened immune systems). Otherwise, doctors are supposed to read the package inserts and the *Physicians' Desk Reference* and keep track of the newest updates through professional journals, the FDA Web site, medical conferences, e-mail alert services, and sales reps' visits. Of course, the slew of recalled drugs in the late 1990s and 2000s proved that warnings—even those in so-called black boxes, the most serious type—do not always work. Doctors do not always pay attention. The label on Propulsid was changed five times, one more dire than the last. Rezulin had three label changes. The drugs finally were recalled in part because physicians were not following the precautions or conducting the tests the labels advised.

When it comes to how products are used, how diseases spread, or how Americans can lead healthier lives, there is no lack of government entities that might have jurisdiction. The states oversee the practice of medicine by licensing physicians. The U.S. surgeon general warns us about lifestyle issues like smoking and sexually transmitted diseases. The Department of Agriculture and the Department of Health and Human Services jointly write dietary guidelines that are usually followed by school lunch nutritionists and other federal programs. (Yes, the FDA is part of HHS, but the guidelines are done by the department as a whole.) If an epidemic breaks out, the Centers for Disease Control will take charge of advising the public on how to avoid exposure. Consumer groups have petitioned the Federal Trade Commission to clamp down on fast food and candy ads aimed at children. The National Institutes of Health does research into basic science and provides funding for other research by outside labs. Even on the local level, some municipalities have organized community weight-loss contests.

Jere Goyan, when he was the commissioner from November 1979 to January 1981, thought a lot about the "how" issues. "I was concerned with what I considered the overmedicated society, that people were looking to a pill for the answer to their problems. They could take a pill for their hypertension or diabetes and not worry about anything else such as diet and exercise. I was particularly concerned about so-called minor tranquilizers." That is still a big worry today, especially as the pharmaceutical industry keeps turning out more and more antidepressants, antianxiety drugs, mood stabilizers, and stimulants, along with all-in-one miracle pills like Provigil and heartburn drugs like Prilosec and Nexium, all of which are then pitched on TV. The drugs are safe and effective, but maybe too effective—too tempting to use.

However, Goyan never really acted on his concerns, largely because, he said, "the FDA does not to my knowledge have the mandate to regulate prescribing. I think that the Public Health Service, NIH, CDC, and others such as the American Heart Association should set standards for drug prescribing."

Yet inch by inch, the post-Goyan FDA has been deliberately moving into the *how*.

How we eat, for instance. It's certainly clear that the nation's unhealthy eating habits are becoming a serious problem. About one-third of Americans are obese and another third overweight, according to the CDC. That puts people at an increased risk for a number of diseases, such as cancer, heart disease, high blood pressure, arthritis, and Type II diabetes; indeed, cases of this kind of diabetes grew by 61 percent from 1993 to 2003. Some scientists argue that obesity itself is a disease, not a behavioral failing. We eat more fast food and fewer home-cooked meals; we get less exercise. So the American diet is definitely a problem. But is it the FDA's problem?

Bob Brackett, head of the Center for Food Safety, bluntly called obesity one of his center's key issues. He explained the rationale this way: "It may not be a disease; that's debatable. It is a public health issue. It sure does result in diseases of various types," or at least contribute to them. "Our mandate is to reduce health risk, not only microbiologically, but [in terms of] eating too much or too little." Thus, the FDA set up its special working group on obesity, headed by the agency's then top PR official, and in March 2004 the group announced its official strategy for combating obesity. Among the recommendations: "Encouraging [food] manufacturers to use dietary guidance statements, such as, 'To manage your weight, balance the calories you eat with your physical activity; have a carrot, not the carrot cake.'" That is, the FDA would give advice to food companies as to how to give advice to consumers—for a product that the FDA does not need to approve before it goes on the market.

Actually, contrary to what Brackett said, it has not been the agency's mandate "to reduce health risk... [in terms of] eating too much or too little." It has never been the FDA's job to make sure fewer people get diabetes, only to make sure that the diabetes pills they take are safe and effective. Its nutrition labels for packaged food provide statistics, not lectures. Maybe it should do more. There is something perverse about running around approving hordes of expensive new medicines instead of trying to ensure that people never need these medicines. It would be like doctors waiting until their patients were actually diabetic and then prescribing metformin, instead of warning them in advance that they were at risk and advising a change in diet. That would be a lousy way to practice medicine. Certainly the FDA, with its experience with diet pills and food labels, has a lot of expertise to contribute to the national obesity conversation. Still, there are other perfectly capable federal agencies whose historic mandates have clearly encompassed giving Americans nutritional advice, most notably the surgeon general and the USDA-HHS committee that writes dietary guidelines.

Or take the idea of risk management—approving highly dangerous drugs only in conjunction with strict limitations on the way they are prescribed. Thalidomide patients like Mike Katz have to follow the patented STEPS program, including promising to use two methods of birth control. Doctors who prescribe Lotronex, the once-recalled drug for irritable bowel syndrome, must get special training and also explain the risks to patients. Women of child-bearing age who fill a prescription for the acne drug Accutane, which can cause birth defects, must have proof of two negative pregnancy tests before they start and monthly tests before each refill. Not only was the FDA now dictating to doctors and pharmacists how to dispense drugs, but it was even getting into patients' bedrooms. In this case, the agency admitted that it was going beyond its usual M.O. but justified the moves under its "safety" rubric: Thalidomide and Accutane are so dangerous for pregnant women that ordinary warnings are not sufficient. (Accutane was also one of the five drugs, along with the cholesterol-lowering medication Crestor, that the controversial FDA safety reviewer David Graham had singled out as particularly worrisome.)

Jeffrey Jump of Xitact, the Swiss company that makes simulation-based systems for training doctors, described another way the FDA gets involved in how physicians do their job. He said that a subsidiary of Johnson & Johnson used a Xitact machine in a demonstration before an FDA advisory committee in the spring of 2004, to prove that the company would be properly training doctors to use its new carotid artery stent for propping open clogged arteries. So the FDA was now approving physicians' medical training.

Even off-label prescribing may come under closer FDA scrutiny—again, for reasons of safety and efficacy, because of the kinds of horrible side effects that have been reported by the parents of the teens on antidepressants, the Knight-Ridder newspaper chain, and others. The FDA had more or less backed away from the whole topic after it was sharply rebuked by the federal district court in 2000, in the Washington Legal Foundation case involving companies that disseminated information about unapproved uses that had been printed in professional journals.

Instead, the FDA had left enforcement to other arms of the government, including several federal prosecutors. But in the summer of 2003, Mark McClellan told the *Wall Street Journal* that he was taking another look at regulating off-label uses. "I'd like to see a better way to get more information on the label," he said. This echoed suggestions by people like Peter Barton Hutt, the former FDA counsel.

McClellan symbolically signaled his new assertiveness overall when he changed the FDA's motto. Instead of the traditional "protecting America's health," it was now "protecting and advancing America's health." The FDA was not just reactive, inspecting the drugs and foods that were brought to it; it would also be proactive, helping drug companies develop new drugs more efficiently, helping generic drugs get on the market faster, helping doctors prescribe more effectively, and helping consumers stay healthy by eating right. Maybe the agency would end up giving itself more work of the traditional kind by enabling pharmaceutical manufacturers to pump out a spate of new drugs more rapidly. Maybe it would end up reducing its workload by forestalling future recalls, or helping make some lifestyle diseases so uncommon that the drug companies would have less incentive to develop new drugs for them. In any case, it sure wasn't Teddy Roosevelt's FDA.

TOBACCO AGAIN?

The Supreme Court settled the issue once and for all in 2000: The FDA has no authority over tobacco. Except that it didn't.

"There is a new group of products coming close to market with [claims of] reduced harm from tobacco," pointed out Steve Galson. (Along those lines, Matthew Myers of the National Center for Tobacco-Free Kids would also include cigarettes like RJ Reynolds's Eclipse, Brown & Williamson's Advance Lights, and Vector Tobacco's Omni.) Should the FDA oversee those health claims? "We've never really established how you set standards for letting a company make claims for reduced harm from tobacco. If they're making a disease claim, I'm thinking we might" have jurisdiction, Galson mused. The Supreme Court, after all, had ruled only on David Kessler's narrow assertion that nicotine is a drug and cigarettes thus are drug delivery systems.

By the same token, it has long been clearly established that if nicotine is used as a drug to help people quit smoking—say, through nicotine gum or patches—the FDA does have the right to regulate it. Even Lester Crawford, ever cautious, allowed that with all the new stop-smoking products, "I must say the landscape has changed. We've been drawn into it."

Besides, the court had left it open for Congress to deliberately grant the FDA jurisdiction over cigarettes, and bills to that effect surfaced in 2003 and again in 2004, tying FDA oversight to a bailout of tobacco farmers. The version passed by the Senate (though killed by the Republican House leadership) in 2004 would have let the FDA regulate cigarette advertising, distribution, labeling, and ingredients and even restrict the amount of nicotine, although the regulators would not have been able to outlaw cigarettes or nicotine entirely. In return, the government would pay tobacco farmers $12 billion to give up antiquated quotas, dating back to the Depression, that kept prices high by limiting how much of their crop the farmers could sell each year. The measures had a mixed base of support from some tobacco-state legislators, some antismoking advocates (Matthew Myers backed the 2004 version but not the earlier one), and just one big tobacco company, Philip Morris. The FDA seemed divided. Galson voluntarily raised the topic in our interview and appeared eager to find a way to take on tobacco, but Crawford was, typically, more hesitant. "It seems to be working pretty well as it is. That's why they formed the Drug Enforcement Administration, and the Bureau of Alcohol, Tobacco, and Firearms. They do the sorts of things that don't seem to fit in the FDA. The last time we got sucked into this, the Supreme Court said no." If Congress ever did pass legislation, Crawford warned, the FDA would need more staff, but he had not calculated how much more.

The logical argument against giving the FDA jurisdiction over tobacco is that tobacco is neither a drug nor a food product. As Sam Kazman, general counsel of the libertarian Competitive Enterprise Institute, put it, "If tobacco is the drug, what is the disease?" Even if you accept Kessler's definition of cigarettes as a device for delivering the addictive drug nicotine—which almost no one but Kessler and his crew does—then tobacco would be more like a controlled substance, not a prescription drug, and thus under the aegis of the DEA.

The logical argument in favor of FDA jurisdiction goes back to McClellan's proactive redefinition of the FDA's mission. There is no question that cigarettes are dangerous to America's health—the health of people who smoke as well as people who breathe in secondary smoke. So, if the FDA's job is to protect and advance the public health, the biggest single step it could take to improve health would be to rein in the product that is the number one cause of death in the United States. That was the impetus that motivated Kessler to begin with.

FIGHTING TERRORISM

After the September 11 attacks on the World Trade Center and Washington, D.C., the FDA, like many government agencies, found its role changed by the nation's war on terrorism. First, there was a panicky public demand for more vaccines, especially at the height of the anthrax scare that rapidly followed September 11. Letters containing spores of the deadly anthrax poison were sent to high-profile politicians and journalists like then Senate Majority Leader Tom Daschle and then NBC news anchor Tom Brokaw, and several people, including two postal workers in Washington, D.C. and a 61-year-old hospital employee in Manhattan, died from handling or inhaling the poison. What if it spread more widely in the next mail delivery? What if terrorists unleashed smallpox or some other plague?

The FDA decided it needed to spur drug makers to develop and produce vaccines faster. Then, if the companies responded, the regulators faced the problem of proving efficacy. There were no Americans walking around with anthrax or smallpox who could participate in standard Phase II clinical trials, and it would hardly be ethical to deliberately infect a few hundred people just to have test subjects.

To get more vaccines available, the agency took on something of the role of colleague of the industry, rather than regulator—a precursor of its "critical path" approach to cooperating with drug makers. As Jesse Goodman explained, "We worked with companies and people that had previously manufactured smallpox vaccine to identify potentially available stocks of older vaccines. There was intensive collaboration bringing together companies, CDC, and the NIH to assess the safety and potency of existing vaccines. Working with NIH clinicians, we conducted trials to see if some of those vaccines could be diluted to stretch out the supply." The FDA also turned its attention to helping companies develop new vaccines. "We set up teams to do everything we could to avoid problems, to streamline the whole process. Going to the factories and providing technical input, at a time much earlier than we would normally do. Sitting down with people early on [at the drug companies and asking], 'Let's be sure we are on the same wavelength. What are the steps you're going to take, what are the facilities you're going to use,' to try to make sure upfront the product will be safe and effective." When he found that only one company was working on the assays necessary to test smallpox vaccines, Goodman assigned two of his staffers to develop more (in another example of the benefits of having the FDA conduct research, albeit the applied type).

With new vaccines now in the pipeline, the FDA agreed to ease up on the efficacy requirement. In cases where Phase II human testing was impossible or unethical, bioterror vaccines would be approved as long as they had been shown to be safe in humans and effective in animals. While no one was surprised at the decision—in fact, it had first been proposed in Jane Henney's time in 1999—it was a step beyond what the FDA had done for AIDS patients two decades earlier. AIDS drugs all had to go through the full range of efficacy testing eventually; the FDA just let people use some of the promising drugs before the tests were completed.

The biggest change in the way the FDA works came from the Public Health Security and Bioterrorism Preparedness and Response Act of 2002, which deputized the agency to protect the national food supply from possible terrorist acts, such as a real-life version of the Great Chilean Grape Scare of 1989. Food regulation has always been, by law, a reactive job. The FDA does not need to approve food products before they can be sold. It kicks in only after the fact, if there seems to be a problem resulting from contaminated, poisoned, or otherwise adulterated food. When something actually happens, as in 2003 when imported green onions from Mexico were suspected of causing an outbreak of hepatitis A at a U.S. restaurant, then inspectors at the Mexican border might block shipments from particular farms and distributors, and the FDA probably will issue consumer warnings.

The bioterrorism law brought a whole new attitude. Food importers now had to alert the agency in advance of all food shipments to the United States—food for animals as well as humans—so that FDA and U.S. Customs staff could inspect any suspect samples. What would pique the inspectors' interest? Bob Brackett would not say—it could be the country a food came from, or just the region, or some characteristic of the food, for instance. But clearly, the FDA was not going to wait for reports of a cluster of *E. coli* cases. Any suspect food could be held for 30 days. Also, facilities that handle food consumed in the United States would have to register with the agency. To cope, the FDA was getting an extra $130 million and hiring 650 new people.

"The FDA has not previously looked systematically for deliberate acts of terror," pointed out Richard Cooper, the former agency chief counsel and now a partner at Williams & Connelly. "It has had to reorient itself for that new responsibility."

Actually, the law's ramifications go beyond terrorism. While the FDA was supposed to be looking specifically for deliberate acts of food tampering, an inspector can hardly distinguish *E. coli* bacteria that might be injected by Islamic *jihadists* from those that grow via more natural causes. Even more absurd, if the inspector did determine that some bacteria were a natural contaminant, he or she would hardly throw the contaminated sample back into the food supply. "We're concerned about keeping the food safe regardless of whether it is intentional or accidental," Brackett noted.

So now food would have to be proved safe beforehand, rather than after the fact. That starts to sound a lot like drug regulation.

Consumer groups, though annoyed that the industry had lobbied the FDA to water down some of the requirements in the bioterrorism law, were basically pleased because they saw it as a backdoor approach to the more aggressive oversight of food they had long wanted—and with an extra $130 million in funding, to boot.

CATCHING UP AFTER THE FACT

The dilemma that the FDA, patients, and doctors have always faced is that clinical trials and the approval process cannot possibly catch all the potential side effects of every drug. Indeed, among more than half of the new medications approved between 1976 and 1985, important side effects were found only after they were on the market, according to the federal Government Accountability Office. It was not until several years after two anemia drugs, Procrit and Aranesp, had been out in general use, and manufacturers decided to test them for an entirely different reason— to see if they helped cancer patients live longer—that it was discovered in the fall of 2003 that they might actually cause higher levels of blood clots and make cancer patients sicker. It took nearly a year after the FDA's approval for the first strong evidence to emerge publicly connecting heart attacks and stroke with Vioxx and even longer for Celebrex.

So how can patients and doctors know whether their medicine is safe? They need to have access to updated information, well after a drug has been out on the market. This means that the FDA has to keep track of drugs long after they are approved. For years the agency has been struggling with better ways to do that. Doctors voluntarily report adverse events to the FDA's MedWatch system, and companies must do so. In addition, some drug approvals, such as those using surrogate markers, require continued post-approval monitoring of patients. In a typical year, the agency gets about 280,000 reports. When troubling patterns emerge, the FDA can commission a full-blown review, as it did with the Columbia University study of antidepressants or David Graham's analysis of Vioxx. But it is widely acknowledged, even by the FDA, that the voluntary, outside reporting is seriously incomplete. Alastair Wood, who has long advocated better data collection, estimated that only five percent of bad side effects are registered; others up that—a little—to 10 percent. (All this is separate from the FDA's efforts, described in Chapter 5, to toughen the requirements for reporting adverse events during clinical trials.) There was also growing concern that problems with devices were not being properly reported, as more and more emergency equipment like heart defibrillators were used by nonprofessionals in offices, schools, and homes. Many critics asserted that PDUFA, the user fee law, made things worse because its funding formula forces the FDA to siphon money away from safety oversight and into new drug reviews—an issue that was unsuccessfully raised by consumer groups back during the law's third renewal.

To its credit, the FDA had occasionally sought extra funding or authority for safety reviews. And it was trying to make the post market data collection easier via electronic prescribing and reporting. Janet Woodcock suggested that such an electronic communication system could also link hospitals and pharmacies to make sure medicines were being dispensed and used properly. The miniature radio-frequency electronic tags that were being tried on OxyContin and other drugs probably would not be much help, because they were aimed at tracking stolen drugs, not side effects. However, in a much creepier experiment with high-tech radio frequency, the FDA in October 2004 gave the go-ahead for Applied Digital Solutions of Florida to implant tiny computer chips under people's skin. The chips have special coding that would supposedly allow doctors faster access to computer files of patients' medical records. Presumably, this technology could someday be used to file records of side effects, too.

Beyond the electronic efforts, the review that the FDA launched of its entire system of overseeing drug safety, after the Vioxx recall, could lead to a better system of reporting post-market problems. Going further, Iowa senator Charles Grassley, outgoing HHS Secretary Thompson, and others suggested that it might not be good enough for one arm of the FDA to review another arm's approvals; an independent safety review board might be needed to avoid the inherent conflict of interest that arises when an agency analyzes its own past decisions. There will always be "denial, rejection, and heat" when safety questions are raised about approved drugs, charged David Graham, the staffer who raised such questions about Vioxx and who claimed higher-ups at the FDA tried to intimidate him. At the least, all the publicity would keep everyone on their toes for a while.

Actually, a lot of the post-market data the FDA needs exists already. The problem is that it is buried in the clinical trials that pharmaceutical manufacturers pay for and design but never publish. These are the most systematic, scientific tabulations of all of a drug's effects, bad and good, and they often are done after the drug is on the market, as well as during the approval process. If a trial shows that a drug works, the company that makes the drug will probably submit the results to medical journals, give copies to sales reps to tote around to doctors, and issue an enthusiastic press release. If a trial does not show any benefit, however, it usually disappears from the face of the earth.

The topic burst into public view in the spring of 2004 just as the FDA was issuing its stricter warnings for antidepressants. Everyone "knew" that there were no studies clearly indicating whether the drugs worked on teens or, conversely, whether the drugs increased the risk of suicide among teens. Then it was revealed that GlaxoSmithKline actually did have some trial data on its drug Paxil that it had never made public. And the FDA had had that information all along.

Suddenly, the FDA was caught in the middle. Companies submit reams of data to the agency, but by law the regulators must keep a lot of that secret. For instance, the FDA gets all results from clinical trials that are conducted as part of a new drug or biologic application. That information stays confidential unless the drug is approved, at which point only summaries are made public, under the theory that disclosing too many details could reveal trade secrets about how the drug was made. As for trials that are conducted after a drug is in use—typically, to get a supplemental application—only the safety data must be reported promptly to the FDA. The effectiveness data can wait until the company actually decides to file for the supplemental application. So, if the company never files, that information will never find is way to Rockville. And if the FDA rejects the application, it is actually banned from making the data public. In the case of off-label prescriptions like the pediatric use of antidepressants, people could keep taking pills even though the manufacturer knew quite well that the pills were useless. And the manufacturer would never have to tell anyone.

Where else could patients and doctors get the information? There were a lot of scattered partial solutions, mainly on the Internet. All current trials for serious or life-threatening conditions must be registered on a Web site run by the NIH's National Library of Medicine. Other arms of the NIH list many of the studies that have been published in medical journals, but of course that leaves out the really secret, unpublished ones, presumably those with the most worrisome results. A handful of drug companies, such as Glaxo Wellcome, a precursor of GlaxoSmithKline, posted some of their own trials on their sites. However, that was clearly insufficient, since GlaxoSmithKline had kept the negative results on Paxil hidden, and in early June 2004, the New York State attorney general, Eliot Spitzer, filed his lawsuit against Glaxo charging fraud for concealing those results. Glaxo replied that it had submitted its studies to the FDA, as required. A week later it promised to make reports of all its Paxil pediatric studies available, and the following week it also said it would create an improved Web site listing all tests ever run on any drugs it marketed. In late August, it settled the New York lawsuit.

For his part, Spitzer first told the *New York Times* he didn't blame the FDA because it had been restricted by court rulings—although, somewhat confusingly, he cited the district court ruling in the Washington Legal Foundation case, which really has nothing to do with whether the FDA can make trial results public. Two and a half months later, the *Times* quoted Spitzer making a 180-degree turnaround and demanding, "where has the FDA been all these years when clinical data has been hidden from public scrutiny? They have simply failed to confront the problem." In the congressional hearings that September, Democrats and Republicans alike denounced the FDA's secrecy.

At any rate, all the scattered data banks and resources were not a real solution. So the American Medical Association called for the federal government to create a single, comprehensive repository of all clinical drug trials performed in the United States. Several U.S. senators and representatives—among them Senator Edward Kennedy of Massachusetts and Representative Henry Waxman of California, the leading Democrats in Congress on health care, and Republican Senator Charles Grassley of Iowa—promptly began writing bills to set up a government database. Even Merck and Johnson & Johnson broke ranks with their fellow Big Pharmas to agree on the basic principle. (Somewhat differently, Lilly promised to disclose extensive information on its own Web site.) A group of 12 leading medical journals announced in September 2004 that they would no longer publish trial results unless the trial was registered in a public database from the start.

And just which government agency should run that database?

The AMA pointed to the Department of Health and Human Services, which basically meant the NIH or the FDA. Democratic Senators Christopher Dodd of Connecticut and Tim Johnson of South Dakota specifically asked those two agencies for comment, and one proposed Senate bill would grant the FDA the power to penalize companies that did not register their trials on the database. Certainly a good case could be made for the NIH to expand its existing Web site through the Library of Medicine. But just as good a case could be made for the FDA, as the only arm of government that actually gets most of the trial results in its own files and knows of almost every drug under development. The concern about trade secrets is hardly insurmountable, since drug companies like GlaxoSmithKline, Merck, Lilly, and Johnson & Johnson seem to be able to work around it.

Drug prices. Ethics. Post-market safety tests. Terrorist attacks. Tobacco. Drug company secrecy. The American diet. How doctors practice medicine. It's a heavy agenda to add to an agency that already encompasses a quarter of the U.S. economy—that complains about not having enough staff or money—that is criticized for being, alternately, too slow or too rushed—and that is having trouble keeping up with fast-changing science. The FDA may be big, but it is not omnipotent.

To make things worse, an agenda of new issues means more occasions for confusing and conflicting turf fights with the Agriculture Department, the NIH, the Drug Enforcement Administration, and all the other agencies that the FDA already overlaps with. It means more opportunity for pressure from various political, industry, consumer, and religious forces, especially since so many of the new issues are the kind of controversial and topical ones that generate intense public interest. The more controversies the FDA steps into, the more its luster will undoubtedly dim. In addition, most of these new responsibilities would require extra training and perhaps extra staff. Yet only the bioterrorism law brings in extra funding. The FDA has to assume, like most other government agencies except the Pentagon, that its budget will always be squeezed.

So why should the FDA take these burdens on?

Because this is what public health has become. These are all issues of intense importance to American health that demand some public policy framework, that cannot be left to chance. Yesterday's century needed the FDA to establish a certain basic level of safety and scientific guidelines for pharmaceutical exploration. But the definition of public health—even of safety and efficacy—changes as science and society change. Today "safety" might also mean topics like: How can we make sure people are informed of all relevant clinical trial results? What can we do to reduce the incidence of diseases? And "efficacy" might mean: How can we make sure people can afford the drugs that we approve? Is there a way to change people's lifestyles, perhaps through diet or antismoking efforts, so that they don't need as many drugs? Should we clone human beings and use their body parts for research? Yes, some of these issues involve broad questions of politics, ethics, and social policy beyond the FDA's traditional scientific mandate. That is exactly why they need the FDA's scientific input, in the same way that the FDA cannot ignore the broader ramifications of the scientific issues it studies.

If the FDA merely approved a drug and ignored those other public health issues, it would not be a real protector of the public health much longer.

While Antigenics was still on clinical hold, I asked Elma Hawkins, who was then vice chairman, what was the most important lesson she had taught the company's employees about the FDA, during those six months that she was commuting from Boston to New York to help them put together their first application. She put her finger to her ear. "Listen," she said. There was a pause.

"I must have said a gazillion times," she went on, "'Do as they say. If they say, "jump," you jump. If they say, "swim," you swim.' The worst thing you can do to the FDA is ignore them. They are a more powerful entity than you. You gain nothing by being their enemy."

So the FDA is a big pain in the neck? An arbitrary dictator?

Not to Elma Hawkins, consumer, shopper, and godmother of two little girls. "I'm glad that somebody is so strict," she said. "I know if the bottle says it's aspirin, it's aspirin. It's important to have an independent eye looking at the safety data, looking at the efficacy data, making sure that if it's tried on a hundred million people, it won't kill a hundred million people."

Acknowledgments

Any book of nonfiction exists only because of all the people who contributed to it. In the case of this book, that means not just the approximately 200 people I interviewed; it also means the assistants who arranged some of those interviews, the friends and relatives who gave me their insights into food and drug regulation, the editors who helped guide me, the other journalists who wrote books and articles that provided background, and the personal circle who kept me going with everything from child care to newspaper clippings to moral support.

I can't possibly thank them all individually—I hope you know who you are! But a few have to be singled out:

Garo Armen, Sunny Uberoi, and everyone at Antigenics, who really opened up their doors and spent a lot of time showing me what it's like to launch a biotech firm and try to move a brand-new drug through the FDA.

Ira Loss of Washington Analysis and Phil Noguchi of the FDA, who have been terrific sounding boards, every time I came back with more (and more) questions.

A number of people who patiently agreed to repeat interviews: former FDA Commissioners Michael Friedman, Jere Goyan, and Mark Novitch; Alastair Wood of Vanderbilt University; Jay Siegel of Centocor; Tom Garvey of Garvey Associates; Mike Myers of Palio Communications;

Boyd Clarke of Neose Technologies; and Jerry Mande of Yale, who dug through his files to find those old transcripts of Senate testimony.

David Goetzl, my former colleague at Crain Communications, who once again helped me decipher the world of advertising.

Judy Messina, another former Crain's colleague, who has been a great source of insight into the biotech world and who also backstopped me by reading over some of the chapters with her expert eye.

Julie Smith Morrow, who helped me understand some of the science behind heat-shock proteins.

Debbie Majerovitz, who gave me a better appreciation of the way SSRIs work in treating depression (and whose good humor is a cure for depression in itself).

Kathleen Quinn of the FDA press office, who worked magic in managing to coordinate so many top officials' schedules to match my trips to Washington.

My editors at Wiley—Jeanne Glasser, who had the great inspiration to look into the FDA; Kevin Commins and Pamela Van Giessen, whose advice provided exactly the direction I needed to give the book its final structure; and copy editor Matt Kushinka, whose sharp eyes saved me from a very red face.

My agent, Susan Barry of the Barry-Swayne Agency, who has always been there with her good cheer and good counsel.

And my husband, Pete Segal, and my son, Joey Hawthorne, who—I promise!—will finally get back their wife and mother (at least until my next book).

Notes

Most of the sources of my material should be fairly self-evident. If anyone is quoted directly or indirectly, that derives from an interview I conducted with the person between June 2003 and August 2004, unless otherwise indicated. When multiple sources offered essentially the same point or observation, I try to make that clear in the text. In many cases, basic facts have been widely reported in history books or current newspaper and magazine articles (for instance, the story of contamination problems at the factory that made the flu vaccine in fall 2004, which is discussed in Chapter 5). Other information is from a source that is implicit in the information—an announcement of an FDA policy comes from an FDA press release, quotes from new FDA guidelines on TV ads come from those guidelines, figures for the FDA budget are from the federal budget.

The notes below are an attempt to give the sourcing for anything that is not obvious, and to give credit when I cite specific books or articles.

In addition, I am using this opportunity to add some technical details and background to certain discussions of drug development and approval.

—Fran Hawthorne

INTRODUCTION

Page vii: *Studies on the other drugs...*

[SSRIs get their name because of the way they work. The brain sends a chemical transmitter called serotonin across the synapses, or spaces, from one nerve cell to another, essentially to create a pleasant, positive mood. Usually, there is excess serotonin, which the transmitting nerve sops up, in a process known as reuptake. One theory of depression is that too much serotonin is sopped up in the reuptake, and not enough is transmitted. So the SSRIs block—or inhibit—that reuptake, thus allowing more of the serotonin to be transmitted.]

Page xii: *The agency warned pregnant women...*

[The ultrasound and cell phone stories have been reported in numerous publications. The information about blood banks came from the story "Panel Calls for West Nile Tests on All U.S.-Stored Blood," Dow Jones Newswires, article 19, 2003, and the information about China is from Joseph Kahn, "Foul Water and Air Part of Cost of the Boom in China's Exports," *New York Times*, November 4, 2003, A1.]

Page xii: New York Times *claimed the new warnings...*

[Gardiner Harris, "Regulators Want Antidepressants to List Warnings," *New York Times*, March 23, 2004, A1]

Page xiii: *"You don't just ask someone to clam up"...*

[Anna Wilde Mathews, "In Debate Over Antidepressants, FDA Weighed Risk of False Alarm," *Wall Street Journal*, May 25, 2004, A1.]

Page xiii: *Temple admitted that all the clinical trials...*

[Gardiner Harris, "FDA Links Drugs to Being Suicidal," *New York Times*, September 14, 2004, A1.]

CHAPTER 1

Page 6: *"I couldn't get over how weird...*

[Laila Kain, "The Scientist," *Hartford Courant*, May 16, 2004.]

Page 6: Armen also had a personal reason...

[Michael Peltz, "Antigenics's Cancer Drug Gives Its Shareholders Indigestion," *Bloomberg Markets Magazine*, January 5, 2004.]

Page 15: *Investors did not blame Armen...*

[Brian Lavery, "2 Top Officers Quit Elan, Troubled Irish Drug Maker," *New York Times*, July 10, 2002, W1. The news about Elan in general has been widely reported.]

Page 17: *(Dyax Corporation, another small firm...*

["FDA Suspends Dyax Cancer Treatment," *New York Times*, May 26, 2004, C4.]

Page 21: *"For investors," wrote* Bloomberg Markets Magazine...

[Michael Peltz, "Antigenics's Cancer Drug Gives Its Shareholders Indigestion," *Bloomberg Markets Magazine*, January 5, 2004.]

CHAPTER 2

Page 28: *Famously, a former commissioner, Dr. Alexander M. Schmidt...*
[There are many references to this speech, which is also attributed to testimony that Schmidt gave to Congress; the citation I used came from Daniel P. Carpenter, "The Political Economy of FDA Drug Review," *Health Affairs*, January–February 2004, p. 54.]

Page 29: *Drugs with the FDA's imprimatur kill...*
[Anna Wilde Mathews, "Vioxx Recall Raises Questions of FDA's Safety Monitoring," *Wall Street Journal*, October 4, 2004, B1.]

Page 30: *the Government Accountability Office (formerly the General Accounting Office)...*
["Strategic Action Plan, Food and Drug Administration," published by the FDA, August 2003, p. 28.]

CHAPTER 3

Page 35:...*as for the other men, who worked in tank rooms full of steam...*
[Upton Sinclair, *The Jungle*, Signet Classic, 2001, p. 102.]

Page 36: *Some Colonial doctors published manuals...*
[Paul Starr, *The Social Transformation of American Medicine*, Basic Books, 1982, p. 32.]

Page 36: *In* Tom Sawyer, *written from 1874 to 1875...*
[Mark Twain, *Tom Sawyer*, Vintage Books, 1991, pp. 82–83.]

Page 37: *Philip J. Hilts, in his history of the FDA...*
[Philip J. Hilts, *Protecting America's Health: The FDA, Business, and One Hundred Years of Regulation*, Alfred A. Knopf, 2003, p. 22.]

Page 37: *As the FDA itself points out...*
["Milestones in U.S. Food and Drug Law History," which I accessed on the FDA Web site at http://www.cfsan.fda.gov/mileston.html.]

Page 39: *As Philip Hilts describes him, Wiley was...*
[Philip J. Hilts, *Protecting America's Health: The FDA, Business, and One Hundred Years of Regulation*, Alfred A. Knopf, 2003, pp. 11, 15.]

Page 39: *The results—severe indigestion, stomach pain...*
[Ibid., 40.]

Page 43: *Nor did the feeble FDA under then Commissioner George P. Larrick...*
Ibid., 137–138, 142.]

Page 43: *Over the next year, Richardson-Merrell would...*
[Ibid., 152–153.]

Page 48: *The soda-drinking public...*
[Ibid., 202–206.]

Page 49: *The FDA's acting commissioner admitted to...*
[Katherine Walsh and Michael Waldholz, "U.S. to Continue Probing Pfizer's Troubled Valve—FDA Chief Admits Agency Had Dealt Improperly with Defective Device," *Wall Street Journal*, February 27, 1990, A3.]

Page 49: *Later that year TPA was approved...*
[Stephen S. Hall, *Merchants of Immortality: Chasing the Dream of Human Life Extension*, Houghton-Mifflin Co., 2003 p. 15.]

Page 51: *Several FDA initiatives to give consumers...*
[Philip J. Hilts, *Protecting America's Health: The FDA, Business, and One Hundred Years of Regulation*, Alfred A. Knopf, 2003, p. 215–217.]

Page 52: *In his 1994 book* The FDA Follies...
[Herbert Burkholz, *The FDA Follies*, Basic Books, 1994, pp. 117–122.]

Page 56: *To Kessler, as he proclaimed in a speech...*
[David Kessler, *A Question of Intent: A Great American Battle with a Deadly Industry*, Public Affairs, 2001, p. 23.]

Page 56: *Kessler, in a book he wrote...*
[Ibid., 30.]

Page 58: *In* A Question of Intent, *he claims...*
[Ibid., 26–30.]

Page 62: *From then on, Henney was in the bull's-eye...*
[Even four years later, opposition to RU-486 still famed. After three deaths—which is not much, out of 360,000 women who used it—conservatives were pushing a Senate bill to "suspend" the drug.]

CHAPTER 4

Page 65: *Federal health officials in the mid-1980s...*
[Much of the information in this example is taken from "Scrambled Eggs: How a Broken Food Safety System Let Contaminated Eggs Become a National Food

Poisoning Epidemic," published by the Center for Science in the Public Interest, May 1997. Information also comes from news stories, FDA announcements, and my own interviews.]

Page 70: *Altogether, Eric Schlosser, the author...*

[Eric Schlosser, *Fast Food Nation: The Dark Side of the All-American Meal,* Perennial/ HarperCollins, 2002, p. 263.]

Page 72: *David Kessler in his book called Cooper...*

[David Kessler, *A Question of Intent: A Great American Battle with a Deadly Industry,* Public Affairs, 2001, p. 175.]

Page 74: *Two-thirds of all the land...*

[Roger Thurow, Scott Kilman, and Gregory L. White, "New Farm Powers Sow the Seeds of America's Agricultural Woes," *Wall Street Journal,* June 18, 2004, A1.]

CHAPTER 5

Page 82: *At the end of this time...*

[This is a number that is frequently cited, based on data from the Center for the Study of Drug Development at Tufts University and the Pharmaceutical Research and Manufacturers of America.]

Page 83: *That's because of the nature...*

[Devices fall into three different classes, depending on the level of risk—from tongue depressors to pacemakers. According to David Feigal, the former director, 90 percent of devices come to market based simply on their design, without any inspection at all. The Devices Center's new "real-time review" streamlines the process even more, to the point of almost being instantaneous: If the paperwork is submitted three weeks in advance and "if the issues are pretty straightforward," reviewers will meet with the manufacturer and make a binding decision on the spot. The meeting can even be done by phone.]

Page 85: *If things do not work out well...*

[Lester Crawford, the acting commissioner of the FDA, began citing statistics along this line repeatedly in speeches in 2004.]

Page 85: *The trials are held in groups...*

[A whole new breed of companies, known as clinical research organizations, sprang up in the late 1990s specifically to conduct these trials, thus giving hospitals and medical schools a jolt of competition. (These are not to be confused with contract research organizations like Alquest, which help guide drug companies through the FDA approval process.) It's not so much for the money: While drug companies pay a per-patient fee that can run $1,000 to $30,000, that typically covers only 5 to 10 percent over the trial's administrative cost. Rather, physicians want a first crack at what could be a promising new cure for their patients. And hospitals and universities want the prestige that comes from being seen as a place that does pioneering work. In the words of Dr. Victor Hatcher, director of the office of clinical trials at New York City's Montefiore Medical Center, "It's part of the mission of a medical center like Montefiore. When oncology patients come, they expect that you ought to have clinical trials. They want to be offered the chance." But there's growing controversy over whether the test sites have given drug companies too much control over the conduct of the trials and the publication of research, as discussed in Chapter 15.]

Page 86: *"Doctors don't want to know..."*

[Peter Jaret, "She Turns Her Pen on Drug Makers," *Los Angeles Times*, August 9, 2004, F1.]

Page 86: *Still, the FDA and Temple held firmly...*

[In August 2004 the FDA added an even more controversial twist to the debate when it approved a stent made by Guidant Corp.—a device that supposedly would prop open the carotid artery in the neck in order to prevent a stroke—after a trial without any control group at all. Instead, all 581 patients in the trial got the stent. The "control" was that Guidant compared their rates of stroke, death, and heart attacks with the historic rates among patients who had undergone the traditional treatment, surgery.]

Page 87: *In 1989 it published guidelines...*

[In the fall of 2003, the agency also announced that it wanted to create a database that would show how men and women react differently to drugs and "track and encourage the inclusion of women in clinical studies." It contracted with seven universities to gather data on how women respond to certain treatments.]

Page 88: *Congress had to pass a special...*

[Testing on children raised so many ethical issues that, soon after the dispute over antidepressants, the FDA created a special Pediatric Ethics advisory subcommittee.]

Page 89: *Dr. Henry I. Miller, a former FDA official...*

[Henry I. Miller, *To America's Health*, Hoover Institution Press, 2000, pp. 65–66.]

Page 91: *Novartis had to change the name...*

[Daniel Vasella, *Magic Cancer Bullet*, HarperBusiness, 2003, pp. 151–153.]

Page 92: *On an offhand suggestion...*

[This information comes largely from my interviews with Irwin Martin but also from Ron Winslow, "The Birth of a Blockbuster: Lipitor's Route out of the Lab," *Wall Street Journal*, January 24, 2000.]

Page 93: *"A meeting of the minds ...*

[This testimony was given in front of the House of Representatives' Subcommittee on Oversight and Investigations, June 13, 2002.]

Page 95: *"A fully paginated document ...*

["Guidance for Industry: Formal Meetings with Sponsors and Applicants for PDUFA Products," published by the FDA, Center for Drug Evaluation and Research and Center for Biologics Evaluation and Research, February. 2000, p. 7.]

Page 99: *Between the second and third reviews ...*

[The committees can also meet after a product is on the market, perhaps to consider new uses or new restrictions, as in the case of antidepressant use by teenagers.]

Page 99: *In one case in 1997 ...*

[This and also the story about the vote on Lotronex come from David Willman, "How a New Policy Led to Seven Deadly Drugs," *Los Angeles Times*, December 20, 2000.

The FDA subsequently invalidated the Lotronex consultant's vote, not because of his consulting ties, but because he was only a temporary appointee. Both Posicor and Lotronex were eventually pulled from the market after numerous deaths and other severe complications were associated with each of them. Less than two years later Lotronex was back, under strict conditions, because patients complained that they had no other treatment for irritable bowel syndrome, the condition it treated. There is more on both drugs in Chapters 7 and 10.]

Page 104: *Drug and device manufacturing plants ...*

[In 2003, the FDA started revamping its regulations to encourage companies to update their equipment and processes. Among other things, it said it would focus on production steps that could directly affect patients' health and promised a corps of inspectors dedicated solely to pharmaceuticals.

In addition, the FDA inspects factories that make vaccines—which are particulary susceptible to contamination—every two years.]

Page 104: *Altogether, agency officials annually ...*

[Jeanne Whalen, Pui-Wing Tam and Sarah Lueck, "Behind Flu-Vaccine Shortage: Struggle to Police Drugs Globally," *Wall Street Journal*, November 5, 2004, A1.]

Page 106: *Although those measures failed ...*

[Congress later added user fee laws for devices (2002) and animal products (2003). But until all the Centers were on equal footing, there was a distinct disadvantage for manufacturers with a combination product that had to be approved by both the Drugs and Devices staffs—say, one of the catheters that uses drugs to dissolve blood clots after a stroke. "When a device needed review from a CDER or CBER person, the reviewer's attention was on user fee products. They had to meet the user fee deadline," said Dr. Susan Alpert, who was director of the FDA's Office of Device Evaluation from 1993 to 1999. So a combination product that did not have to be done within PDUFA's six-month deadline was a low priority for the review staff, compared with a PDUFA drug. Alpert left the FDA to become vice president of regulatory affairs and compliance at Medtronic, Inc., a devices maker in Minneapolis.]

Page 106: *CBER was generally slower than CDER...*

[In 2003 the median review time for priority products at CBER was 12.1 months, significantly slower than the Drugs Center's 7.7 months, according to FDA data. CBER also reviews far fewer drugs in a typical year: For instance, it reviewed 16 drugs in 2001, 21 in 2002, and 22 in 2003, versus 66, 78, and 72, respectively, for CDER. Dr. Jesse Goodman, CBER's director, disputed the criticism, arguing that the products that Biologics reviews are usually complex and new. He also pointed out that having a smaller number of drugs can actually drag down the median review time, because "when you have an outlier, it makes the statistics very unreliable. The Center," he added, "has met all its PDUFA goals and deadlines." There is more on this topic in Chapter 11.]

Page 106: *James C. Greenwood, who at that time was...*

[The following summer he was named president of the biotech industry's trade group.]

CHAPTER 6

Page 112: *Nervously, the vice president...*

[Much of the story of the return of thalidomide has been widely reported, and parts also came from my interviews with John Jackson, Graham Burton, Gilla Kaplan, Mike Katz, and Michael Friedman. But I want to particularly cite one source for this section on the victims' reaction: Deepti Hajela, "Giving Thalidomide a Second Chance," Associated Press, June 1998.]

Page 116: *...multiple myeloma is the second-most common...*

[The data on multiple myeloma and also leprosy come from a variety of sources, including Celgene, the American Cancer Society, and *The Merck Manual of Medical Information*, Merck & Co., 1997, pp. 779 and 891.]

Page 117: *For instance, the newspaper chain reported...*

[Alison Young and Chris Adams, "Off-label Use Growing," *St. Paul Pioneer Press*, November 2, 2003.]

Page 118: *For years the medical community...*

[Leila Abboud, "Off-Label Treatments, New Drugs Target Mysterious, Debilitating Fibromyalgia," *Wall Street Journal*, August 3, 2004, D1.]

Page 119: *But as Temple testified...*
[Chris Adams and Alison Young, "FDA Rules Becoming Irrelevant," *St. Paul Pioneer Press*, November 4, 2003.]

Page 119: *Knight-Ridder reported that one Celgene sales rep...*
[Ibid.]

Page 120: *law enforcement officials have investigated...*
[The law enforcement investigations of marketing practices at a number of pharmaceutical companies have been widely reported, but the specific reference to Provigil comes from Amy Barrett, "This Pep Pill Is Pushing Its Luck," *BusinessWeek*, November 1, 2004, p. 76.]

Page 120: *A one-time sales rep for a small California biotech...*
[Andrew Pollack, "Suit by Former Employee Charges Promotion of Drug's Off-Label Use," *New York Times*, May 12, 2004, C1. The information about Neurontin has been widely reported.]

CHAPTER 7

Page 129: BusinessWeek *in February 2002 described...*
[Catherine Arnst, "Where ImClone Went Wrong," *BusinessWeek*, February 18, 2002, p. 68.]

Page 138: *DiMasi came up with his total...*
[Fran Hawthorne, *The Merck Druggernaut*, John Wiley & Sons, p. 64.]

Page 138: *Using an entirely different system...*
[Ibid., 65–66.]

Page 138: *In 2004, Pfizer made eyes pop...*
[Scott Hensley and Ron Winslow, "Pfizer Makes $800 Million Bid to Reshape Heart-Care Market," *Wall Street Journal*, April 8, 2004, A1.]

Page 139: *Consumer groups, meanwhile, tended...*
[Fran Hawthorne, *The Merck Druggernaut*, John Wiley & Sons, pp. 67–68.]

Page 139: *Ann Campbell, an Alabama research scientist...*
[This was posted on the Web site PharmaLive on March 24, 2004, reprinted from *Law Review Weekly*, and from a press release from the office of U.S. Attorney Alice H. Martin in the northern district of Alabama.]

Page 139: *No wonder CDER spends over $45 million...*

[Anna Wilde Mathews, "FDA Plans Major Review of Procedures," *Wall Street Journal*, November 5, 2004, A3.]

Page 140: *The long string of recalls and withdrawals...*

[David Willman, "How a New Policy Led to Seven Deadly Drugs," *Los Angeles Times*, December 20, 2000.]

Page 141: *The story of Merck's arthritis blockbuster Vioxx...*

[Most of this has been widely reported. The two citations from the *Wall Street Journal* are: Anna Wilde Mathews and Barbara Martinez, "E-Mails Suggest Merck Knew Vioxx's Dangers at Early Stage," November 1, 2004, A1, and Anna Wilde Mathews, "Did FDA Staff Minimize Vioxx's Red Flags?" November 10, 2004, B1.]

CHAPTER 8

Page 145: *And in politics, the pharmaceutical industry...*

{Figures about the industry's clout, including the number of lobbyists, are cited frequently by the media. The information about spending $150 million a year in lobbying and $5 million just to lobby the FDA came from Robert Pear, "Drug Companies Increase Spending on Efforts to Lobby Congress and Governments," *New York Times*, June 1, 2003.]

Page 146: *Hinchey specifically cited "unprecedented activity...*

[The quote is from a press release issued by Congressman Hinchey on July 13, 2004.]

Page 146: *Tossing out years of government...*

[Robert Pear, "In a Shift, Bush Moves to Block Medical Suits," *New York Times*, July 25, 2004, A1.]

Page 147: *There was, in fact, an explicit concern...*

[Robert Temple, "Development of Drug Law, Regulations, and Guidance in the United States," in *Governmental Regulation of Drugs*, 1995, p. 1646.]

Page 149: *The* Wall Street Journal *in July 2004 reported...*

[Anna Wilde Mathews and Thomas M. Burton, "After Medtronic Lobbying Push, the FDA Had Change of Heart," *Wall Street Journal*, July 9, 2004, A1.]

Page 157: *In a paper published in the* American Journal of Political Science...

[Daniel P. Carpenter, "Groups, the Media, Agency Waiting Costs, and FDA Drug Approval," in *American Journal of Political Science*, July 2002, pp. 490–505.]

Page 158: *Nine years earlier, in 1994...*

[David Dranove and David Meltzer, "Do Important Drugs Reach the Market Sooner?" *RAND Journal of Economics*, Autumn 1994, pp. 402–423.]

Page 159: *The newspaper cited an agency publication...*

[David Willman, "How a New Policy Led to Seven Deadly Drugs," *Los Angeles Times*, December 20, 2000.]

Page 159: *When the consumer group Public Citizen...*

[Peter Lurie and Sidney M. Wolfe, "FDA Medical Officers Report Lower Standards Permit Dangerous Drug Approvals," Public Citizen, December 2, 1998.]

Page 162: *Daniel Carpenter of Harvard has studied...*

[Daniel P. Carpenter and Marc Turenne, "Why Do Bigger Firms Receive Faster Drug Approvals?" presented at the Harvard-MIT Workshop on Positive Political Economy, March 16, 2001.]

Page 165: *In fact, critics charged that during...*

[Sheryl Gay Stolberg, "FDA Officials Press Legislators to Oppose Bill on Importing Less Expensive Drugs," *New York Times*, July 25, 2003.]

Page 166: *The small staff in the FDA's Office...*

[Heather Won Tesoriero, "Fake-Drug Sites Keep a Step Ahead," *Wall Street Journal*, August 10, 2004, D4.]

Page 167: *Moreover, an estimated 3.5 percent...*

[Mary Kissel, "Labeling Rules Likely for Food Allergies," *Wall Street Journal*, July 7, 2004, D1.]

Page 167: *Sixty-two percent of the people polled...*

[Kate Zernike, "Is Obesity the Responsibility of the Body Politic?" *New York Times*, November 9, 2003.]

Page 169: *In 2001 the FDA and the food industry...*

[Sarah Ellison, "Blood Sugar, Sugar Alcohol and the FDA," *Wall Street Journal*, July 25, 2004, B1.]

Page 171: *One of the weirdest and most obscure...*

[Most of the information in the section about shellfish comes from "Death on the Half Shell," by the Center for Science in the Public Interest, June 2001, as well

as my interviews with Caroline Smith DeWaal and Joseph Madden, the ISSC
Web site, and *The Merck Manual*.]

Page 174: Britain's Prince Charles joined...
[Peter Pringle, *Food, Inc.*, Simon & Schuster, 2003, p. 117.]

Page 175: *As the journalist Peter Pringle...*
[Ibid., 170.]

CHAPTER 9

Page 182: *In the case of silicone-filled breast implants...*
[There is a lot of varying data on the risks from silicone-filled implants. These
particular numbers come from Gina Kolata, "Company Making Case to Allow
Breast Implants," *New York Times*, October 11, 2003. However, other articles
have cited different numbers—for instance, an FDA report in 2000 showing that
two-thirds of the women studied had suffered from ruptured implants.]

Page 185: *There are several controversial postscripts...*
[Of course I used numerous sources for this paragraph. Among the docu-
ments from the George family lawsuit are a Parke-Davis "Record of FDA
Contact," dated August 7, 1995, from Mary Taylor of Parke-Davis, with the
quote about how Alexander Fleming of the FDA would be willing to "ease Dr.
Gueriguian out."

Other documents: an e-mail dated December 2, 1996, from Fleming to Irwin
Martin of Parke-Davis about Gueriguian's report on Rezulin, saying, "I have
attached an encryped [sic] WordPerfect 5.x draft (typos and all) of his review.
Please mark it up as quickly as you can this morning with whatever comments you
would like me to consider."

Also, an e-mail dated December 4, 1996, from Martin to Fleming, beginning,
"Zan—received your recent e-mails. Glad to see the pressure to use John's
[Gueriguian] document has been relieved. Regarding the presentation next week.
Do you see us introducing each of the PM issues with our position..." and fur-
ther strategizing.

Also, an e-mail dated September 16, 1998, from Martin to two colleagues at
Parke-Davis about his dinner with "Zan" Fleming.

More information came from my interviews with people quoted in this chapter (some of whom asked not to be identified), David Willman, "How a New
Policy Led to Seven Deadly Drugs," *Los Angeles Times*, December 20, 2000.]

Page 187: *Woodcock told the* Los Angeles Times...
[Ibid., Today, Pfizer (which bought Warner-Lambert in 2000) often cites the new
drugs as the reason Rezulin was withdrawn. For instance, in a press release July
2, 2004, about a class action lawsuit settlement, the company said: "Rezulin was

voluntarily withdrawn from the market in March 2000 after two newer medicines became available that were comparable in effectiveness and that appeared to have fewer side effects."]

CHAPTER 10

Page 192: *Nevertheless, Odwalla won praise...*

[For instance, the e-mail newsletter *Business Respect*, which bills itself as "the free email newsletter on Corporate Social Responsibility," wrote up a case study in which it pronounced, "Odwalla stands as an example of best practices that few can match." In 1998 *San Francisco* magazine named Odwalla "Best Brand Name" in its annual "Best of the Bay Area" issue.]

Page 203: *Writing in the January–February 2004 issue...*

[Daniel P. Carpenter, "The Political Economy of FDA Drug Review," *Health Affairs*, January–February 2004, pp. 56–57.]

Page 203: *No wonder that in his July 2002...*

[Daniel P. Carpenter, "Groups, the Media, Agency Waiting Costs, and FDA Drug Approval," in *American Journal of Political Science*, July 2002, pp. 490–505.]

Page 204: *... at one point in 2004...*

[Denise Grady, "Heeding a Call to Test Breast Cancer Treatments," *New York Times*, July 26, 2004, A1.]

Page 204: *"By just about any measure...*

[Daniel P. Carpenter, "The Political Economy of FDA Drug Review," *Health Affairs*, January–February 2004, p. 57.]

Page 205: *In his* American Journal of Political Science...

[Daniel P. Carpenter, "Groups, the Media, Agency Waiting Costs, and FDA Drug Approval," in *American Journal of Political Science*, July 2002, p. 500.]

Page 206: *According to the FDA, Australian mice...*

[This information came in an appendix to a story by Tamar Nordenberg, "Cell Phones and Cancer: No Clear Connection," published in *FDA Consumer*, November–December 2000.]

CHAPTER 11

Page 212: *During the unsuccessful campaign...*

[David Kessler, *A Question of Intent: A Great American Battle with a Deadly Industry*, Public Affairs, 2001, pp. 299, 303, 306, 325.]

Page 212: *Mark McClellan and staffers...*

[Sheryl Gay Stolberg, "FDA Officials Press Legislators to Oppose Bill on Importing Less Expensive Drugs," *New York Times*, July 25, 2003.]

Page 215: *No other commissioner had...*

[Elisabeth Bumiller, "A Spokesman Son, a Tell-All Dad, a Mum Mom," *New York Times*, September 15, 2003, A14.]

Page 216: *By contrast, months before he was named...*

[To give just two examples: The Fifth Annual David A. Winston Lecture at the National Press Club, October 20, 2003, and a speech at the MedAdNews Pharmaceutical Leadership Forum, an industry conference, November 17, 2003.]

Page 216: *During the 2004 election...*

[Jackie Calmes, "Washington Wire, *Wall Street Journal*, October 15, 2004, A4, and also John Harwood, "Washington Wire, *Wall Street Journal*, October 29, 2004, A4.]

Page 220: *According to the* Wall Street Journal, *he participated...*

[Leila Abboud, "FDA Official Criticized Agency for Scrutiny of Contraceptive," *Wall Street Journal*, June 18, 2004, B4.]

Page 223: *Several groups of health professionals...*

[Mireya Navarro, "Experts in Sex Field Say Conservatives Interfere with Health and Research," *New York Times*, July 10, 2004.]

Page 223: *The National Academy of Sciences even held an all-day...*

[David Brown, "Panel Debates Politics' Role in Scientists' Appointment," *Washington Post*, July 22, 2004.]

Page 223: *As the* New York Times *put it...*

[Joel Brinkley, "Out of Spotlight, Bush Overhauls U.S. Regulations," *New York Times*, August 14, 2004, A1.]

Page 225: Even an executive from Bristol-Myers Squibb...

[Andrew Pollack, "New Tacks in Cancer Treatment Show Promise in 2 Clinical Trials," *New York Times*, June 2, 2003, A1.]

Page 226: *Moreover, it was Pazdur who in December 2001...*

[It has been widely reported that Bristol-Myers and Waksal were tipped off by an insider at the FDA. One source for Pazdur's role is Justin Gillis, "Source of Tip on ImClone Drug Is Identified," *Washington Post*, June 17, 2002.]

Page 227: *On top of all that, Pazdur had been...*

[This information comes from a range of public sources, including the *Houston Business Journal*, the *Houston Chronicle*, and M. D. Anderson. Mendelsohn's connections to ImClone and Anderson have been widely reported.]

Page 230: As Robert Essner, the chief executive of the big drug company...

[Andrew Osterland, "Taking a Dose of Strong Medicine," *Institutional Investor*, May 2004, p. 24.]

CHAPTER 12

Page 234: *In the mid-1960s the Division of Biological Standards approved...*

[Meyer and Parkman's development of the vaccine and the problems of conflict of interest that ensued have been widely reported, but the comparison of their vaccine with the human-cell version comes specifically from Stephen S. Hall, *Merchants of Immortality: Chasing the Dream of Human Life Extension*, Houghton-Mifflin Co., 2003, pp. 32–33.]

Page 245: *Some researchers were effectively adding...*

[Andrew Pollack, "In Drug Research, Some Guinea Pigs Are Now Human," *New York Times*, August 4, 2004, A1.]

CHAPTER 13

Page 254: *According to the writer Paul Starr in his book...*

[Paul Starr, *The Social Transformation of American Medicine*, Basic Books, 1982, pp. 129–133.]

Page 261: *In a study released in November 2001...*

["Prescription Drugs and Mass Media Advertising, 2000," National Institute for Health Care Management.]

Page 262: *Nexium is actually half of the molecule...*

[The story of Nexium and Prilosec has been discussed in many news articles. A good overall look comes from Gardiner Harris, "As a Patent Expires, Drug Firms Line Up Pricey Alternative," *Wall Street Journal*, June 6, 2002, A1.]

Page 263: *When* Prevention *magazine queried 1,222 Americans...*

["International Survey on Wellness and Consumer Reaction to DTC Advertising of Rx Drugs," *Prevention*, 2000–01, pp. 52–55.]

Page 263: *"You have people walking in to doctors saying...*
[Fran Hawthorne, *The Merck Druggernaut*, John Wiley & Sons, p. 164.]

Page 264: *"If doctors think it's medically reasonable...*
[Ibid, 164.]

Page 264: *"Medicines aren't like shampoo or perfume...*
[Erin N. Marcus, "When TV Commercials Play the Doctor," *New York Times*, January 3, 2003.]

Page 270: *"I was surprised how minor they were...*
[Robert Ehrlich, "A Little Evolution from the FDA," rxinsight.com, February 6, 2004.]

Pages 270/271: BusinessWeek *magazine suggested that...*
[John Carey, "Drug Ads Need Stronger Medicine," *BusinessWeek*, February 9, 2004, p. 84.]

Page 271: *Even an industry insider like Bob Ehrlich...*
[Robert Ehrlich, "FDA Hearings: New DTC Action Coming?" rxinsight.com, September 12, 2003.]

Page 272: *former governor Howard Dean of Vermont—who is also...*
[From a speech by Howard Dean in Council Bluffs, Iowa, on October 14, 2003.]

CHAPTER 14

Page 273: *In 1996 the regulators had approved 53...*
[The 2003 statistics come from the FDA. The earlier data are from "Prescription Drugs and Intellectual Property Protection," National Institute for Health Care Management, August 2000.]

Page 274: *Derived from a toxin...*
[*The Merck Manual of Medical Information*, Merck & Co., 1997, p. 516.]

Pages 276/277: *"Schering-Plough's Clarinex illustrates...*
["Profiting from Pain: Where Prescription Dollars Go," Families USA, July 2002, p. 11.]

Page 277: *"We think most experts would agree...*
[Arnold S. Relman and Marcia Angell, "America's Other Drug Problem," *The New Republic*, December 16, 2002, p. 32.]

Page 278: *By relaxing muscles and easing pain...*

[Donald G. McNeil Jr., "Wrinkles Gone? New Uses Studied for Botox," *New York Times*, March 2, 2003, A1. Botox's approval for severe underarm sweating was officially announced by the FDA.]

Pages 278/279: *As Bob Temple wrote in the September 19, 2000...*

[Robert Temple and Susan S. Ellenberg, "Placebo-Controlled Trials and Active-Control Trials in the Evaluation of New Treatments," *Annals of Internal Medicine*, September 19, 2000, p. 460.]

Page 280: *To Marcia Angell, the former...*

[Peter Jaret, "She Turns Her Pen on Drug Makers," *Los Angeles Times*, August 9, 2004, F1.]

Page 280: *AstraZeneca also had 11 separate patents...*

[Arnold S. Relman and Marcia Angell, "America's Other Drug Problem," *The New Republic*, December 16, 2002, p. 38.]

Page 281: *In fact, when Bristol-Myers Squibb in 2000...*

[Gardiner Harris and Chris Adams, "Drug Manufacturers Step Up Legal Attacks That Slow Generics," *Wall Street Journal*, July 12, 2001, A1.]

Page 284: *"Some people believe the FDA should leave...*

[From McClellan's speech at the MedAdNews Pharmaceutical Leadership Forum, November 17, 2003.]

CHAPTER 15

Page 286: *He repeated his message in a slew...*

[To give just a few examples: the speeches cited above at the National Press Club, October 20, 2003, and at the MedAdNews Pharmaceutical Leadership Forum on November 17, 2003, as well as a speech to the Drug Information Association in Ottawa, Canada, November 18, 2003.]

Page 288: *Families USA, for instance, published analyses...*

["Profiting from Pain: Where Prescription Dollars Go," Families USA, July 2002, and also "Enough To Make You Sick," Families USA, 2001.]

Page 289: *When he and four other academics...*

[Peter J. Neumann, Kara Zivin Bambauer, Vijay Ramakrishnan, Kate A. Stewart, and Chaim M. Bell, "Economic Messages in Prescription Drug Advertisements in Medical Journals," *Medical Care*, 2002, pp. 840–803.]

Page 292: *"In wanting to improve our bodies...*
["Beyond Therapy: Biotechnology and the Pursuit of Happiness," President's Council on Bioethics, October 2003. The quotes come from the sections "Essential Sources of Concern" and "General Reflections."]

Page 292: *"Suppose a drug without side effects...*
[Gregg Easterbrook, "Tolstoy and the Beltway," *The New Republic*, January 26, 2004, p. 35.]

Page 297: *indeed, cases of this kind of diabetes...*
[The statistics come from the Centers for Disease Control.]

Page 299: *But in the summer of 2003...*
[David Armstrong, "How Drug Directory Helps Raise Tab for Medicaid and Insurers," *Wall Street Journal*, October 23, 2003, A1.]

Page 304: *In a typical year...*
[Anna Wilde Mathews, "Vioxx Recall Raises Questions of FDA's Safety Monitoring," *Wall Street Journal*, October 4, 2004, B1.]

Page 304: *There was also growing concern that problems with devices...*
[Barry Meier, "Flawed Device Places FDA Under Scrutiny" *New York Times*, December 15, 2004, A1.]

Page 306: *For his part, Spitzer first told...*
[Gardiner Harris, "Spitzer Sues a Drug Maker, Saying It Hid Negative Data," *New York Times*, June 3, 2004, A1.]

Page 306: *Two and a half months later, the* Times...
[Gardiner Harris, "Glaxo Agrees to Post Results of Drug Trials on Web Site." *New York Times*, August 27, 2004, C4.]

Bibliography

Books

Angell, Marcia, M.D. *The Truth About the Drug Companies: How They Deceive Us and What to Do About It.* Random House, 2004.

Atwood, Margaret. *Oryx and Crake.* Nan A. Talese/Doubleday, 2003.

Avorn, Jerry, M.D. *Powerful Medicines: The Benefits, Risks, and Costs of Prescription Drugs.* Knopf, 2004.

Berkow, Robert, M.D., ed. *The Merck Manual of Medical Information* (home edition). Merck Research Laboratories, 1997.

Bovard, James. *Lost Rights: The Destruction of American Liberty.* St. Martin's Press, 1994.

Boyer, Paul. *The American Nation.* Holt Rinehart and Winston, 2001.

Burkholz, Herbert. *The FDA Follies.* Basic Books, 1994.

Byers, Michael. *Long for the World.* Houghton Mifflin Co., 2003.

Cohen, Jay S., M.D. *Over Dose: The Case Against the Drug Companies.* Jeremy P. Tarder/Putnam, 2001.

Compton's Encyclopedia, 1997.

Crichton, Michael. *Jurassic Park.* Ballantine Books, 1990.

Crichton, Michael. *Prey.* Avon Books, 2002.

Critser, Greg. *Fat Land: How Americans Became the Fattest People in the World.* Mariner Books/Houghton Mifflin, 2003.

Greider, Katharine. *The Big Fix: How the Pharmaceutical Industry Rips Off American Consumers.* Public Affairs, 2003.

Griffinhagen, George. *150 Years of Caring*. American Pharmaceutical Association, 2002.

Hall, Stephen S. *Merchants of Immortality: Chasing the Dream of Human Life Extension*. Houghton Mifflin Co., 2003.

Hawthorne, Fran. *The Merck Druggernaut: The Inside Story of a Pharmaceutical Giant*. John Wiley & Sons, Inc., 2003.

Hilts, Philip J. *Protecting America's Health: The FDA, Business, and One Hundred Years of Regulation*. Alfred A. Knopf, 2003.

Huxley, Aldous. *Brave New World*. HarperPerennial/Harper Collins, 1960.

Kessler, David. *A Question of Intent: A Great American Battle with a Deadly Industry*. Public Affairs, 2001.

Lieberman, Trudy. *Slanting the Story: The Forces That Shape the News*. The New Press, 2000.

Miller, Henry I., M.D. *To America's Health: A Proposal to Reform the Food and Drug Administration*. Hoover Institution Press, 2000.

Ozeki, Ruth. *All Over Creation*. Penguin Books, 2003.

Perlin, David, PhD., and Ann Cohen. *Dangerous Diseases and Epidemics*. Alpha, 2002.

Pringle, Peter. *Food, Inc.: Mendel to Monsanto—The Promises and Perils of the Biotech Harvest*. Simon & Schuster, 2003.

Schlosser, Eric. *Fast Food Nation: The Dark Side of the All-American Meal*. Perennial/HarperCollins, 2002.

Sinclair, Upton. *The Jungle*. Signet Classic, 2001.

Smith, Ian. *The Blackbird Papers*. Doubleday, 2004.

Starr, Paul. *The Social Transformation of American Medicine*. Basic Books, 1982.

Teitelman, Robert. *Gene Dreams: Wall Street, Academia, and the Rise of Biotechnology*. Basic Books, 1989.

Twain, Mark. *Tom Sawyer*. Vintage Books, 1991.

Vasella, Daniel, M.D. *Magic Cancer Bullet: How a Tiny Orange Pill Is Rewriting Medical History*. HarperBusiness, 2003.

Reports and Articles

In my research, I read hundreds of newspaper and magazine articles from a range of publications. This list highlights some of the most important, along with papers from academic journals and other reports.

Carpenter, Daniel P. "Groups, the Media, Agency Waiting Costs, and FDA Drug Approval." *American Journal of Political Science* 46, no. 3 (July 2002).

Carpenter, Daniel P. "The Political Economy of FDA Drug Review." *Health Affairs* 23, no. 1 (January–February 2004).

Carpenter, Daniel P., and Marc Turenne. "Why Do Bigger Firms Receive Faster Drug Approvals?" Presentation at the Harvard-MIT Workshop on Positive Political Economy, March 16, 2001.

Center for Science in the Public Interest. "Death on the Half Shell: The Failure of Regulators and the Shellfish Industry to Prevent Deaths and Illnesses from Gulf Coast Shellfish" (June 2001).

Center for Science in the Public Interest. "Genetically Engineered Foods: Are They Safe?" *Nutrition Action Health Letter* 28, no. 9 (November 2001).

Center for Science in the Public Interest. "Outbreak Alert! Closing the Gaps in Our Federal Food-Safety Net" (September 2002).

Dahl, Elizabeth, and Caroline Smith DeWaal. "Scrambled Eggs: How a Broken Food Safety System Let Contaminated Eggs Become a National Food Poisoning Epidemic." Center for Science in the Public Interest (May 1997).

Danzon, Patricia, and Michael Furukawa. "Prices and Availability of Pharmaceuticals: Evidence from Nine Countries." *Health Affairs* (October 2003).

DiMasi, Joseph A. "Risks in New Drug Development: Approval Success Rates for Investigational Drugs." *Clinical Pharmacology & Therapeutics* (May 2001).

DiMasi, Joseph A., Ronald W. Hansen, Henry G. Grabowski, and Louis Lasagna. "Research and Development Costs for New Drugs by Therapeutic Category: A Study of the U.S. Pharmaceutical Industry." *Pharmacoeconomics* (February 1995).

Dranove, David, and David Meltzer. "Do Important Drugs Reach the Market Sooner?" *RAND Journal of Economics* 25, no. 3 (Autumn 1994).

Families USA. "Profiting from Pain: Where Prescription Drug Dollars Go" (2002).

Fenichel, Robert R. "How Hypertensive Drugs Get Approved in the U.S.," from *Hypertension: A Companion to Brenner & Rector's The Kidney*, eds. Suzanne Oparil, Michael A. Weber, Richard Zorab, and W. B. Saunders (2000).

Galambos, Louis, and Jane Eliot Sewell. "Confronting AIDS: Science and Business Cross a Unique Frontier." Merck & Co., 1997.

Garvey, Thomas, and Freddie Ann Hoffman. "Food, Cosmetic, and Medical Product Classification in the United States." Presentation at the Second Pan-American Conference on Drug Regulatory Harmonization, November 3–4, 1999.

Hubbard, Tim, and James Love. "A New Trade Framework for Global Healthcare R&D." *PloS Biology* 2, no. 2 (February 2004).

Kazman, Sam. "Deadly Overcaution." *Journal of Regulation & Social Costs* 1, no. 1 (September 1990).

Kazman, Sam. "Saying Yes to Drugs." *Journal of Regulation & Social Costs* 2 (June 1992).

Kessler, David A., Jerold R. Mande, F. Edward Scarbrough, Renie Schapiro, and Karyn Feiden. "Developing the 'Nutrition Facts' Food Label." *Harvard Health Policy Review* 4, no. 2 (Fall 2003).

Lurie, Peter, and Sidney M. Wolfe. "FDA Medical Officers Report Lower Standards Permit Dangerous Drug Approvals." *Public Citizen* (December 2, 1998).

Milne, Christopher-Paul. "The Pediatric Studies Incentive: Equal Medicines for All." Tufts Center for the Study of Drug Development (April 2001).

National Institute for Health Care Management. "Prescription Drugs and Intellectual Property Protection" (August 2000).

National Institute for Health Care Management. "Prescription Drugs and Mass Media Advertising" (November 2001).

Neumann, Peter J., Kara Zivin Bambauer, Vijay Ramakrishnan, Kate A. Stewart, and Chaim M. Bell. "Economic Messages in Prescription Drug Advertisements in Medical Journals." *Medical Care* 40, no. 9 (2002).

Neumann, Peter J., Karl Claxton, and Milton C. Weinstein. "The FDA's Regulation of Health Economic Information." *Health Affairs* 19, no. 5 (September–October 2000).

Noguchi, Philip D. "From Jim to Gene and Beyond: An Odyssey of Biologics Regulation." *Food and Drug Law Journal* 51 (1996).

Peltz, Michael. "Antigenics's Cancer Drug Gives Its Shareholders Indigestion." *Bloomberg Markets* (January 5, 2004).

President's Council on Bioethics. "Beyond Therapy: Biotechnology and the Pursuit of Happiness" (October 2003).

Relman, Arnold S., and Marcia Angell. "America's Other Drug Problem." *The New Republic* (December 16, 2002).

Slaughter, Ed, and Martha Schumacher. "International Survey on Wellness and Consumer Reaction to DTC Advertising of Rx Drugs." *Prevention* (2000–2001).

Stewart, Kate A., and Peter J. Neumann. "FDA Actions against Misleading or Unsubstantiated Economic and Quality-of-Life Promotional Claims." *Value in Health* 5, no. 5 (2002).

Temple, Robert. "Development of Drug Law, Regulations, and Guidance in the United States," from *Governmental Regulation of Drugs* (1995).

Temple, Robert. "Special Study Designs: Early Escape, Enrichment, Studies in Non-Responders." *Communications in Statistics* (1994).

Willman, David. "How a New Policy Led to Seven Deadly Drugs." *Los Angeles Times* (December 20, 2000).

Wood, Alastair J. J., C. Michael Stein, and Raymond Woosley. "Making Medicines Safer—The Need for an Independent Drug Safety Board." *The New England Journal of Medicine* 339, no. 25 (December 17, 1998).

Index

This book is due on the last date stamped below.
Failure to return books on the date due may result
in assessment of overdue fees.

MAY 0 8 2012		
MAY 0 6 REC'D		
FEB 2 3 2015		
FEB 1 6 REC'D		
FINES	.50 per day	